GREAT EMPIRES

AN ILLUSTRATED ATLAS

GREAT
EMPIRES
AN ILLUSTRATED ATLAS

NATIONAL GEOGRAPHIC

WASHINGTON, D.C.

CONTENTS

CONTENTS

INTRODUCTION

From a 21st-century perspective, great empires seem to be a thing of the past. The term "empire" conjures images of swords and gunships, silk-robed dictators in luxurious palaces, treasure ships carrying gold from the exploited to the exalted. But empires have shaped world history in more than militaristic ways. They have forged connections among diverse peoples to the enrichment of civilization.

An empire is typically defined as a political unit with an extensive territory, or a number of territories and peoples, governed by a single supreme authority. Empires can be land based or maritime, sedentary or nomadic, defensive or offensive. They are among the oldest forms of political structure, dating back to ancient Mesopotamia in the third millennium B.C. Many lasted for centuries: Rome ruled for 600 years; Byzantium for 1,000; China, in successive dynasties, for more than 2,000. By contrast, many of today's nation-states are perhaps 50 to 150 years old—just pups, by historical standards.

Identifying empires in history can be difficult: Just how large does a territory have to be to make it empire size? How long lasting? How diverse according to population? The lines can be blurred. Did the Phoenicians govern an empire or a network of trading cities? Did early Egyptian rulers hold sway over a single nation or many? Does modern imperialism—the United States in the Philippines, the Soviet Union in Eastern Europe—fit the same model? Depending on your criteria, the world has known more than 150 empires in its time, including such now obscure entities as the Irish empire of Brian Boru and the realm of the Wari of Peru.

Thus it was not easy to pick the empires featured in this book. We wanted to include the familiar empires that are generally considered "great," whether in size or cultural influence, but we also wanted to shed light on some cultures that don't get as much attention: North African empires, for instance, or those of Southeast Asia. We included empires that had a distinctive cultural stamp, but excluded some, particularly industrial-era ones, that were linked primarily by commercial ties or temporary military domination. Napoleon, though he named himself an emperor and conquered diverse territories, never really forged a coherent or long-lasting empire. Alexander, by contrast, died young, but Hellenistic lands in the Middle East bore his stamp for centuries. The Maya are not included because no single Maya city-state dominated the Yucatán the way the Aztec did central Mexico or the Inca did Peru. Those dynamic Maya city-states were instead like ancient Athens and Sparta—great rivals that prevented each other from achieving imperial supremacy.

Organizing the empires into chapters and sections presented another challenge. Modern atlases typically arrange countries by continent, even while acknowledging that continents are artificial geographical creations with arbitrary boundaries. But empires, by their very nature, span wide areas and cross continental boundaries. Maritime empires are not even contiguous. And the long lives of most empires can make it difficult to place them into traditional historical categories such as ancient, medieval, or modern.

Shah Jahan (left) sits regally astride his mount. Painted by Frederick Martin, ca 1912.

Nevertheless, we've sorted our empires into geographical and historical bins to keep track of their relationships in space and time.

Looking at history in terms of these huge political entities allows us to see patterns on a broad scale. As diverse as these empires are, study of their growth and administration reveals many similarities. Military power is one of the most obvious. Particularly before the age of exploration, empires were land based and grew primarily through military conquest. Rome's famed armies spread its influence in every direction, from Asia to the British Isles. Its soldiers not only subdued foreigners by force of arms but also built roads, maintained aqueducts, and settled into distant lands, intermarrying with locals to produce generations of loyal Roman citizens. The Mongols assembled possibly the greatest military force the world has known, overcoming armies from the Balkans to the Pacific with their fast-moving horsemen. Aztec soldiers were famed for their ferocity; Chinese forces maintained the vast boundaries of their empire for thousands of years. In more recent times, purely military conquest gave way in many places to technological and commercial conquest, as rapidly industrializing countries reached out to seize resources: gold, sugar, spices, opium, oil, and more.

Imperial armies were often led by revered commanders: Julius Caesar, Alexander, Cyrus, Genghis Khan, Saladin. The semilegendary status and charisma of these leaders helped establish a central authority and solidarity within a widespread empire. When rulers were seen as divine or semidivine, as in Egypt, China, and India, it reinforced their claim to power.

With great empires come great administrative responsibilities: taxation, finance, infrastructure, transportation, education. The empires that lasted longest were often those with the best civil servants. China's Confucian meritocracy served it well for centuries; Byzantium became known for its vast bureaucracy, which held the empire together even when emperors in Constantinople were weak or incompetent. The nomadic Mongols, on the other hand, lacked any experience at settled governance, and their empire disintegrated accordingly.

Certain features appear again and again across empires. First-class roads and communications are among them. Roman roads held the empire together. So well built were they that they can still be seen and used across Europe. India's Emperor Ashoka linked trading centers across his empire with roads adorned by shade trees, wells, and inns. The Inca government at Cusco maintained thousands of miles of fine roads, as did the Persian and subsequent Islamic empires. Postal carriers, spies, merchants, and armies benefited. Imperial governments also frequently enforced standardization among weights, measures, and time, smoothing the path of commerce. One of the emperor Shi Huangdi's accomplishments was to standardize the width of China's cart axles, so that wheels would match ruts in his empire's roads.

Many of the most successful—that is, long-lived and stable—empires were marked by their ability to incorporate diverse populations, making use of their varied skills. Pre-Christian Rome, whose imperium is at the root of the English word "empire," was an early example. Emperor Claudius and his successors even added provincial citizens to the august Roman senate. To the protests of Italian senators, Claudius replied (according to Tacitus): "We had unshaken peace at home; we prospered in all our foreign relations, in the days when Italy beyond the Po was admitted to share our citizenship, and when, enrolling in our ranks the most vigorous of the provincials, under color of settling our legions throughout the world, we recruited our exhausted empire. Are we sorry that the Balbi came to us from Spain, and other men not less illustrious from Narbon Gaul? Their descendants are still among us, and do not yield to us in patriotism. What was the ruin of Sparta and Athens, but this, that mighty as they were in war, they spurned from them as aliens those whom they had conquered?"

Other empires maintained a strict separation between "superior" conquerors and "inferior" conquered peoples. This distinction is seen most commonly in more modern, colonial empires. Colonial powers in the New World, Africa, and Asia might see conquered populations as fodder for forced labor, or as heathens ripe for religious conversion, but rarely did they admit them to equal status.

Looking at world history through the wide-angle lens of empire formation reveals a process both enriching and destructive. Empire building almost always means war and death. Millions upon millions have been slaughtered, raped, and enslaved in the quest for territory and wealth. The Mongols piled up actual hills of skulls; Aztec eviscerated tens of thousands atop their temples. Egyptian and Chinese laborers toiled and died for their emperors' grand creations; African slaves suffered on American plantations. And empires, jostling for supremacy, can precipitate conflict on a grand scale, as seen in the world wars of the 20th century.

Empires also have been the engines of productive change throughout history. The world's religions, technologies, crops, arts, and languages have spread along imperial highways. Sometimes this was intentional. The Mongols, for all their ferocity, succeeded in part because they sought out foreign artisans, incorporated their technology, and respected their beliefs. More often it was an unavoidable by-product of the mix of cultures. Slaves shipped to distant lands enriched their new cultures with music, languages, foods, and stories. Beauty itself traveled imperial roads, as when exquisite Ming vases reached European tables or Arab architecture transformed southern Spain.

Sometimes violently, sometimes gradually, empires have merged human populations. The words we speak, the meals upon our tables, the places in which we worship, the clothes we wear, and more can be traced back to the ebb and flow of imperial power. Even our chromosomes bear witness to these connections. Many North Americans, for instance, have been surprised to discover a little piece of Mongol DNA in their genes.

We don't think of ourselves as creatures of empire now, in the 21st century, on a planet divided into 195 nations. But empires of every description—creative and destructive, grand and cruel, brutal and benevolent—have shaped our world. ✺

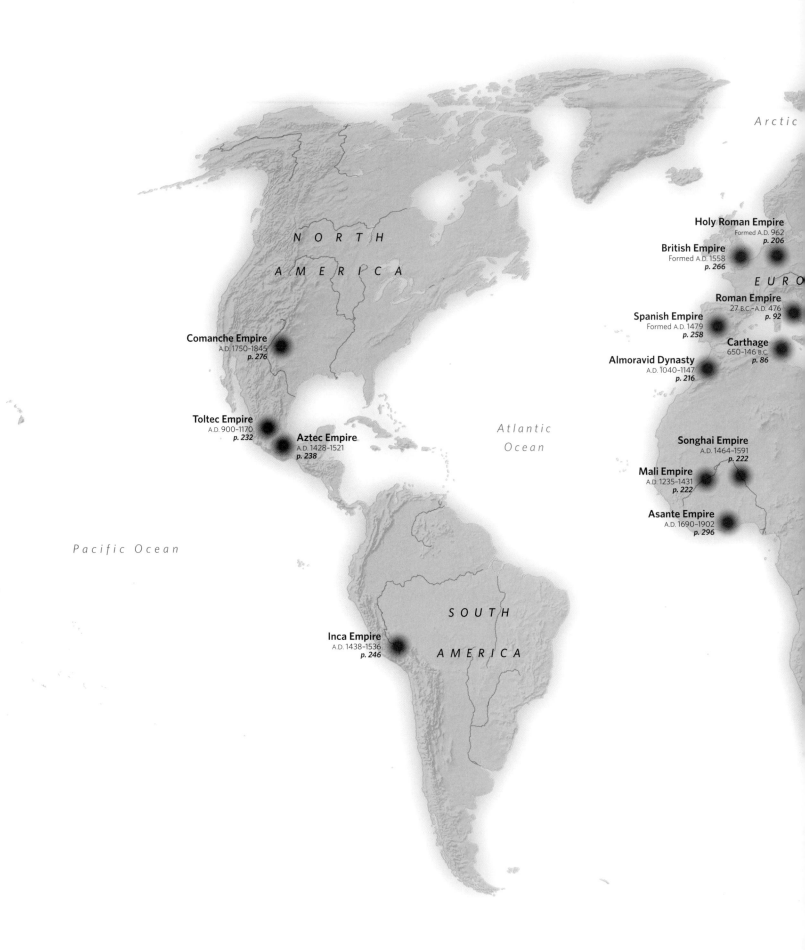

Arctic

NORTH
AMERICA

Holy Roman Empire
Formed A.D. 962
p. 206

British Empire
Formed A.D. 1558
p. 266

EUROP

Roman Empire
27 B.C.–A.D. 476
p. 92

Spanish Empire
Formed A.D. 1479
p. 258

Carthage
650–146 B.C.
p. 86

Almoravid Dynasty
A.D. 1040–1147
p. 216

Comanche Empire
A.D. 1750–1845
p. 276

Songhai Empire
A.D. 1464–1591
p. 222

Toltec Empire
A.D. 900–1170
p. 232

Aztec Empire
A.D. 1428–1521
p. 238

Mali Empire
A.D. 1235–1431
p. 222

*Atlantic
Ocean*

Asante Empire
A.D. 1690–1902
p. 296

Pacific Ocean

SOUTH

Inca Empire
A.D. 1438–1536
p. 246

AMERICA

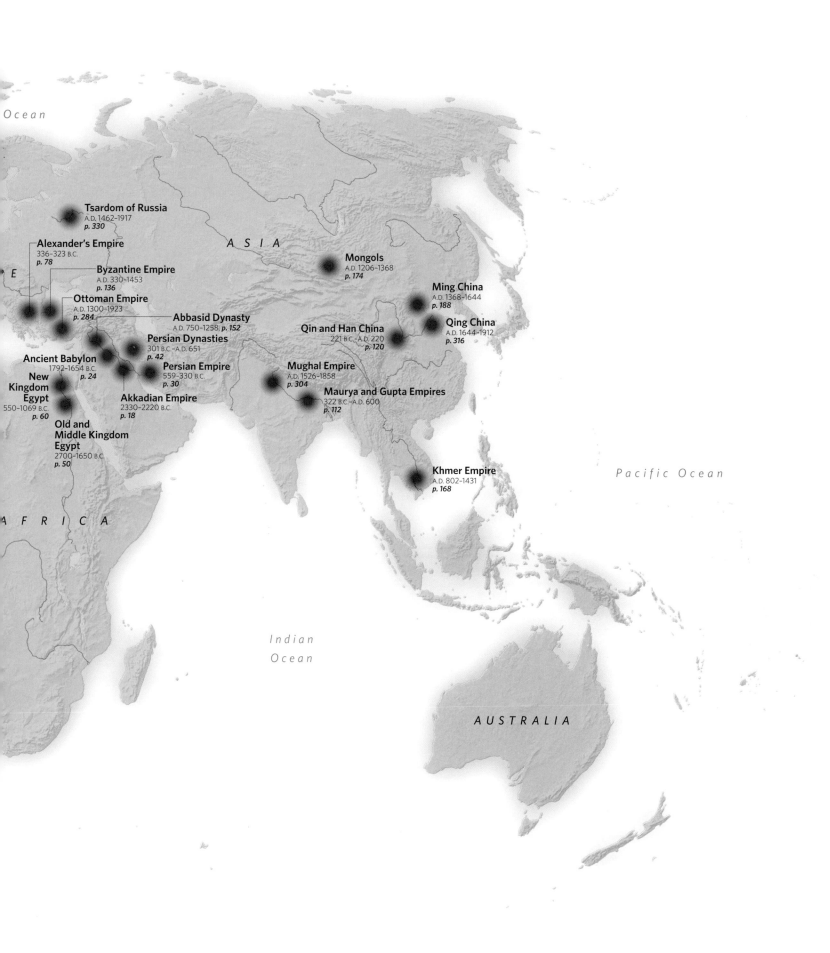

Tsardom of Russia
A.D. 1462–1917
p. 330

Alexander's Empire
336–323 B.C.
p. 78

ASIA

Mongols
A.D. 1206–1368
p. 174

Byzantine Empire
A.D. 330–1453
p. 136

Ming China
A.D. 1368–1644
p. 188

Ottoman Empire
A.D. 1300–1923
p. 284

Abbasid Dynasty
A.D. 750–1258, *p. 152*

Qin and Han China
221 B.C.–A.D. 220
p. 120

Qing China
A.D. 1644–1912
p. 316

E

Persian Dynasties
301 B.C.–A.D. 651
p. 42

Ancient Babylon
1792–1654 B.C.
p. 24

Persian Empire
559–330 B.C.
p. 30

Mughal Empire
A.D. 1526–1858
p. 304

Maurya and Gupta Empires
322 B.C.–A.D. 600
p. 112

New Kingdom Egypt
550–1069 B.C.
p. 60

Akkadian Empire
2330–2220 B.C.
p. 18

Old and Middle Kingdom Egypt
2700–1650 B.C.
p. 50

Khmer Empire
A.D. 802–1431
p. 168

Pacific Ocean

AFRICA

Indian Ocean

AUSTRALIA

PART I

2600 B.C. - A.D. 500

The world's first empires arose not long after the dawn of civilization, which occurred more than 5,000 years ago as complex societies emerged, first in Mesopotamia and Egypt and later in other Mediterranean lands, India, and China. Those well-organized societies engaged in irrigation projects and other public works, built cities—one of the hallmarks of civilization—promoted artistry and trade, and recorded transactions, laws, and legends. Such advances enhanced the authority of rulers, who used writing to glorify their deeds and impose law and order, claimed a share of the wealth produced by traders, artisans, and farmers, and used that bounty to support men they conscripted for public projects and military service.

Most great empires of the ancient world grew up along rivers—the Tiber in Italy where Rome took shape, the Nile in Egypt, the Tigris and Euphrates in Mesopotamia, the Indus in India, and the Yellow and Yangtze in China. Like rivers at flood stage, those empires sometimes caused devastation as they grew mightier and engulfed one country after another. Once mature, however, they often brought order and prosperity to lands they encompassed, facilitating the exchange of goods, ideas, and beliefs.

MARE
SIRI
A
CVM

CIPRVS

PCIACVM ·

PHOENICIA

SVRIA

Castiotis

Palmirena

Curua siria

Betania

IVDEA

galilea

Samaria

Raypheni

ARABIA

Zoara

Petra

PETREA

Pharo

NTANA

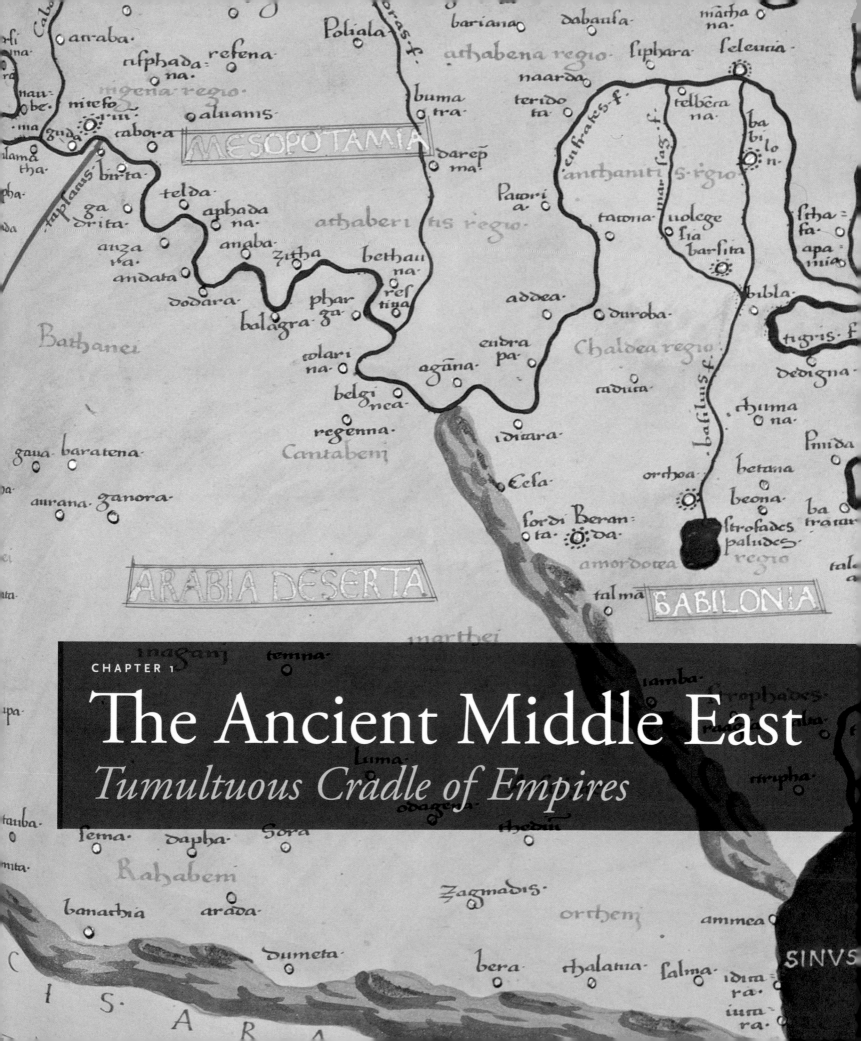

CHAPTER 1

The Ancient Middle East

Tumultuous Cradle of Empires

AKKADIAN EMPIRE
Sargon's Legacy

King Sargon of Akkad founded the world's first empire around 2330 B.C. in Mesopotamia, the fertile land between the Tigris and Euphrates Rivers. Akkad lay just north of Sumer, the southernmost region of Mesopotamia, bordering the Persian Gulf. The Sumerians developed a civilization a thousand years before Sargon's time, featuring irrigation works that made parched land fertile, a writing system using wedge-shaped characters called *cuneiform* and well-organized city-states dominated by towering mud-brick temples called *ziggurats*. The Akkadians intermingled with the gifted Sumerians, emulating and ultimately outdoing them. This process, in which ambitious people residing at the margins of an old and accomplished society became its masters, was to be repeated throughout history by great empire-builders, including the Romans who conquered Greece and the Mongols who seized China.

Many kings followed in the path of Sargon and ruled over Mesopotamia and surrounding lands, including Hammurabi of Babylon and Cyrus the Great of Persia, founder of an empire

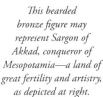

This bearded bronze figure may represent Sargon of Akkad, conqueror of Mesopotamia—a land of great fertility and artistry, as depicted at right.

that embraced the entire region known today as the Middle East. An emperor by definition was a ruler who asserted authority over other rulers and held sway over multiple countries and cultures. Cyrus and his Persian successors were hailed as "king of kings" because they subjugated the monarchs of many lands, including Babylonian rulers who had earlier exiled rebellious Jews from their homeland. Cyrus allowed those exiles to return to their promised land. The Jews praised the Persian emperor in scripture as a savior to whom God gave power over other kingdoms so that he would restore them to Jerusalem and allow them to rebuild their temple. In later times, Christians used the splendid imperial title to honor their Messiah as "King of kings and Lord of lords" (1 Timothy 6:15).

Sargon and his successors bequeathed to the world a concept of power that involved much more than military might. They commanded obedience not just by winning battles and striking fear into their foes but also by imposing order, dispensing justice, and serving as earthly representatives of gods their subjects dreaded and revered. Ultimately, the accomplishments

ca 3500 B.C. Cities develop in Sumer, forming the basis for Mesopotamian civilization.

ca 2330 B.C. Sargon of Akkad conquers Sumer and goes on to expand his domain.

ca 2250 B.C. Naram-Sin, Sargon's grandson, takes power.

ca 2100 B.C. Ur-Nammu of Ur takes command of Sumer and Akkad.

ca 1800 B.C. Babylon, a city-state in Akkad, emerges as an imperial power.

ca 2500 B.C. Royal burials at the Sumerian city-state of Ur include human sacrifices.

ca 2280 B.C. Sargon dies, bequeathing control of his empire to his heirs.

ca 2220 B.C. Akkadian Empire collapses following the death of Naram-Sin.

ca 2000 B.C. Ur destroyed by invading Elamites.

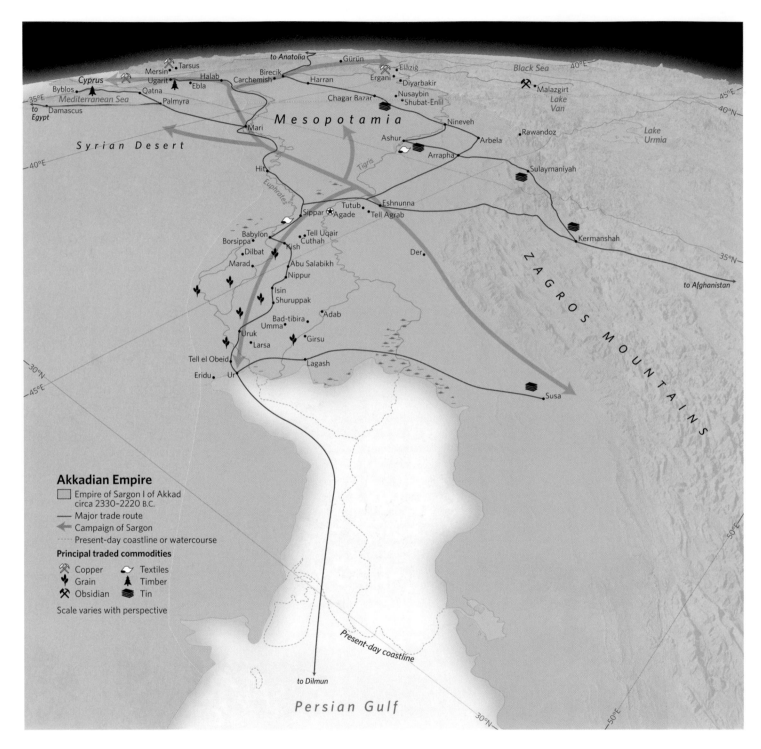

Akkadian Empire

⬚ Empire of Sargon I of Akkad
circa 2330–2220 B.C.

— Major trade route

← Campaign of Sargon

⋯ Present-day coastline or watercourse

Principal traded commodities

⚒ Copper   🗇 Textiles

🌿 Grain   🌲 Timber

⚒ Obsidian   ▦ Tin

Scale varies with perspective

of emperors were overshadowed in the minds of many devout Middle Easterners—including Jews, Christians, Zoroastrians, and Muslims—by the idea of a supreme ruler in heaven, greater than any power on earth.

According to legend, Sargon of Akkad began life as a foundling, abandoned by his mother, a priestess who gave birth to him in secret and set him adrift on a river in a reed basket. The infant was discovered by a common laborer, a "drawer of water," who dipped his bucket in the river and saved the boy, whom he raised as his adopted son. As a young man tending his father's garden, he was visited by Ishtar, goddess of desire, fertility, storms, and warfare, who loved him. Inspired by her, he rose from obscurity and took the world by storm.

The purpose of this legend was to show that Sargon—whose name means "rightful king" in Akkadian—was entitled to rule

> *"To build a house, to build a woman's chamber,*
> *to have implements, to kiss the lips*
> *of a small child are yours, Inanna,*
> *To give the crown, the chair and the scepter*
> *of kingship is yours, Inanna"*
>
> ENHEDUANNA'S HYMNS TO INANNA

Mesopotamia, however humble his origins. Akkadians had long been understudies of the Sumerians, from whom they learned much before emerging first as their rivals and ultimately as their rulers. Before Sargon took power, the powerful Sumerian city-states of Ur and Uruk had to contend with Kish to their north, in Akkad, near modern-day Baghdad.

Sargon began his ascent to power as a trusted cupbearer to the king of Kish, whom he overthrew. He then led troops against the great rival ruler to the south, Lugalzagesi, who had brought all of Sumer under his command. Lingering animosity between Sumerian city-states, which had long been at odds, may have hampered Lugalzagesi in his struggle against Sargon, who captured him and placed a yoke around his neck. An inscription commemorating the victory boasted that Sargon defeated 50 other rulers on his way to the Persian Gulf, where he "washed his weapons in the sea."

Sargon sent Akkadian governors to rule Sumerian cities and instructed them

The goddess Inanna, portrayed here, was celebrated in hymns by Sargon's daughter Enheduanna.

Akkadians and Sumerians waged war in chariots drawn by horses like that shown trampling an enemy in this mosaic.

ENHEDUANNA

After conquering Sumer, Sargon made his daughter, Enheduanna, the high priestess of the moon god Nanna in Ur. Hers was a position of great importance, for Nanna was the patron deity of that city-state, and his daughter Inanna—known to Akkadians as Ishtar—was revered as the goddess of love and war. Like other Mesopotamian deities, she was a volatile figure, who brought fertility and bounty as well as death and destruction. Sargon himself was said to have been visited and inspired by Ishtar as a young man, and his daughter composed hymns to the goddess that were inscribed on tablets and endured. That makes Enheduanna the first author whose name is known to us. In one of her hymns, she praises the goddess as "that singular woman the unique one / who speaks hateful words to the wicked / who moves among the bright shining things / who goes against rebel lands / and at twilight makes the firmament beautiful all on her own."

The massive walls of this structure unearthed at Tell Brak in northern Mesopotamia indicate that it was designed to fend off attackers.

TELL BRAK

Since the 1930s, archaeologists have been excavating at Tell Brak, a site in northeastern Syria containing the remnants of one of the oldest cities in Mesopotamia. Tells are mounds formed by the debris of ancient settlements established at the same site over eons. Relics of more recent settlements are found near the top of these mounds, while vestiges of older settlements are nearer the bottom.

Archaeologists have found evidence of an impressive city at Tell Brak that arose around 4000 B.C. and housed artisans who crafted luxury goods and religious objects. The so-called Eye Temple, built around 3500 B.C., contained figurines with staring eyes that may represent gods or worshipers. This city developed earlier than many cities to the south in Sumer and Akkad, where empires later took shape. Sumer and Akkad fostered powerful rulers with large armies not because they contained the first cities in the region but because rival city-states developed in close proximity and competed fiercely with each other.

When Sargon of Akkad conquered

Idols found at the Eye Temple at Tell Brak include a staring figure with a conical cap, which may represent a god.

all of Mesopotamia, Tell Brak became an administrative center. His grandson, Naram-Sin, built an imposing palace or fortress with walls more than 30 feet thick. It may have been used to store tribute collected by Akkadian officials. Naram-Sin boasted in an inscription that he was "king of the four quarters, king of the universe." He may not have ruled the universe, but his empire extended for nearly 500 miles from Ur to Tell Brak and encompassed what Mesopotamians considered the civilized world.

to tear down the walls around those cities. By lowering such barriers and unifying his realm, he promoted commerce within Mesopotamia and between that region and lands such as India. Merchants there prospered through maritime trade, shipping pearls, ivory, and other treasures to Mesopotamia in exchange for goods such as wool and olive oil. Copper, silver, and other precious metals served such traders as currency. Societies had not yet devised coinage, so instead, the metal was weighed on a scale to determine its value. Sargon used taxes he collected from merchants to pay his soldiers and support royal artists and scribes, who glorified his deeds in sculptures and inscriptions.

Sargon ruled for more than 50 years and founded a dynasty that held firm through the reign of his grandson, Naram-Sin, who crushed a rebellion and declared himself a god. Here, as elsewhere in the ancient

Akkadian cylinder seal of lapis lazuli (above, left) from a royal cemetery in Ur creates the impression in clay (right). A monument (below) shows the victorious King Naram-Sin wearing a conical helmet with bull's horns.

> *"Do not speak ill, speak only good. Do not say evil things, speak well of people. He who speaks ill and says evil—people will waylay him because of his debt to Shamash. Do not talk too freely, watch what you say."*
>
> THE AKKADÊAN PRECEPTS, CA 2200 B.C.

world, supreme rulers who made other kings their subjects sometimes demanded not just to be treated *like* gods but rather to be worshiped as actual deities. Such imperial cults could last for centuries, as in the case of the Roman Empire. But the Akkadian dynasty collapsed soon after the death of Naram-Sin, and his cult perished with him. Power reverted to Mesopotamian city-states, each of which had a patron deity to whom the local ruler paid homage. The Sumerian king Ur-Nammu, who came to power around 2100 B.C., built a majestic ziggurat in Ur dedicated to the moon god Nanna and established a dynasty that dominated Sumer and Akkad for nearly a century. Ur was later eclipsed by a city that became the capital of an empire that rivaled Sargon's in scope and would long be renowned for its power and glory—Babylon.

BABYLONIAN EMPIRES
From Hammurabi to Nebuchadnezzar II

The wealth and splendor of Mesopotamia made it an irresistible target for nomadic groups living at its margins, including Elamites to the east and Amorites to the west. By 1800 B.C., Amorites from the Syrian desert had infiltrated much of Mesopotamia, including Akkad and the fast-rising city-state of Babylon, located on the Euphrates River near Kish. Amorites spoke a Semitic language related to Akkadian and were quick to embrace Akkadian and Sumerian culture. The Amorite ruler Hammurabi, crowned king of Babylon in 1792, was both an avid warrior and a shrewd administrator who honored the traditions of Sumer, Akkad, and other lands he brought under his authority.

Like Sargon, Hammurabi first moved south and conquered Sumer before seizing control of northern Mesopotamia. He could be merciless to enemies, destroying cities that defied him. But he also provided unity and stability to his newly founded empire by compiling a code of laws, or legal precedents, that applied to all his subjects. Inscribed in stone on a monument

A figure dedicated to Hammurabi (above). Babylon regained glory under Nebuchadnezzar II, whose throne room was adorned with strutting lions (right).

showing Hammurabi being blessed by the sun god Shamash, the code governed domestic disputes as well as crimes committed outside the home. Its purpose, he declared, was to cause justice "to rise like the sun over the people, and to light up the land."

Hammurabi's Code was based partly on Sumerian laws but prescribed harsher penalties than were customary in Sumer for some offenses, including death or mutilation for crimes by commoners resulting in bodily injury. Like the ancient Israelites, who traced their origins to Mesopotamia, the desert-dwelling Amorites may once have applied the principle of "an eye for an eye, and a tooth for a tooth" to all those who harmed others. By Hammurabi's time, however, the law favored people of wealth and rank, who were required only to pay a fine if they injured commoners.

Hammurabi's Code also favored men over women. Adultery by a husband might go unpunished, but an unfaithful wife would be sentenced to execution by drowning.

Despite such inequities, the laws promulgated by Hammurabi

1792 B.C. Hammurabi becomes king of Babylon and begins forging an empire.

1595 B.C. Hittites descend from the north and conquer Babylon.

ca 900 B.C. Assyrians emerge as the dominant force in Mesopotamia and surrounding lands.

612 B.C. Babylonians defeat Assyrians and inherit their empire.

539 B.C. Babylon falls to Cyrus the Great of Persia.

BABYLONIAN EMPIRE

ca 1750 B.C. Hammurabi dies, leaving his code of laws as his chief legacy.

ca 1120 B.C. Nebuchadnezzar I takes power and launches a brief Babylonian revival.

689 B.C. King Sennacherib of Assyria destroys Babylon, which is later rebuilt.

586 B.C. Jerusalem falls to the Babylonian army of Nebuchadnezzar II.

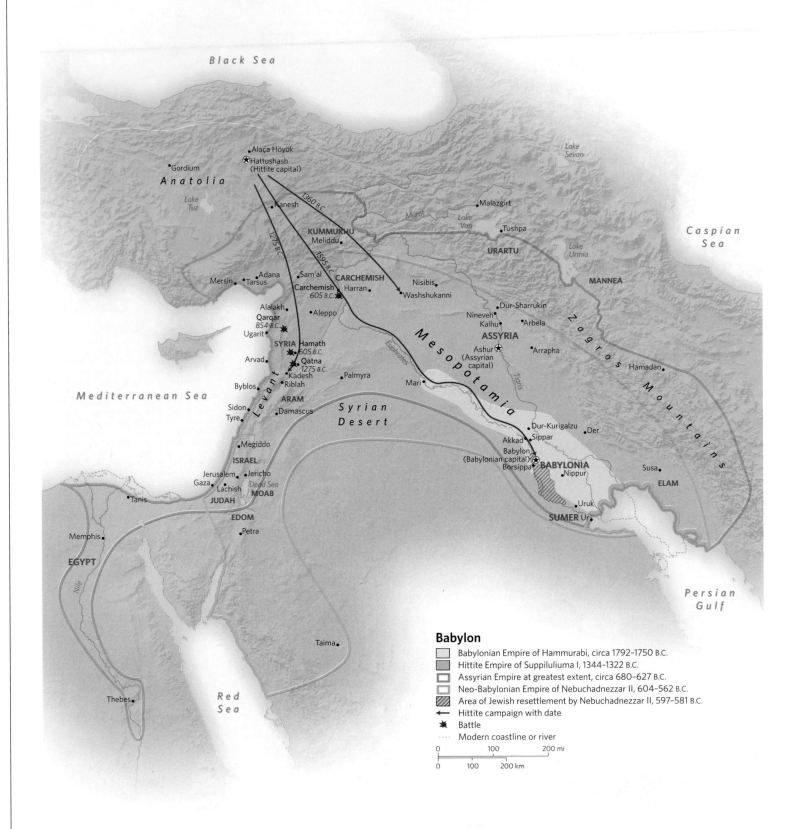

Black Sea

Caspian Sea

Gordium

Alaça Höyük
⊛ Hattushash
(Hittite capital)

Anatolia

Lake Tuz

Kanesh

1360 B.C.

KUMMUKHU
Meliddu

Murat

Lake Van

Malazgirt

Tushpa

URARTU

Lake Urmia

MANNEA

Mersin   Adana
Tarsus

Sam'al
Carchemish   CARCHEMISH
605 B.C.   Harran

Nisibis

Washshukanni

Dur-Sharrukin

Nineveh
Kalhu   Arbela

ASSYRIA

Arrapha

Zagros Mountains

Hamadan

Alalakh
Qarqar
854 B.C.
Ugarit

Aleppo

SYRIA   Hamath
605 B.C.
Arvad   Qatna
1275 B.C.
Kadesh
Byblos   Riblah

Mediterranean Sea

Palmyra

Euphrates

Mari

Ashur
(Assyrian
capital)

Mesopotamia

Tigris

Sidon
Tyre   Damascus

Levant

ARAM

Syrian Desert

Megiddo

ISRAEL

Jerusalem   Jericho
Gaza   Lachish
JUDAH   *Dead Sea*   MOAB

Dur-Kurigalzu
Der
Akkad   Sippar
Babylon
(Babylonian capital)   ⊛ BABYLONIA
Borsippa   Nippur

Susa

ELAM

EDOM

SUMER   Ur

Memphis

EGYPT

Petra

Nile

Red Sea

Taima

Tanis

Thebes

Persian Gulf

Babylon

☐ Babylonian Empire of Hammurabi, circa 1792–1750 B.C.
☐ Hittite Empire of Suppiluliuma I, 1344–1322 B.C.
☐ Assyrian Empire at greatest extent, circa 680–627 B.C.
☐ Neo-Babylonian Empire of Nebuchadnezzar II, 604–562 B.C.
▨ Area of Jewish resettlement by Nebuchadnezzar II, 597–581 B.C.
← Hittite campaign with date
⊛ Battle
‑ ‑ ‑ Modern coastline or river

0   100   200 mi
0   100   200 km

offered some protection to women, commoners, and slaves. For example, wives abused by their husbands could sue for divorce, and all defendants were at least somewhat shielded from false testimony by a law prescribing the death penalty for witnesses who committed perjury. Setting laws down in writing discouraged judges from ruling arbitrarily and promoted the idea of justice as universal and enduring. Many emperors throughout history, from Hammurabi to Napoleon Bonaparte, issued law codes in an effort to unite realms that contained people of many different customs and conceptions of justice, and to discourage them from taking the law into their own hands. Hammurabi's Code did not allow for personal acts of vengeance, and that alone was a significant contribution to law and order.

However accomplished they were as lawgivers, Hammurabi and other ancient conquerors lived by the sword and often died by the sword. They were not bound

An Assyrian artist versed in Babylonian and Sumerian lore carved this image of the mythic hero Gilgamesh taming a lion.

by any concept of international law, and there were no rules restraining kings or emperors from attacking each other, even when they had formed alliances and pledged eternal friendship. For instance, Hammurabi turned against his ally the king of Mari, a flourishing city on the upper Euphrates River, and destroyed his palace and a temple to Shamash, which was inscribed with curses on anyone who desecrated the shrine, asking the gods to cut the offender's throat and annihilate his offspring. In strife-torn Mesopotamia, such curses were often fulfilled. Hammurabi's dynasty lasted only a few generations before it was undermined by rebels and toppled by conquerors as ruthless as he had been.

In 1595 B.C., Babylon was sacked by Hittites who swept down from Asia Minor, the area known in ancient times as Anatolia and in recent times as Turkey. The Hittites were one of many groups of Indo-Europeans who spoke related languages and migrated in waves from the

THE CODE OF HAMMURABI

Hammurabi's Code was not equitable, because it did not treat people of all ranks equally. But it embodied a principle that remains central to our modern conception of justice: the idea that laws and punishments should be set down in writing and made known to those who are charged with offenses as well as to their accusers and judges, who must abide by the code. "Let the oppressed, who has a case at law, come and stand before this my image as king of righteousness," Hammurabi proclaimed in writing on the monument pictured below, inscribed with his law code: "Let him read the inscription, and understand my precious words: The inscription will explain his case to him; he will find out what is just, and his heart will be glad." Even those who could not read—a large segment of the populace—benefited when laws and penalties were committed to writing and judges could not then alter them at will to suit their prejudices.

The sun god Shamash hands the scepter of authority to Hammurabi on this stele inscribed with his code.

> *"If any one receive into his house a runaway male or female slave of the court, or of a freedman, and does not bring it out at the public proclamation of the major domus, the master of the house shall be put to death."*

CODE OF **HAMMURABI**

BABYLONIAN MATHEMATICS

Babylonians developed a method of computation based on the number 60 that served as the basis for the 60-second minute, the 60-minute hour, and the 360-degree circle. Fractions were denoted as portions of 60, with 30 representing one-half, 20 one-third, 15 one-fourth, 12 one-fifth, and 10 one-sixth. Babylonian students could easily calculate that one-sixth (10) plus one-third (20) equals one-half (30). Babylonian numerals were superior to Roman numerals for math because all numbers from one to ten were designated by a different numeral and numbers above ten were designated by compound numerals whose value depended on their position from left to right. That facilitated addition, subtraction, and other operations. Babylonians solved problems such as determining the length of the hypotenuse of a right triangle—a solution that anticipated the Pythagorean theorem (credited to the Greek Pythagoras) by more than a thousand years.

A clay tablet inscribed around the time of Hammurabi shows calculations of the sort Babylonians made to arrive at a version of the Pythagorean theorem.

An artist's rendering of the fabled Hanging Gardens of Babylon evokes the splendor of that city, rebuilt following its destruction by Assyrians in the early seventh century B.C.

Eurasian steppes above the Black Sea and Caspian Sea, where they domesticated horses and harnessed them to war chariots. Another branch of Indo-Europeans called Aryans gave their name to Iran, where many settled while others advanced into Afghanistan and India. The Hittites who stormed Babylon soon withdrew to Asia Minor with their booty, leaving Mesopotamia prey to other invaders.

Babylonian power revived briefly around 1100 B.C. under King Nebuchadnezzar I and his successors. In centuries to come, however, the region was dominated by their northern rivals, the Assyrians—a warlike people who embarked on far-ranging conquests. By the seventh century B.C., their domain extended all the way from Mesopotamia to Egypt, but Assyrian rulers such as King Sennacherib were unable to maintain so vast an empire for long. To compel obedience, they relied mainly on intimidation, which cowed some subjects but drove others to rebel. That included the resurgent Babylonians, who rebuilt their city after it was destroyed by Sennacherib in 689 B.C. and toppled their Assyrian masters in 612. They, too, faced rebellions such as that mounted in Judah, which was all that remained of the former kingdom of Israel after earlier Assyrian conquests. Troops sent by King Nebuchadnezzar II to put down that uprising stormed Jerusalem and carried captives to Babylon, characterized in the Bible as a land of oppression: "O daughter Babylon, you

devastator! Happy shall they be who pay you back what you have done to us!" (Psalms 137:8).

Neither the Babylonians nor the Assyrians were as barbaric as their victims made them out to be. They were creators and

builders as well as destroyers, drawing on the cultural and artistic traditions of Mesopotamia to promote literature and learning and embellish their cities with monuments and gardens. Some Jewish exiles who settled in Babylon found it to their liking and chose to remain there even after they were allowed to return to their homeland. Beyond Mesopotamia, however, few subjects of the Assyrians or Babylonians relished living under their punishing regimes or regretted their downfall. To control diverse lands and peoples without resorting repeatedly to armed force required a ruler as skilled at governing as he was at waging war. Such was the king who founded the Persian Empire and surpassed the Babylonians.

PERSIAN EMPIRE
Cyrus the Great and His Successors

Like Sargon of Akkad, the Persian conqueror Cyrus the Great, born around 585 B.C., was a storied figure whose dramatic ascent to power inspired legends. By one account, he was of royal birth but was sent secretly to be raised by shepherds when the king of the Medes, to whom Persians were then subject, dreamed that Cyrus would overthrow him and ordered the infant killed. Both the Persians and the Medes spoke Indo-European languages and were descendants of Aryans who entered Iran from the north. Centuries later, Nazi Germany constructed a fiction of a superior Aryan race, but in reality, these people had much in common with other groups in the region. Like Semitic tribes such as the Amorites or the nomadic Israelites described in the Book of Genesis, they were mostly pastoralists who herded sheep or cattle and followed their herds from place to place. Presiding over them were priests, known as *magi* among the Persians, and nobles or chieftains who gained wealth and prestige by waging war. The legend of Cyrus's upbringing linked him both

An inscribed cylinder (above) tells how Cyrus the Great captured Babylon. His successor Darius I ruled at the Iranian city of Susa in a court adorned with winged sphinxes (right).

to that warrior elite and to common Iranians who followed their flocks, signifying that he was close to all his subjects and tended to their needs like a good shepherd.

The first Persian kings may have been elected by a council of tribal chieftains. By the time Cyrus took the throne in 559, however, kingship was hereditary, passed down through the Achaemenid dynasty to which he belonged. After mounting a successful rebellion against the king of the Medes, Cyrus became the ruler of all Iranians, whose skill at fighting on horseback gave his army great mobility. He next campaigned against Lydia, a country rich in gold, located in Asia Minor near the Aegean Sea. According to the Greek historian Herodotus, Lydia's fabulously wealthy king, Croesus, launched the war with Persia after being assured by a soothsayer that he would destroy a great kingdom. The prophecy came true, but it was his *own* kingdom that fell when Cyrus besieged Croesus and his troops at their capital, Sardis, and captured the city in 546.

559 B.C. Cyrus the Great becomes king of the Persians and leads them against their overlords, the Medes.

539 B.C. Cyrus takes Babylon and becomes master of Mesopotamia.

525 B.C. Persian troops led by Cambyses conquer Egypt.

490 B.C. Greek troops repulse Persian invaders at Marathon.

330 B.C. Alexander the Great shatters Persian Empire.

546 B.C. Cyrus defeats King Croesus of Lydia.

529 B.C. Cyrus dies in battle and is succeeded by his son Cambyses.

522 B.C. Darius I seizes power following the death of Cambyses.

480 B.C. Persian fleet led by Darius's successor, Xerxes, defeated by Greeks at Salamis.

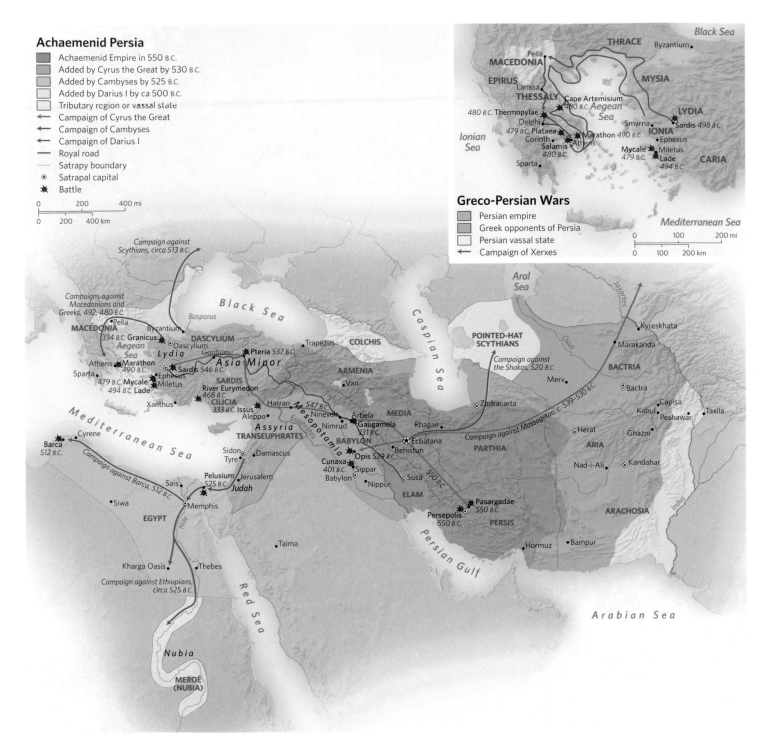

Achaemenid Persia

- Achaemenid Empire in 550 B.C.
- Added by Cyrus the Great by 530 B.C.
- Added by Cambyses by 525 B.C.
- Added by Darius I by ca 500 B.C.
- Tributary region or vassal state
- ← Campaign of Cyrus the Great
- ← Campaign of Cambyses
- ← Campaign of Darius I
- — Royal road
- — Satrapy boundary
- ⊙ Satrapal capital
- ✴ Battle

Greco-Persian Wars

- Persian empire
- Greek opponents of Persia
- Persian vassal state
- ← Campaign of Xerxes

After conquering lands surrounding Mesopotamia, Cyrus closed in on Babylon, which was weakened by internal divisions after King Nabonidus elevated another god above that city's patron deity, Marduk. Many Babylonians turned against their king and saw no reason to oppose

Cyrus, who was known to spare those who yielded to him. In 539, they opened their gates to the Persians, who entered the city "in peace, amidst joy and jubilation," according to an inscription touting Cyrus's triumph. Cyrus reassured Babylonians by publicly worshiping their beloved Marduk,

just as he won the gratitude of other people he conquered by restoring images of gods seized in battle and allowing exiles from Judah and other kingdoms to return home.

Cyrus the Great died in 529 while campaigning against defiant tribes around the Caspian Sea. He would be remembered

> *"Marduk, the great lord,*
> *rejoiced at [my good] deeds,*
> *and he pronounced a sweet blessing over me,*
> *Cyrus, the king who fears him,*
> *and over Cambyses, the son [my] issue,*
> *[and over] my all my troops,*
> *that we might live happily*
> *in his presence, in well-being."*

CYRUS CYLINDER

not just as a mighty conqueror but also as a magnanimous victor who won over those he defeated by showing them mercy. One measure of his greatness was the esteem in which he was held in later years by the Greeks despite the bitter wars they waged against his Persian successors. In the words of the Greek author Xenophon, "he honored his subjects and cared for them as if they were his own children; and they, on their part, revered Cyrus as a father."

Cyrus's son and heir, Cambyses, enlarged the empire by invading Egypt—which had regained power since rebelling against Assyria a century earlier—and conquering that kingdom in 525. The Persians, little known before Cyrus launched his campaigns, were now masters of the Middle East. But that alone did not assure them of lasting glory. Throughout history, many such empires left little impression on posterity. Some collapsed quickly after the death or defeat of their architect; others survived for a generation or two before crumbling.

One reason empires were short-lived was that they were often ruled by men who prided themselves on leading armies to bat-

tle and embarked on long campaigns to expand their realms or put down rebellions. Such lengthy absences allowed plots and power struggles to develop within the palace. After conquering Egypt, for instance, Cambyses spent three years securing his grip on that country and advancing south-

A golden Persian earring inlaid with turquoise and other precious stones reflects the wealth acquired by Cyrus and his successors.

ward up the Nile into Nubia. Meanwhile, a rebellion, possibly led by his brother and successor Bardiya, was brewing against him at home. Upon learning of the plot in 522, Cambyses rushed back, but he died on the way. When Bardiya died as well, the man who then took the throne, Darius, claimed that Cambyses had ordered Bardiya killed after discovering his brother's treachery. Darius may well have staged a coup against Bardiya, however, and then shifted the blame to Cambyses.

Some Persians considered Darius a murderous usurper, and many subjects in distant lands saw this as an opportunity to rebel. This succession crisis left the empire in turmoil and might have shattered it had not King Darius I been

THE WEALTH OF CROESUS

These coins, stamped with royal emblems, were issued in Lydia around the time of Croesus.

Not many ancient rulers were as rich as Croesus, king of Lydia in Asia Minor. His kingdom contained large deposits of electrum, an alloy of gold and silver, which he used to issue coins—a practice that originated in Lydia and Greece a century or so before Croesus took power around 560 B.C. His conspicuous wealth made him the subject of legends. According to the Greek historian Herodotus, he met with the wise Athenian ruler Solon and asked if wealth did not ensure happiness. "He who possesses great store of riches is no nearer happiness than he who has what suffices for his daily needs," Solon replied, "unless he continue in the enjoyment of all his good things to the end of life." The defeat of Croesus by Cyrus the Great was viewed by Herodotus as proof that wealth does not guarantee fulfillment. ✍

Darius unified his empire by issuing coins like the one shown here and building roads used by merchants and messengers traveling between his mountainous Iranian homeland and the Aegean Sea.

Ten Thousand Immortals

The Persian army was led by an elite corps known as the Ten Thousand Immortals, because any who died were promptly replaced, so their number remained constant. They had special privileges and were rewarded handsomely. "Every man glittered with the gold which he carried about his person in unlimited quantity," wrote Herodotus in his account of the wars waged against the Greeks by the Persians Darius I and Xerxes. "They were accompanied, moreover, by covered carriages full of their women and servants, all elaborately fitted out. Special food, separate from that of the rest of the army, was brought along for them on dromedaries and mules." They were well armed with bows, spears, and daggers, but not as heavily armored as the Greek troops. Whereas the Greeks had bronze helmets and thick wooden shields, the Ten Thousand Immortals wore turbans and carried wicker shields that offered less protection in close combat.

Darius formed a contingent of 1,000 men within the Ten Thousand Immortals to serve as imperial guards, portrayed here at his court in Susa.

as shrewd as he was ruthless. By his own account, his troops crushed nine uprisings in the first three years of his reign. After restoring order to his realm, Darius expanded it by advancing its eastern frontier to the Indus River and its western boundary beyond the Bosporus, the strait separating Asia from Europe. More significant than his conquests, however, were the steps he took to consolidate the vast dominion, demonstrating an organizational genius rivaled by few ancient or modern rulers.

Adopting a system initiated by Cyrus, Darius divided the Persian Empire into more than 20 provinces called satrapies, governed by satraps he appointed. The local officials who served under each satrap were mostly natives of that province and ran their districts without much interference from their Persian overlords. One of the main responsibilities of satraps was to collect taxes—annual levies that replaced the irregular tribute payments demanded by the rulers of other ancient empires. When demands for tribute were too heavy, they caused resentment and rebellion; when they were too light, kings had difficulty funding their army and administration unless they found new lands to plunder. By imposing regular taxes, Darius sought to avoid those extremes. The success of this system depended on the loyalty and integrity of satraps, who could cause turmoil if they overtaxed subjects to enrich

*"It is said that as many days as there are
in the whole journey, so many are the men and horses
that stand along the road, each horse
and man at the interval of a day's journey;
and these are stayed neither by snow nor rain nor heat
nor darkness from accomplishing
their appointed course with all speed."*

HERODOTUS DESCRIBING THE PERSIAN MESSENGER SYSTEM

PERSEPOLIS

The magnificent palace complex of Persepolis, located near Shiraz, Iran, was inaugurated by Darius around 518 B.C., completed a century later, and destroyed by the conquering army of Alexander the Great in 330 B.C. According to the Greek author Plutarch, Alexander needed 5,000 mules and 20,000 camels to make off with the loot from Persepolis. Over the centuries, artists and curiosity-seekers visited the ruins, but systematic excavations did not begin until 1931. Despite the looting and burning by Alexander's men, archaeologists and the Iranian workers assisting them unearthed historical treasures at Persepolis in the form of inscriptions, splendid sculptures carved in relief and other works of art, and the remains of buildings, which allowed them to reconstruct portions of the palace.

Lining the walls of a stairway leading to the vast Apadana, or reception hall, were reliefs showing envoys from more than 20 countries carrying tribute to the king of kings, including Bactrians offering him camels and Indians loaded down with gold dust. The Harem of Xerxes included a relief showing that king fighting a lion and contained more than 20 apartments, which may have been occupied by his wives or consorts. The pride he and his father, Darius, took in Persepolis is evident in proclamations they had inscribed there. Ahura Mazda and other gods willed that this great fortress should be built, Darius proclaimed: "And so I built it. And I built it secure and beautiful and adequate, just as I was intending to." ⌀

Sculpted in relief, Persian nobles ascend a stairway reconstructed by archaeologists at Persepolis, built by Darius I and his successors.

themselves or fund campaigns against the emperor. To guard against that, Darius dispatched secret agents to spy on his distant appointees. He also formed a trusted imperial guard of a thousand men within a larger elite corps of Persian troops called the Ten Thousand Immortals.

Both taxation and trade were facilitated by coins Darius issued, a practice he adopted from Lydian and Greek rulers. Unlike gold or silver ingots that had to be weighed to determine their value, Persian coins—stamped with an idealized image of Darius as a warrior, drawing his bow—had a fixed value and were easily exchanged.

Traders, troops, and imperial spies moved quickly about the Persian Empire on roads built by Darius and his successors. The greatest of those was the Royal Road, which extended for more than 1,500 miles from Ephesus on the Aegean Sea to Susa in western Iran, the empire's administrative center. Other roads led south from Susa to Pasargadae, Cyrus's former stronghold and burial place, and to Persepolis, where Darius and his successors built a splendid palace complex. Caravans of traders riding donkeys or camels took about three months to traverse the Royal Road, but royal dispatches could be relayed from Susa to Ephesus in a week by express riders.

Darius presided at court with great pomp, seated on a high throne below a purple canopy. "By the grace of Ahura Mazda am I king," declared Darius, who claimed a divine right to rule granted him

> *"I replied: 'Firstly, I am Zarathushtra, A veritable opponent of the evil-doer, but a powerful friend of the good, am I.'"*
>
> ZARATHUSTRA,
> FROM *USHTAVAITI GATHA*

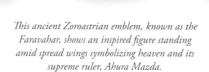

This ancient Zoroastrian emblem, known as the Faravahar, shows an inspired figure standing amid spread wings symbolizing heaven and its supreme ruler, Ahura Mazda.

by Ahura Mazda, the supreme deity of Zoroastrianism, a religion based on the teachings of the Iranian prophet Zoroaster. Although Zoroastrians recognized the existence of other gods or spirits, some good and some demonic, Ahura Mazda surpassed them all and embodied truth, justice, and wisdom. He reigned as king of kings in heaven, as Darius did on earth. Although Darius did not impose his beliefs on people of other

faiths, Zoroastrianism influenced Judaism and later Christianity, whose followers shared with Zoroastrians a belief in heaven and hell and the coming of an apocalypse, or day of judgment, when the fate of all souls would be decided.

For more than three decades, Darius remained lord of the Middle East. People there had long been ruled by kings or emperors who wielded power over many cities or countries and, like Darius, claimed to be divinely inspired, if not actually divine. When Persian forces advanced west to the Aegean Sea and crossed into Europe, however, they entered the Greek world, consisting of independent city-states with inhabitants who resisted imperial domination. Before Athens instituted democracy in the fifth century B.C. by allowing all free male citizens to elect their leaders, many Greek city-states were ruled by tyrants, who seized power and functioned as dictators. Some of them were popular figures who overthrew oligarchies (ruling councils of aristocrats) and won favor among citizens. But Greeks did not worship these tyrants, nor bow to rulers who considered themselves immortal or invincible—sins of pride for which ambitious men who soared too high or reached too far were punished by the gods in Greek myths and tragedies.

Darius overreached after the Ionians—residents of Greek city-states along the eastern shore of the Aegean Sea—rebelled against him in 499 B.C. Although he suppressed that revolt, he then set out to punish the Athenians and others on the Greek mainland who had aided the Ionians. Like

"In the month of Muharrem I set out for Khorasan, in order to oppose the invasion of the Uzbeks, and advanced by way of Ghurbend and Shibertu."

THE MEMOIRS OF **BABUR**,
EVENTS OF THE YEAR A.H. 912

An artist's rendering of the Battle of Marathon shows surging Greeks, at left with spears raised, overcoming their Persian foes.

many emperors who succeeded continually in battle, he grew overconfident and thought his troops were superior to any challenge. His army was considerably larger than the opposing Greek forces, but the Athenians were fighting on their own turf and outmaneuvered their foes in 490 at Marathon, inflicting a stinging defeat on the Persians. Darius died in 486 before he could launch another campaign against the Greeks or put down an uprising in Egypt, where rebels were encouraged to learn that the Persians were not unbeatable.

Darius's son and successor, Xerxes, brutally suppressed the revolt in Egypt as well as a rebellion in Babylon, where his troops destroyed the shrine of Marduk, the god honored earlier by Cyrus the Great. Such stern measures led the Greeks to denounce Xerxes as a despot who lacked the wisdom and restraint of Cyrus and foolishly thought his powers were limitless. According to Herodotus, Xerxes vowed not just to avenge the defeat at Marathon and conquer Greece but also to extend Persian territory as far as "heaven reaches. The sun will then shine on no land beyond our borders; for I will pass through Europe from one end to the other."

Xerxes made meticulous preparations for war against the Greeks. For three years, he amassed troops from various countries and assembled a huge fleet of galleys—warships propelled by oars. Yet he and his commanders found it hard to supply and coordinate their sprawling

MARATHON: A RACE TO DIE FOR

According to legend, in 490 B.C. a Greek soldier was sent as a messenger from the battlefield at Marathon to announce the defeat of Persian invaders to the anxious people of Athens, some 26 miles away. Arriving, he cried, "We have won!" with his last breath and dropped dead. When the Olympic Games were revived in 1896, the marathon race inspired by that feat became a competitive event.

At the ancient Greek Olympian games, athletes vied in other contests of military significance, including hurling the discus and the javelin. For the most part, those contests served as a peaceful outlet for the intensely competitive Greeks, who were expected to suspend all hostilities during the games, held once every four years. After defeating the Persians, however, the city-states of Athens and Sparta renewed their old rivalry and drew their allies into the long and bitter Peloponnesian War. The games continued, but they were often shadowed by conflict and controversy, much like those held in recent times of international tension at cities such as Berlin, Munich, and Moscow. In 420 B.C., Sparta was barred from participating, and the games were conducted under armed guard.

A torchbearer leads the way in a spirited race depicted on a Grecian urn.

forces. Greek galleys, defending their home waters, caught the much larger Persian fleet in a narrow strait at Salamis in 480 and won a smashing victory. Disheartened, Xerxes sailed away with what remained of his navy, leaving his army to be defeated at Plataea in 479 by Greeks who had vowed to fight to the death and "put freedom before life."

This campaign marked the end of Persian expansion and demonstrated that even the mightiest empires had their limits, imposed by geography and human nature, or the tendency of men to fight harder for their own land than when campaigning on foreign ground for a remote emperor

Persian chariots like this golden model were drawn by horses.

who might not even speak their language. Xerxes withdrew to his palace at Persepolis, where he was assassinated in 465.

Persian power declined under Xerxes' successors, who overtaxed their subjects

and as a result faced frequent rebellions. Darius III, the last king of the Achaemenid dynasty founded by Cyrus, wilted under the blistering assaults of Macedonians led by their inspirational commander, Alexander the Great, who conquered the Persians in 330 B.C. and made their empire his own. Two centuries of Persian rule left a deep impression, however, and much of the region would remain under Persian influence or control for a thousand years to come.

An embattled warrior stands beside a charioteer with harness in hand in a Greek depiction of the fighting that brought Alexander the Great victory over Darius III and doomed the Persian Empire.

DAILY LIFE

WATER TO THE DESERT

Unlike Mesopotamia, whose Tigris and Euphrates Rivers provided water via canals to nourish fields and cities, arid and mountainous Persia had no major interior waterways. Agriculture and settlement were made possible by irrigation tunnels called *qanats*, which moved water down from underground sources at high elevations. Vertical shafts were excavated at regular intervals to remove soil and provide ventilation to laborers as they dug the tunnel, which sloped gently down to the outlet, eliminating the need for pumps. Qanats were in use during the reign of Cyrus the Great and his successors and became more elaborate over time. Bridges such as the one shown at left, incorporating arches like those used in Roman aqueducts to distribute the weight and keep the structure from collapsing, carried water from the outlets of qanats across ravines to distant villages. Qanats similar in design to those constructed by the ancient Persians still provide water to parched regions of Iran and other countries today.

This aqueduct in central Iran was linked to an irrigation tunnel called a qanat.

PERSIAN DYNASTIES
Seleucids, Parthians, and Sasanids

Following the death of Alexander the Great in 323 B.C., his top generals vied for control of his empire and carved it up. Greece and neighboring Macedonia—which had absorbed Greek culture and was now exporting it to conquered lands—went to Antigonus. Egypt fell to Ptolemy, founder of a dynasty that ruled the land of the Nile until the death of Queen Cleopatra three centuries later. The remainder of Alexander's realm was claimed by Seleucus, who became Persia's new monarch and ruler of most of the Middle East, with the exception of Egypt. To do so, he had to battle his Macedonian rivals as well as former Persian subjects who were weary of imperial domination and did not want another king of kings.

Like Alexander, Seleucus invaded India but had to pull back, under pressure from Chandragupta Maurya, founder of the first Indian empire. After agreeing to a truce and ceding to Chandragupta areas north of the Indus River formerly under Persian control, he received 500 war elephants in compensation. He used those fearsome animals, capable of crushing a man's head under foot, to defeat his

Seleucus I, portrayed above on a coin in battle gear, acquired war elephants in India. According to biblical accounts, Seleucid troops later used elephants against Jewish rebels, as depicted at right.

archrival, Antigonus, in 301 and win control of Syria. He then went on to conquer Asia Minor. Following his death in 281, he was deified, common to Macedonians whose kings were cult figures.

The empire established by Seleucus I, founder of the Seleucid dynasty, combined elements of Greek or Hellenistic culture with Persian traditions. In a ceremony staged by Alexander the Great shortly before his death, Seleucus had wed a Persian noblewoman named Apama while Alexander married the daughter of Darius III and several of his generals wed other Persian princesses. Although Seleucus later took other wives or mistresses, as was customary for rulers in much of the ancient world, Apama was the mother of his heir, Antiochus I. Seleucid kings were thus partly of Persian descent, and they adopted the Persian administrative system by appointing satraps to govern their provinces and collect taxes. True to their Macedonian heritage, however, they founded cities dominated by Greek-speaking colonists, including Antioch in Syria and Seleucia, their capital on the Tigris River. Greeks formed an elite group, often resented by natives subjected to Greek customs.

323 B.C. Alexander the Great dies, triggering a power struggle between Seleucus and other Macedonian generals.

301 B.C. Seleucus defeats Antigonus and extends his domain from Iran to the Mediterranean.

281 B.C. Seleucus I dies, bequeathing power to his son, Antiochus I, of the Seleucid dynasty.

165 B.C. Jewish rebels led by Judas Maccabeus defy Antiochus IV and take Jerusalem.

139 B.C. Mithradates I leads Parthians to defeat Demetrius II and supplant the Seleucids.

64 B.C. Romans conquer Syria and threaten Parthians in Mesopotamia.

53 B.C. Parthians crush invading Roman army at Carrhae in Mesopotamia.

A.D. 224 Persian rebels led by Ardashir I, founder of the Sasanid dynasty, oust last Parthian king.

A.D. 651 Arab conquerors bring Sasanid rule to an end.

Eleazar occidit elephante e ipe mortuus fuit

Primi machab vi°

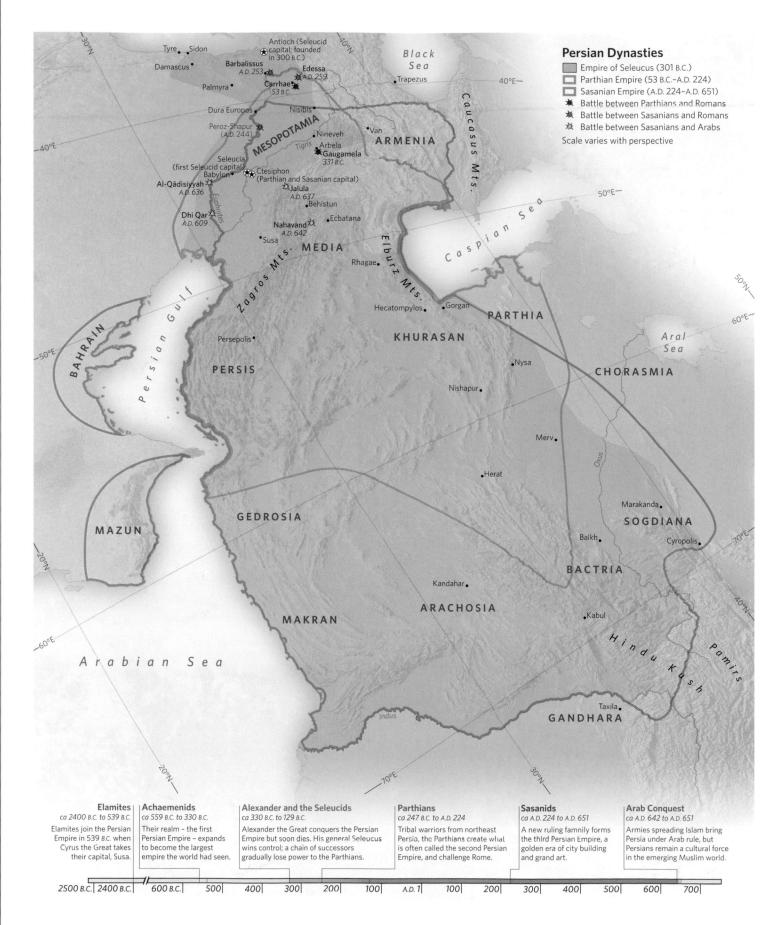

Persian Dynasties

- Empire of Seleucus (301 B.C.)
- Parthian Empire (53 B.C.–A.D. 224)
- Sasanian Empire (A.D. 224–A.D. 651)
- ✹ Battle between Parthians and Romans
- ✷ Battle between Sasanians and Romans
- ✸ Battle between Sasanians and Arabs

Scale varies with perspective

Tyre • Sidon
Antioch (Seleucid capital; founded in 300 B.C.)
Damascus •
Barbalissus *A.D. 253*
Edessa *A.D. 259*
Palmyra •
Carrhae *53 B.C.*
Dura Europos
Nisibis •
Peroz-Shapur *(A.D. 244)*
MESOPOTAMIA
Nineveh • Van
Tigris
Arbela
Gaugamela *331 B.C.*
ARMENIA
Seleucia (first Seleucid capital)
Babylon •
Ctesiphon (Parthian and Sasanian capital)
Al-Qādisiyyah *A.D. 636*
Jalula *A.D. 637*
Behistun
Dhi Qar *A.D. 609*
Nahavand *A.D. 642*
Ecbatana
Euphrates
Susa •
MEDIA
Rhagae •
Black Sea
Trapezus •
Caucasus Mts.
Caspian Sea
Elburz Mts.
Hecatompylos •
Gorgan •
PARTHIA
KHURASAN
Aral Sea
CHORASMIA
Nysa •
Nishapur •
Persepolis •
PERSIS
Zagros Mts.
BAHRAIN
Persian Gulf
Merv •
SOGDIANA
Marakanda •
Balkh •
Cyropolis •
Herat •
MAZUN
GEDROSIA
BACTRIA
Kandahar •
ARACHOSIA
Kabul •
MAKRAN
Hindu Kush
Pamirs
Arabian Sea
Indus
Taxila •
GANDHARA

Elamites *ca 2400 B.C. to 539 B.C.*	**Achaemenids** *ca 559 B.C. to 330 B.C.*	**Alexander and the Seleucids** *ca 330 B.C. to 129 B.C.*	**Parthians** *ca 247 B.C. to A.D. 224*	**Sasanids** *ca A.D. 224 to A.D. 651*	**Arab Conquest** *ca A.D. 642 to A.D. 651*
Elamites join the Persian Empire in 539 B.C. when Cyrus the Great takes their capital, Susa.	Their realm – the first Persian Empire – expands to become the largest empire the world had seen.	Alexander the Great conquers the Persian Empire but soon dies. His general Seleucus wins control; a chain of successors gradually lose power to the Parthians.	Tribal warriors from northeast Persia, the Parthians create what is often called the second Persian Empire, and challenge Rome.	A new ruling family forms the third Persian Empire, a golden era of city building and grand art.	Armies spreading Islam bring Persia under Arab rule, but Persians remain a cultural force in the emerging Muslim world.

2500 B.C. | 2400 B.C. | 600 B.C. | 500 | 400 | 300 | 200 | 100 | A.D. 1 | 100 | 200 | 300 | 400 | 500 | 600 | 700

King Antiochus IV was a devotee of Greek culture who, after quelling an uprising in Jerusalem, forbade Jews to worship Yahweh and erected an altar to the Greek god Zeus in their temple. Shocked by this sacrilege, rebels led by Judas Maccabeus took Jerusalem in 165 B.C. and tore down that altar, rededicating the temple to Yahweh and keeping up their struggle until their province of Judea won independence.

That Jewish rebellion was just one of many challenges faced by Seleucid rulers as their empire weakened and crumbled. A greater threat came from Rome, whose formidable legions were advancing east around the Mediterranean. During the first century B.C., the Romans completed their conquest of the Mediterranean world by subjugating Egypt, Judea, and Syria—the last bastion of the Seleucids, who resided there after losing control of Iran and Mesopotamia. Those eastern lands, which had formed the core of the old Persian Empire, fell to the expansive Parthians, whose warriors fanned out on horseback from northern Iran, confounding foes with their dazzling skills as cavalrymen.

Once a province within the Persian and Seleucid Empires, Parthia broke free and became an empire in its own right under King Mithradates I, who defeated and captured the Seleucid ruler Demetrius II in 139 B.C. Having established his supremacy, he spared Demetrius—who was later freed— and offered him his daughter in marriage. Mithradates also dealt mercifully with the many Greeks who had settled in the lands he ruled and had feared reprisals under this new regime.

The Parthians had little reason now to beware of Greeks, but they had good cause to fear those who had conquered Greece—the far-ranging Romans, who after encircling the Mediterranean began advancing toward the Persian Gulf. The Parthians were a loosely organized society whose kings had limited authority over local chieftains or clan leaders. They never amassed enough offensive strength

Ishtar, Assyrian and Babylonian goddess, 4th century B.C.

ANTIOCHUS AND STRATONICE

In his later years, Seleucus I offered his young wife Stratonice in marriage to his son and heir, Antiochus. According to Plutarch, Antiochus had fallen for his stepmother and was so ashamed and lovesick he was pining away. His condition was diagnosed by a physician, who noticed that when Stratonice was near, Antiochus's "voice faltered, his face flushed up, his eyes glanced stealthily, a sudden sweat broke out on his skin, the beatings of his heart were irregular and violent, and, unable to support the excess of his passion, he would sink into a state of faintness, prostration, and pallor." Seleucus declared, "It would be well for me to part not only with Stratonice, but with my empire, to save Antiochus." Yet he may have had another reason: His marriage to Stratonice was part of a pact with her father, the Macedonian ruler Demetrius I, with whom Seleucus was now at odds. ✎

Antiochus languishes in the presence of the lovely Stratonice in a painting by Swiss artist Angelika Kauffmann.

PARTHIAN SHOTS

Persians prided themselves on their expertise at mounted warfare. From the time of Cyrus the Great to the reign of the Sasanid ruler Ardashir II nearly a thousand years later, no warriors who emerged from Iran on horseback were more adept than the Parthians. Among their tactics was the Parthian shot, in which they turned and fired arrows backward at pursuers with deadly accuracy while galloping away.

Sturdy Parthian horses could bear cavalrymen equipped with heavy weapons and armor. At the Battle of Carrhae, those troopers smashed into Roman infantrymen while light cavalry swept around their flanks, firing arrows and raising blinding clouds of dust. As the Roman historian Tacitus related, the foot soldiers "could neither see clearly nor speak plainly, but being crowded into a narrow compass . . . were shot, and died no easy nor even speedy death." Of 40,000 Roman soldiers, fewer than 10,000 survived. Parthians were such renowned horsemen that long after they fell from power, Ardashir II had himself portrayed firing a Parthian shot.

Ardashir II strikes the pose made famous by Parthian cavalrymen on a silver dish from the late fourth century A.D.

to strike against the Roman threat, but when Romans invaded their territory, the Parthians banded together and defended themselves furiously. At the Battle of Carrhae, waged in northern Mesopotamia in 53 B.C., they scored a stunning victory, all but annihilating the opposing Roman army.

Unfortunately for the Parthians, the Romans never forgot such defeats and went to great lengths to avenge them. On

> *"Of all the days in the year, the one which they celebrate most is their birthday. It is customary to have the board furnished on that day with an ampler supply than common... They are very fond of wine, and drink it in large quantities."*
>
> HERODOTUS, ON THE CUSTOMS OF THE PERSIANS, CA 430 B.C.

several occasions, Roman legions sacked the Parthian capital, Ctesiphon, burning and looting, slaughtering men in droves, and carrying off thousands of women and children as slaves. The Parthians refused to surrender to the Romans, but the attacks weakened them and their rulers, who faced insurrections.

Among the rebels vying for power were Persians in southern Iran, who hoped to restore the fabled empire founded by Cyrus the Great. In A.D. 224, a Persian prince named Ardashir toppled the last Parthian monarch and proclaimed himself king of kings. Rulers of the dynasty he founded, known as the Sasanids for a revered ancestor of Ardashir I, considered themselves heirs to Cyrus the Great and Darius I and sought

to recapture past Persian glory by bringing provinces and their satraps under tighter imperial control, fostering trade, patronizing artists and scholars, rebuilding cities, erecting monuments, and reestablishing Zoroastrianism as the official religion. They were fortunate to achieve power while Rome was gradually losing strength and posed less of a threat.

Although this new Persian empire was never as large as the old one, the Sasanids remained masters of Iran and Mesopotamia for more than four centuries before they were defeated in 651 by Arabs devoted to Islam. Under Muslim rule, the Persian ideal of governing firmly but equitably and promoting commerce, artistry, and learning endured, inspiring the Abbasid dynasty that made its capital at Baghdad in Mesopotamia—the cradle of civilization and the hearth in which empires were forged for more than 3,000 years. Politically and culturally, imperial Persia had as profound an impact on the Middle East as imperial China did on the Far East and imperial Rome did on Europe.

In a monumental relief near Persepolis, the god Ahura Mazda, far right, invests power in Ardashir I, founder of the Sasanid dynasty, by handing him a crown.

PHAROS

CHAPTER 2

Egypt on the Rise

Lords of the Nile

OLD AND MIDDLE KINGDOMS
Pyramids of Power

"No one rebels against me in all lands," declared Queen Hatshepsut, one of the few women ever to rule Egypt in her own right. "All foreign lands are my subjects." When she had those words inscribed on a monument around 1470 B.C., she was exaggerating the extent of her power, as many monarchs did. Her New Kingdom empire had evolved from the unified state of the Old Kingdom, becoming a domain that reached from Nubia in the south to Syria in the north. But the Egyptians never made the people of Mesopotamia or more distant lands their subjects or rivaled the feats of later empire-builders such as the Persians or Romans.

The majesty of Egypt lay not in the scope of its conquests but in the remarkable stability and persistence of this proud kingdom, which raised its pharaohs to great heights long before it became a great empire. Despite the heavy demands Egyptian rulers placed on those who waged their wars and built their monumental tombs and temples, rebellions were infrequent. One dynasty succeeded another over the centuries with few radical changes in practices or beliefs. Pharaohs reigned as god-kings, and the order they imposed was viewed by people of all ranks as a gift from heaven. A society deeply concerned with the next life and achieving immortality, Egypt came as close as any ancient kingdom to reigning for an eternity and inspiring everlasting awe.

In the beginning, Egypt was not one country, but two. Lower Egypt, situated along the lower Nile River where it branches out to form the delta, was known as the Black Land because it was a marshy area, abounding in wildlife. Upper Egypt, upriver to the south, was the Red Land because it was largely desert—except for a fertile floodplain along the Nile. The river was swelled in summer by monsoon rains falling in the highlands of East Africa and overflowed, leaving a fertile layer of silt. By raising dikes and digging canals, villagers in Upper Egypt managed those floodwaters and increased the amount of land under cultivation, harvesting enough grain to support those who toiled in the fields as well as merchants,

The conqueror Narmer, standing here beside the falcon god Horus, unified Egypt. Later Old Kingdom rulers built pyramids like those at Meidum (right).

ca 3100 B.C. Egypt unified by Narmer.

ca 2550 B.C. Khufu of 4th dynasty erects Great Pyramid at Giza.

ca 2050 B.C. Mentuhotep II of Thebes reunites Egypt, inaugurating Middle Kingdom.

ca 2600 B.C. Djoser of Egypt's 3rd dynasty buried in Step Pyramid at Saqqara.

ca 2150 B.C. Old Kingdom collapses and Egypt fractures.

ca 1650 B.C. Hyksos invasion brings Middle Kingdom to an end.

PEOPLE

IMHOTEP

Imhotep, who served as vizier (chief counselor) to King Djoser of Egypt's 3rd dynasty, was a man of many talents. Trained as a scribe, he won renown as a scholar, priest, and physician. But he is best remembered as the architect of Djoser's magnificent tomb—the Step Pyramid at Saqqara, completed around 2600 B.C. Earlier royal tombs had been low structures called *mastabas*, made of mud brick. Imhotep designed a stone structure with six levels, each narrower than the one below. As one inscription described the building, it was a staircase for the king, so that his spirit "may mount up to heaven thereby." Later Egyptian architects refined Imhotep's design by creating pyramids with smooth sides. So great was Imhotep's reputation as a physician and wonder-worker that he was deified in later times and worshiped at temples—an extraordinary honor for an Egyptian who was not of royal blood. ✍

Egyptians prayed to images of Imhotep like this statuette, asking him to heal them.

artisans, and other specialists. Here as in Mesopotamia, strong rulers emerged. They oversaw those irrigation projects, claimed part of the harvest to support their troops and officials, and used the navigable Nile to extend their authority over distant communities. About 3100 B.C., a king from Upper Egypt known as Narmer (sometimes referred to as Menes) conquered the delta and became Lord of the Two Lands, a title

meaning "great house," referring both to the palace and the king.

As pharaohs grew more powerful, they associated themselves with a deity even higher and mightier than Horus: the solar god Re. The sun was revered in many lands, but it had special significance in sun-baked Egypt, where it dispersed the annual floods, bringing life to the land. The sun traveled through a dark underworld each

> *"Hail to thee, O Nile! Who manifests thyself over this land, and comes to give life to Egypt! Mysterious is thy issuing forth from the darkness, on this day whereon it is celebrated!"*
>
> —HYMN TO THE NILE, CA 2100 B.C.

held proudly by his successors for centuries.

The kingdom that Narmer founded extended from the Mediterranean Sea some 500 miles south to the First Cataract of the Nile. This was not yet an empire, because its people made up a single, coherent society, sharing a common culture, language, and script, which featured alluring characters called *hieroglyphs*. But ruling a kingdom of this size involved some of the same methods used elsewhere by emperors and their scribes to command obedience, including portraying the king as a sacred figure. Early Egyptian cities were less populous than those in Mesopotamia and did not evolve into distinct city-states. But each had its own patron deity to whom the inhabitants prayed. The patron deity of Hierakonpolis—the city in Upper Egypt from which Narmer hailed—was Horus, a soaring spirit pictured as a falcon. Horus watched over Egypt's first pharaohs, a term

night to rise anew each dawn, a phenomenon viewed by Egyptians as a miraculous resurrection. Myths portrayed pharaohs as sons of this sun god—conceived when Re impersonated their father the king and impregnated the queen—and promised that their eternal spirit would rise up after death and join Re in heaven. That mythology, spelled out in hieroglyphs, was a matter of faith for pharaohs and their followers. But it was also a form of propaganda, designed to make the king's subjects worship and obey him and place their duties to the pharaoh above their obligations to any other lord or god.

Around 2700 B.C., Egypt moved beyond its formative phase—when rulers of its first two dynasties secured their hold on the land—and entered the golden age of the Old Kingdom. The concept of divine kingship was now firmly established, and pharaohs staked their claim to immortality

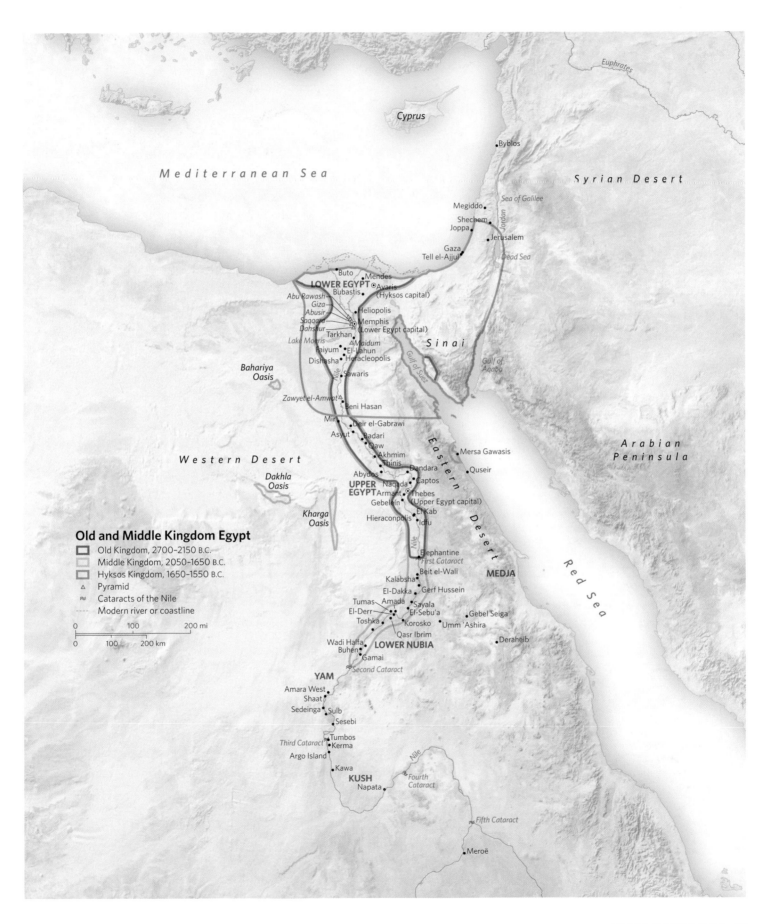

Byblos

Mediterranean Sea

Syrian Desert

Cyprus

Euphrates

Megiddo
Sea of Galilee

Shechem
Joppa

Jerusalem

Jordan

Gaza
Tell el-Ajjul

Dead Sea

Buto • Mendes
LOWER EGYPT
Bubastis • Avaris
(Hyksos capital)

Abu Rawash
Giza
Abusir
Saqqara
Dahshur
Tarkhan
Heliopolis
Memphis
(Lower Egypt capital)

Sinai

Lake Moeris
Faiyum • El-Lahun
Dishasha
Maidum
Heracleopolis

Sawaris

Gulf of Suez
Gulf of Aqaba

Bahariya
Oasis

Zawyet el-Amwat
Beni Hasan

Mir
Deir el-Gabrawi
Asyut • Badari
Qaw
Akhmim
Thinis

Western Desert

Dakhla
Oasis

Abydos • Naqada
UPPER
EGYPT
Captos
Armant • Thebes
Gebelein (Upper Egypt capital)
Hieraconpolis • El-Kab
Idfu

Dandara
Captos

Mersa Gawasis

Quseir

Arabian
Peninsula

Eastern Desert

Kharga
Oasis

Nile

Elephantine
First Cataract

Beit el-Wali

MEDJA

Red Sea

Kalabsha
El-Dakka • Gerf Hussein
Tumas
Amada • Sayala
El-Derr • El-Sebu'a
Toshka • Koresko
Qasr Ibrim

Gebel Seiga

Umm 'Ashira

Deraheib

Wadi Halfa
Buhen **LOWER NUBIA**
Gamai

Second Cataract

YAM

Amara West
Shaat
Sedeinga • Sulb
Sesebi

Tumbos
Third Cataract Kerma
Argo Island
Kawa
KUSH
Napata

Nile

Fourth
Cataract

Fifth Cataract

Meroë

Old and Middle Kingdom Egypt

▢ Old Kingdom, 2700–2150 B.C.
▢ Middle Kingdom, 2050–1650 B.C.
▢ Hyksos Kingdom, 1650–1550 B.C.
△ Pyramid
≈ Cataracts of the Nile
---- Modern river or coastline

0   100   200 mi
0   100   200 km

Camels cross the sandy plain at Giza as the sun rises over the Great Pyramid of Khufu and the nearby pyramid of his successor, Khafre.

THE GREAT PYRAMID

Constructed around 2500 B.C. to hold the remains of King Khufu of the 4th dynasty, the Great Pyramid at Giza contains more than two million stone blocks weighing on average about two and a half tons each. Archaeologists continue to investigate how those huge limestone and granite blocks were hefted into place. They came from distant quarries, up to 500 miles away, and must have been transported down the Nile to Giza on barges. Some sort of ramp was probably used to haul them up the sides of the emerging pyramid, which rose to a height of 481 feet. Within the magnificent and impressive structure are passageways leading to the King's Chamber, containing a stone sarcophagus for the pharaoh's remains. The tomb was robbed ages ago, leaving no mummy or grave treasures. So-called air shafts leading from the King's Chamber to the surface of the pyramid may have been intended not for ventilation but to allow the king's spirit to ascend to heaven.

Tens of thousands of laborers toiled for two decades constructing this great monument. Teams of workers with names such as "Victorious Gang" left their titles inscribed on the blocks. Many were peasants, conscripted to labor on the pyramid seasonally. The Greek historian Herodotus, who visited Egypt around 450 B.C., wrote that Khufu's name was "odious, even to posterity," for the labors he imposed on those who cut and transported the stones and built the Great Pyramid: "100,000 men were thus employed at a time, and they were relieved by an equal number every three months." Herodotus was repeating stories told to him thousands of years after Khufu died, but building such monuments must indeed have been taxing on Egypt and its people. That may explain why later pharaohs built smaller tombs than those erected at Giza by Khufu and his 4th-dynasty successors.

by erecting massive tombs to hold their mummified remains. (If a spirit was not housed in a well-preserved body, it might be lost, Egyptians feared, and never fulfill its destiny.)

Pharaohs of the 4th dynasty signaled their lofty ambitions by building towering, smooth-sided pyramids, whose shape mimicked the sun's slanting rays as they pierced the clouds. According to an inscription, the Great Pyramid of King Khufu—erected about 2550 at Giza, near the Old Kingdom capital of Memphis—was designed to elevate his spirit so that it would "ascend to heaven as the eye of Re." That hypnotic image, which can be found on the U.S. dollar bill, achieved immortality even if the rulers buried in such tombs—many of which were later plundered and left vacant—did not.

Pyramids, obelisks, and other symbols of Egyptian might became lasting emblems of power and permanence, associated later with national heroes such as George Washington and with imperial glory seekers such as Napoleon, who invaded Egypt and marveled at monuments that would continue to dazzle onlookers long after the sun set on his ambitions.

The Egyptian workers who built those pyramids were conscripts, not slaves, and they may well have taken pride in the results of their efforts. But the burden placed on the kingdom by these massive projects, which took decades to complete, could not be sustained by later rulers. Kings of the 5th and 6th dynasties were buried in smaller pyramids, hastily constructed. Egyptian nobles, meanwhile, were acquiring more wealth and power in relation to the pharaoh and erecting impressive tombs

"Speak the truth; do the truth: for it is great, it is mighty, it is everlasting. It will obtain for you merit, and will lead you to veneration."

—THE TALE OF THE ELOQUENT PEASANT, CA 1800 B.C.

Many Egyptian tombs contained paintings like this one, symbolically offering the spirit of the deceased nourishment in the form of bread, meat, and drink.

of their own. Eventually, many Egyptians with the means to do so would arrange to have their bodies mummified after death and placed in coffins containing funerary texts—spells designed to aid them when they entered the underworld and stood in judgment before Osiris, the god who ruled that shadowy kingdom and offered eternal life to those who proved worthy.

Egypt grew stronger and more stable when the king no longer towered so high above his subjects that he alone was deemed worthy of a glorious afterlife. In time, pharaohs, officials, priests, scribes, soldiers, and common people would all have their place in an orderly social hierarchy that endured because it afforded those at lower levels, on whose efforts rulers depended, security in this life and some hope of salvation after death. Before Egypt achieved that stability, however, it underwent upheaval. About 2150 B.C., the Old Kingdom collapsed. Persistent drought may have caused famine and unrest. Local rulers vied with each other for supremacy until King Mentuhotep II of Thebes reunited Egypt by force of arms around 2050, inaugurating the Middle Kingdom.

Egypt emerged as an imperial power under Mentuhotep II and his successors, who sent troops south into Nubia. Earlier pharaohs had dispatched trading or raiding parties into Nubia to obtain gold, ivory, ebony, and other treasures. But Egyptians now established a permanent military presence there by building fortresses such as Buhen, a huge structure bristling with battlements and surrounded by a moat. Situated near the Second Cataract of the Nile, well upriver from the traditional boundary between Egypt and Nubia, it

THE EGYPTIAN DIET

In Egypt as in other Middle Eastern lands, bread was the staff of life. Fields along the Nile, nourished by the river's annual floods and the silt left behind, were among the most fertile in the ancient world. Egypt suffered occasional famines, but peasants here often produced enough wheat and barley to meet the needs of their own population and other people around the Mediterranean. Wheat was made into bread, and barley was used to brew beer. Egyptians supplemented their diet by fishing and hunting fowl. They also raised cattle, but meat was consumed mostly by the wealthy. Bread and beer were prepared on large estates by servants or slaves and at home by women, who sometimes had to make a small amount of food go a long way. In an ancient Egyptian tale, a peasant setting out on a six-day journey gives eight bushels of grain to his wife: "Behold, two bushels of grain shall be left for bread for you and the children," he tells her. "But make for me six bushels into bread and beer for the days that I shall be on the road."

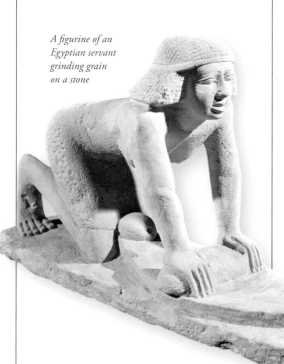

A figurine of an Egyptian servant grinding grain on a stone

This romantic painting of the Nile by 19th-century French artist Charles-Théodore Frère portrays Egypt as little changed since ancient times.

served as a frontier outpost, offering refuge to traders and guarding against attempts by Nubians or other foreigners to raid Egyptian towns. Later pharaohs advanced that frontier and brought most of Nubia under Egyptian control. Some Nubians were captured and enslaved, but Egyptians did not reserve such treatment only for black Africans living to their south. They also enslaved light-skinned people from western Asia. Many Nubians remained free and came to terms with their Egyptian overlords, serving them capably as soldiers or local officials and adopting their customs and beliefs. Eventually, Nubians would emerge from under Egypt's shadow and build pyramids to house the remains of their own rulers.

Pharaohs of the Middle Kingdom also made armed incursions into Palestine, the biblical land of Canaan, although they did not fortify and hold that country as they did Nubia. Instead, many people from Palestine and beyond began infiltrating the Nile Delta. Around 1650 B.C., intruders of Asiatic origin known as the Hyksos, meaning "rulers of foreign lands," took control of the delta. Riding horse-drawn chariots like the Hittites who would soon storm Babylon, they overpowered Egyptian forces. Looking back on that invasion more than a thousand years afterward, the Egyptian historian Manetho characterized the Hyksos as barbarians who "burned our cities ruthlessly, razed to the ground the temples of

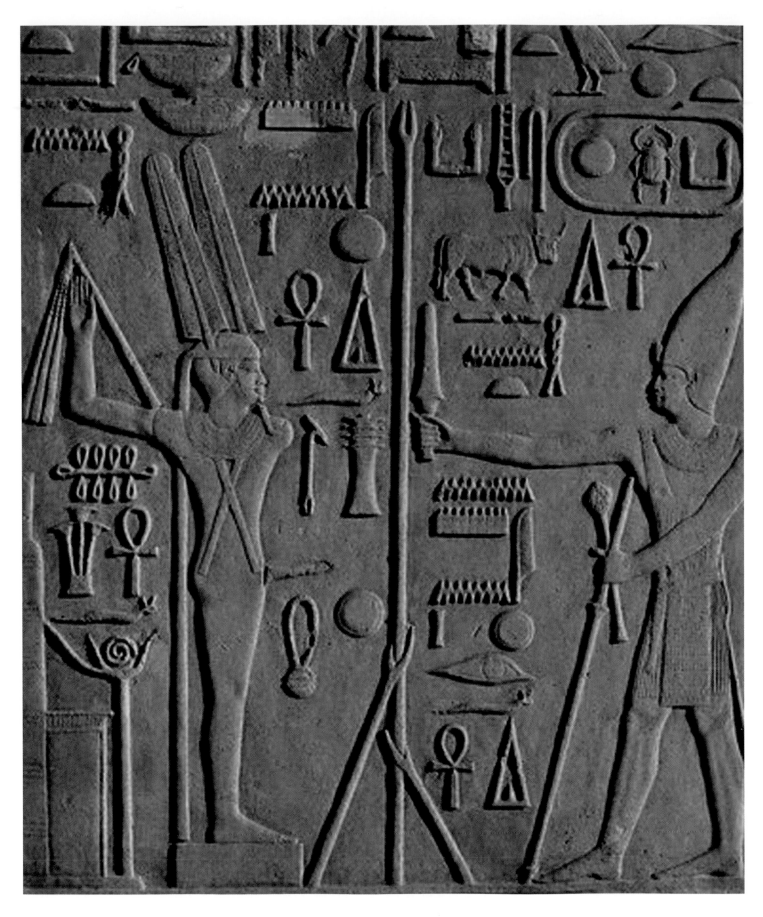

Pharaoh Senusret I of the Middle Kingdom stands at right facing the god Amun in this relief at Karnak, a temple complex in Thebes.

our gods, and treated all the natives with a cruel hostility, massacring some and leading into slavery the wives and children of others." Such brutal measures were practiced by many ancient conquerors, of course, and the Hyksos were by no means the worst offenders.

After occupying Lower Egypt and establishing their capital at Avaris, the Hyksos refrained from attacking the rulers of Upper Egypt in Thebes. Instead, they demanded tribute from the Thebans and took their princesses as wives. Far from dragging Egypt back into barbarism, the Hyksos prodded the country forward by introducing new technology, including chariots and bronze weapons. Those innovations

were adopted and exploited by Egyptians when they wearied of paying tribute to the foreigners and set out to defeat them.

King Kamose of Thebes launched that campaign, vowing to save Egypt and "smite the Asiatics." He died before completing the conquest, though, leaving as heir his young relative Ahmose, who may still have been under the care of his mother, Queen Ahhotep. Ahmose later praised her in writing as one who cared for Egypt and "looked after her soldiers," suggesting that she served as regent until he matured and took command. When Ahmose expelled the Hyksos from the delta around 1550, the triumph marked the dawn of the New Kingdom, whose rulers concluded that the best way to prevent another invasion from western Asia was to compete there for imperial supremacy.

A modern artist's rendering of the expulsion of the Hyksos shows triumphant Egyptians overlooking the defeated invaders.

MILITARY MIGHT

Model chariot and team from an Egyptian tomb

LEARNING FROM THE ENEMY

The invading Hyksos introduced to Egypt horse-drawn chariots like the model shown here, with one man holding the reins and another carrying a shield and weapon. Before long, Egyptians adopted such chariots and used them to expel the Hyksos. That victory marked the dawn of the New Kingdom, during which Egyptian charioteers waged war abroad and expanded their empire. Mighty New Kingdom pharaohs such as Ramses II led those forces on campaigns and had themselves portrayed heroically riding chariots into battle and vanquishing their foes. Ramses II may have been the model for the proud king referred to simply as Pharaoh in the Bible, who loses his army when the sea that God parted to allow the Israelites to escape Egypt closes over his pursuing chariots, drowning "the horsemen and all the host of Pharaoh" (Exodus 14:28).

NEW KINGDOM
Egypt's Imperial Heyday

King Ahmose I inaugurated the triumphant New Kingdom around 1550 B.C. when he drove the Hyksos out and pursued them into Palestine, capturing their fortress at Sharuhen. He also reasserted Egyptian control over Nubia, which had broken free during the tumultuous Hyksos era. The conquests of Ahmose and his successors enriched pharaohs and their forces, who claimed spoils and tribute from lands they conquered and took captives as slaves. Commanders who served the king faithfully were granted high positions as royal officials or governors, replacing troublesome nobles who had formerly served as governors and vied with pharaohs for power.

Like earlier pharaohs, rulers of the New Kingdom claimed descent from Egypt's supreme deity—an honor now held by Amun, the patron god of Thebes, whose cult incorporated that of Re, favored during the Old Kingdom. The magnificent temple complex at Karnak, located on the outskirts of Thebes, was the center of this powerful religious sect, which owned vast tracts of land throughout

This ankh-shaped mirror symbolizing the breath of life was among the treasures entombed with New Kingdom pharaohs such as Ramses II (right).

Egypt, huge herds of livestock, and dozens of workshops where laborers produced bread, beer, and linen garments for the priesthood. Pharaohs donated to this cult part of what they gained through conquest. Priests returned the favor by making offerings at monuments that glorified Amun (sometimes referred to as Amun-Re) and the rulers devoted to him, including mortuary temples located near the entrance to royal tombs, hewn out of cliffs across the Nile from Thebes. Unlike the soaring pyramids of old, these tombs were hidden to prevent grave robbers from pilfering the treasures deposited in burial chambers to afford rulers a luxurious afterlife.

The campaigns that brought Egypt wealth and imperial glory were holy wars, waged by pharaohs who trusted in Amun and other honored deities to grant them victory over foes who worshiped lesser gods. About 1457 B.C., King Thutmose III put his faith to the test by campaigning against rebels in Palestine and Syria. His grandfather, Thutmose I, had swept through those lands with his army and forced princes there to pay Egypt tribute. But Thutmose III faced lingering opposition in the region from

- **ca 1550 B.C.** Ahmose I of Thebes expels Hyksos, reunites Egypt, and ushers in New Kingdom.
- **ca 1457 B.C.** Thutmose III, now ruler in his own right, secures Palestine and Syria for Egypt.
- **ca 1275 B.C.** Ramses II leads Egyptian forces against Hittites in great chariot battle at Kadesh.
- **1070 B.C.** New Kingdom breaks apart.
- **667 B.C.** Assyrians invade Egypt, ending Nubian rule.

- **1479 B.C.** Queen Hatshepsut becomes regent for King Thutmose III and later clings to power.
- **ca 1350 B.C.** Amenhotep IV, renamed Akhenaten, devotes himself exclusively to god Aten.
- **1156 B.C.** Ramses III dies, marking beginning of the end for New Kingdom.
- **ca 750 B.C.** Nubians from kingdom of Kush take control of Egypt.

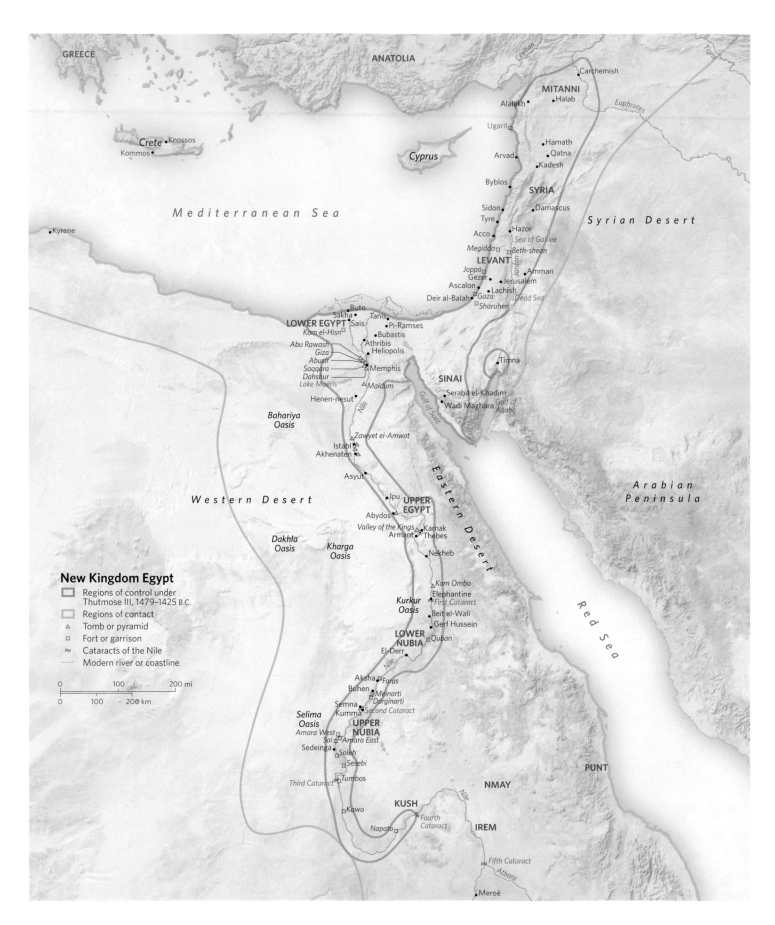

GREECE

ANATOLIA

MITANNI

Carchemish

Alalakh • Halab

Euphrates

Tigris

Ugarit

Hamath

Crete • Knossos

Cyprus

Arvad • Qatna

Kommos •

Kadesh

Byblos

SYRIA

Syrian Desert

Mediterranean Sea

Sidon • Damascus

Tyre

Acco • Hazor

• Kyrene

Sea of Galilee

Megiddo • Beth-shean

LEVANT

Joppa

Gezer • Amman

Ascalon • Jerusalem

Deir al-Balah • Lachish

Buto

Gaza

Sakha

Dead Sea

Tanis

Sharuhen

LOWER EGYPT • Sais • Pi-Ramses

Kom el-Hisn

Bubastis

Abu Rawash

Athribis

Heliopolis

Giza

• Timna

Abusir

Memphis

Saqqara

SINAI

Dahshur

Lake Moeris

Maidum

Serabit el-Khadim

Gulf of Suez

Wadi Maghara

Gulf of Aqaba

Henen-nesut

Bahariya Oasis

Nile

Arabian Peninsula

Zawyet el-Amwat

Istabl

Akhenaten

Asyut

Western Desert

Ipu

UPPER EGYPT

Eastern Desert

Abydos

Valley of the Kings

Karnak

Armant • Thebes

Dakhla Oasis

Kharga Oasis

Nekheb

Kom Ombo

Red Sea

Elephantine

First Cataract

Kurkur Oasis

Beit el-Wali

Gerf Hussein

LOWER NUBIA

Quban

El-Derr

Nile

Aksha • Faras

Buhen

Meinarti

Dorginarti

Semna

Kumma Second Cataract

Selima Oasis

UPPER NUBIA

Amara West

Sai • Amara East

Sedeinga

Soleb

Sesebi

Third Cataract • Tumbos

Nile

NMAY

Kawa

KUSH

IREM

Napata

Fourth Cataract

PUNT

Fifth Cataract

Atbara

Meroë

New Kingdom Egypt

▢ Regions of control under Thutmose III, 1479–1425 B.C.

▢ Regions of contact

△ Tomb or pyramid

▢ Fort or garrison

≈ Cataracts of the Nile

- - - Modern river or coastline

0   100   200 mi

0   100   200 km

powerful rivals, including the Hittites in Asia Minor and the kingdom of Mitanni in northern Mesopotamia, which sought to expand at Egypt's expense by encouraging this rebellion.

Thutmose III was urged by his officers to take a roundabout route to Megiddo, a hilltop city in Palestine where his foes were camped, overlooking the main road from Egypt to Syria. Instead, he insisted on advancing directly through a treacherous mountain pass at Aruna to show that he had no fear of being attacked there by the rebels he despised. According to an inscription at Karnak touting his feats, he declared: "I swear, as Re loves me, as my father Amun favors me . . . my majesty shall proceed on this Aruna road." Yielding to his wishes, his officers replied dutifully: "We are followers of your majesty wherever your majesty goes! A servant follows his lord."

The pharaoh rode up front during that perilous advance to show that he completely trusted in the gods to protect him and his troops, who indeed made it through the pass unscathed. Then he entered battle at Megiddo "on a chariot of fine gold, decked in his shining armor," dazzling and intimidating his opponents, who soon gave up the fight and retreated to their last bastion of safety within the city walls. Gathering up prisoners, weapons, and chariots abandoned by their foes, his troops "jubilated and gave praise to Amun for the victory

he had given to his son." After a lengthy siege, Megiddo fell to the Egyptians, and the rebel leaders crawled on their bellies in supplication before Thutmose, whose triumph they believed demonstrated the power of his father Amun "over all foreign lands."

Thutmose III went on to humble the king of Mitanni by driving his forces from Syria, securing that country temporarily for the Egyptians, who still had to reckon with the formidable Hittites. The long struggle between those two powers culminated around 1275 B.C. when Egyptian troops led by King Ramses II met Hittites in battle at Kadesh, a stronghold in Syria. The Egyptian army consisted of four divisions, named for the gods Amun, Re, Ptah, and Seth. Ramses was up front with the Amun division when Hittite charioteers surprised the Re division to his rear and routed it. According to a flattering account composed at his command, Ramses saved the day by turning his chariot on the Hittites and overwhelming them: "His majesty slaughtered them in their places; they sprawled before his horses; and his majesty was alone, none other with him."

Unlike the account commissioned earlier by King Thutmose III, which gave some credit for his victory at Megiddo to his "valiant army," Ramses' inscription portrayed him as a superhuman figure, scattering the Hittites with no help from his troops. In truth,

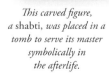

This carved figure, a shabti, *was placed in a tomb to serve its master symbolically in the afterlife.*

The Rosetta Stone, with hieroglyphs at top

DECIPHERING HIEROGLYPHS: THE ROSETTA STONE

Ancient Egyptian inscriptions mystified modern historians until the Rosetta Stone was discovered in 1799 during Napoleon's invasion of Egypt and its Egyptian text was deciphered. The stone—inscribed in 196 B.C. during the reign of King Ptolemy V of Egypt—contained the same text in Greek (the official language of the Ptolemaic dynasty), hieroglyphs (the original Egyptian script), and demotic (a cursive Egyptian script derived from hieroglyphs). Nevertheless, deciphering the hieroglyphs took two decades. English Egyptologist Thomas Young achieved an early breakthrough by identifying Ptolemy's name as a cartouche (a set of hieroglyphs contained within an oval) at several places in the text. French linguist Jean-François Champollion expanded on Young's work and cracked the code by determining that some hieroglyphs represent objects or concepts while others are phonetic, representing syllables in the spoken language.

> *"Lo, the god knows me well,*
> *Amun, Lord of Thrones-of-the-Two-Lands;*
> *He made me rule Black Land*
> *and Red Land as reward,*
> *No one rebels against me in all lands.*
> *All foreign lands are my subjects."*
>
> INSCRIPTION OF **QUEEN HATSHEPSUT** AT KARNAK

This chest, shaped like a cartouche and inscribed with sacred symbols, was entombed with King Tutankhamun.

the battle at Kadesh was no great victory. It was at best a draw for his hard-pressed soldiers, who withdrew from Syria afterward. Eventually, he concluded a peace treaty with the Hittite king, sealed when that monarch promised to send his daughter to join Ramses' harem, bringing a large dowry. When Ramses wrote to inquire when that princess would be arriving with her gifts, she dictated her own response,

chiding him for mentioning the dowry. "My brother possesses nothing?" she asked the conspicuously wealthy king. "That you, my brother, should wish to enrich yourself from me is neither friendly nor honorable!"

This alliance revealed more about Egypt's imperial ambitions than the deceptive account of Ramses' "victory" at Kadesh. Although rulers of the New Kingdom boasted that all lands were subject to them, they were largely content with dominating neighboring lands such as Palestine and Nubia, which provided them with tribute and also served as buffers, shielding them from raiders or invaders. Unlike the Persians and Romans, who rose from obscurity and set out to prove themselves in battle by subduing one distant country after another, Egyptians possessed a mighty kingdom long before they acquired an empire. They showed little interest in conquering the wider world as long as their homeland was secure and their neighbors bowed to them. Ramses had won a concession when the Hittite king offered his daughter to him in marriage. But this was a compromise between two longtime foes, not a conquest for

Queen Hatshepsut had herself portrayed here as a king, wearing a beard that linked pharaohs to the god Osiris.

Egyptians. They owed their success not just to their military prowess but also to their diplomatic skills, demonstrated by pacts that brought to the king's household princesses from many lands. (As long as Egypt remained a great power, Egyptian princesses were not given as wives to foreign rulers.)

When pharaohs returned from campaigns to their palace, they left behind the masculine world of battle and bravado and entered a realm where women were prominent. The most important women in the imperial family were the king's mother—who might serve as regent if he succeeded his father as a boy—and the king's principal wife. Males born to this principal wife were first in the line of succession, but princes born to secondary wives in the harem sometimes reached the throne. A principal wife who produced no male heir by her husband before he died might remain

KARNAK

The colossal Egyptian temple complex of Karnak at Thebes was not among the original Seven Wonders of the World, unlike the Great Pyramid of Giza. Many tourists today, however, find the scale and grandeur of Karnak beyond anything they have ever seen. Its hypostyle hall—framed by pillars 80 feet high and encompassing 54,000 square feet—reflects the pride and ambition of Pharaohs Seti I and Ramses II, who were largely responsible for constructing it. Officially, such monuments were meant to honor the gods—in this case, Amun, the New Kingdom's supreme deity. But because pharaohs claimed Amun as their father and patron, they were in fact glorifying themselves as well as the god when they erected such tributes to him.

Karnak was the site of a dramatic annual ceremony called the Opet Festival, which occurred in the season when the Nile flooded, an occasion of utmost importance for the ancient Egyptians and a time of thanksgiving. The pharaoh accompanied an image of Amun from the god's Great Temple at Karnak to the Luxor Temple at the far end of Thebes. There the king underwent a mysterious ritual that seemingly renewed his powers and confirmed that he was the god's true son and heir. Priests of Amun, who oversaw bakeries, breweries, and other assets within the temple complex, took this occasion to share their bounty with the people, who received bread and beer and expressed their thanks by praising Amun and his earthly embodiment, the pharaoh.

Karnak, situated along the Nile in Thebes, stands today as a towering monument to rulers of the New Kingdom and their patron deity, Amun.

"Double the food your mother gave you,
Support her as she supported you;
She had a heavy load in you,
But she did not abandon you."

THE INSTRUCTION OF **ANI**

The head of this staff bears the image of a Nubian captive.

a prominent figure if she served as regent to a youngster he conceived with one of his secondary wives. Such was the case with Queen Hatshepsut, who broke with tradition by strategizing to retain her power even after the heir placed under her regency came of age.

Hatshepsut was the daughter of King Thutmose I, who did much to expand the Egyptian empire, and she became the principal wife of King Thutmose II, her half-brother. Incestuous marriages were not the rule among Egyptian royalty, but they had the advantage of uniting two descendants of a king who was considered to be a god and producing offspring of the highest breeding. Royals who wed their siblings found precedents in Egyptian mythology, including the marriage of the god Osiris to his sister Isis, who, after her husband was dismembered by his scheming brother Seth, put Osiris back together and restored him to life. For that feat and for preventing Seth from murdering her child Horus—destined to rule Egypt as a god and guide its first pharaohs—Isis served as an inspiration for Egyptian women, especially the queens.

Unlike Isis, Hatshepsut had no prince by her husband-brother, who left her with only a daughter when he died in 1479 B.C. His designated heir—the boy who would later win glory at Megiddo as King Thutmose III—was the son of a secondary wife who lacked the exalted ancestry of his

Women wash clothing in the Nile in this painting by Eugène Alexis Girardet, another French Orientalist painter who portrayed Egypt as timeless and eternal.

SO WHAT?

SACRED CATS

Many animals figured prominently in Egyptian culture and mythology, but no domesticated animal was held in higher esteem than the cat. They were useful because they preyed on mice and rats, but they were also treasured as pets. The Egyptian term for cat was *miu*, a name probably derived from their mewing sound. A female cat was *miut*, which was also a term of endearment for girls, like "kitten."

Among the Egyptian deities associated with felines was Bastet, a goddess originally portrayed with the head of a lion. Bastet achieved prominence after the collapse of the New Kingdom when her cult center, Bubastis, became politically important. According to Greek historian Diodorus Siculus, who wrote in later times, anyone who killed a cat in Egypt was "condemned to death, whether he committed this crime deliberately or not." Many cats were mummified and buried in cemeteries dedicated to Bastet. ✍

Ancient Egyptian cat mummy

> *"Homage to thee, Osiris, Lord of eternity,*
> *King of the Gods, whose names are manifold,*
> *whose forms are holy, thou being of hidden*
> *form in the temples, whose Ka is holy."*
>
> —THE PAPYRUS OF ANI
> (THE EGYPTIAN BOOK OF THE DEAD)

regent, Hatshepsut. Only the king's rightful male heir was entitled to call the god Amun his father, but by wedding Thutmose II, Hatshepsut had earned the title "god's wife," or wife of Amun, thus strengthening her connection to Egypt's supreme deity. She may have resented the fact that her husband's successor was the child of a woman she considered far beneath her. She acted less like that boy's temporary overseer and more like Egypt's rightful ruler, referring to herself as "mistress of the Two Lands."

Regencies were supposed to end when the boy-king reached maturity. As that transition loomed, however, Hatshepsut threw caution aside and declared herself pharaoh, adopting all the emblems and titles associated with kingship except the label "Mighty Bull." She went so far as to claim Amun as her father, authorizing an account that described how the god conceived her by impersonating King Thutmose I and impregnating her mother. Amun meant for her to take charge of Egypt, she insisted: "I acted under his command; it was he who led me."

A few women had ruled Egypt before Hatshepsut, but they were obscure successors to kings who evidently had no male heirs. For her to assert priority over Thutmose III was a radical move in this conservative society and could not have

DAILY LIFE

This mummy, known as the Younger Lady, was identified as the mother of King Tutankhamun through DNA testing.

MUMMIES

Mummification was not performed to comfort the family and friends of the deceased, as embalmers do today when they preserve a body for viewing and burial. Its purpose was to provide a lasting home for the immortal soul of the deceased, which would embark on heavenly journeys, then return to the entombed body for nourishment in the form of real or symbolic offerings of food and drink. Mummification was a sacred task, performed by priests, who first removed the perishable internal organs and placed them in a vessel called a canopic jar that would be buried with the mummy. They then dried and preserved the body using a salt called *natron*, swathed it in fragrant oil, coated it with resin, and wrapped it in linen. Coffins and the walls of tombs were inscribed with spells, or sacred texts, which helped ensure that the deceased would achieve immortality and sail across heaven in spirit with the sun god Re. "I shall sail rightly in my bark," proclaimed one such text. "I am lord of eternity in the crossing of the sky."

Illustrated texts like this one in the tomb of Amenhotep II served as spiritual guides for the deceased.

been achieved unless she had support from high officials at court, who risked losing power, if not their lives, if she yielded to Thutmose. She could not match her father's conquests by leading troops to battle, a role reserved for men, although her commanders conducted some military campaigns. Her proudest venture, however, portrayed on the walls of her mortuary temple, was a trading expedition she dispatched to the land of Punt, along the Red Sea. It returned laden with gold, ivory, myrrh (prized as

incense), and a menagerie of exotic animals, including monkeys, apes, panthers, giraffes, and baboons.

Hatshepsut did not banish Thutmose III—officially, he served as her co-ruler—but she overshadowed him. He may have waited patiently for her to die, or he may have plotted against her and hastened her departure, which occurred two decades or so after she became regent. Now about 30, Thutmose took power and followed in his grandfather's footsteps by achieving victories in Palestine and Syria.

A tomb relief portraying a solar boat, or bark, in which spirits of the dead would sail across heaven

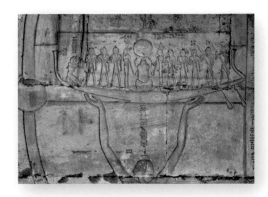

Queen Hatshepsut may have contributed to those imperial feats by strengthening his drive to triumph in battle, an arena where she as a woman could not venture.

Other brilliant and fearless women later figured prominently in the history

"*Your dawning is beautiful
in the horizon of the sky,
O living Aten, Beginning of life!
When You rise in the Eastern horizon,
You fill every land with Your beauty.*"

AKHENATEN, "HYMN TO ATEN"

Life-giving rays emanate from solar disks representing Aten at a temple erected by Akhenaten, who worshiped Aten exclusively.

of the New Kingdom, including Queen Tiy, the daughter of an army commander. She became the principal wife of King Amenhotep III. Tiy was portrayed by sculptors at Amenhotep's mortuary temple seated at his side on a shared throne, suggesting that their union was a royal partnership in which both the king and the queen were worthy of reverence. Their son, crowned Amenhotep IV, paid similar tribute to his principal wife, Nefertiti, who joined him when he left Thebes around 1350 B.C. to devote himself to Aten (a radiant deity inhabiting the solar disk), whom he worshiped to the exclusion of all other gods at a new capital, Akhetaten ("Horizon of Aten"), under a new name, Akhenaten ("He Who Serves Aten"). He

was said to be the author of the "Hymn to Aten," which offers high praise to the god from "your son who came from your body." Akhenaten portrayed Aten as his father much as earlier pharaohs claimed to be the son of Amun or Re. This cultural revolution was too much for traditionalists, and Akhenaten was later vilified as a heretic by rulers who restored the old forms of worship, honoring various gods.

Preoccupied with spiritual matters, Akhenaten did little to bolster the Egyptian empire. Although he fathered numerous daughters, he failed to provide a male heir, leaving the throne to his sons-in-law Smenkhare, who survived Akhenaten by only a few months, and young Tutankhamun, who would be remembered largely for the spectacular treasures later found in his tomb. They were among the last rulers of the accomplished 18th dynasty, which

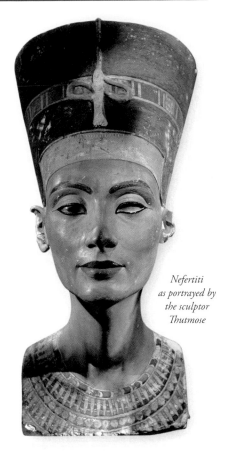

Nefertiti as portrayed by the sculptor Thutmose

THE EXALTED NEFERTITI

No queen was portrayed more often in Egyptian paintings and sculptures than the lovely Nefertiti. She became a virtual goddess in Akhenaten's new cult, although officially Aten was the only deity. Egyptians prayed to her, and she may have helped fill the void left when the cults of goddesses were suppressed.

Although Akhenaten had only one god, he did not limit himself to one wife. Inscriptions tell of another woman, named Kiya, who appears on monuments with Akhenaten and may have rivaled Nefertiti. Later in Akhenaten's reign, however, references to Kiya were scratched out and replaced with the names of Nefertiti's daughters. Nefertiti evidently solidified her position as the king's principal wife—an exalted figure closer to Akhenaten and his heavenly father, Aten, than any woman on earth. ✍

Egyptian kings and queens wore a majestic uraeus like this one, representing a rearing cobra.

was founded by Ahmose I and endured for nearly three centuries.

No king did more to father sons and heirs and sustain his royal lineage than Ramses II of the 19th dynasty, who lived up to the title Mighty Bull by siring more than 100 princes and princesses by the many wives in his harem before he died in 1221 after a 67-year reign. Keeping a large harem, as Ramses did, increased the chances that a king would produce male heirs. It also had diplomatic advantages. A foreign ruler who gave his daughter to the pharaoh might prove more cooperative and less likely to turn against him. But harems could also undermine the pharaoh and his great house by becoming centers of plots against the king and his rightful successor.

One such conspiracy was aimed at Ramses III of the 20th dynasty, who took the throne about 1187 and succeeded in repelling invasions by Libyans from the west, as well as mysterious intruders called the Sea Peoples, who swept down from the northern Mediterranean. In his later years, one of his secondary wives plotted with other women in the harem and officials at court to kill the king and place her son by him on the throne instead of his designated successor. The plotters were apprehended, but Ramses III died soon afterward, either of natural

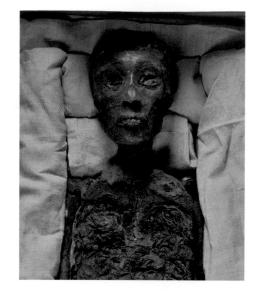

A forensic artist used the mummy of Tutankhamun (top) as a model to portray the young king as he appeared before he died (above).

causes or because the conspirators succeeded in their scheme.

Ramses III was the last imposing ruler of imperial Egypt. The challenges he faced before he died in 1156, including threats from abroad and treachery at home, continued to plague the New Kingdom until it collapsed around 1070. Egypt still had kings, but they were no longer Lords of

Linen gloves found in Tutankhamun's tomb

the Two Lands. One dynasty governed Lower Egypt from Tanis, a city in the Nile Delta, while high priests of Amun-Re in Thebes—who were allowed to marry and have children—formed a rival dynasty and controlled Upper Egypt.

This was an age of transition and turmoil throughout the Near East. Contributing to the upheaval were advances in the technology of ironworking, which yielded stronger weapons than those made of bronze. The main source of iron ore in the Near East was Asia Minor. When the Hittite empire collapsed there around 1200 B.C. under pressure from the Sea Peoples, those invaders and other rising military powers gained greater access to the ore and became increasingly skilled at forging it. Although Egypt succeeded in repelling the Sea Peoples, some of them occupied the Mediterranean coast above the delta. Known as Philistines, they lent their name to Palestine and bequeathed their expertise as ironworkers to the Israelites, who solidified a kingdom under David and Solomon about 1000 B.C. Having lost control of Palestine, the Egyptians had no buffer against aggressive powers such as the Assyrians, who gained strength in Mesopotamia during this tumultuous Iron Age and eventually shattered the kingdom of Israel, threatening to do the same to Egypt.

Meanwhile, Egypt was subject to take-overs that were friendly compared with the hostile advances of the Assyrians and later conquerors. Like other imperial forces, the Egyptian army had recruited many men from countries it conquered or campaigned against, including Libyans and Nubians. Many of those recruits adopted Egyptian customs, and some settled in Egypt. As

KING TUT'S TREASURES

Howard Carter made one of the most celebrated archaeological discoveries ever when he unearthed the tomb of King Tutankhamun in 1922. The young king's mummy and most of the treasures buried with him had escaped centuries of grave robbers, who stripped bare many other ancient burial vaults. Until recent times, many mummies were stolen and reduced to powder because they were thought to have medicinal properties. One French king reportedly mixed mummy powder with rhubarb and had some every day, hoping that it would render him invulnerable.

Intact mummies such as King Tut's, containing DNA and a complete skeletal structure, have revealed much about the genealogy and medical condition of ancient rulers. Using x-rays, archaeologists detected two injuries that could have been fatal to Tutankhamun—an indentation at the back of skull that some have interpreted as evidence of murder, and a fracture in the left leg that could have caused gangrene.

What most impressed and captivated the public, though, was not Tut's mummy, but the splendid offerings buried with him, described by Carter as a "strange and wonderful medley of extraordinary and beautiful objects." The greatest and perhaps now most iconic treasure was the king's death mask (below), containing more than 20 pounds of gold. Other items buried with him to ensure that he remained strong, wealthy, and well fed in the afterlife include a leopard-skin cloak, two jars of honey, four game boards, six chariots, eight shields, 12 loaves of bread, 30 wine jars, 34 loincloths, 46 bows, and 116 baskets of dried fruit. ✎

The death mask of King Tut shows him wearing the royal uraeus and the black eye shadow favored by both men and women in ancient Egypt.

the kingdom weakened, commanders of foreign origin gained political clout. About 950, a Libyan chieftain named Sheshonk from Bubastis, a city in the Nile Delta where Libyan recruits had settled and were now largely Egyptianized, became king of Lower Egypt. He and his successors tried to win over the rulers of Upper Egypt in Thebes through marriage alliances with high priests there. Thebans remained wary of the Libyans, however, and employed Nubian forces to fend them off. Around 750, King Piye of Kush (as Nubia was now known) entered Thebes unopposed and took power, reassuring the populace by worshiping Amun-Re at Karnak. He

went on to defeat the Libyans in the north and establish a Nubian dynasty whose rulers honored Egyptian traditions and differed little from earlier pharaohs except in complexion.

In 667, Assyrians invaded Egypt and ended Nubian rule. Thereafter, Egypt was prey to one great imperial power after another, a bitter fate for a kingdom whose rulers once portrayed all foreign lands as subject to them. Periodically, Egyptians regained control of their country, only to be conquered anew—by Cambyses of Persia in 525, Alexander the Great of Macedonia in 332, and finally the Roman emperor Octavian, or Augustus

The New Kingdom was still flourishing when Ramses II erected this massive temple at Abu Simbel, but began to decline not long after he died.

Caesar, whose invasion in 30 B.C. drove Queen Cleopatra to suicide and reduced Egypt to a Roman province. Such was the power and persistence of Egyptian culture and beliefs that Cleopatra, last ruler of the Macedonian dynasty founded by Alexander's general Ptolemy, likened herself to the goddess Isis. When she died, the kingdom of Egypt expired with her. But the legend of Cleopatra survived, as did the cultural legacy of the 30 dynasties that preceded hers over 3,000 years, leaving a monumental impression on the world.

DAILY LIFE

AN ETERNAL GAME

Judging by scenes like the one at left—from the tomb of Queen Nefertari, principal wife of Ramses II—Egyptians could think of few better ways to spend eternity than by playing senet, possibly the world's oldest board game. Senet sets like the one shown below, with boards divided into 30 squares and pieces like those used in later times for chess, have been found in Egyptian tombs dating back 5,000 years. The game took on great meaning for players, who saw it as a fateful contest that could determine their future in this life and the next. In a text called the Satirical Papyrus, a lion is shown playing senet with an antelope and appears to be gloating, as if anticipating victory over its prey. An Egyptian hieroglyph that depicts a senet board means "to endure." Indeed, to win at senet in the afterlife was to defeat death and endure forever.

Above, Queen Nefertari plays senet on a board similar to the one at right, found in Tutankhamun's tomb, equipped with a sliding compartment to hold its wooden pieces. Nefertari's unseen opponent may represent a challenge she must overcome in spirit before achieving the glorious afterlife awaiting her.

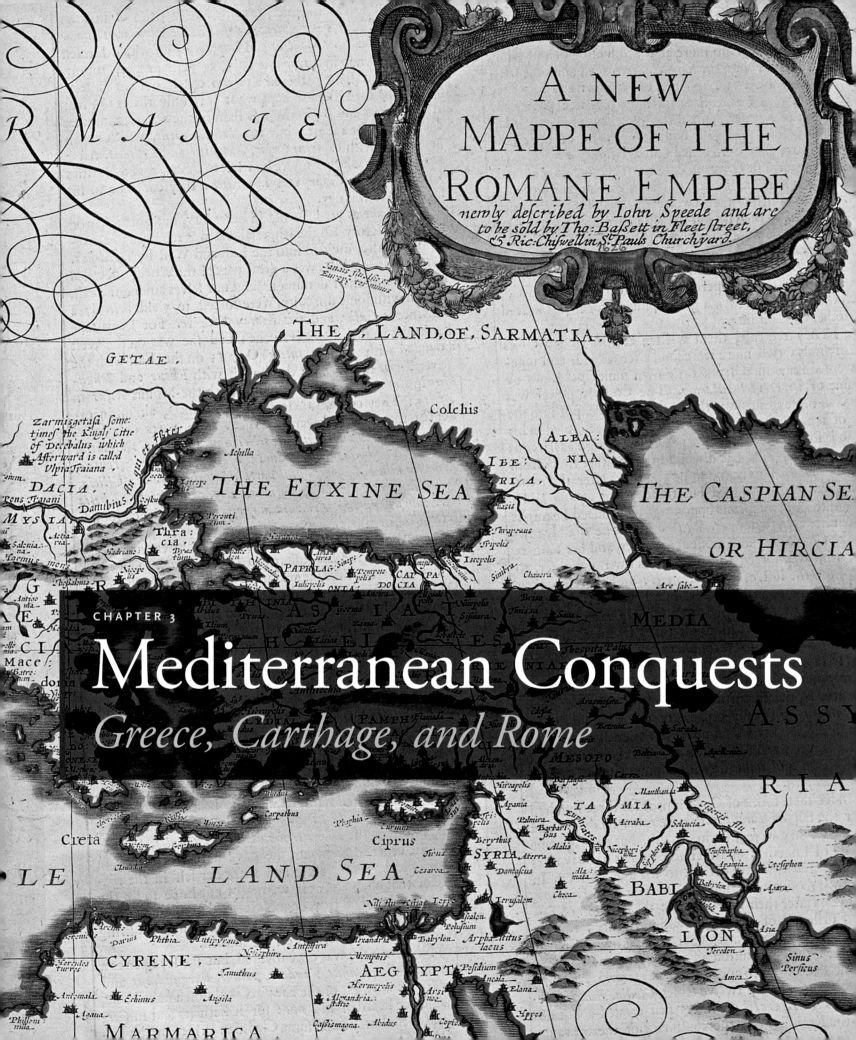

CHAPTER 3

Mediterranean Conquests
Greece, Carthage, and Rome

ALEXANDER'S EMPIRE

A Conqueror for the Ages

The empire that Alexander the Great forged was not long lasting, but his heroic deeds were legendary. When Julius Caesar was a young man, wrote the Greek author Plutarch, he read an account of the exploits of Alexander that reduced him to tears. "Do you think I have not just cause to weep," Caesar said, "when I consider that Alexander at my age had conquered so many nations, and I have all this time done nothing that is memorable?" Unlike Alexander, who won great victories long before he died at the age of 33, Caesar did not conquer Gaul and cross the Rubicon to become dictator of Rome until he was past 50. But the desire to emulate Alexander and achieve lasting fame and glory drove Caesar and other ambitious Romans to expand their empire until it embraced the entire Mediterranean world and much of Europe.

The Roman Empire was not built in a few years the way Alexander's empire was, but it was larger and longer lasting, bequeathing to the modern world languages, laws, and traditions

Tetradrachme of King Philip II of Macedonia (above) on horseback wearing a kausia *(hat) and a cape. Alexander the Great on his horse Bucephalus (right).*

such as citizenship, fostered in the city-states of ancient Greece, Italy, and other Mediterranean lands. The great city-state of Carthage, on the North African coast, founded colonies around the western Mediterranean and vied with Rome for imperial supremacy, until it was crushed by its rival and reduced to rubble. That conquest allowed Julius Caesar and his successors to lay claim to the legacy of Alexander and build one of the greatest empires of all time.

The stage was set for Alexander's conquests when Greeks defeated the invading Persians in the fifth century B.C., then ended up fighting ruinously among themselves, leaving an opening for the Macedonians to their north. Athens, which led the struggle against Persia, used its naval power afterward to dominate other Greek city-states and demand tribute. Some Greeks resisted Athenian imperialism and backed its adversary Sparta.

Sparta, located on the Peloponnesus, a peninsula at the southern tip of Greece, was not a democracy like Athens. It was a highly regimented society led by two kings, who alternated

356 B.C. Alexander is born to King Philip II of Macedonia.

ca 340 B.C. Philip II conquers Greece.

334 B.C. Alexander begins campaign against Persian Empire.

327 B.C. India is invaded by Alexander.

323 B.C. Alexander dies of fever, prompting a struggle between his top generals, who carve up his empire.

ca 342 B.C. Greek philosopher Aristotle serves as Alexander's tutor.

336 B.C. After his father is assassinated, Alexander becomes king.

331 B.C. Alexander's army defeats Persians and their ruler, Darius III, at Gaugamela.

325 B.C. Alexander withdraws from India.

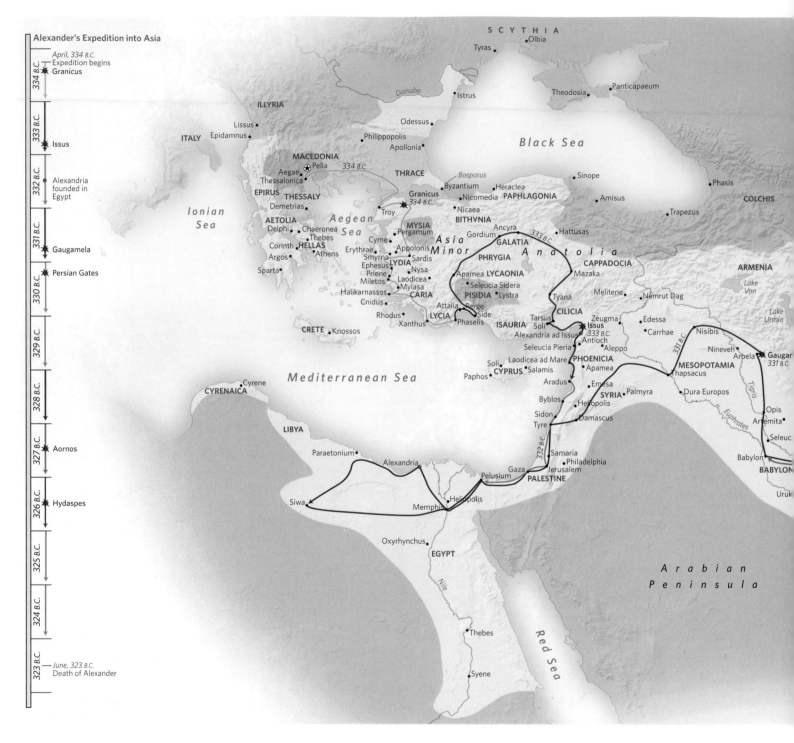

Alexander's Expedition into Asia

April, 334 B.C.
Expedition begins
334 B.C. ✴ Granicus

333 B.C. ✴ Issus

332 B.C. • Alexandria founded in Egypt

331 B.C. ✴ Gaugamela

330 B.C. ✴ Persian Gates

329 B.C.

328 B.C.

327 B.C. ✴ Aornos

326 B.C. ✴ Hydaspes

325 B.C.

324 B.C.

323 B.C. — *June, 323 B.C.*
Death of Alexander

as commanders of the army and shared political power with an aristocratic council of elders and an assembly of citizens. Like their Athenian counterparts, however, Sparta's citizens were free men. Women and slaves were not eligible for citizenship in the Greek world, and citizen-soldiers fought hard to uphold their rights. Sparta used its military might to subdue surrounding communities and make the inhabitants Helots (serfs who toiled for Spartans), while Athenians acquired many slaves.

The struggle between Athens and Sparta, known as the Peloponnesian War, dragged on for decades. Sparta and its allies secured victory in 404 B.C. by making concessions to their former Persian enemies, who helped equip them to defeat the Athenian navy. Democracy withered in Athens during that long war, and many city-states on both sides of the conflict were left weak and

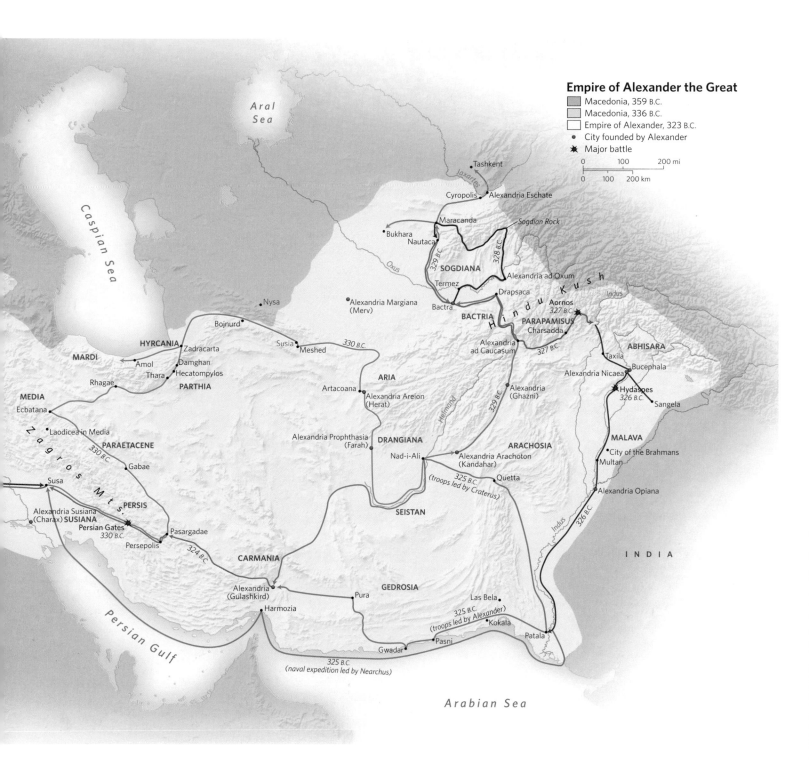

Empire of Alexander the Great

- Macedonia, 359 B.C.
- Macedonia, 336 B.C.
- Empire of Alexander, 323 B.C.
- • City founded by Alexander
- ✴ Major battle

0 100 200 mi
0 100 200 km

Aral Sea

Caspian Sea

Tashkent

Cyropolis • Alexandria Eschate

Maracanda

Bukhara
Nautaca
Sogdian Rock

329 B.C.   328 B.C.

SOGDIANA

Alexandria ad Oxum

Nysa   Termez

Alexandria Margiana
(Merv)   Bactra   **BACTRIA**

Bojnurd   **Hindu Kush**   Indus

Drapsaca   Aornos
327 B.C.

HYRCANIA   **PARAPAMISUS**
Zadracarta   Susia   Charsadda
Meshed   330 B.C.   327 B.C.

MARDI   Damghan   Alexandria   **ABHISARA**
Amol   Hecatompylos   ad Caucasum   Taxila
Thara   Bucephala

Rhagae   **PARTHIA**   Alexandria Nicaea
ARIA   Alexandria
Artacoana   (Ghazni)   ✴ Hydaspes

MEDIA   Alexandria Areion   326 B.C.
Ecbatana   (Herat)   Sangela

Laodicea in Media   329 B.C.
PARAETACENE
330 B.C.   Alexandria Prophthasia   **DRANGIANA**   **MALAVA**
(Farah)   **ARACHOSIA**   • City of the Brahmans
Gabae   Multan
Nad-i-Ali   Alexandria Arachoton
Susa   (Kandahar)   325 B.C.
PERSIS   Quetta   (troops led by Craterus)   Alexandria Opiana
Alexandria Susiana
(Charax) **SUSIANA**   **SEISTAN**   Indus
Persian Gates   326 B.C.
330 B.C.   Pasargadae
Persepolis   324 B.C.   **INDIA**

CARMANIA

Alexandria   Las Bela
(Gulashkird)   Pura   **GEDROSIA**   325 B.C.
Harmozia   (troops led by Alexander)
Kokala
Persian Gulf   Patala
Gwadar   Pasni
325 B.C.
(naval expedition led by Nearchus)

Arabian Sea

---

unstable. Their decline created a vacuum that was filled by the dynamic King Philip II of Macedonia, who subdued Greece around 340. He bequeathed that world and its culture to his son Alexander, who was tutored by the great Greek philosopher Aristotle. According to Plutarch, Alexander kept a copy of Homer's *Iliad* annotated by Aristotle "with his dagger under his pillow, declaring that he esteemed it a perfect portable treasure of all military virtue and knowledge."

The precocious Alexander was already a seasoned commander in the Macedonian army when he became king at the age of 20 in 336 following his father's assassination. Greeks who wanted to be citizens, not subjects, saw this as an opportunity to break free and rebelled. The young monarch crushed that uprising by storming the defiant city of Thebes,

> *"... in his love of glory, and the pursuit of it, he showed a solidity of high spirit and magnanimity far above his age."*
>
> PLUTARCH, ON ALEXANDER THE GREAT, *ALEXANDER* (WRITTEN A.D. 75)

north of Athens, slaughtering thousands of its inhabitants and enslaving the rest. Greeks then bowed to his authority, and some enlisted to fight for him, but the core of his army was Macedonian and fiercely loyal.

In 334, Alexander set out to conquer the Persian Empire, which was no longer as formidable as it once was, but remained a behemoth, far larger and more populous than Alexander's kingdom. His army numbered only about 40,000 men, but it was a versatile force including hard-charging cavalry on whom he relied mightily, light infantry armed with bows or javelins, and heavily armed foot soldiers who wielded spears and formed a phalanx, advancing relentlessly behind raised shields. Alexander deployed his troops with great skill and earned their devotion by leading them in battle and suffering several wounds. His Persian opponents, by contrast, were often conscripts or mercenaries who lacked the dedication and determination of his own men.

Crossing the Bosporus into Asia Minor, Alexander visited Troy—the fabled city where his Homeric hero Achilles won glory—before routing a Persian force consisting largely of Greek mercenaries. He showed those soldiers of fortune no

mercy but posed as the liberator of Greek cities in Asia Minor that had rebelled against Persia in the past and now hoped for freedom. When they opened their gates to Alexander, they were exchanging one imperial master for another, but many people preferred to be under his rule than Persian domination. Intent on stopping

Alexander's cavalrymen clash with troops mounted on elephants during his invasion of India, which ended with his withdrawal.

Alexander before he advanced down the Mediterranean coast, the Persian emperor Darius III led an army to the Gulf of Issus in 333 but suffered a humiliating defeat, retreating so hastily that he behind left his retinue, including members of his family, who were seized as hostages.

Refusing to make peace unless Darius yielded to him as emperor, Alexander moved south along the sea toward Egypt, vowing to "defeat the Persian fleet on land" by seizing any ports that opposing ships might use to contest his advance. One port that refused to yield to him was Tyre, a Phoenician city on the coast of Lebanon from which colonists had set out across the Mediterranean to North Africa and founded Carthage. Alexander laid siege to Tyre for seven months before capturing the city. He met with a warmer reception in Egypt, where he was hailed for delivering the country from Persian rule and honored as a god-king like the pharaohs of old—veneration he considered his due.

Having secured the Mediterranean coast, Alexander advanced east into Mesopotamia, where Darius awaited him on the plain of Gaugamela in 331 with replenished forces that far outnumbered their Macedonian foes. Once more, however, Alexander demonstrated that a small army acting in concert was superior to a sprawling one that lacked cohesion. When a gap opened in the Persian ranks, he and his Companions—elite cavalrymen who were like brothers to him—dashed into the breach, splitting the opposing army in two. Defeated and disgraced, Darius

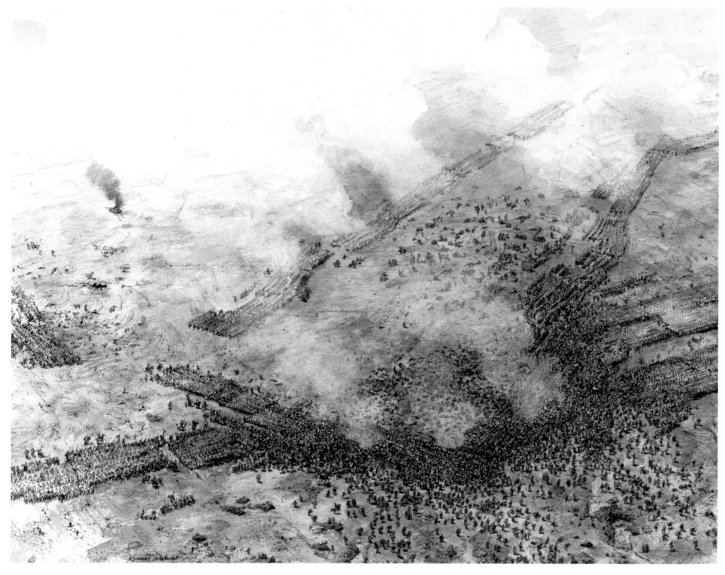

An artist's rendering of the Battle of Gaugamela shows rectangular Macedonian phalanxes amid clouds of dust raised by cavalry and charioteers.

ALEXANDER'S ARMY

Alexander's success owed much to his skillful coordination of infantry and cavalry. His heavy infantry units were armed with shields and spears and arrayed in a phalanx. The classic Macedonian phalanx consisted of 16 rows of 16 men each, forming a solid square that could resist attack from any direction. If soldiers at the perimeter fell, men stepped up to replace them. Alexander's infantry was often assigned to hold the center of the line and prevent enemy breakthroughs while cavalry on either flank swept forward. When required, however, rectangular phalanxes could adopt another formation such as a wedge and take the offensive.

Alexander himself led cavalry charges riding Bucephalus, a horse he grew up with. During his conquest of the Persian Empire, Plutarch wrote, Alexander spared old Bucephalus and used another horse when "riding about and marshalling some part of his phalanx, or exhorting or instructing or reviewing his men . . . but whenever he was going into action, Bucephalus would be led up, and he would mount him and at once begin the attack." During his climactic battle with Persian king Darius III at Gaugamela, Alexander waited to advance until opposing charioteers had assailed his infantry and been driven back. He then led a furious charge that routed Darius and the troops guarding him. As Plutarch related: "When they saw Alexander close at hand and terrible, and driving those who fled before him upon those who held their ground, they were smitten with fear and scattered."

PARMENIO

Macedonian general Parmenio served as patron and protector of young Alexander, whose father was assassinated when he was 20. Alexander himself was at risk of assassination, but Parmenio sided with him and had the culprits seized and executed. More than 30 years older than Alexander, Parmenio counseled the young king to marry and produce an heir before he waged war on the Persians. It was good advice, because Alexander later died without a Macedonian heir, which set the stage for a bloody power struggle between his generals that fractured his empire. Alexander, however, was too impatient for glory to delay his campaign against the Persians for domestic or dynastic reasons.

Parmenio was Alexander's second in command. In battle, Parmenio led the cavalry on one wing and played a supporting role while Alexander commanded the other wing and mounted heroic charges. Alexander would not tolerate a rival, and Parmenio's position as the conqueror's right-hand man placed him at risk. After the Persians' defeat, Parmenio's son Philotas was accused on slender evidence of conspiring against Alexander and executed. Parmenio, the man who had been like a second father to the young king and shielded him, was judged guilty by association, and Alexander had him put to death. ✍

Alexander tramples an enemy in a frieze on the Alexander Sarcophagus, which celebrated his conquests but did not serve as his coffin.

died at the hands of a Persian assassin a year later.

By adding the vast Persian realm to his kingdom on the Balkan peninsula, Alexander forged a Eurasian empire of unprecedented scope. Yet this was not enough for him. One Greek lesson he failed to heed was the danger of hubris, striving arrogantly for more than any man was meant to achieve. After subduing Bactria in what is now Afghanistan and wedding Roxana, the daughter of a Bactrian chief, he invaded India in 327 and crossed the Indus River, the farthest frontier of the old Persian Empire. But when monsoon rains arrived and mired them in mud, his weary troops grew feverish and mutinous. In 325, he turned back, bringing his last major campaign to an ignominious end.

Gold chalice with the emblem of Alexandria, Egypt

Alexander's genius was military, not political or diplomatic. In the few years remaining to him before his death in 323, he made fitful efforts to organize his huge empire. He admired his former Persian foes for their imperial accomplishments and hired Persian bodyguards, officers, and officials. He also added Persian princesses to his list of wives, after Roxana, and wed dozens of his commanders to Persian noblewomen. Many Macedonians felt he placed too much trust in people they still viewed as enemies, and Greeks consented only reluctantly to his demand that he be recognized as divine

like some Near Eastern monarchs. "If Alexander wishes to be a god," Spartans observed skeptically, "let him be a god."

Alexander's empire fractured after he died. But the Macedonian dynasties established by his generals Ptolemy in Egypt and Seleucus elsewhere in the Near East had a profound impact on that region by infusing it with Greek culture and Greek colonists. Among the many Middle Eastern cities founded by Macedonians or Greeks was Alexandria in Egypt, commissioned by Ptolemy as his capital and dedicated to Alexander. That port's great library and museum embodied the cosmopolitan spirit of the larger Greek world that Alexander brought into being.

The third dynasty that emerged under Antigonus when Alexander's generals divided his realm did not last long. Greeks never fully accepted imperial rule by Macedonians and tried to break free, only to fall subject to a greater power when Romans took control of their country in the second century B.C. By embracing the concept of citizenship and applying it to other Italians, Romans created a republic nearly as strong politically as it was militarily. Civic pride combined with military prowess put Rome almost in a class by itself—with the notable exception of its great rival, Carthage.

This medieval Italian depiction of the emerging city of Alexandria, founded in Egypt after Alexander's death by his general Ptolemy, testifies to the enduring legacy of the great Macedonian conqueror.

CARTHAGE

Rome's Imperial Rival

Beginning in 264 B.C. and continuing on and off for more than a century, Rome and Carthage engaged in an epic struggle, known as the Punic Wars because Carthaginians were of Punic, or Phoenician, origin. The Phoenicians were merchants and seafarers who fanned out from the coast of Lebanon across the Mediterranean. Among the goods they offered in trade were the famed cedars of Lebanon, used to build ships and palaces, and fabrics tinted with an alluring reddish-purple dye the Greeks called *phoenix,* a term also applied both to a mythical bird of that fiery color and to the Phoenician people. Culturally, their most important export was their phonetic alphabet, consisting of 22 consonants and much simpler to learn than the hundreds of characters Egyptian or Mesopotamian scribes had to master to write in hieroglyphs or cuneiform. The Greeks added vowels to that alphabet, which helped promote literacy.

Like the Greeks, the far-ranging Phoenicians founded distant colonies, the greatest of which was Carthage, situated across from Sicily on the coast of present-day Tunisia. By 300 B.C.,

The Phoenicians bequeathed to Carthage a script like that inscribed on the ritual object above and a tradition of trade and colonization in ships like the reconstruction at right.

Carthage was the maritime master of the western Mediterranean, equipped with a large merchant fleet and a formidable navy. It had little reason to fear Rome, which had no navy. But the Romans were growing ever stronger as they used armed force and diplomacy to become the dominant partner in alliances with other Italians. Before long, they had extended their authority south to the Strait of Messina, which separates the Italian mainland from Sicily.

The First Punic War began when Romans ferried troops across the strait and challenged Carthage for control of Messina and other Sicilian cities. They won some battles, but they knew they had no chance of defeating Carthage and its navy without a war fleet of their own—so they built one. The Romans modeled their ships on a Carthaginian galley they seized after it ran aground, but added to that design an ingenious device: a heavy wooden gangplank called a *corvus* (Latin for "crow") that could be winched up and dropped down on an enemy ship with such force that a metal spike at its base would penetrate the deck, fixing the gangplank in place and allowing Roman forces to storm the vessel.

ca 800 B.C. Phoenician colonists establish Carthage.

264 B.C. Rome challenges Carthage for control of Sicily, beginning the First Punic War.

218 B.C. Second Punic War begins; Carthaginian commander Hannibal invades Italy.

202 B.C. Romans defeat Carthaginians at Zama and force them to yield, ending Second Punic War.

146 B.C. Third Punic War ends with destruction of Carthage.

ca 500 B.C. Carthaginians occupy Cadiz and colonize other places in Spain.

241 B.C. First Punic War ends with Rome in control of Sicily.

216 B.C. Hannibal defeats Roman army at Cannae.

149 B.C. Romans set out to annihilate Carthage, launching Third Punic War.

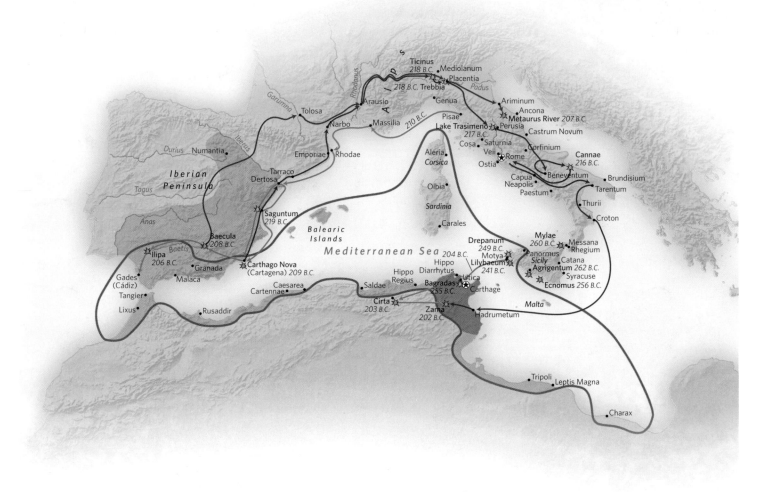

Carthage
- ☐ Carthage, 264 B.C.
- ☐ Carthage, 218–201 B.C.
- ■ Carthage, 201 B.C.
- ✳ Roman victory
- ✳ Carthaginian victory
- ← Campaign of Hannibal, 219–202 B.C.
- ← Campaign of Hasdrubal, 208–207 B.C.
- ← Campaigns of Scipio Africanus, 210–206 and 204–202 B.C.

0   100   200 mi
0   100   200 km

The device could not be used in rough seas and made ships heavier and more unstable. But it helped the upstart Roman navy gain victories and bought time for construction of a better fleet, which won control of the seas off Sicily in 241 and forced Carthage to surrender that island.

This defeat was costly for Carthage, which had to pay tribute to Rome and was slow to compensate its mercenaries, who rebelled after the war. That revolt, put down by the Carthaginian general Hamilcar Barca, underscored a crucial distinction between Carthage and Rome.

The Romans relied on citizen-soldiers and acquired an increasingly large pool of them by extending citizenship to their Italian allies, while Carthaginians were reluctant to grant citizenship to other people within their empire and relied heavily on mercenaries. To sustain the struggle against

> *"[Hamilcar] then, by dint of a spirit confident and incensed against the Romans, contrived, in order more easily to find a pretext for going to war with them, to be sent as commander-in-chief with an army into Spain, and took with him thither his son Hannibal, then nine years old."*
>
> CORNELIUS NEPOS, *LIVES OF EMINENT COMMANDERS*

Rome, Carthage needed new sources of wealth and manpower. These it found in Spain, where Hamilcar secured control of much of the Iberian Peninsula and its resources, including vast deposits of silver.

Spain served as the base for Hamilcar's son Hannibal when that brilliant general set out to defeat Rome in the Second Punic War, which began in 218. Carthage was no longer a great naval power, but its Spanish treasure allowed Hannibal to assemble a formidable army, including mercenaries from North Africa, Spain, and Gaul—a country encompassing modern-day France and environs and inhabited by Celtic tribes. Some of those recruits were motivated not just by the pay they received but also by hatred for Rome, notably the Celts Hannibal enlisted as his forces marched from Spain to northern Italy, a former Celtic stronghold. Hannibal's daring advance through the Alps with at least 40,000 troops and dozens of war elephants became legendary. As Roman historian Livy described it: "At the head of the column were the cavalry and elephants. Hannibal himself, with the pick of the infantry, brought up the rear, keeping his eyes open and alert for every contingency."

Hannibal's invasion stunned the Romans. In 216, he dealt them a staggering defeat in the Battle of Cannae by drawing back the endangered center of his line to form a pocket in which the oncoming Romans were trapped when his resilient forces swept around their flanks

PEOPLE

HAMILCAR BARCA

Best known as the father of Hannibal, Hamilcar Barca (*barca* means "lightning") was a brilliant commander in his own right who restored the fortunes of Carthage following its defeat by Rome in the First Punic War. Roman chronicler Cornelius Nepos portrayed Hamilcar as a warmonger who hated the Romans and required young Hannibal to swear an oath never to befriend them. Anxious Romans viewed Hamilcar's Spanish campaign as the prelude to an invasion of Italy—a nightmare that later materialized when Hannibal crossed the Alps with his army. In fact, Rome bore as much responsibility for the Second Punic War as Carthage did. Stripped of Sicily and other colonies by Rome and forced to pay heavy indemnities following the first war, Carthage faced a bleak future until Hamilcar conquered much of Spain and acquired its mineral wealth. In the process, though, he antagonized Rome, which would not tolerate a rival to its imperial ambitions.

Urged on by Hamilcar Barca, young Hannibal vows defiance to Rome in this painting by Giovanni Battista Pittoni.

> *"Hannibal so cherished in his mind the hatred which his father had borne the Romans, and which was left him, as it were, by bequest, that he laid down his life before he would abate it."*

CORNELIUS NEPOS, *LIVES OF EMINENT COMMANDERS*

and enveloped them—one of the most celebrated maneuvers in military history. His strategic objective was to demoralize Rome's Italian allies and cause them to defect. And some did defect to him in southern Italy, where Hannibal and his army held out for more than a dozen years.

In the end, Hannibal was forced to abandon Italy by a general as bold as he

was, Publius Cornelius Scipio. Scipio took the offensive against Rome's enemies in Spain and later crossed to North Africa, reckoning that Hannibal would have to meet him there to defend his capital. He overcame Hannibal's vaunted cavalry—which included skilled horsemen from Numidia in North Africa—by inducing Numidians to switch sides and fight for

Rome in the Battle of Zama, waged in 202 not far from Carthage. By crushing Hannibal there, Scipio won the war and the honorific "Africanus." Carthage ceded to Rome all its territories outside Africa and disbanded its army, but continued to profit from trade.

In 150, Carthage raised troops to fend off assaults by Rome's ally Numidia. That provided a pretext for the Third Punic War (149–146), launched at the urging of Roman orator Marcus Porcius Cato, who declared, "Carthage must be destroyed!" And so it was, in a punishing campaign that ended when Romans razed the city and sold much of its population into slavery.

A 17th-century painting of a battle during the Second Punic War shows one of Hannibal's elephants rampaging through Roman troops.

HANNIBAL'S ELEPHANTS

When Hannibal and his army set out from Spain to cross the Alps into Italy, they brought along some three dozen war elephants. These functioned much like tanks today, using their bulk to smash through enemy lines. Elephants were not indigenous to Spain, though, so where they came from remains a matter of debate. The only species native to North Africa was fairly small and would have been of limited use. Hannibal's animals might have come from sub-Saharan Africa, but elephants from there are not easily trained, especially in the skills required for battle. Indian elephants, on the other hand, can be trained and were widely used in warfare. Persians employed some against Alexander the Great, and his general Seleucus brought hundreds back to the Middle East from the Indus Valley. Those may have been the ancestors of the animals Hannibal used.

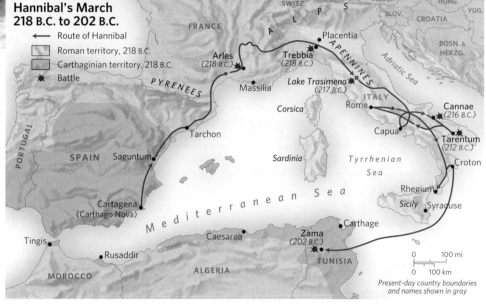

Hannibal's March 218 B.C. to 202 B.C.
← Route of Hannibal
Roman territory, 218 B.C.
Carthaginian territory, 218 B.C.
✴ Battle

Present-day country boundaries and names shown in gray

Soldiers and elephants trudge through a snowy Alpine pass during Hannibal's march to Italy, where he fought for more than a decade.

Crossing the Alps was as difficult for Hannibal's elephants as it was for his troops, who had to cope with cold nights, steep icy paths, and hostile tribesmen. "The elephants proved both a blessing and a curse," wrote the Roman historian Livy, "for though getting them along the narrow and precipitous tracks caused serious delay, they were nonetheless a protection to the troops, as the natives, never having seen such creatures before, were afraid to come near them."

About 20 elephants survived the trek and made it to Italy to battle the Romans. Only one elephant, named Surus ("the Syrian"), was still alive when Hannibal's long Italian campaign ended.

ROMAN EMPIRE
Rise of the Caesars

Rome crushed Carthage in 146 B.C., the same year in which it completed its conquest of Greece and Macedonia. The Roman Empire now embraced parts of two continents, Europe and Africa, and would soon expand into Asia. Politically, however, Rome was still a republic, governed by rules laid down centuries earlier after it rebelled against the Etruscans, who had dominated much of Italy from around 800 to 500 B.C. As rulers of Rome, Etruscans had enhanced that city on the Tiber River by paving its streets, erecting public buildings, and introducing a script based on the Greek alphabet. Romans, however, longed to be rid of their masters. According to legend, they ousted their last Etruscan king, Tarquin the Proud, after his son raped a virtuous Roman woman named Lucretia.

After gaining independence in 509, Rome became a republic—a state governed publicly and collectively by its citizens. It was not a democracy like Athens, which gave each citizen an equal vote. Common Roman citizens, known as plebeians, originally had far less say in government than did

Romans were influenced by the culture of the Etruscans, who crafted the gold clasp above, and the Greeks, who inspired Roman architecture and painting (right).

patricians—aristocrats who dominated the Roman Senate and controlled a special assembly that elected two consuls annually to rule Rome for the year. Those consuls were granted *imperium,* supreme power, including the right to command troops. To prevent a consul from abusing that power and making himself king, he was allowed to bring troops into the city only when celebrating a triumph, during which he was hailed for his feats as *imperator* (supreme commander) before yielding power. As Rome grew mightier, the rewards of commanding troops and winning victories increased substantially, as did the risk that a Roman general might use his army to occupy the capital and reign permanently as imperator—the source of the English emperor, meaning one holding supreme power for life.

Roman conquests endangered the Roman Republic not just by tempting successful commanders to abuse their power but also by flooding Italy with slaves from conquered lands and enriching landlords who owned slaves at the expense of poor farmers who relied on their own labor. In the past, Rome had eased social tensions by granting plebeians the right to

509 B.C. Rome achieves independence from Etruscans and becomes a republic.

146 B.C. Romans destroy Carthage and complete conquest of Greece and Macedonia.

44 B.C. Assassination of Caesar leads to civil war.

A.D. 117 Emperor Trajan dies, with Roman Empire at its greatest extent.

A.D. 476 Rome falls to Germanic invaders.

ca 275 B.C. Southern Italy comes under Roman rule.

49 B.C. Julius Caesar crosses the Rubicon with his army and becomes Rome's dictator.

31 B.C. Octavian (Augustus Caesar) defeats Mark Antony and Queen Cleopatra of Egypt and becomes emperor.

A.D. 212 Roman citizenship extended to all within the empire who are not slaves.

The Roman Empire

- ▨ Roman Territory, 201 B.C.
- ▨ Gains by 100 B.C.
- ▨ Gains by 44 B.C.
- ▨ Gains by A.D. 14
- ▨ Gains by A.D. 117
- ▨ Region temporarily held by Rome, with dates
- ▨ Vassal of Rome
- ⌐⌐⌐ Fortified frontier
- —— Roman road

- ◉ Provincial capital
- ⚓ Legion headquarters
- ⚓ Major naval base
- ✷ Battle of the Samnite Wars (343–290 B.C.)
- ✷ Battle of the 1st Punic War (264–241 B.C.)
- ✷ Battle of the 2nd Punic War (218–202 B.C.)
- ✷ Battle of the Macedonian Wars (214–148 B.C.)
- ✷ Battle of the Roman-Germanic Wars (113 B.C.–A.D. 439)
- ✷ Battle of Julius Caesar's Civil War (49–45 B.C.)
- ✷ Other major battle

0   100   200 mi
0   100   200 km

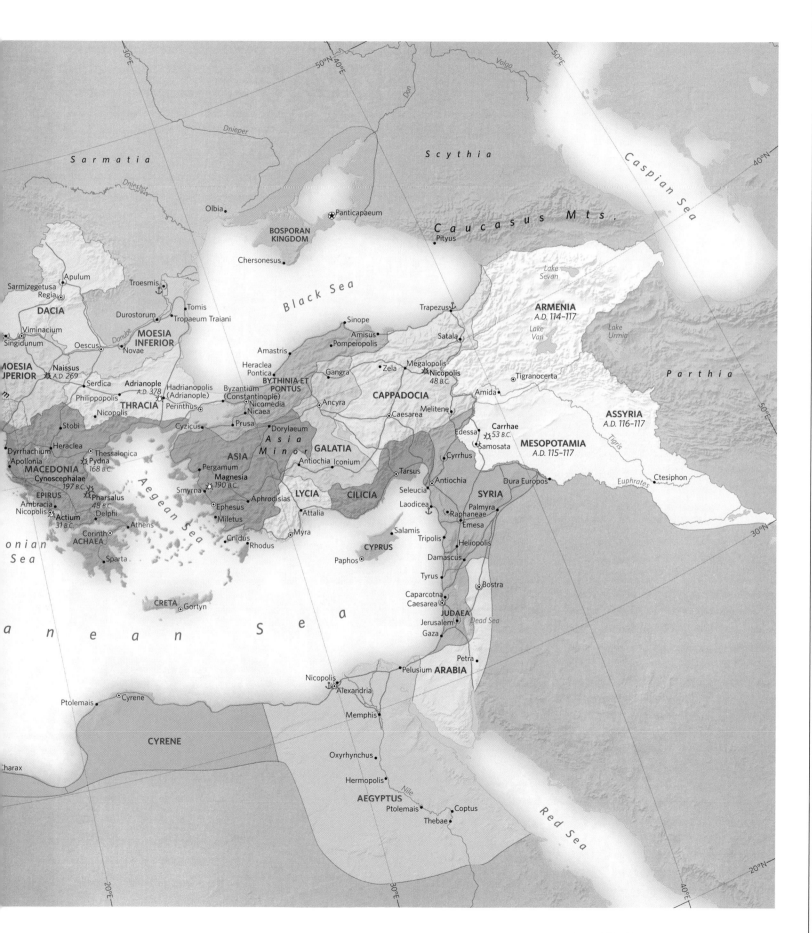

S a r m a t i a

S c y t h i a

Caspian Sea

Dnieper

Dniester

Olbia

Panticapaeum

BOSPORAN KINGDOM

C a u c a s u s   M t s.

Pityus

Chersonesus

Black Sea

Trapezus

Lake Sevan

ARMENIA
A.D. 114–117

Apulum

Sarmizegetusa
Regia

Troesmis

Tomis

Sinope

Satala

Lake Van

Lake Urmia

DACIA

Durostorum

Tropaeum Traiani

Amisus

Pompeiopolis

P a r t h i a

Viminacium

Danube

MOESIA INFERIOR

Amastris

Zela

Megalopolis

Nicopolis
48 B.C.

Tigranocerta

Singidunum

Oescus

Novae

Heraclea
Pontica

Gangra

Amida

**MOESIA
UPERIOR**

Naissus
A.D. 269

**BYTHINIA-ET
PONTUS**

CAPPADOCIA

ASSYRIA
A.D. 116–117

Serdica

Adrianople
A.D. 378

Hadrianopolis
(Adrianople)

Byzantium
(Constantinople)

Ancyra

Melitene

Edessa

Carrhae
53 B.C.

Philippopolis

THRACIA

Perinthus

Nicomedia

Nicaea

Caesarea

Samosata

MESOPOTAMIA
A.D. 115–117

Nicopolis

Cyzicus

Prusa

Cyrrhus

Tigris

Stobi

A s i a   M i n o r

Dorylaeum

GALATIA

Antiochia

Dura Europos

Euphrates

Ctesiphon

Heraclea

Thessalonica

ASIA

Pergamum

Antiochia
Iconium

Tarsus

Antiochia

SYRIA

Palmyra

Dyrrhachium
Apollonia

Pydna
168 B.C.

Magnesia
190 B.C.

Seleucia

Raphaneae

MACEDONIA

Cynoscephalae
197 B.C.

Smyrna

Aphrodisias

LYCIA

CILICIA

Laodicea

Emesa

EPIRUS

Pharsalus
48 B.C.

Ephesus

Attalia

Salamis

Tripolis

Heliopolis

Ambracia
Nicopolis

Delphi

Miletus

CYPRUS

Damascus

Actium
31 B.C.

Athens

Cnidus

Myra

Salamis

Tyrus

Bostra

Corinth

ACHAEA

Rhodus

Paphos

Caparcotna
Caesarea

*onian
Sea*

Sparta

JUDAEA

a n e a n   S e a

Jerusalem

Dead Sea

CRETA
Gortyn

Gaza

Petra

Pelusium

ARABIA

Nicopolis
Alexandria

Ptolemais
Cyrene

Memphis

CYRENE

Oxyrhynchus

harax

Hermopolis

Nile

AEGYPTUS

Ptolemais
Coptus

Thebae

Red Sea

REFORMING THE ROMAN ARMY

When Gaius Marius became consul in 107 B.C., he faced the problem of defending a sprawling empire with an army that still operated as if Rome were a small republic confined to the Italian peninsula. In a tradition that reflected the elitism of the Roman Republic, only landowners were allowed to serve in the army. Citizens of wealth and status disdained the lower classes and did not trust them to defend a country in which they had little stake. By Marius's time, however, the landed class was shrinking as wealthy slave owners expanded their estates at the expense of poor farmers. One option for Rome was to increase its reliance on foreign troops, who fought as auxiliaries in Roman armies—but that could leave the empire at the mercy of those very foreigners. Imperial powers that relied heavily on foreign soldiers often ended up being dominated by them, as happened in Egypt after the New Kingdom collapsed.

Marius created a professional army in which the only requirement for service was Roman citizenship. Poor Romans flocked to enlist and received equipment and pay. If their armies triumphed, they could hope to share in the spoils of conquest and receive land grants when they retired. Besides increasing the pool of men available to serve, this had other benefits. Henceforth, the bulk of the army was made up of common citizens accustomed to hardship and prepared to perform laborious tasks such as building roads when they were not marching and fighting. Marius reduced the army's reliance on cumbersome supply wagons and had soldiers carry most of what they needed on their backs. They became known as "Marius's mules."

The danger in these reforms was that soldiers would grow more loyal to the generals who rewarded them with spoils and land than they were to Rome's political leaders. Professional armies soon became the tools of Roman dictators and engaged in civil wars.

A 19th-century painting by Saverio Altamura portrays the army of Marius celebrating a victory. Marius defeated Germanic tribes and later became embroiled in a civil war against Lucius Cornelius Sulla, backed by Romans who opposed Marius's reforms.

Roman troops wage war in this relief carved on the Arch of Constantine, erected in Rome to commemorate Emperor Constantine's victory in A.D. 312 over his rival, Maxentius. Such civil wars were frequent in the last days of the Roman Republic and occurred occasionally in later imperial times.

elect representatives and hold high office, including consulships. Some men of modest origins became as rich and powerful as members of the hereditary nobility. But that did not reduce tensions between the rich and the poor.

In the late second century B.C., two brothers from a noble family, Tiberius and Gaius Gracchus, proposed reforms that included redistributing public land—much of it acquired through conquest—from wealthy landholders to poor farmers and granting full citizenship to Rome's Italian allies, who had legal rights but could not vote or hold office. Those proposals met with fierce opposition from conservative Romans, who were unwilling to share their land or privileges with others and assailed the brothers, both of whom died violently. As their fate demonstrated, the political process was breaking down, leaving issues that divided the public to be thrashed out by armies and generals. The status of Italian allies who fought for Rome but remained second-class citizens was resolved only after they rebelled in 91 B.C. Romans settled that conflict by offering full citizenship to all loyal Italian freemen. Harder to resolve was the conflict between wealthy landlords and those with little or no land. Soldiers without land looked for rewards to their commanders, who returned from conquests abroad to vie for supremacy at home.

Among those ambitious generals was Gaius Marius, who rose to become consul with the support of common citizens. He broke with tradition by allowing Romans who did not own property to enlist as soldiers. After campaigning successfully against hostile German tribes, he returned with his troops to Rome and pressed the Senate to grant land to his troops. His great rival was Lucius Cornelius Sulla, favored by conservatives hostile to Marius's reforms. In 88 B.C., Sulla marched on Rome with his

Julius Caesar, portrayed here as a conqueror wearing a breastplate, rewarded his army with the spoils of war, then used his loyal troops to seize power.

army and forced Marius into exile, igniting a civil war. Marius and his forces returned to Rome while Sulla was off campaigning in Asia and executed their political opponents. Sulla regained control of Italy when he returned and struck back by drawing up a list of thousands of his enemies, who were proscribed, meaning that any Roman could kill them and claim their property.

That bloodbath and Sulla's dictatorship left the Roman Republic near collapse. The great question was not whether the republic would fall, but which commander would gain supremacy and put the wounded polity out of its misery.

Few Romans would have chosen young Julius Caesar as the man most likely to succeed on a grand scale and dominate their world. His early accomplishments as an officer and politician were overshadowed by those of Pompey the Great, who earned that title in his mid-20s and invited comparison with Alexander the Great. Pompey reconquered Spain from a rogue Roman general, helped crush a slave rebellion led by the gladiator Spartacus, cleansed much of the Mediterranean of pirates, and secured Asia Minor, Syria, and Judea for Rome before returning in triumph to the capital in 61 B.C. His reputation was immense, but he lacked the political skill and cunning of Caesar, who forged a three-man alliance known as the First Triumvirate with Pompey and Marcus Licinius Crassus, one of the richest men in Rome.

Caesar, at about 40, was the youngest member of the triumvirate—and neither as wealthy as Crassus nor as esteemed as Pompey. But he won popularity as a candidate for office by shrewdly using borrowed money to stage spectacular gladiatorial combats. In 59 B.C., he became the first of the three to be elected consul. He pushed through reforms that benefited Pompey's troops and other citizens in need of land by allowing angry veterans who supported

WINING AND DINING

Unlike the Greeks, whose banquets or drinking parties were often all-male affairs, Romans gathered for festive meals in groups that frequently included men, women, and children. Guests reclined on couches and, in wealthy households, were served by slaves. After nibbling on delicacies that included eggs, oysters, fish, and fowl, diners tossed the shells and bones aside. Wine flowed freely, often mixed with honey or water, allowing people to imbibe without becoming drunk. Sometimes, the women and children retired early, and the men who remained might be entertained by courtesans.

Romans were of two minds about the lavish banquets. Some thought that their society was too extravagant for its own good and that Rome was going soft. Others embraced the philosophy "Eat, drink, and be merry, for tomorrow we die." Such epicureans savored pleasures but did not necessarily approve of eating or drink to excess. Romans prized self-control and pitied those who were slaves to their appetites or passions.

Scenes like this sometimes occurred after Roman banquets, when men who had had plenty to drink let their togas down in mixed company.

The Roman Colosseum, completed in A.D. 80, held more than 50,000 spectators, who watched gladiatorial contests and other blood sports staged by rulers to divert the populace.

those measures to gather menacingly in Rome, where they intimidated the Senate. Some of Caesar's political maneuvers were illegal and left him open to prosecution when he stepped down as consul. He eluded that threat by taking command of Roman forces on the frontier. By leaving Pompey and Crassus behind in Rome, he risked losing out to them politically, but he needed a great military victory to win lasting glory and therefore set out to conquer the long-defiant Gauls, Celts who lived in modern-day France.

By 53 B.C., after five years of relentless campaigning, Caesar had seemingly completed his conquest. But Gauls of various tribes banded together belatedly under a defiant chieftain named Vercingetorix and nearly overcame Caesar before he besieged their fortress at Alesia in 51 and captured their leader. Hauled off to Rome and paraded in chains through the streets there before being ritually strangled, Vercingetorix was one of more than a million Gauls killed or enslaved by legions loyal to Caesar, whose crushing victory rivaled anything Pompey ever accomplished in battle. The third member of their triumvirate, Crassus, had died in a disastrous campaign against the Parthians in Mesopotamia, leaving Pompey and Caesar to compete for supremacy. Roman orator Marcus Tullius Cicero, who revered the republic and hoped to preserve it, called the looming contest "the greatest struggle that history has ever known" and

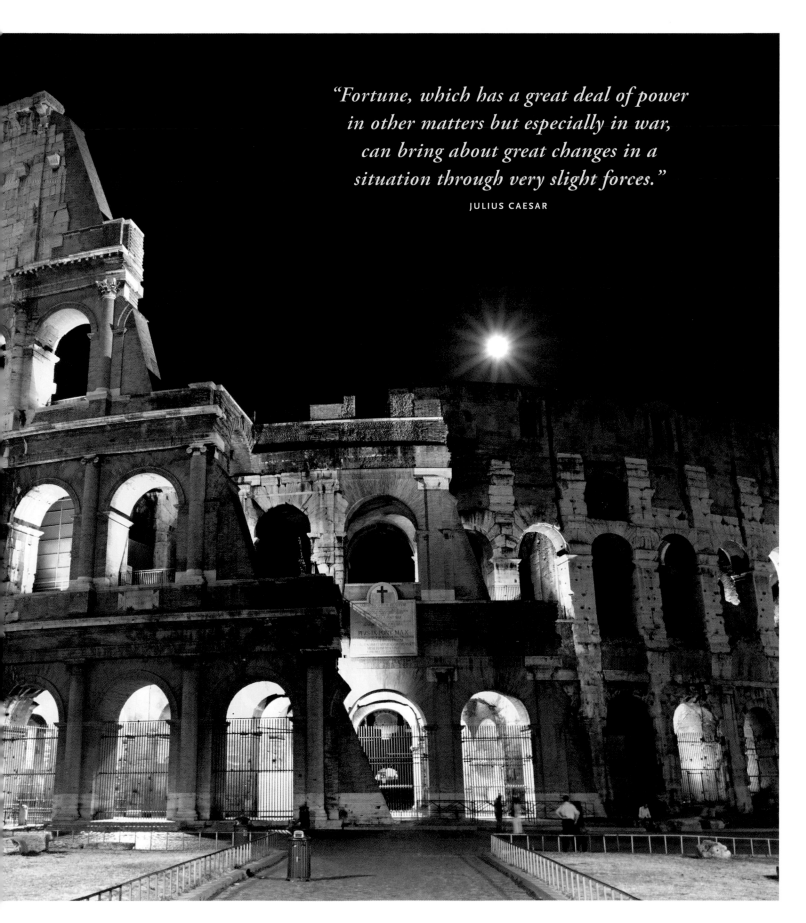

"Fortune, which has a great deal of power in other matters but especially in war, can bring about great changes in a situation through very slight forces."

JULIUS CAESAR

Hadrian's Wall in northern England was built in the second century A.D. to shield Roman Britain from hostile Celtic tribes.

feared the outcome, whichever man won: "Victory will bring many evils in its wake, including the certainty of a despot."

In January 49, Julius Caesar and his army crossed the Rubicon River, which marked the southern boundary of Cisalpine Gaul, beyond he which he could not legally command troops. By doing so, he defied the Senate in Rome, dominated by conservatives of noble ancestry who counted on Pompey to protect their interests. Lacking support from the Roman masses, who favored Caesar, Pompey and his forces left Italy to seek support in Greece and Macedonia. He assembled an army twice the size of Caesar's, but the conqueror of Gaul was now Pompey's superior in battle and defeated him decisively at Pharsalus in 48. Fleeing to Egypt, Pompey was betrayed and killed as he came ashore.

Unlike some earlier Roman generals who engaged in civil wars, Caesar was magnanimous to his opponents, including Marcus Junius Brutus, a supporter of Pompey who went on to achieve political prominence with Caesar's blessing. However, when Caesar was proclaimed perpetual dictator,

Brutus, the descendant of a Roman hero who had helped overthrow the city's last Etruscan king centuries earlier, turned against Caesar and led conspirators in the Senate who assassinated him in 44 B.C. They acted in the name of the Roman Republic, threatened by Caesar's tyranny. But the republic was dead, and their desperate effort to revive it only resulted in the rise of another almighty Caesar.

In his will, Caesar named as heir his 18-year-old nephew, Octavian. Like his uncle, who courted the powerful Pompey before challenging him, Octavian formed an alliance with—and would later do battle with—an older and more accomplished figure, Mark Antony, who had served as a general under Caesar. Octavian and Antony formed the Second Triumvirate

"At the sight of the city utterly perishing amidst the flames Scipio burst into tears, and stood long reflecting on the inevitable change which awaits cities, nations, and dynasties, one and all, as it does every one of us men."

POLYBIUS, *THE THIRD PUNIC WAR, 149-146 B.C.,* [THE HISTORIES, BOOK XXXVI-XXXIX]

with another of Caesar's aides, Marcus Aemilius Lepidus, who proved inept and was overshadowed by his partners.

Antony and Octavian inaugurated their alliance by doing away with political opponents, including Cicero, who denounced Antony in the Senate and paid with his life. Then they went after Caesar's assassins, who fled Rome when the populace turned against them. Antony

commanded the army that defeated those diehard republicans at Philippi in 42 and chose to remain there in Greece as ruler of Rome's wealthy eastern provinces. Octavian returned to rule Italy, where his forces put down an uprising led by members of Antony's family.

Relations between the two partners-turned-rivals worsened when Antony, after marrying Octavian's sister, carried on a

SO WHAT?

THE ROMAN CALENDAR

The traditional Roman calendar had 12 months based on the lunar cycle and was shorter than the solar year. Extra days were sometimes added between one year and the next to bring the months in line with the seasons, but this was not done systematically. By the time Julius Caesar became dictator, the Roman calendar was three months ahead of the solar cycle. On the date of the harvest festival, for instance, the crops were still green. Caesar set things right by adding nearly 90 days to the year 46 B.C. He then introduced his Julian calendar, with a year of 365 days and an extra day every fourth year.

After his death, Caesar was deified. Like the gods Janus (January) and Mars (March), he had a month dedicated to him—Julius (July), the month in which he was born. The following month (August) was later renamed to honor his nephew, Augustus Caesar.

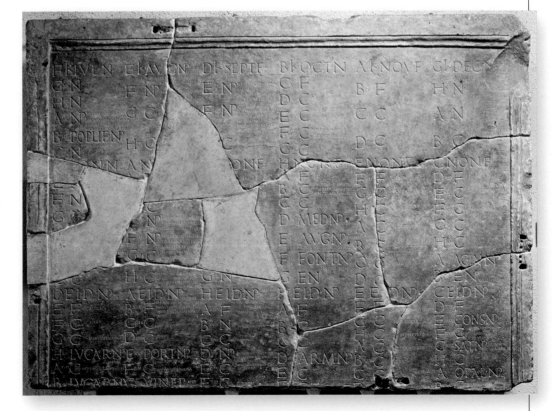

Roman calendars were carved in stone, but that did not stop mighty rulers such as Julius Caesar from altering them.

sensational affair with Queen Cleopatra of Egypt, who achieved power and sought to preserve it by charming and disarming Roman conquerors. After being placed on the throne by Julius Caesar, she had entertained him royally and given birth to a boy she named Caesarion, implying that he was Caesar's son. Now Antony had children by her, bequeathed eastern provinces to them, and acknowledged Caesarion as Caesar's true heir in defiance of Octavian's claim.

Octavian denounced Antony as a man at the mercy of a foreign queen and waged war on that couple. Although not a great general like his uncle, Octavian excelled as commander in chief by entrusting campaigns to gifted officers. One such was the accomplished admiral Marcus Agrippa, who trapped the fleet of Antony and Cleopatra at Actium off the coast of Greece in 31. Abandoning their doomed forces, they retreated to Egypt, where the lovers committed suicide as Octavian closed in on them.

The victorious Octavian took Egypt as his personal province and had Caesarion put to death. Returning to Rome in triumph, he added the title Augustus (meaning "sacred" or "exalted") to his adopted surname Caesar and remained imperator for life. The vast Roman Empire, long contested by consuls and generals, was now firmly in the grasp of an emperor.

Like Darius I of Persia, Augustus Caesar was an organizational genius whose administrative accomplishments surpassed his military feats. He reassured those citizens who feared tyranny and looked back longingly on the Roman Republic by preserving its institutions, including the Senate. He reorganized that body to include representatives from throughout Italy and allowed it to exercise some real responsibilities, including appointing

The eruption of Mount Vesuvius in A.D. 79 buried the city of Pompeii in ash, preserving for posterity the remains of its buildings and inhabitants.

proconsuls to govern Roman provinces not under the emperor's direct control. Augustus maintained authority over the Senate and its appointees, however, by serving for many years as consul as well as supreme commander and by taking on the powers of a tribune—an office created centuries earlier to protect the rights of common citizens that allowed him to veto any measure he found objectionable.

Although Roman citizens now had little say in how their government was run, they still had legal rights, including the right to defend themselves in court and to appeal the verdict to a higher tribunal. Roman women were second-class citizens, with fewer rights than freemen, but they were legally entitled to inherit wealth, which some used to engage in business. Augustus promoted traditional Roman family values and exercised his prerogative as emperor and paterfamilias—a father ruling over his family—by forcing his daughter Julia to wed her stepbrother Tiberius and later exiling her for adultery when she rebelled. Yet even Augustus had to yield occasionally to his determined wife, Livia, who like other Roman matrons greatly influenced her husband and children.

The ultimate source of Augustus Caesar's power was the army. Far from seeking to enlarge those forces, which were bloated by civil war, he reduced the number of legions from 60 to 28, amounting to some 150,000 men in all, and settled veterans in colonies that helped Romanize distant provinces. He worked to consolidate the empire by securing its borders in some places and advancing them in regions where hostile tribes threatened. The greatest challenge he faced during his

VILLAS OF POMPEII

Pompeii and nearby Herculaneum, both buried by the A.D. 79 eruption of Mount Vesuvius, were popular resorts for wealthy Romans, who built villas along the Bay of Naples where they could enjoy the vistas and ocean breezes. Roman villas such as the one diagrammed here had an atrium at the entrance. An opening in the roof of the atrium allowed sunlight to enter on fair days. In foul weather, rain filled a pool beneath the skylight. Beyond the atrium lay a courtyard called the peristyle, containing a garden where residents could sit, stroll, or dine. Living rooms and bedrooms were tastefully furnished and beautifully decorated with frescoes and mosaics.

Visitors to Pompeii today can view the remains of such estates, including the Villa of the Mysteries, so called for frescoes depicting a mysterious ritual. Among the figures portrayed there is Dionysus, the Greek god of wine, rapture, and fertility, whose devotees included women called maenads. The frescoes show women participating in an initiation rite of some kind. Brides may have undergone the ritual before marriage to seek fertility.

The gracious villas of Pompeii reflect the wealth that prominent Romans accumulated as their empire expanded. Some prospered through trade, which flourished when the Mediterranean Sea became, in effect, a Roman lake. Others grew rich by amassing prizes of war, including slaves from conquered lands, who toiled for their owners in fields, workshops, or mines. ✒

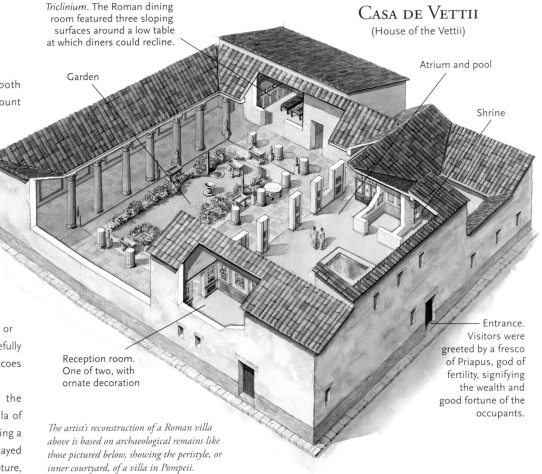

CASA DE VETTII
(House of the Vettii)

Triclinium. The Roman dining room featured three sloping surfaces around a low table at which diners could recline.

Garden

Atrium and pool

Shrine

Entrance. Visitors were greeted by a fresco of Priapus, god of fertility, signifying the wealth and good fortune of the occupants.

Reception room. One of two, with ornate decoration

The artist's reconstruction of a Roman villa above is based on archaeological remains like those pictured below, showing the peristyle, or inner courtyard, of a villa in Pompeii.

Rings found on the fingers of a woman who died following the eruption of Mount Vesuvius in 79

46-year reign came in A.D. 9, five years before he died, when Roman forces who had crossed the Rhine and marched deep into Germany were ambushed. Augustus sent Tiberius to quell that uprising, led by a German chieftain named Arminius who had been granted Roman citizenship before he rebelled. Roman troops pulled back to the Rhine afterward, and Augustus advised his successors to keep the empire's frontiers as he left them.

Notwithstanding battles in Germany and other contested regions, Augustus initiated a largely peaceful era known as the Pax Romana, which lasted for nearly two centuries as Rome imposed order on a world long convulsed by conflict. Lands that were once plundered by Roman troops became tranquil

Vase with grapevine motif, found at Pompeii

provinces, subject to taxation but spared devastation unless they rebelled. Trade flourished and cities prospered as Augustus and his successors built roads, aqueducts, baths, and amphitheaters, or circuses, to entertain the urban masses, who often received grain doles to keep them from rioting. The Roman poet Juvenal scoffed that Romans who once took an active part in government now cared only for "bread and circuses." But ritualized carnage by gladiators and wild animals in coliseums was better than bloodshed in the streets. Roman engineering brought the attractions of urban life to provincial cities such as Lyon in Gaul. This helped transform conquered subjects into complacent Roman citizens. The privilege of citizenship was gradually extended until it was granted to all free men and women within the Roman Empire in 212.

One imperial problem Augustus did not solve was how to ensure an orderly succession. Having no son of his own, he designated as his heir Tiberius, Livia's son by a previous marriage. His later years as emperor were marred by murderous

---

DAILY LIFE

The Pont du Gard in southern France was erected by Romans in the first century B.C. to supply water to the city of Nemausus (Nîmes).

AQUEDUCTS

The growth of Rome and other cities around the Roman Empire was made possible by aqueducts, which supplied fresh water to urban areas that would otherwise have been limited to local sources that could not have supported populations of up to one million, in Rome's case, and were often polluted. Engineers who designed aqueducts like the one shown here used the principle of the arch to distribute the weight of the structure and relied on gravity to carry water from sources at higher elevations to the city, where it flowed through lead pipes to fountains and baths. Public baths promoted public health and were a popular diversion. Many featured both cold and warm pools, heated by furnaces circulating water beneath the tiles. In the late days of the empire, when Rome was besieged by Germanic invaders, all but one aqueduct was cut off. The city's public water supply remained inadequate throughout the Middle Ages.

Laborers pick grapes in this mosaic from the Roman province of Gaul (France), a wine-producing region then as it is today.

intrigue, which haunted the Julio-Claudian dynasty instituted by Augustus. Tiberius's dynastic successors included just one worthy ruler—Claudius, who invaded Britain and created an efficient imperial bureaucracy staffed by well-educated freedmen (emancipated slaves). His accomplishments were overshadowed by the excesses of the despots who preceded and followed him, Caligula and Nero, who were so despised that even the Praetorian Guard, assigned to protect the emperor, turned against them.

Nero's suicide in 69 prompted a brief civil war that was won by Vespasian, a gifted general of modest origins whose short-lived Flavian dynasty ended in 96 with the assassination of his brutal son

Domitian. The elderly senator who took his place, Nerva, lived only two years but set a worthy precedent by adopting an accomplished heir, Trajan. A commander of Spanish origin, Trajan was the first man born outside Italy to rule the Roman Empire, which he brought to its greatest extent by conquering Dacia (known today as Romania for its Roman occupiers) and advancing into Mesopotamia. He died in 117 without realizing his ambition of matching the Near Eastern conquests of Alexander the Great. The Roman Empire now far exceeded Alexander's empire, however, reaching from the Persian Gulf all the way to Britain.

Shortly before his death, Trajan followed Nerva's example and adopted an experienced heir, his cousin Hadrian, who took a defensive stance by withdrawing forces from Mesopotamia and erecting Hadrian's Wall—a massive barricade shielding Roman Britain from hostile Celtic tribes to the north—and other fortifications. Those measures signaled that the empire had reached its limit of expansion and now faced the daunting task of holding off raiders and invaders lured by the wealth and fertility of Rome's provinces. A devotee of Greece, Hadrian adorned Athens with monuments and celebrated what would later be called the Classical Age, which began with the literary and artistic achievements of ancient Greece and continued in Roman times as architects, sculptors, poets, and philosophers followed Greek precedents. The Roman author Virgil, for example, traced the legendary history of Rome back to the fall of Troy in his epic poem, *The Aeneid,* modeled after Homer's *Iliad* and *Odyssey.* Roman philosophers such as Marcus Aurelius, a protégé of Hadrian who himself later became emperor, were deeply influenced by Greek schools of thought such as Stoicism, whose followers sought to lead lives governed by reason rather than passion and to calmly accept what fate decreed.

DAILY LIFE

SLAVERY

The Roman Empire relied heavily on slave labor. By one estimate, slaves made up a quarter of the population in Rome. Some slaves were brutally exploited, including those who toiled in mines or on galleys, pulling oars. Slaves who fought as gladiators faced such a high risk of death or mutilation that they rebelled under the leadership of Spartacus in the first century B.C. and were crucified by the thousands when their revolt was crushed. Other slaves were better treated, particularly those who worked as domestic servants. Educated Greeks served as tutors and scribes for wealthy Romans and were sometimes rewarded with freedom. All slaves were at the mercy of their masters, however, and were subject to severe penalties, including a law calling for every slave in a household to be put to death if one of them murdered the master. In one notorious case, 400 slaves were executed after one of them killed his master in a fit of rage.

Domestic slaves, like one shown here at right combing a girl's hair, often fared better than those who performed menial labor. Some slaves wore a collar (inset) promising a reward to anyone who returned them to their master if they fled.

PEOPLE

JULIAN THE APOSTATE

When Emperor Constantine embraced Christianity in the early fourth century A.D., there were still many worshipers of other deities throughout the empire. Paganism briefly regained official favor when Constantine's nephew Julian (above) became emperor in 360. Although indoctrinated as a Christian, he renounced the faith, and so was called Julian the Apostate. Christians suffered discrimination during his brief reign, but unlike earlier Roman rulers, he did not persecute them. Steeped in the classical culture of ancient Greece and Rome, Julian hoped to revive that tradition, but he died in 363 while campaigning in Persia and did not alter history. Christianity reemerged as the official Roman religion and remained dominant around the Mediterranean until the rise of Islam.

In the long run, however, Greek ideas had less impact on the Roman world than did beliefs emanating from the troubled province of Judea, where Jews rejected the cult of the divine emperor, instituted during the reign of Augustus, and refused to honor any deity but Yahweh, their one God. Some Jews rebelled against Roman rule and suffered devastating reprisals. Others, such as Jesus of Nazareth and his disciples, acknowledged the political authority of Rome but honored God as the supreme spiritual authority, greater than any power on earth. By worshiping Jesus as *Christ*—a Greek term meaning "anointed one" or messiah—and hailing him as "king of kings," Christians challenged the idea that the emperor was almighty. Many were persecuted and died for their faith, believing that martyrdom would unite them with the resurrected Christ and earn them salvation. Christianity brought together people of different classes, including slaves, and grew stronger as the empire declined.

There were many reasons for that decline, which began in the third century. Trade routes that linked Rome and its western provinces to Asia became conduits for epidemics that devastated cities and disrupted commerce. Tax revenue failed to cover the costs of administering and defending this vast empire. When rulers responded by debasing their currency—decreasing the amount of precious metals in coins they minted—people began to reject that currency and revert to barter. During the fourth century, nomadic tribes overran the empire's poorly defended frontiers. A migration of Huns from central to western Europe in the early fifth century displaced Vandals, Visigoths, and other Germanic tribes, who then overwhelmed Italy.

The fall of Rome to Germanic invaders in 476 did not bring an end to the entire

> *"I warn you, youths of Rome, learn the noble arts ...*
> *a woman will give her hand, won by eloquence."*
>
> OVID, *THE ART OF LOVE*

empire, whose eastern power base had separated from the faltering western empire. That partition had begun under Emperor Diocletian, whose successor, Constantine, founded a new imperial capital in 330 at a site called Byzantium on the Bosporus Strait, where Europe meets Asia. Known as Constantinople (later renamed Istanbul), it was less exposed to Germanic migrations than Rome and closer to the ports and bazaars of the Near East, which remained relatively stable and prosperous while western Europe suffered. It was also closer to the birthplace of Christianity—which Constantine adopted as the state religion—and to Egypt and Lebanon, which had large Christian populations. As Rome weakened and collapsed, Constantinople flourished and emerged as capital of the Byzantine Empire, which combined Roman traditions with Greek customs and upheld Christianity, once a persecuted sect but now the imperial faith.

A 17th-century painting by French artist Pierre Puget portrays the baptism of Emperor Constantine as a Christian.

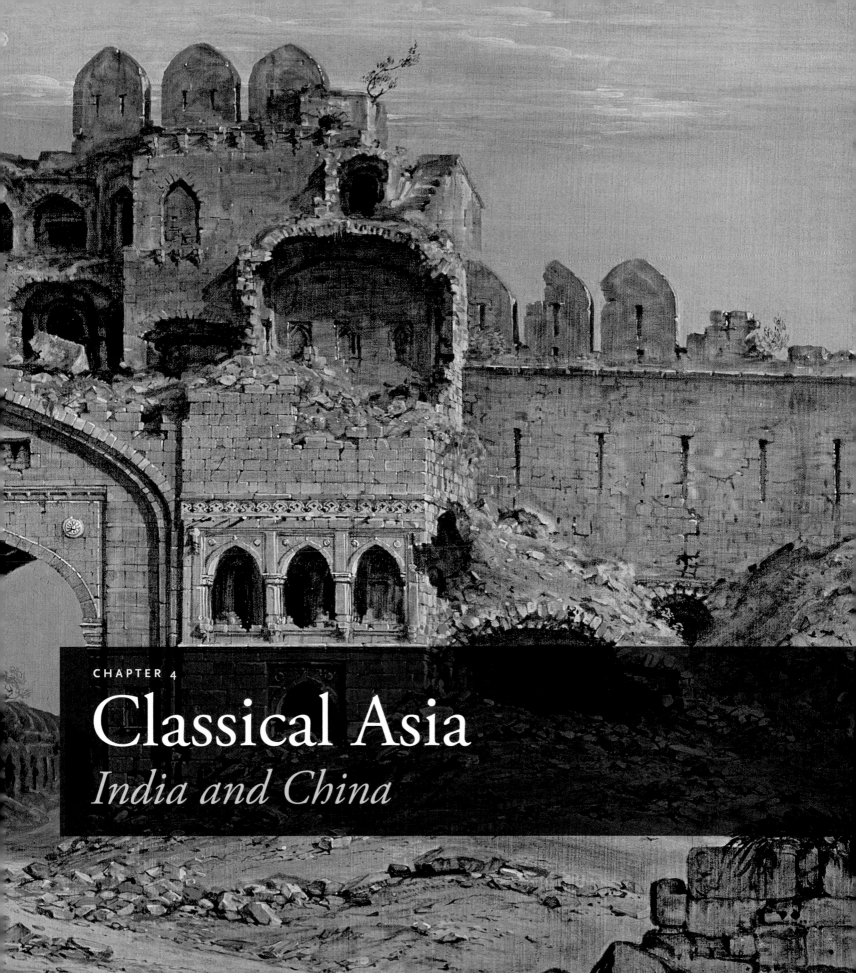

CHAPTER 4

Classical Asia
India and China

MAURYA AND GUPTA EMPIRES
Strength and Spirituality

The requisites of government are that there be sufficiency of food, sufficiency of military equipment, and the confidence of the people in their ruler," said Confucius, according to the devoted students who collected his teachings in *The Analects*. His concise evaluation could serve as a guide to the rise and fall of the classical empires of India and China. At the same time that Greek and Roman civilizations were encircling the Mediterranean, the first widespread empires took shape in the east. And food, armies, and strong rulers were the keys to the survival of these Asian civilizations.

By 325 B.C., Alexander the Great had crossed the Indus River into the Punjab in northwest India, evicting Persian overlords along the way. But when his sick and footsore troops rebelled against marching any farther, the Macedonians returned home, leaving behind a power vacuum.

Northern India was an agricultural land, settled by Aryan migrants who had brought with them a sacred language, Sanskrit, and a hierarchical society divided into castes—priests

Following the departure of Alexander the Great (above), India entered a golden age of culture (right, paintings from the Ajanta caves).

(brahmins), aristocratic warriors (kshatriyas), merchants and artisans (vaishyas), peasants (shudras), and "untouchables." More than a dozen states jostled for control of the Ganges Valley, with its fertile lands and river trade routes. Alexander's visit barely disturbed them—there is no mention of him in Indian histories—but it did bring together briefly two of the most powerful men in the ancient world: Alexander himself and Chandragupta Maurya, known to the Greeks as Sandrakottos.

Chandragupta had been born into an impoverished family, probably in the Punjab. He must have been a conspicuously promising youth, however, because he was soon taken under the wing of an ambitious brahmin, Kautilya. It was while he was a student in the city of Taxila that he apparently met Alexander and, according to some stories, angered the Macedonian with his brash advice. But his cockiness may have been warranted, because by 322 B.C. he had allied with local leader in the Punjab and overthrown the Nanda rulers of the powerful state

325 B.C. Alexander the Great's troops leave India.

300 B.C.–A.D. 100 Buddhism spreads throughout India.

200 B.C.–A.D. 650 Ajanta caves decorated by Buddhist artisans.

A.D. 320 Gupta dynasty founded by Chandra Gupta I.

ca A.D. 550 Gupta dynasty ends.

ca 321 B.C. Mauryan dynasty begins as Chandragupta Maurya takes the throne.

268–232 B.C. Ashoka rules Mauryan Empire.

185 B.C. Mauryan dynasty comes to an end.

ca A.D. 380 Chandra Gupta II comes to the throne.

Mauryas and Guptas

- Mauryas under Chandragupta, circa 297 B.C.
- Mauryas under Ashoka, circa 260 B.C.
- Guptas under Samudra Gupta, circa A.D. 370
- Additions to Gupta Empire by Chandra Gupta II, circa A.D. 410
- → Southern campaign of Samudra Gupta, circa A.D. 360
- → Route of Hun attack, circa A.D. 505-511

of Magadha, ascending to the throne in about 321.

For the next decades, Chandragupta steadily took over northern and central India, eventually dominating an area from the borders of Persia and the Himalayas south almost to the tip of the subcontinent—one of the largest empires in history. In 305, Seleucus, one of Alexander's generals, attempted to invade from the west and was repulsed. Seemingly there were no hard feelings: Seleucus returned the land he had overrun, and in return, Chandragupta gave him 500 elephants.

Before he departed with his pachyderms, Seleucus appointed an ambassador named Megasthenes to the Mauryan court. Megasthenes' accounts, relayed by later historians, portray the Mauryan lands as fertile, producing cotton and sugarcane, and its people as law-abiding, sober, and

> *"Here [in my domain] no living beings are to be slaughtered or offered in sacrifice. Nor should festivals be held, for Beloved-of-the-Gods, King Piyadasi, sees much to object to in such festivals."*
>
> EMPEROR ASHOKA,
> FROM THE FIRST OF THE 14 ROCK EDICTS

industrious. Much of the empire's calm administration may be due to Kautilya, who continued as Chandragupta's counselor and is believed to be the main author of the *Arthashastra*, a collection of writings on economics and statecraft that rival the later Machiavelli's in cool-eyed pragmatism. Kings, according to the treatise, should be virtuous, energetic, and watchful. "If a king is energetic, his subjects will be equally energetic. If he is reckless, they will not only be reckless likewise, but also eat into his works. Besides, a reckless king will easily fall into the hands of his enemies. Hence the king shall ever be wakeful." Kings must divide their days, Kautilya said, among work, education, and pleasure, making sure to set aside time each day to meet with their spies.

The *Arthashastra* reflects the empire's Hindu social structure: Penalties for harming brahmins, for instance, are much harsher than those for harming peasants. But the newer doctrines of Buddhism and Jainism were also gaining influence. According to legend, Jainism's strict practices of simplicity and self-denial attracted even the emperor. Around 297, having ceded the throne to his son Bindusara, Chandragupta is said to have retreated to a Jain monastery and fasted to death.

It was Chandragupta Maurya's grandson Ashoka and another religion—Buddhism—that reinvigorated the Mauryan empire. Having apparently killed off some of his brothers, rival claimants to the throne, Ashoka became emperor in 268 B.C. Around 260, he led a military campaign to conquer the kingdom of Kalinga, site of valuable trade routes. Accounts claim that 100,000 were killed in the conquest. This may be an exaggeration, but what is not exaggerated is the change to the emperor's outlook after the battles. According to Ashoka's own writings, he was "deeply pained by the killing, dying, and deportation that take place when an unconquered country is conquered." As a result of his sympathy for the people's suffering, Ashoka renounced military conquest and other forms of violence, including cruelty to animals. He became a patron of Buddhism, supporting the spread of the doctrine through India while urging tolerance toward all sects. Reportedly he even sent his own son and daughter as missionaries to Sri Lanka.

PEOPLE

The ambitious Kautilya provided advice and counsel to help his protégé Chandragupta rise from obscurity to emperor.

KAUTILYA

Kingmaker and shrewd adviser, Chandragupta's mentor Kautilya is credited for much of the emperor's success. Yet few facts are known about Kautilya, also known as Chanakya, and those are interlaced with legend.

Born around 350 B.C., Kautilya was evidently a brahmin, an intelligent, solitary man who was educated at Taxila and familiar with medicine and Greek and Persian culture. As teacher and minister, he guided Chandragupta both in warfare and in statecraft. According to legend, Kautilya devised a way to defeat the Nanda kingdom after seeing a young boy eat his chapati by nibbling around the edges. Thereafter, Chandragupta wore away the Nanda by first taking over their dependent kingdoms.

The masterful 15-section *Arthashastra (The Science of Material Gain)* is attributed to Kautilya, although in its present form it probably has several authors in addition to the Mauryan minister.

THE AJANTA CAVES

Carved into volcanic cliff faces of the Wagurna River valley, some 65 miles northeast of Aurangabad in western India, are 29 artistic treasures of the Gupta era: the Ajanta caves. They were occupied for some 850 years beginning about 200 B.C. by Buddhist monks and artisans, who filled them with painted and sculpted depictions of the Buddha and his life.

The supple, dancing forms show Buddha in a variety of incarnations, including as an elephant; balanced and intricate, they represent a high point in Indian classical art. Inscriptions show that much of the art was sponsored by wealthy patrons, nobles, and merchants who wished to acquire merit in what was perhaps an otherwise worldly life.

As Buddhism gave way to Hinduism in India, the caves were abandoned. They were largely ignored until 1819 when an English officer, John Smith, rediscovered them while tiger hunting. He couldn't resist leaving his mark, writing "John Smith, April 1819" in pencil on the walls.

"Too much desire brings pain. Death and rebirth are wearisome ordeals, originating from our thoughts of greed and lust. By lessening desires we can realize absolute truth and enjoy peace, freedom, and health in body and mind."

THE SECOND AWAKENING, TEXT FROM MAHAYANA BUDDHISM

Ashoka's edicts, carved into stones and pillars around the country, exhorted the citizens to generosity, justice, and mercy. He was not an unworldly ruler, however. He efficiently managed a centralized government from his capital at Pataliputra (near present-day Patna). A large bureaucracy collected taxes, inspectors reported back to the emperor, irrigation expanded agriculture, and, in a familiar hallmark of ancient empires, excellent roads were built connecting key trading and political centers. Ashoka even ordered that the roads be provided with shade trees, wells, and inns.

Ashoka was an inspirational figure, but his Mauryan successors had neither his charismatic personality nor his ability to hold onto land. By 185 B.C., southern states had broken away, Bactrian Greeks had moved into northwestern states, and the Mauryan dynasty had disappeared.

Between the death of the Mauryan Empire and the birth of the next great dynasty, the Guptas, there were five centuries of poorly documented history. India reverted to a patchwork of states, beset in the north by invaders from Bactria, Parthia, and elsewhere. Even so, trade flowed across the subcontinent; the arts, notably sculpture and literature, flourished. The stage was set for the next empire, which nourished the arts as much as it did the body politic.

The new empire took shape through the bonds of marriage. A chief from the kingdom of Magadha named Chandra Gupta (no relation to Chandragupta Maurya)

Gupta-dynasty coin

The arched Cave 26 of the Ajanta caves is filled with fine Buddhist carvings.

Emperor Ashoka (right) gained fame not only for his able administration but also for his conversion to nonviolence.

"Riches and honors are what men desire. If they cannot be obtained in the proper way, they should not be held. Poverty and baseness are what men dislike. If they cannot be avoided in the proper way, they should not be avoided."

THE SUPERIOR MAN IV.5, CONFUCIUS, ANALECTS

Terra-cotta figure from the Mauryan era

married Princess Kumaradevi of the powerful Licchavi family in a neighboring kingdom about A.D. 308. By 320, he ruled over a significant portion of northeastern India with the title *maharajadhiraja,* or king of kings. Their son, Samudra Gupta, greatly expanded the Gupta Empire during his long reign, from about 330 to 380. A vigorous warrior, with the "prowess of his arm that rose up to pass all bounds," according to a contemporary inscription, he conquered roughly the eastern half of India. His son, Chandra Gupta II, after possibly killing off his brother, succeeded

The Dhamek Stupa in Sarnath
marks the spot where the Buddha
gave his first sermon.

century, noted the overall contentment among the Indian population. "The people are very well off, without poll tax or official restrictions . . . The kings govern without corporal punishment . . . Throughout the country the people kill no living thing nor drink wine, nor do they eat garlic or onions, with the exception of Chandalas [untouchables] only."

Although Fa noted the presence of many Buddhist monasteries, the Gupta monarchs were Hindu, and during the Gupta years and afterward, Hinduism gained ground relative to Buddhism. In both Buddhist and Hindu sanctuaries, the arts of mural painting and sculpture flourished. Still notable today are the Ajanta caves—Buddhist cave temples containing outstandingly intricate and richly colored wall paintings—as well as the sculptures of the Buddha at the sacred site of Sarnath in Uttar Pradesh. The Sanskrit language had a new flowering in classical literature. The writer Kalidasa, who probably lived during the reign of Chandra Gupta II, is considered one of India's greatest authors. His epic poetry and drama in Sanskrit include the drama *Abhijnanashakuntala (The Recognition of Shakuntala),* a tragic love story.

to the imperial throne and extended his rule to the west coast, with its key harbors. Trade flourished and crafts and banking were closely administered by a strict system of guilds.

Fa Xian, a Buddhist monk who traveled through Gupta realms in the fourth

Fruitful but brief, the Gupta Empire fell to a foe that had brought down more than one civilization: nomadic warriors from Central Asia. Invading the Punjab and Kashmir around 510, the Huns defeated Gupta armies in a realm that was already fragmenting, ending early India's golden age.

SO WHAT?

NUMERALS

Today's familiar numerals—0 through 9—are sometimes referred to as "Arabic numerals," but more properly they could be called "Indian," or "Hindu-Arabic," numerals, because classical India seems to be the source for both the shape of our numerals and for some of the basics of their use.

Mathematical and astronomical texts from India dating between the second and eighth centuries A.D. show that today's numeric system—including the use of a zero, the idea of negative numbers, and the use of decimal-place values—was developed in classical India before being filtered through Islamic cultures. The shapes of numerals themselves also evolved over the centuries on the subcontinent, from Kharosthi numerals, similar to Roman numerals, to Brahmi and then to Gwalior, whose forms look like those of today. Zero was originally designated by a dot and called *sunya,* meaning "empty."

Islamic scientists embraced the system, but European politicians remained suspicious of it for centuries, resisting the use of "ciphers" (a word taken from the Arabic *sifr,* "zero") until about the 16th century.

١	٢	٣
1	2	3

✕	⟩	Ʒ
4	10	20

⌐	ല
100	1000

*Examples of Kharosthi numerals,
precursors of today's Roman numerals.*

QIN AND HAN
Defining a Culture

China already had a long history by the time its states were unified under its first emperor. Settlements in the valleys of the Yellow and Yangtze Rivers had grown into an agricultural civilization, with fertile central lands that were barricaded by deserts, steppes, and mountains to the north and west, and by the sea to the east.

Between the fifth and third centuries B.C., a time known as the Period of the Warring States, at least seven kingdoms battled for supremacy in east-central China. The state of Qin, based in the Sichuan plains, eventually won out in 221 B.C., under the leadership of the ruthless King Zheng. The victorious Zheng, said by later historians to be born to a merchant's concubine, gave himself the title Qin Shi Huangdi, First Qin Emperor.

With a ferocious force of character, the emperor set out to mold his diverse territories into a single unit mutely obedient to his will. He divided the lands into 36 command areas, each supervised by a governor, a military commander, and an imperial inspector who all reported to him. In an early example of the rule that one should keep one's friends

Early Han jade phoenix pendant (above). Emperor Wudi leaves his palace (right).

close and one's enemies closer, Shi Huangdi relocated hundreds of thousands of influential families from their home provinces to the capital, Xianyang, where he could keep an eye on them. Weapons were confiscated and melted down. A new imperial currency was issued. Weights and measures were standardized—even wagon axles were built according to a standard measure, so as to fit within the ruts in China's roads. Chinese writing was also made uniform, so that all words with the same meaning in the country's varied languages would be represented by the same characters.

The emperor ruthlessly suppressed dissent. Learning that some scholars used texts from the past to criticize his policies, Shi Huangdi had all books except those on medicine, agriculture, forestry, or divination confiscated or burned. Some accounts say that 460 scholars were rounded up and executed. Citizens of all ranks were encouraged to inform on one another, with those convicted of crimes being either executed, mutilated, or put to hard labor.

Hard labor was, in fact, the lot of much of China's population. Qin armies numbered in the hundreds of thousands, mobilized to defend against Xiongnu nomads

---

551–479 B.C. Life span of Confucius (Kong Fuzi).

206 B.C.–A.D. 9 Western Han dynasty rules from Chang'an.

ca 85 B.C. Sima Qian writes *The Records of the Grand Historian*.

A.D. 25–220 Eastern Han dynasty rules from Luoyang.

A.D. 184–208 Yellow Turban rebels attack the Han government.

221–210 B.C. Qin empire consolidated by Qin Shi Huangdi.

124 B.C. Emperor Wudi founds the first imperial university.

A.D. 9–23 Wang Mang, a reformer, rules during an interregnum.

A.D. 189 Palace eunuchs slaughtered.

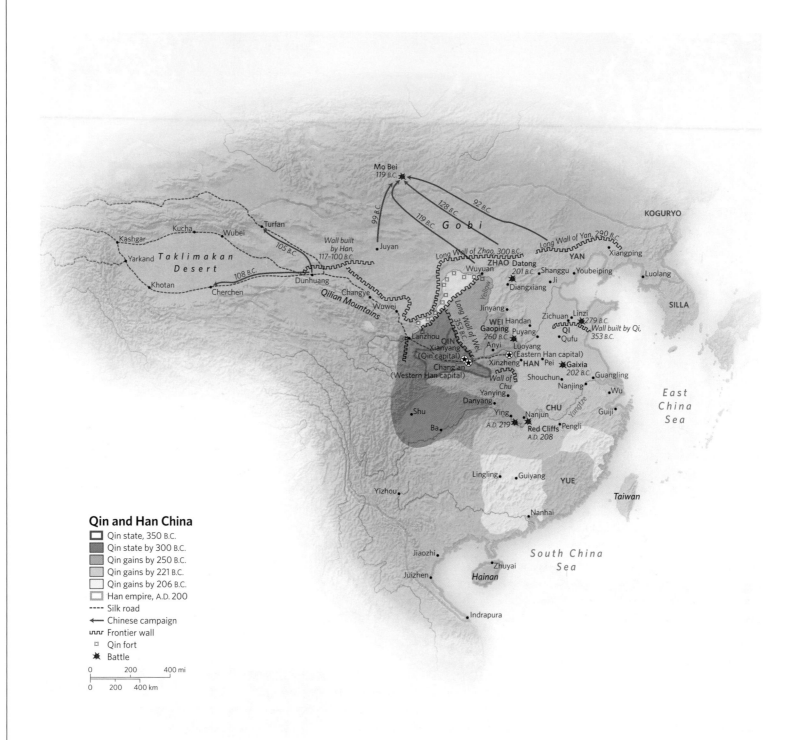

Qin and Han China
- ☐ Qin state, 350 B.C.
- ▨ Qin state by 300 B.C.
- ▨ Qin gains by 250 B.C.
- ▨ Qin gains by 221 B.C.
- ☐ Qin gains by 206 B.C.
- ☐ Han empire, A.D. 200
- ---- Silk road
- ← Chinese campaign
- ᴗᴗᴗ Frontier wall
- ▫ Qin fort
- ✳ Battle

0 200 400 mi
0 200 400 km

in the north and other tribes in the south. Hundreds of thousands more toiled to build palaces, canals, roads, and, according to Han historian Sima Qian, "border defenses along the [Yellow] river, constructing 44 walled district cities overlooking the river and manning them with convict laborers . . . The whole line of defenses stretched over 10,000 *li* [more than 3,000 miles]." This last project, in which many workers died, was the beginning of the Great Wall.

Not surprisingly, the autocratic emperor was the target of several assassination attempts. Perhaps in response, he became obsessed with the idea of immortality. According to Sima, his advisers counseled him that the herbs of immortality would not work for him until he could move about unobserved—after which he built walkways and passages connecting his

> *"The determined scholar and the man of virtue*
> *will not seek to live at the expense of humanity.*
> *They will even sacrifice their lives to preserve their humanity."*
>
> JEN (HUMANENESS) XV.8, CONFUCIUS, ANALECTS

palaces so that he could travel in seeming invisibility. Possibly the most megalomaniacal of his projects was his enormous tomb and buried terra-cotta statues, constructed at tremendous cost by 700,000 forced-labor conscripts. They consisted of a host of thousands of life-size terra-cotta soldiers, archers, chariots, weapons, horses, officials, servants, and even entertainers such as musicians and a strong man—but not a single woman. The tomb and statues were unfinished at the time of the emperor's death in 210.

Chaos followed his death. Shi Huangdi's heirs turned on one another, ministers assassinated other ministers, and nobles, generals, and peasants formed clashing armies. By 202, one peasant-turned-general had carried the day. Liu Bang, known henceforth by the title Han Gaozu, founded a dynasty that lasted for more than 400 years and shaped later Chinese empires.

Where Qin Shi Huangdi's government had embraced a legalist philosophy, emphasizing a strict rule of law enforced by punishment, the Han rulers turned to Confucianism. Confucius (Kong Fuzi) lived during the Zhou dynasty, 300 years before the Han, but his teachings became

A Han-era print depicts a benevolent divinity offering longevity and glory.

increasingly influential after his death. He held that all people had a duty to serve their families and communities in accord with the natural harmonies of life. Each person had a proper role to play in society: "Let the ruler be a ruler and the subject a subject."

Compassion and justice were the core of right behavior; virtue and merit would be rewarded.

Reinforcing as it did the idea of obedience to the hierarchy, Confucianism appealed to the Han rulers. And the belief that people should rise according to merit inspired countless young men to work diligently to climb through the growing ranks of Chinese bureaucracy. In 165 B.C., Chinese officials began to administer a civil service exam to select candidates for government office. In 124, Emperor Wudi (the "Martial Emperor") oversaw the creation of the first imperial university, created to train men from the provinces, typically sons of landowners, in the techniques of government.

Wudi was the sixth of the Han rulers. Reigning for more than 50 years from 141, he built the empire not only internally, through Confucian principles, but also externally through aggressive military campaigns. The Xiongnu nomads of the north—fine horsemen and archers—were a perpetual threat that he was determined to eliminate. Earlier emperors had attempted to placate the raiders with expensive gifts and diplomatic marriages; Wudi sent armies. Up to 100,000 men at a time struggled with the nomads in costly battles, although the Han continued to placate them with tribute as well, including silk that was then traded to the West along the silk roads. Eventually, Han troops pushed back the Xiongnu, and Han colonists occupied former Xiongnu territories in the north and west. To the south, Wudi conquered or reconquered territory in southern China and much of Vietnam and Korea.

Wudi's expensive campaigns led him to increase taxes on businesses and institute state monopolies on iron, salt, and wine. These actions, combined with a cultural revulsion toward merchants as a class, had the possibly unintended effect

"All under heaven are of one mind, single in will. Weights and measures have a single standard, words are written in a uniform way."

SIMA QIAN,
THE EMPEROR'S STONE INSCRIPTION,
LANGYA TERRACE

of discouraging the growth of specialized industries and cities. China remained heavily agricultural even when other civilizations urbanized. Innovation and technology did not die out during the Han era, however. The earliest examples of paper—made from hemp—date to Wudi's reign, and the invention of a ship's rudder allowed for easier navigation of trade routes.

The arts also flourished under the Han. Bronze work, long a strength of Chinese artists, continued to develop in curving vessels and the proud figures of galloping horses. Ceramics began to employ lead-based glazes of green, yellow, brown, and celadon. Miniature ceramic houses, servants, and soldiers have been found in Han-era tombs. Lacquerware—cups, bowls, trays—was particularly valuable. Up to 100 thin coats of the toxic substance—made from the caustic sap of a native lacquer tree—might be applied to an object, one coat per day, before the item was ready.

Literature was represented particularly by masterful histories, such as that of Sima Qian. His *Records of the Grand Historian*

Emperor Sinen-Li of Han dynasty with scholars who are translating classical texts

Traces of the original pigment are still visible on the faces of kneeling archers from the pits around Qin Shi Huangdi's tomb.

THE TERRA-COTTA WARRIORS

In 1974, workers digging a well near the Chinese city of Xi'an, in the province of Shaanxi, unearthed a figure more than 2,000 years old: a life-size soldier made of terra-cotta. Authorities soon found more, *many* more, such buried figures—thousands of clay soldiers, as well as horses, chariots, and even metal weaponry, still shiny. Arrayed in military formation, seemingly ready for battle, the soldiers bore traces of the bright paint that must once have enlivened them. Although formed from standardized pieces, they were evidently finished by hand so that no two figures looked exactly alike.

Six thousand soldiers and chariots fill one excavated pit; more than 1,000 clay cavalrymen, horses, and wooden chariots are packed in another. Lower-ranking warriors range from five feet eight inches to six feet two inches in height; commanders are six and a half feet tall. Other pits contain the bones of humans and horses, terra-cotta grooms, and real hay.

This ancient army was stationed just east of a necropolis surrounding the tomb of Qin Shi Huangdi and was apparently a stand-in for the afterlife with which he was obsessed. The tomb and surroundings were probably begun soon after he took power and remained unfinished at his death. Clay figures fill the ground just around the tomb, as well, but *Soldiers in the terra-cotta army* these are not soldiers—rather, they represent acrobats and musicians who it seems would keep the emperor company into death, while the soldiers kept guard outside.

A statue of Confucius portrays him in a thoughtful pose.

CONFUCIUS

The teacher and philosopher known to the West as Confucius was born Kong Qiu in 551 B.C. His family may once have been aristocratic, but they had apparently fallen on hard times, because Kong took menial jobs as a young man. Nevertheless, he excelled as a scholar, learning ritual, music, the classics, mathematics, and more.

"Simple and unassuming in manner," according to accounts, Kong believed that education and reflection led to virtue, and that those who aspired to command others should cultivate moral authority in themselves. He rose rapidly through government ranks to become minister of justice in the state of Lu. After falling out of favor, he gathered a wide circle of disciples who knew him as Kong Fuzi (Master Kong). These pupils recorded his words in *The Analects*, a collection of ethical concepts that guided Chinese governments for millennia. He died in 479, leaving behind perhaps 3,000 devoted students.

An illustration depicts the hordes of craftsmen necessary to create the First Emperor's tomb and terra-cotta army.

is a vivid picture of centuries of Chinese history. Sima's epic was completed over 18 years, despite an episode in which he fell so far out of favor with the emperor as to be castrated. Chinese poetry included the descriptive fu style; even the famed warlord Cao Cao wrote fu poetry with sensitive reflections on the melancholy beauty of nature. Music and dance with string instruments accompanied banquets and temple ceremonies.

Emperor Wudi understood that his power was always threatened by that of the great aristocratic families. His policy of advancement through merit was one attempt to combat that; another was his decree that inherited property should be divided equally among all heirs. This applied not only to the great families but also to small farmers. As a result, many farms became fragmented as populations grew, shrinking to the point where farmers had to sell their plots to wealthier landowners and become tenants, increasing the power of the wealthy.

After Wudi's death in 87 B.C., a series of weak emperors and strong empresses took control, reigning over an increasingly discontented populace. In A.D. 9, a regent of the child emperor seized power himself, instituting a

A statue of a chimera—an animal hybrid—from an Eastern Han tomb

Emperor Wudi (left), who supported education and the arts, welcomes a man of letters.

brief interregnum in the Han dynasty. Wang Mang was a reformer who attempted to cut court expenses, redistribute land, and reform the currency. A scholar and inflexible Confucian, he executed three of his own sons for breaking the law. Eventually nature and society both turned against him; Yellow River floods, famines, peasant uprisings, and opposition from the deposed royal family led to a rebellion in 23. Rebels cornered Wang and his troops in the imperial palace in Chang'an, where the emperor was killed in a hand-to-hand sword fight.

The victor was a member of the royal family, who restored Han rule in 25 as Emperor Guangwu. Historians refer to the earlier, pre-Wang era as the Former, or Western, Han. Beginning with Guangwu, who moved his capital to Luoyang in the east, the dynasty is known as the Later, or Eastern, Han.

For a time, the new Han rulers restored stability. Reforms to land distribution and taxes eased the burdens of the peasantry to some extent, as did the introduction of such crops as alfalfa and grapes. But within a century, the court began to be taken over by a group that had long held influence in the background: eunuchs.

MILITARY MIGHT

BLOOD-SWEATING HORSES

Around 126 B.C., one of Emperor Wudi's officials, Zhang Qian, returned from an expedition into Central Asia with a tale that aroused the Martial Emperor's acquisitive instincts. The people of Ferghana, Zhang said, bred the finest horses ever seen—tall, strong, and fast, with great stamina. Descended from celestial creatures, they sweated blood in the summer.

Wudi devoted three years and two expensive military campaigns to acquiring the horses from Ferghana. Eventually he won an agreement to take home 3,000 blood-sweating horses of ordinary quality, as well as ten of the finest for breeding. From these, he produced a superb line of horses that could outperform the enemy's smaller variety.

Modern equine experts believe the breed in question was the Akhal-Teke, still greatly valued today. The bloody sweat may have come from parasites that burrowed into the horses' thin skin in the summer.

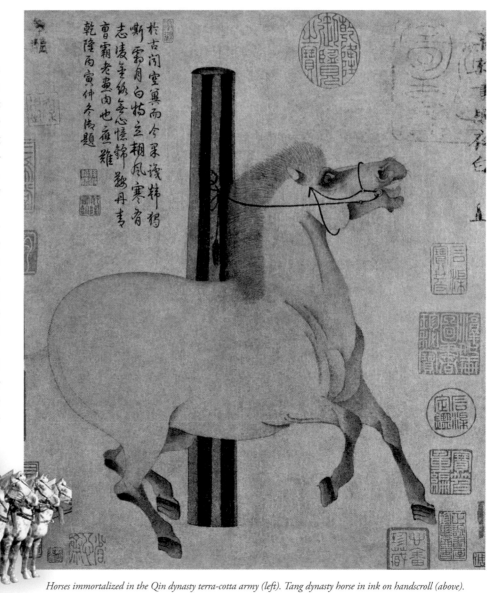

Horses immortalized in the Qin dynasty terra-cotta army (left). Tang dynasty horse in ink on handscroll (above).

> *"Yet only to teach men and not to teach women – is that not ignoring the essential relation between them?"*

BAN ZHAO PAN CHAO, *LESSONS FOR WOMEN*

Believed to be harmless due to their lack of posterity and family connections, eunuchs had access to the innermost reaches of the court, including the women's chambers. In 124, they managed to place a child on the throne, and in the 160s, they banned or killed hundreds of outer court officials. In retaliation, in 189, imperial relatives stormed the palace and slaughtered 2,000 beardless men on the assumption they were eunuchs.

Western Han terra-cotta chickens, found in a grave

Bereft of a strong central government, the citizenry again suffered from famines and bandits. From the late second century into the third, members of the secret Yellow Turban society led an uprising in eastern and central China. Led by Daoist faith healer Zhang Jue, they pillaged the countryside before attacking the court at Luoyang in 184. By the next year, the disorganized court managed to rally troops to defeat the rebels in a series of bloody battles. Nevertheless, Yellow Turban uprisings continued in various provinces into the third century. The famed general Cao Cao (noted above for his poetry) briefly gained control in 207 with the aid of huge armies and navies before his defeat in battle at Red Cliffs along the Yangtze River around 208. In 220, the last Han emperor abdicated, and the country broke apart into three kingdoms. China struggled through rebellions and short-lived dynasties until the advent of the Tang in 618.

Han Gaozu, the founder of the Han dynasty, was born a peasant. He became known as a tough but pragmatic emperor.

DAILY LIFE

A Han-dynasty model of a herdsman and his penned goats

A FARMER'S LIFE

Peasant farmers were the core of Chinese agricultural society, and their lives were brutally hard. "They labor at plowing in the spring and hoeing in the summer, harvesting in the autumn and storing food in winter . . . Through all four seasons they never get a day off . . . No matter how hard they work they can be ruined by floods or droughts, or cruel and arbitrary officials . . . They are forced to sell their fields and houses, even their children and grandchildren, to pay their debts," reported Chao Cuo in 178 B.C.

Although by Han times peasants used plows with iron tips and were aided by oxen and donkeys, the work of farming while also paying taxes and performing mandatory government labor was still grinding. Dividing land among multiple heirs eventually reduced farms to untenable sizes, and frequent droughts and floods devastated them. Banditry and rebellion followed, and peasant uprisings were a threat that lasted into the 20th century.

PART II

500-1500

Not even the grandest empire lasts forever. In decay and conflict, new cultures took hold in the Middle Ages. Seemingly eternal Rome was displaced by Byzantium, the New Rome. Christianity pushed out local gods and goddesses throughout Europe and then faced holy conflict with a new creed—Islam—in Europe, the Middle East, and Africa. To the east, trade cross-pollinated cultures in India, Southeast Asia, and China, while Europe lingered in what used to be called the Dark Ages. Eventually, the Mongols, seen as uncivilized by their enemies, pushed established powers such as the Khmer into insignificance. For their own time, those proud hordes held sway over vast Asia, but their grasp inevitably weakened, and new powers triumphed. Perhaps the only constant was that all these kings ruled over many generations of poor peasants. Great technological advances—firearms, printing presses, and ships that could cross the oceans—would soon bring more upheaval. Meanwhile, in the Americas, other empires built cities, traded, and fought, still unbeknownst to the Old World.

THE MIDDLE AGES

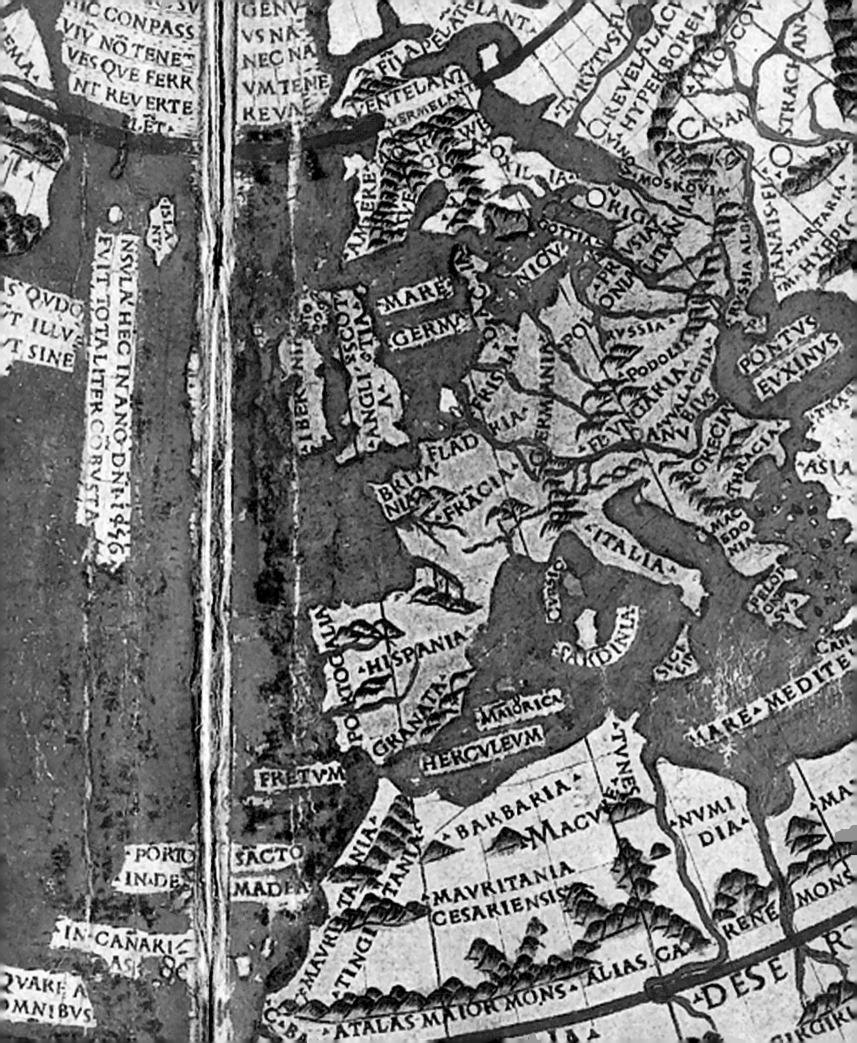

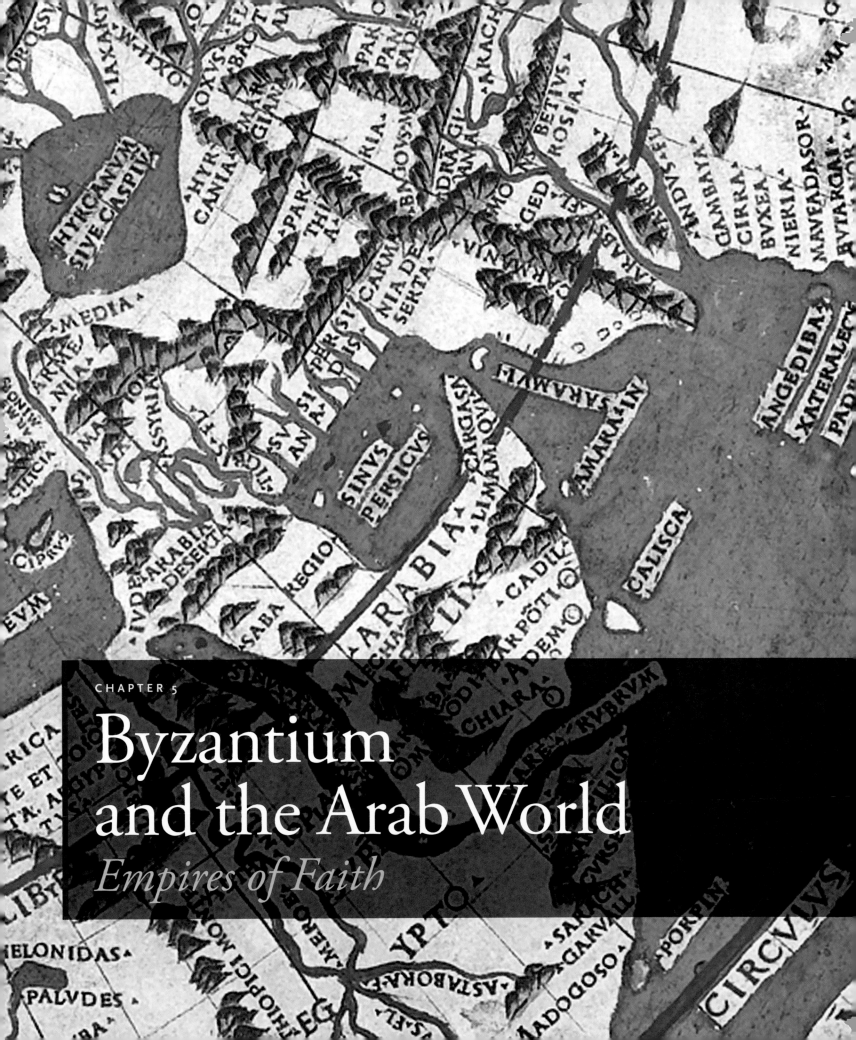

CHAPTER 5

Byzantium and the Arab World

Empires of Faith

BYZANTINE EMPIRE
Creating the New Rome

During the Age of Faith that dawned when Byzantine emperors in Constantinople embraced Christianity and Islam arose in Arabia, Christians and Muslims had at least one thing in common: They all credited their victories to heaven. "Praise be to God . . . Praise to him who has caused our enemies to perish and brought to us our inheritance from Muhammad our Prophet," said the brother of Abu al-Abbas, founder of the Abbasid dynasty, who in 750 overthrew the caliph who ruled the Muslim world. As descendants of Muhammad's uncle, Abu al-Abbas and his heirs claimed the right to rule a vast Islamic empire in the name of Allah and his Prophet. But they were not the only ones who thought God was on their side. That belief was shared by opposing Muslims who denied their legitimacy as well as by Christians of various persuasions, including Orthodox soldiers of the Byzantine Empire who clashed with Muslim armies and Catholic crusaders from western Europe who set out to secure the Holy Land for their faith and ended up sacking Constantinople.

Silver birds clasp red velvet in a Byzantine brooch (above). Emperor Justinian (right, in a mosaic from Ravenna, Italy) directed the early expansion of the Byzantine Empire.

Underlying the religious conflicts between Muslims, Orthodox Christians, and Roman Catholics were cultural differences rooted in past imperial rivalries. Muslim rulers were heirs to the proud imperial legacy of Persia and followed Persian precedents by advancing west and challenging Europeans for control of the Mediterranean world. Byzantine emperors drew inspiration from the accomplishments of their classical Greek predecessors and Alexander the Great, who infused the Near East with Greek culture. Crusaders from western Europe fought to restore the glory of Rome— once the hub of an empire far surpassing that of Alexander or his Persian rivals—and bring Jerusalem and other sites sacred to Christians, Muslims, and Jews under Roman Catholic authority.

When the Roman emperor Constantine founded the great city on the Bosporus Strait that would bear his name, he did not think of it as Greek or Byzantine. He called it New Rome, for it was modeled after the empire's capital on the Tiber River. This new capital, which was dedicated in A.D. 330 at a site called Byzantium and became

330 Emperor Constantine founds city of Constantinople.

537 Hagia Sophia, the great church, built by Justinian.

717–741 Leo III reigns as emperor.

976–1025 Basil II, the Bulgar Slayer, reigns.

1453 Constantinople falls to Ottomans.

527–565 Emperor Justinian rules, with Theodora as empress.

550s Silk production begins after empire gains secret from China.

726–843 Icon controversy splits Byzantium.

1054 Schism splits Roman Catholic and Orthodox Churches.

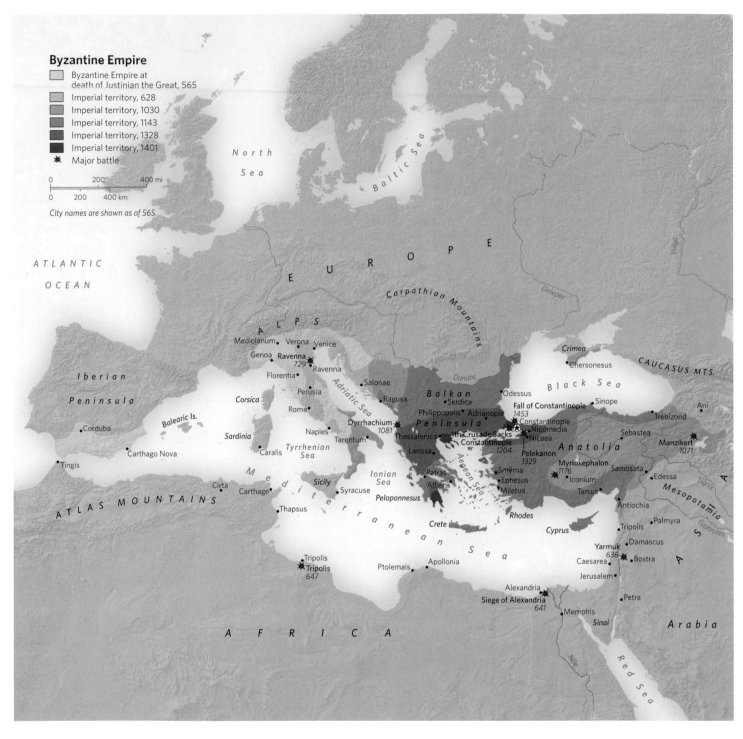

Byzantine Empire

- Byzantine Empire at death of Justinian the Great, 565
- Imperial territory, 628
- Imperial territory, 1030
- Imperial territory, 1143
- Imperial territory, 1328
- Imperial territory, 1401
- ★ Major battle

0   200   400 mi

0   200   400 km

City names are shown as of 565.

known as Constantinople, was more defensible than Rome and closer to wealthy eastern provinces such as Egypt, the source of much of the grain that fed Rome and later Constantinople. Furthermore, Rome remained a largely pagan city, containing not only Christian churches but also

shrines devoted to various gods and goddesses. After converting to Christianity, Constantine angered Romans who held other beliefs by refusing to participate in a pagan procession. He then left Rome for good to build an imperial city that would glorify both his power and his faith.

Constantine had succeeded in reuniting the Roman Empire by armed force, but it soon divided again into eastern and western halves. Constantinople endured as capital of the eastern half, known as the Byzantine Empire, while Rome and its western empire fell to Germanic invaders in

> *"Everybody ... stepped from his rank and found he was now at liberty to walk roads where before there had been no path ... The government was like a Queen surrounded by romping children."*
>
> **PROCOPIUS,** *THE SECRET HISTORY*

the fifth century. Rulers in Constantinople avoided a similar fate by buying off the Goths and members of other Germanic tribes, granting them land, and even enlisting them as troops to repulse other invaders. Byzantine emperors also relied heavily on soldiers from former Roman provinces in the Balkans such as Macedonia and Illyria, extending from what is now Albania to Croatia. Those Romanized recruits were favored over Germans in Constantinople, and some rose to positions of trust.

After the death of Emperor Anastasius in 518, an Illyrian of humble origins called Justin, who served as commander of the palace guard, took power in Constantinople. Elderly and childless, he adopted as heir his energetic nephew, Peter Sabbatius, who assumed the name Justinian. Fluent in Latin, Justinian spoke Greek haltingly, but that was no great handicap in a city whose leading figures still considered themselves Romans. The civic center of Constantinople was adorned with classical monuments like the Roman Forum and a coliseum called the Hippodrome, where charioteers belonging to two teams, the Blues and the Greens, competed to the roars of their fans. Justinian was well versed in Roman law and Christian theology. But he also enjoyed popular pastimes such as plays and chariot races and fell in love with an actress named Theodora, who like other members of her profession had an unsavory reputation. According to the Byzantine historian Procopius, "no role was too scandalous for her to accept without a blush." Nonetheless, the two wedded after Justinian prevailed upon his uncle to amend a law forbidding men of high rank from marrying actresses.

In 527, he succeeded the deceased Justin as emperor and Theodora became empress. Unlike the old Roman Empire, where rulers' wives played no official role, the Byzantine Empire that Justinian solidified and expanded was more like ancient Egypt, where queens were honored and sometimes exercised power. Justinian would be remembered for codifying Roman law and publishing an authoritative digest of statutes that provided a legal framework for many later European societies. But Theodora also furthered the cause of justice by pressing for laws protecting girls from enslavement and abolishing the death penalty for women convicted of adultery.

Without her, Justinian might have been driven from the throne in 532 when Constantinople rose up against him.

Among the grievances of the populace were food shortages that distressed the poor and the elimination of tax exemptions for the wealthy. The revolt began in the Hippodrome while Justinian was present. Fans of both teams, the Blues and the Greens, who normally shouted "*Nika!*—Victory!" only to cheer on their side, raised that cry together in defiance of the emperor, who fled to the palace while they took to the streets. Justinian was about to abandon the city to the mob when

Justinian's nephew and heir, Justin II, presented this reliquary, said to contain a piece of the True Cross, to the Vatican.

Theodora urged him to stay and fight. "Every man who is born into the light of day must sooner or later die," she declared, by Procopius's account, "and how can an Emperor ever allow himself to become a fugitive?"

Heeding her, Justinian held his ground and called on a trusted general, Belisarius, to crush the revolt. Troops herded rioters back into the Hippodrome and slaughtered some 30,000 people there. Finding much of the city reduced to rubble, Justinian proceeded to reconstruct Constantinople. His greatest monument was the Hagia Sophia ("holy wisdom"), a

A page from a medieval copy of the Code of Justinian

domed structure of breathtaking height that became the glory of Byzantine Christianity—known as the Orthodox Church after it broke with Roman Catholicism in the 11th century. Long before that, however, Byzantine Christians evolved their own rites and recognized their emperor and the patriarch of Constantinople as their spiritual leaders, rather than the bishop of Rome, honored by Roman Catholics as pope.

Even as he rebuilt the capital, Justinian set out to reclaim large parts of the old Roman Empire lost to Germanic tribes.

Soon after Belisarius crushed the Nika Revolt, Justinian sent him to challenge the Vandals, who had descended into Spain and Italy before crossing to Africa, where they occupied the coast of present-day Tunisia and Algeria. Like other new states formed by Germanic invaders, the Vandal kingdom was politically unstable. Exploiting the rift between a ruler who had just seized power and the king he ousted, Belisarius defeated the Vandals within months and went on to attack the Ostrogoths in Italy, who were at odds following the death of their dynamic leader, King Theodoric the Great. In 540, they

In a scene from a fresco by Raphael, Justinian receives a book of Roman law that will form part of his new law code.

ARCHAEOLOGY

St. Catherine's Monastery, almost 1,500 years old, stands at the base of Mount Sinai on Egypt's Sinai Peninsula.

ST. CATHERINE'S MONASTERY

Built between 527 and 561 on the orders of Emperor Justinian, St. Catherine's is one of the world's oldest continuously inhabited Christian monasteries. It was constructed by the pious emperor at the rocky foot of Egypt's Mount Sinai on the spot where Moses is said to have seen the burning bush. Relics of St. Catherine of Alexandria, whose body was supposedly discovered on top of the mountain, are contained there along with those of more than 170 other saints.

The monastery survived religious upheavals and passing armies due in part to its sturdy granite walls, up to 115 feet high. These shelter a plant held to be the original burning bush, as well as church buildings and a mosque. Within the buildings are perhaps the greatest treasures of all: a wealth of religious artwork, including mosaics, icons, chalices, and reliquaries, and a huge collection of illuminated manuscripts, the largest such repository outside the Vatican.

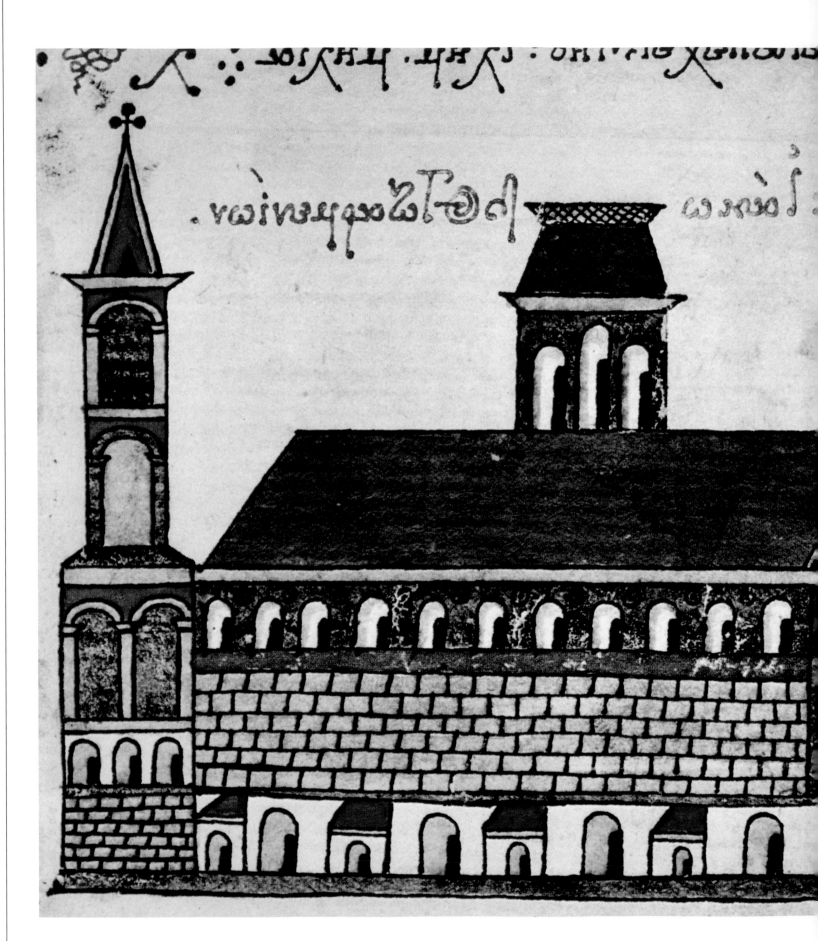

The monastery of St. John of the Armenians was just one of many founded on the peninsula of Mount Athos, a spiritual center for the Orthodox Church.

yielded to Belisarius and invited him to become their monarch, an offer he declined in deference to Justinian.

By the time Justinian died in 565, the Byzantine Empire nearly encircled the Mediterranean. But this was a classic case of imperial overexpansion. The tax burden Justinian placed on his subjects to finance military campaigns was too great, and his successors lacked the funds and forces to defend distant provinces. Lombards of Germanic origin crossed the Alps in 568 and occupied much of northern and central Italy except for a corridor extending from Rome to Ravenna, a port on the Adriatic Sea that remained a Byzantine stronghold until the eighth century. Similar advances were made by Bulgars and other invaders who swept down from the vicinity of the Danube River and seized large parts of the Balkans. But the greatest threat came from the Near East, where Sasanid Persians intent on matching the feats of Cyrus the Great and other Persian conquerors of old wrested Syria, Palestine, and Egypt from Byzantine forces in the early seventh century. They threatened to overrun Asia Minor, known to Greeks as Anatolia or "the land to the east." If Anatolia fell, Constantinople itself would be in peril.

Rising to that challenge came the Byzantine emperor Heraclius, who took power

BLUES VS. GREENS

Among the legacies of the Roman Empire in Byzantium was the immensely popular sport of chariot racing. Races in the city's Hippodrome were one of the few events at which common people could actually view the emperor. Originally four teams—the Whites, Reds, Blues, and Greens—competed in the arena, but eventually the Blues and Greens came to dominate the sport. Wearing their distinctive colors, charioteers on the same team would cooperate to force the other team's chariots to crash. Star charioteers earned good money and could be lured away by rival teams.

Like English football teams, the Blues and Greens developed belligerent fan bases that split the city between them. Fights regularly broke out between the factions. "The members [of each faction] fight with their opponents not knowing for what reason they risk their lives, but realizing full well that even when they vanquish their opponents in brawls, they will be carted off to prison and that, after they have suffered the most extreme tortures, they will be killed," wrote the historian Procopius. These conflicts reached a violent high point during the Nika Revolt in 532, when the factions briefly joined forces in a failed attempt to bring down Emperor Justinian.

Driving teams of horses, charioteers competed for public adulation and wealth in Constantinople's Hippodrome.

Livestock farming flourished in inland areas of the Byzantine Empire (above). Silk (the material of the imperial dalmatic robe below) was one of the key exports of the Byzantine economy.

in 610 and divided his homeland of Anatolia into military districts, each one commanded by a general who recruited troops and rewarded them with land. This system was later extended to other parts of the Byzantine Empire and bolstered its defenses without increasing the tax burden. Heraclius advanced against the Persians and won victories in Mesopotamia that toppled the Persian king in 628. The prolonged struggle between Byzantines and Persians left both sides weaker, however, and vulnerable to Muslim forces advancing from Arabia. Egypt, Palestine, and other former Byzantine provinces along the eastern Mediterranean coast fell readily to the Muslims, who showed greater tolerance toward Jews and members of nonconformist Christian sects than Byzantine rulers had. In 651, Muslims conquered Persia and added that prize to an Islamic empire that now embraced the entire Near East with the exception of Anatolia.

Stunned by their losses to Muslims, Byzantine rulers wondered if God was punishing them for their sins—in particular, for their devotion to icons, sacred images, which iconoclasts (opponents of icons) thought was excessive and violated the biblical commandment against worshiping images. Iconoclasts noted that Islam prohibited such images and feared

HAGIA SOPHIA

The soaring, light-filled structure of Hagia Sophia (also known as the Church of the Holy Wisdom) has been a church, a mosque, and a museum. Its interior reflects this changing history in a rich mix of Christian and Muslim artistic and architectural elements.

Two Christian churches were built and destroyed on the site, near the imperial palace, before Emperor Justinian asked Greek mathematicians Isidore of Miletus and Anthemius of Tralles to design this third, long-lasting edifice. The church was constructed in only six years, and when it opened in 537 it was one of the largest cathedrals in the world. Justinian is said to have boasted, "Solomon, I have outdone thee."

The rectangular basilica is topped by a huge central dome, 160 feet high and 101 feet across. The dome rests on a series of arches and semi-domes and in its airy magnificence has been likened to the dome of heaven. Gilding, multicolored marble and stone inlays, and brilliant mosaics decorate the interior. When the Ottoman Empire defeated the Byzantines in 1453, the church became a mosque. Whitewash covered the figural art, and Islamic roundels were eventually hung from the dome. Now, the mosaics in the upper galleries are being restored and can once again be seen. The building on Aya Sofya Square is now part of a UNESCO World Heritage site that includes several locations in Istanbul. Visitors can tour Hagia Sophia from Tuesday through Saturday.

Perched atop scaffolding, artists carefully piece together Hagia Sophia's mosaics.

Hagia Sophia is topped by a vast dome, under which is an arcade of 40 windows. Elevated galleries were once set aside for women.

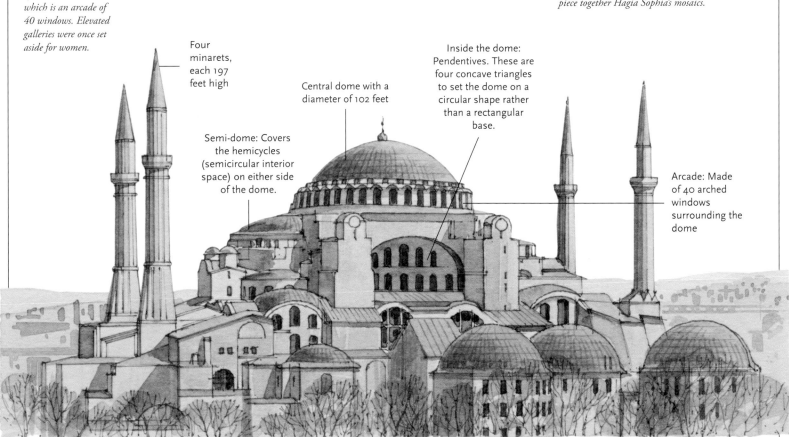

Four minarets, each 197 feet high

Semi-dome: Covers the hemicycles (semicircular interior space) on either side of the dome.

Central dome with a diameter of 102 feet

Inside the dome: Pendentives. These are four concave triangles to set the dome on a circular shape rather than a rectangular base.

Arcade: Made of 40 arched windows surrounding the dome

that God would continue to grant Muslims victories until Christians, too, ceased worshiping icons. Iconoclasm was embraced by Emperor Leo III, who repulsed Muslims besieging Constantinople in 718. He owed that victory in part to the use of Greek fire, a compound that, when set aflame, terrorized opposing forces on land or water. But Leo attributed his military success to God and felt he now had a sacred duty to strip churches and monasteries of paintings and sculptures representing Christ, the Virgin Mary, and other revered figures. Byzantine soldiers favored that prohibition, hoping that God would reward them with more victories. But many other Christians were appalled, including women who took to the streets of Constantinople to protest the removal of their beloved icons. This bitter religious controversy divided the empire, with some rulers favoring iconoclasm and others opposing it. Finally, in 843, Empress Theodora reversed the policy of her late husband, Emperor Theophilus, and restored icons permanently to Byzantine shrines.

By rejecting iconoclasm, Byzantines affirmed their devotion to artistry, a vital element of Greek culture since ancient times. In addition to crafting icons, Byzantine artisans manufactured fine jewelry and glassware and shimmering silk fabrics, which had earlier been produced only in China. By one account, silkworms were introduced to the Byzantine Empire

A gold coin depicts Irene as "empress" (basilissa); some coins also named her "emperor" (basileus).

in the sixth century by itinerant Christian monks who smuggled their eggs out of China. Byzantines also honored Greek scholarly traditions by studying and copying the works of ancient Greek philosophers, scientists, playwrights, and poets, literature that might otherwise have been lost to posterity.

Politically, the Byzantine Empire made up for the loss of remote territories around the Mediterranean by becoming a more cohesive and well-organized state. Its

imperial bureaucracy was so elaborate and complex that the word *byzantine* came to mean "intricate." Its armies regained strength and seized territory in and around Syria from Muslim forces in the tenth century. But the main objective of rulers in Constantinople was to reclaim the northern Balkans from Bulgars and other invaders. Basil II, who became emperor in 976, earned the title "Bulgar Slayer" for punishing campaigns that imposed Byzantine authority and beliefs on what is now Bulgaria and reestablished the Danube River as the empire's northern frontier. He reportedly ordered Bulgar troops he defeated to be blinded, leaving only a few

---

EMPEROR IRENE

Byzantine ruler Irene (circa 752–803) left a distinct stamp on history during her 22-year reign. Born in Athens, she married Byzantine emperor Leo IV in 769. Upon his death, she became guardian of and coemperor with their ten-year-old son, Constantine IV. From the start, her rule was beset by enemies within and without. Known to be a supporter of the use of icons (banned since 730 by Emperor Leo III), she fought off an effort by iconoclasts to depose her in her first year. By 787, she restored the worship of icons, earning the support of church traditionalists. In the meantime, she struggled with incursions by the Franks in one direction, and the Abbasid caliphs in another.

Young Constantine, as he grew, attempted to seize control. In 790, his supporters proclaimed him sole ruler, but in 792 his mother engineered a conspiracy to arrest and blind her son. He died soon thereafter. Irene then reigned as sole emperor for five years, reportedly contemplating a marriage with Charlemagne that would have dramatically reunited the two halves of the former Roman Empire (supposedly this arrangement was

Irene sits in council with her son and one-time coemperor, Constantine IV.

foiled by someone close to the throne). In 802, Byzantine courtiers conspired against her and removed her from the throne, naming her finance minister, Nikephoros, as emperor. Irene was exiled to the island of Lesbos, where she died the following year.

Byzantine styles appear in art from a ceiling in Ravenna, Italy. Ravenna was part of the empire from the sixth through eighth centuries.

soldiers with a single eye to lead the rest back to their horrified ruler, Samuel, who died in disgrace. For all his brutality, Basil was also a shrewd diplomat who extended Byzantine influence to Russia by coming to terms with Grand Prince Vladimir of Kiev. Vladimir married Basil's sister and converted from paganism to Christianity, which took an Orthodox form in Russia as it did in Greece.

The Byzantine Empire declined following the death of Basil II in 1025, in large part because its internal

The sardonyx, gilt, enamel, and pearl chalice of Emperor Romanos II

resources proved insufficient to meet external threats. The reorganization of Anatolia and other areas into military districts, governed by generals, resulted in a social system resembling the feudalism of western Europe, where barons acquired fiefdoms in exchange for their military services to dukes or kings and peasants became their vassals. Byzantine nobles amassed large estates, commanded their own troops, and sometimes rebelled against Constantinople. Emperors found it increasingly difficult to collect revenue and raise armed forces as more and more land and laborers

became the property of those nobles, to do with as they wished.

During the 11th century, new threats to the Byzantine Empire emerged on several fronts. To the west, Normans of Viking ancestry entered the Mediterranean in longships and occupied Sicily and southern Italy. The Byzantines were left without a foothold in Italy, for Rome and Ravenna had become papal states—bastions of the Roman Catholic Church, which broke with the Orthodox Church when leaders of the two denominations excommunicated

---

Emperor Basil II ("The Bulgar Slayer") stands triumphant over prostrate Bulgars, in a frontispiece from an 11th-century Byzantine Psalter.

MILITARY MIGHT

THE VARANGIAN GUARD

In 988, Emperor Basil II faced one of the greatest crises of his reign: The troops of a rebel general, Bardas Phocas, were encamped across the Bosporus from his capital. Basil appealed to Prince Vladimir I of Kiev for aid, promising him the hand of his sister in return. Vladimir sent him 6,000 Varangians, expert Viking mercenaries who had settled in Russia.

After defeating the rebel troops, many of the Varangians stayed on to become the elite personal guards of Basil and successive Byzantine emperors. Well paid and with no local sympathies, they were famous both for their loyalty and for their prowess with the sword and battle-ax. In the midst of battle, the guard would cluster around the emperor in a fearsome wall of defense.

After William the Conqueror took England, disaffected Anglo-Saxons filtered into the guard as well. During the Crusades, however, European forces defeated the Varangians, and they faded from historical view.

Ninth-century emperor Theophilus used mercenary guards that may have included Vikings, precursors to the Varangians.

BYZANTIUM AND RUSSIA

Byzantium had a powerful and permanent influence on the religion, art, and culture of Russia. In the 860s, Byzantine missionaries Cyril and Methodius, Greek brothers, devised the script now known as Cyrillic, which allowed the formerly illiterate Slavic peoples to read and write in their own languages. Christian writings, translated into local languages, helped convert many Slavs to Orthodox Christianity—a process accelerated after Vladimir I of Kiev converted as well. Orthodox missions spread throughout Russia.

As Kiev became a more powerful trading state, Russian and Byzantine merchants became well acquainted, situated as they were along a nexus of East-West trade routes. Byzantine art and architecture also colonized the young Russian state; the art of icons became a Russian specialty, and the onion domes that characterize traditional Russian architecture may have been an attempt to copy the domes of Constantinople.

St. Basil's Cathedral in Moscow displays the onion domes that may have been a legacy of Byzantium.

Ottoman forces besiege the walls of Constantinople in 1453. The Ottoman conquest brought an end to an empire more than 1,000 years old.

each other in 1054. Nonetheless, they soon found a common enemy in the Seljuk Turks: Muslims who seized control of Baghdad from caliphs of the Abbasid dynasty and advanced into Anatolia, where they routed Byzantine forces in 1071 and occupied that country, known today as Turkey. In 1095, the Byzantine emperor Alexius I appealed to Rome for aid, hoping that Catholics would help defend Constantinople against the Turks. Instead, Pope Urban II launched a broader campaign, aimed at ousting Muslims from the Holy Land and seizing Jerusalem.

The ensuing Crusades disrupted and weakened the Byzantine Empire, which suffered the ultimate indignity when the wealthy Italian city-state of Venice, a commercial rival, funded the Fourth Crusade and induced Catholic soldiers to sack Constantinople in 1204. As the Orthodox bishop of Ephesus related, "Even the Great Church of God [Hagia Sophia] and the imperial palace, were filled with men of the enemy, all of them maddened by war and murderous in spirit." Having lost their grip on the Holy Land and undermined Byzantine authority, Crusaders cleared the way for Turks of the emerging Ottoman Empire. During the 14th century, Ottoman forces crossed the Bosporus and occupied much of the Balkans before besieging and capturing Constantinople in 1453. Among the victims of the siege was Emperor Constantine XI, the last ruler to bear the name of the city's founder before this Greek capital of Roman origins fell to the Turks and became Istanbul.

"*Tears fell from [the Sultan's] eyes
as he groaned deeply and passionately:
'What a city we have given over to
plunder and destruction!'*"

KRITOVOULOS, *HISTORY OF MEHMED THE CONQUEROR*

HOUSE OF ISLAM
Umayyads, Abbasids, and Fatimids

From its inception, Islam was both a religious and a political movement, concerned with how the faithful should be guided and governed. Muhammad, born around 570 in Mecca, the commercial and spiritual hub of Arabia, served as judge and military commander of the *ummah*—the community of believers that grew up around him—as well as their prophet. He began to attract followers around the age of 40, when he experienced a revelation in which he recognized Allah, the same God worshiped by Jews and Christians, as supreme. His insistence that Arabs worship Allah to the exclusion of all other gods set him at odds with powerful figures in Mecca, and he fled for his life to Medina, where his movement gained strength. In 630, he and his forces took Mecca and removed pagan idols from the Kaaba, which became the central shrine of *Islam,* which means "submission"—to God and his word, as revealed by Muhammad and inscribed in the Koran.

Muhammad left no designated successor when he died in 632.

A camel-shaped glass flask from the Umayyad dynasty (above). Historian Abu-Zayd visits a Muslim village (right).

His disciple and father-in-law, Abu Bakr, became *caliph* (deputy) and completed the task of uniting the tribes of Arabia under Islam. They had long battled one another, and some rebelled after Muhammad's death by renouncing Islam or refusing to pay taxes. Abu Bakr forced them to submit, however, and prohibited them from warring on other Muslims within *dar al-Islam,* the "house of Islam." Instead, the Arabs turned their energies outward and forged an empire.

No more than 50,000 men took part in the Arabs' initial conquests, but they excelled at mounted warfare, often relying on camels, which were more durable than horses in the desert and better suited for carrying supplies. And they struck at the right time, when rival Byzantine and Sasanid Persian forces had exhausted each other and the Near East was up for grabs. Neighboring Syria had many Arab inhabitants and became the first target of Arab forces, who seized Damascus in 636. From there, they fanned out, wresting Palestine and Egypt from the faltering Byzantines by 642 and Mesopotamia and Persia from

- **ca 570** Prophet Muhammad born in Mecca; he dies in Medina in 632.
- **750–1258** Abbasid dynasty rules from Baghdad.
- **786–809** Caliph Harun al-Rashid rules in Baghdad.
- **1055** Seljuk Turks under Tughril Beg oust Shiites from Baghdad.
- **1258** Mongols invade, ending the Abbasid dynasty.

- **661–750** Islam expands under the Umayyad dynasty.
- **756** Abd al-Rahman makes Cordoba, Spain, his capital.
- **969** Fatimids, a Shiite dynasty, conquer Egypt.
- **1187** Saladin retakes Jerusalem from Christian crusaders.

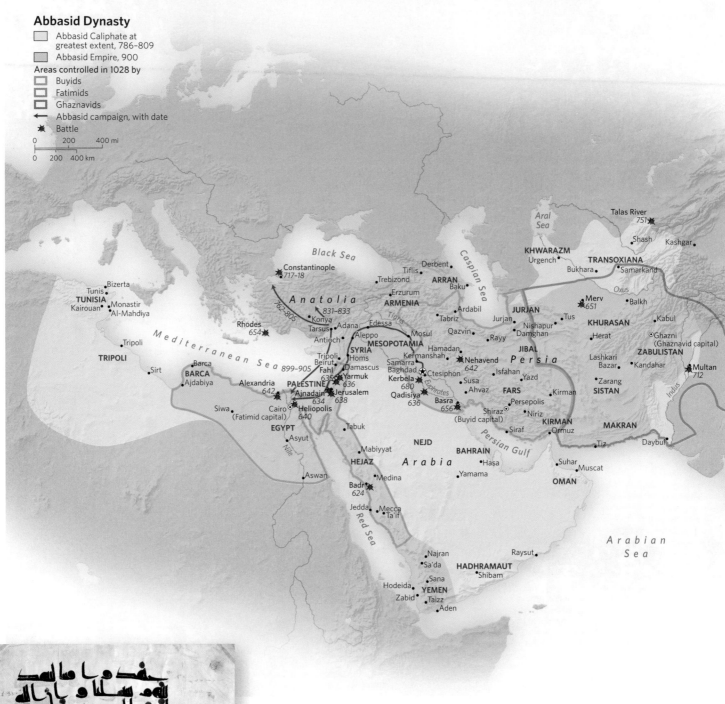

Abbasid Dynasty

Abbasid Caliphate at greatest extent, 786–809
Abbasid Empire, 900

Areas controlled in 1028 by
- Buyids
- Fatimids
- Ghaznavids

← Abbasid campaign, with date
✴ Battle

0   200   400 mi
0   200   400 km

The Koran, shown here in a fragment dating from the Abbasid dynasty, was compiled in the seventh century.

the defunct Sasanid dynasty by midcentury.

Many cities yielded without a fight to the advancing Arabs. Like most soldiers in those times, they looted their defeated foes, but they did so systematically: All booty was registered before it was distributed to warriors and others, with one-fifth of the proceeds going to the caliph to fund his government. Muslim forces established garrisons in lands they conquered and were joined there by Arab civilians who helped populate those strongholds. Conversions to Islam were largely voluntary. Thus, it took centuries for countries such as

An illustration from an Iranian manuscript depicts the first three Shiite imams: Ali and his sons Hassan and Hussein.

Egypt with strong ties to other faiths to become predominantly Muslim. Jews and Christians were tolerated as "people of the Book," whose biblical scriptures and prayers honored the one true God, and they were allowed to continue worshiping as they had before, so long as they paid a special tax required of non-Muslims. Those nonbelievers sometimes opposed their Muslim rulers, but the sharpest civil strife occurred within the house of Islam when dissident Muslims challenged the legitimacy of caliphs, who were growing increasingly wealthy and powerful.

Controversy began during the reign of Uthman, who became caliph in 644. A leader of the influential Umayyad family in Mecca, which had initially opposed Muhammad before embracing the prophet and his message, Uthman filled top government posts with family members and enriched them in the process. He died at the hands of rebels in 656, and civil war ensued between the succeeding caliph, Ali—Muhammad's cousin, son-in-law, and leading disciple—and his opponents, including Umayyads who hoped to regain power. Following Ali's assassination in 661, Umayyads established a dynasty without the support of Shiites, those Muslims who revered Ali and believed that only his descendants were entitled to rule the house of Islam.

The Muslim world continued to expand under the powerful Umayyad caliphs, who made Damascus their capital. Muslim armies advanced eastward into Central Asia and northern India and westward across North Africa before crossing to Spain in the early 700s.

When Abu al-Abbas defeated Umayyad forces in 750 and founded the Abbasid dynasty, he alienated Shiites who had joined in the rebellion hoping that a descendant of Ali would become caliph. Abbasids came from a different branch of Muhammad's family, and by keeping the caliphate within that branch, they excluded Ali's heirs from power. Abbasids and their supporters believed that caliphs were political rather than spiritual guardians of the Islamic world. Thus, descent from a member of Muhammad's family helped legitimize caliphs, but they did not have be descendants of the prophet's disciple Ali to rule righteously. Muslims of that opinion became known as Sunnis, or traditionalists, because they held the

THE BATTLE OF TALAS RIVER

A little-known but pivotal clash between Muslim and Chinese forces in Central Asia, the Battle of Talas River, had profound implications for the balance of power in Asia and the spread of technology in Europe. The silk roads that passed through Central Asia brought prosperity to both the Abbasid empire and the Tang dynasty of China. When a dispute broke out between the two small kingdoms of Ferghana and Chach, the Chinese sent in forces to support Ferghana, while Chach asked the Muslims for aid.

In July 751, Chinese and Muslim armies met at the Talas River in what is now Kazakhstan. After five days of battle, the larger Muslim army prevailed. Chinese armies retreated, and China would never regain its influence over the region. Gradually, Islam replaced the area's former patchwork of religions.

Just as important as the victory, perhaps, were the Chinese papermakers taken captive by the Muslims. These artisans passed on their skills to Islamic craftsmen, and from them papermaking spread to Persia, Egypt, and Europe. Paper replaced vellum in books and, in its cheapness and ease of use, helped spread information and literacy through the Western world. ❧

Chinese artisans form sheets of paper from bamboo. The Chinese were making paper for at least 700 years before the rest of the world.

traditional view that early caliphs other than Ali had in fact been rightful rulers. The conflict between Sunnis and Shiites would deepen and ultimately divide the house of Islam. But it did not prevent Abbasid caliphs from restoring order to the Islamic world and building on the imperial foundation laid by their predecessors.

The Umayyads continued to have some influence. Abd al-Rahman of the Umayyad family fled from Damascus when his dynasty fell to the Abbasids, eventually ending up as ruler of Muslim Spain. He took Cordoba as his capital and transformed it into a cultural and commercial center that surpassed any Christian city in western Europe in the early Middle Ages. Among its monuments were the

A camel caravan rests amid tents (right). These caravans were the lifeblood of the vast medieval Islamic trading network.

THE GREAT MOSQUE AT SAMARRA

In 836, the unpopular Abbasid caliph al-Mutasim left Baghdad and created a new capital city for his caliphate at Samarra, on the Tigris River some 77 miles north of Baghdad. Under al-Mutasim and his seven successors, the ancient city was reborn and rebuilt, with a palace, gardens, and mosques. The city's status as capital was short-lived—that honor returned to Baghdad in 892—but Samarra retained a reputation as a holy center.

Time has erased many of the city's structures, but among the most famous of the remaining buildings is the Great Mosque. Built by the caliph al-Mutawakkil between 847 and 861, the original mosque was one of the world's largest, measuring 409,000 square feet. Its outer wall of baked brick was supported by 44 towers; the interior held marble columns and was probably decorated with glass mosaics. A fountain rose in the courtyard.

Much of the main mosque has disappeared, but its most striking feature remains. The great minaret, 89 feet from the mosque's north face, stands 180 feet high. Winding from its wide base to the narrower summit is a spiral ramp that leads to a windowed vestibule. The building, so different from the delicate spires of modern minarets, harks back to the Mesopotamian ziggurats of Iraq's early history.

A spiral ramp winds five times around the minaret (right) of the Great Mosque. Abstract patterns in stucco (inset) were typical of Samarran decoration.

Ibn Tulun built this elegant Cairo mosque in the ninth century (right). Arab astrolabes (inset) were often used to find the direction of Mecca.

IBN SINA

Persian physician, philosopher, and polymath Ibn Sina, known to the West as Avicenna, was born in 980 near Bukhara in present-day Iran. According to his autobiography, by the age of ten he had memorized the Koran; by the age of 18 he had cured the sultan of Bukhara of a mysterious ailment and was granted access to the sultan's extensive library.

Ibn Sina went on to write some 240 works on philosophy, medicine, mathematics, astronomy, and other subjects. Among his most famous texts are *The Canon of Medicine* and an encyclopedia of science and metaphysics, in which a Neoplatonist philosophy is grounded in the theology of Islam. Translated into Latin, both his philosophical treatise *The Cure* and his well-organized medical text *The Canon* had a long-lasting influence on European scholarship.

Ibn Sina's personal life was as extravagant as his professional one. Immodest and convivial, he enjoyed wine and women. By some accounts, his death in 1037 was hastened by opium administered by a slave. ✍

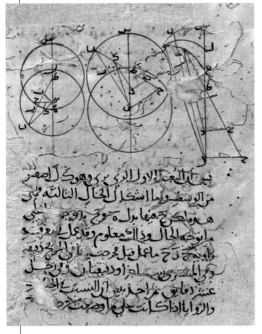

A 19th-century transcription of Ibn Sina's work illustrates astronomical motion.

Great Mosque of Cordoba, one of the largest structures in the Muslim world, and a library containing 400,000 volumes.

The Umayyad dynasty might have lasted longer had its caliphs all been as dynamic and outgoing as Abd al-Rahman. But later rulers of the dynasty were isolated figures, who lived luxuriously in their palaces and entrusted the affairs of government to Arab chieftains holding lucrative positions. Arabs who were not part of that wealthy military elite denounced caliphs and their coterie for violating the spirit of Islam, which placed the needs of the community above personal gain and required Muslims to aid the poor. Others at odds with the Umayyads included many non-Arab Muslims, who were excluded from high offices and the accompanying financial rewards.

Imperial dynasties that came to power by toppling old ruling families have often made a fresh start by moving to a new capital. The Abbasids thus moved the government from Damascus to Mesopotamia, the age-old heartland of empires, home to Sumerian, Akkadian, Babylonian, Assyrian, Macedonian, and Persian sovereigns over the preceding 3,000 years. Abbasids built their new capital, Baghdad, on the Tigris River, near the former Sasanid Persian capital of Ctesiphon and not far from ancient Babylon. Laced with irrigation canals, this was a fertile area that nourished fast-growing cities. It was also fertile ground for Islam, which won numerous converts in what is now Iraq

"A knowledge of causes is a knowledge of secret things, because the secret is a knowledge of the existence of a thing before it comes into being."

IBN SINA,
*ON THE HARMONY OF
RELIGIONS AND PHILOSOPHY*

and in neighboring Iran, birthplace of the Persian Empire. Many of the soldiers who helped Abu al-Abbas win power came from Khurasan in northeastern Iran, where Arab troops and colonists intermingled and intermarried with Iranians to produce a new Islamic society.

Geographically, Baghdad was not much farther from Mecca than was Damascus, the Umayyad capital. But culturally, Abbasid caliphs were entering a different world, one long dominated by Persians of one dynasty or another. Unlike the Umayyads, the Abbasids trusted in Muslims who were not Arabs, hiring Persian clerks and administrators and patronizing Persian artists and scholars. Like well-educated Muslims of all ethnic backgrounds, those Persians knew Arabic, the sacred language of the Koran and the official language of the Islamic empire. Under the Abbasids, Arabic literature and scholarship flourished at courts and universities where Muslims from various lands gathered, producing works of poetry, fiction, and philosophy as well as important treatises on mathematics, astronomy, and other sciences.

Mesopotamia had long been a commercial crossroads, linking India, China, and other lands of the Far East with the Mediterranean world. Under Abbasid rule, that commerce expanded. Camel

Cloisonné jug given to Charlemagne by Harun al-Rashid

caravans plied the Oriental trade routes known as silk roads, and mariners equipped with compasses and astrolabes (used to determine latitude) navigated the Persian Gulf, Arabian Sea, and Indian Ocean, introducing Islam to ports in East Africa and Southeast Asia. Muslim merchants helped disseminate crops native to the Far East such as rice, sugarcane, oranges, lemons, and bananas westward to Africa and Mediterranean lands. They also engaged in the slave trade, which brought black Africans as well as Turks from Central Asia and Slavs from eastern Europe into service as laborers, soldiers, concubines, and household retainers. Under sharia—an Islamic legal and moral code derived from the Koran—Muslims were allowed to hold non-Muslims as slaves but were required to treat them well and encouraged to free them. Just as in the Roman Empire, some freed slaves rose to high positions.

Traders brought caliphs in Baghdad treasures from many lands and increased their revenue through the taxes they paid. Abbasid rulers were as fond of wealth and luxury as any of their Umayyad predecessors, but such behavior was customary in Mesopotamia, where emperors had long lived in splendor and dazzled onlookers. One scholar who visited the palace in Baghdad found the caliph cloaked in gold and seated on an ebony throne: "To the right of the throne hung nine collars of gems . . . and to the left were the like, all

of famous jewels." Like emperors in China and other lands, Abbasid rulers kept a harem of wives and concubines, watched over by eunuchs. Some of those consorts were influential, including a freed slave named al-Khayzuran who became the wife of one caliph and the mother of another, Harun al-Rashid, who reigned in Baghdad from 786 to 809. Harun's opulent court inspired the colorful tales collected under the title *One Thousand and One Nights* and made an impression on the distant Holy Roman emperor Charlemagne, who reportedly sent envoys to Baghdad and received gifts from the caliph that included monkeys and an elephant. Mindful of the blame cast on Muslims who failed to share

CONNECTIONS

ISLAMIC BANKING

Merchants from Europe to Africa to China followed trade routes across the Islamic world, circulating among ports, oases, and crossroads cities. Silk, spices, jewelry, furs, amber, ceramics, livestock, textiles, slaves, and more were exchanged in a thriving commercial economy. Entrepreneurs banded together to form partnerships and share the risks of business investments.

Abbasid banks responded with a new level of sophistication. Like banks today, they loaned money to new businesses, brokered investments, and exchanged currencies. Although Islamic law prohibits excessive interest or usury, medieval banks were allowed to charge interest in some cases. They expanded the system of letters of credit, or *shah*—the origin of today's English word check. Although letters of credit had been in use since classical times, the Islamic banks, with multiple branches of the same institution, spread the practice through their domain, allowing merchants to trade with each other at a distance without the need to carry easily stolen hoards of coins.

Envoys returning to Europe from the court of Caliph Harun al-Rashid brought gifts to Emperor Charlemagne, including ivory chess pieces and an intricate water clock.

their wealth with those in need, caliphs maintained hospitals in Baghdad for the sick and mentally ill, who were treated free of charge and given money when they were well enough to return home.

Abbasid rulers were less concerned with expanding their vast empire than preserving it, but that proved impossible over the centuries. Like Persian emperors of old, they sent out agents to spy on the governors of distant provinces and see that they did not use taxes they collected or troops they commanded to advance their own interests. But that did not prevent provincial chieftains from breaking away and forming their own dynasties. Spain remained a separate Muslim kingdom under the Umayyad ruler Abd al-Rahman and his successors. Other countries slipped

from the grasp of Abbasid caliphs during the ninth and tenth centuries—notably Egypt, a loss Baghdad could ill afford. That wealthy and populous land fell to a Shiite dynasty known as the Fatimids, named for

Muhammad's daughter Fatimah, wife of the revered Ali. Their movement gained strength after Harun's son, the caliph al-Ma'mun, tried to reconcile Shiites to Abbasid rule by naming as his successor a

PEOPLE

OMAR KHAYYAM

Known now mainly for his poetry, translated as *The Rubaiyat of Omar Khayyam*, the Persian scientist Ghiyath al-Din Abu al-Fath 'Umar ibn Ibrahim al-Nisaburi al-Khayyami (1048–1131) was famous in his own time as a mathematician and astronomer. In his 20s, Khayyam had already written a groundbreaking work on mathematics, "Treatise on Demonstration of Problems of Algebra," which discusses the solution to cubic equations by means of intersecting conic sections.

Not until many years after his death did Khayyam's quatrains *(robaiyat)* come to light, and some scholars still question whether he was the author. In 1859, the English writer Edward FitzGerald published his translation of the verses, which contemplate the fleeting nature of life:

> The Moving Finger writes, and, having writ,
> Moves on: nor all thy Piety nor Wit
> Shall lure it back to cancel half a Line,
> Nor all thy Tears wash out a Word of it.

A Persian portrait of Omar Khayyam shows the scholar in a thoughtful mood.

Mongols under Hulegu Khan besiege Baghdad in 1258, ending Abbasid rule (above). A sculpted female figure wears court dress (left).

descendant of Ali, who was later poisoned to death. The caliph was suspected of killing him to appease rebels in Baghdad opposed to that would-be successor, and the scandal further alienated Shiites.

In 909, a Fatimid imam (spiritual leader) who called himself al-Mahdi ("divinely guided") took control of Tunisia. His successors gathered strength and advanced east, conquering Egypt in 969 and building a new capital there: Cairo, near Giza and the other ancient cities

where the Egyptian pharaohs once ruled. The Fatimids' ultimate goal was to topple the Abbasid dynasty and bring the entire Muslim world under their political and spiritual leadership. After seizing Mecca and Damascus, however, they were thwarted in the 11th century by Seljuk Turks, who were now the real masters of Baghdad, having reduced caliphs there to figureheads.

Turks from Central Asia had long served as soldiers under Abbasid rulers, who like many emperors in other times and places recruited warlike tribesmen at their frontiers. They benefited from their services in the short term, but ended up entrusting the defense of their realm to foreigners who did not always remain their obedient servants. By 1055, the decrepit Abbasid dynasty was powerless without Turkish forces, who had converted to Islam as Sunnis and were eager to fight for their faith. When Tughril Beg, the leader of a Turkish faction called the Seljuks, ousted Iranian Shiites called Buyids from

SALADIN

Kurdish-born ruler Saladin (Salah al-Din, 1137–1193), a devout Sunni Muslim, became the sultan of Egypt, Syria, Palestine, and Yemen in an era when Muslim forces were divided and fractious, and when key holy cities had fallen to Christian crusaders. He reunited the Islamic forces as much by the strength of his personality—firm, but generous and fair—as by his decisive military campaigns. To his Christian opponents, he became a byword for chivalry.

Saladin's greatest achievement was the retaking of Jerusalem in 1187 from the Franks, who had held the city for 88 years. Although Muslims bitterly remembered the crusaders' slaughter of the city's people in 1099, Saladin spared Jerusalem's Christian and Jewish inhabitants. His armies pressed the Frankish forces back to the coast, fighting English commander Richard the Lion-Hearted to a draw. Saladin, exhausted, soon died. Having given away all his wealth to the poor, he left too little money to pay for his own funeral. ✏

Sultan Saladin, brave and honorable, became a hero even to his European foes because of his chivalrous treatment of his enemies.

Women appeal to Saladin for mercy during the battle for Jerusalem in a 19th-century painting by Alexandre-Evariste Fragonard.

Baghdad, the grateful Abbasid caliph recognized him as sultan, or chieftain, and invited him to campaign against the Fatimids. With the army at their command, the sultan and his Turkish successors held the keys to Baghdad, and caliphs became their wards, who continued to live royally but had no real authority.

> **"Within a short time, Saladin had conquered almost the whole Kingdom of Jerusalem."**
>
> ANONYMOUS,
> *THE CAPTURE OF THE HOLY LAND BY SALADIN*

After repulsing the Fatimids and occupying Syria and Palestine, Seljuk Turks expanded the Islamic world by seizing Anatolia from the Byzantine Empire. The ensuing Crusades diminished their power and brought a new Muslim sultan to the fore: Saladin, a commander of Kurdish origin who turned against his Fatimid masters, seized control of Egypt in 1171, and went on reclaim Jerusalem from Christian crusaders in 1187. At his death five years later, Saladin's realm reached from Egypt to Syria. Yet Turks retained control of Anatolia, and from that contested borderland at the outskirts of Asia emerged a new Turkish dynasty, known as the Ottomans. In centuries to come, their forces would lay claim to much of the old Muslim world and advance deep into Europe.

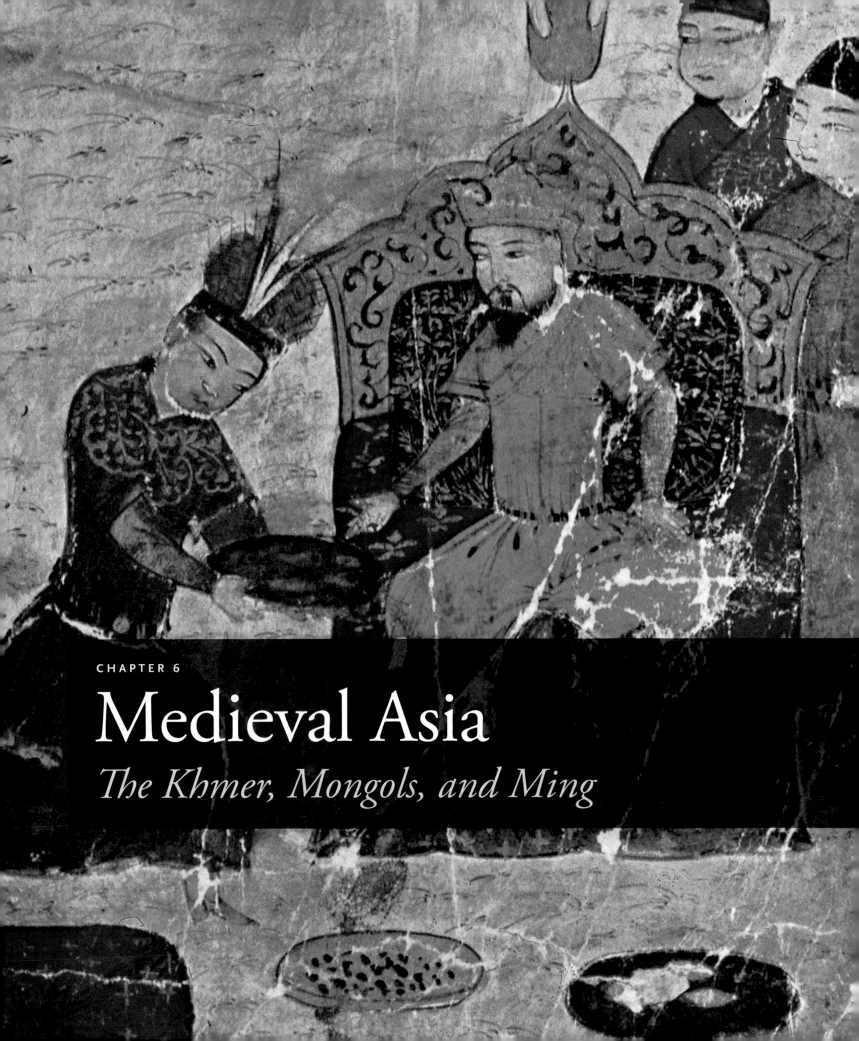

CHAPTER 6

Medieval Asia

The Khmer, Mongols, and Ming

KHMER
An Empire of Temples

The title Khan means "Great Lord of Lords," and certainly he has a right to this title; for everyone should know that this Great Khan is the mightiest man, whether in respect of subjects or of territory or of treasure, who is in the world today," wrote Marco Polo of the Mongol emperor Khubilai Khan. This was not medieval hyperbole. As great khan, Khubilai ruled over an empire stretching from the Pacific to the Mediterranean. While Europe was struggling to rebuild after the collapse of the Roman Empire, Asia was witnessing a flowering of powerful civilizations from Southeast Asia to China and across the steppes to the Black Sea.

Early in the first millennium A.D., the peninsulas and islands that now make up Vietnam, Laos, Cambodia, Thailand, Malaysia, and Myanmar (Burma) became a crossroads of trade between the South China Sea and the Indian Ocean. Indian merchants introduced their culture to the region—Sanskrit, architecture, and, most significantly, the Hindu religion and the idea of the ruler as god-king.

Cambodian stone carvings depicting the birth of Buddha (above) and King Jayavarman at Bayon Temple near Angkor (right)

Indian influences shaped the loosely organized kingdom of Funan, which grew up around the lower Mekong River in the first century A.D. Flowing out of southwest China, the Mekong winds its way to the South China Sea through subtropical lands that alternate between dry winters and wet, monsoon-drenched summers. One Mekong tributary runs into Cambodia's huge lake, Tonle Sap, which quadruples in size every flood season. By the sixth century, migrants from the north were pushing into the fertile river valley. The Funan kingdom dissolved, and for a time invaders from Java controlled the area. Eventually they were replaced by a larger, more powerful, and more centralized empire: the Khmer, ruling from the kingdom of Angkor.

Like some other legendary leaders, the founder of the Angkor kingdom began his career in exile. Jayavarman II (circa 770–850) was either a prisoner or a hostage at the Hindu court of Java before he returned to the lower Mekong plain as a vassal of the Javanese around 800. Within two years, he had thrown off Javanese domination and established

First–sixth centuries A.D. Indian culture comes to Cambodia via traders.

877–ca 890 Indravarman I fills the throne.

ca 890–ca 910 Yasovarman I rules and builds Angkor Thom.

1113–ca 1150 Angkor Wat built in reign of Suryavarman II.

1432 Khmer routed by Thais.

802–835 First Khmer king, Jayavarman II, reigns.

881 "Temple mountain" of Bakong dedicated in Angkor.

ca 1004–1050 Suryavarman I rules, extending empire into Thailand.

1177 Jayavarman VII retakes Cambodia and promotes Buddhism.

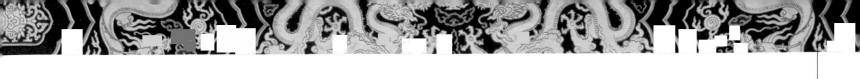

himself not only as ruler of the Khmer people but also as a *devaraja*—a divinely anointed king. At Mount Kulen, northeast of Tonle Sap, he built his first capital, crowned with square towers. Soon he moved closer to the lake and built another capital, Hariharalaya, featuring even larger, stepped-pyramid Hindu temples.

Jayavarman's son inherited the throne, but in 877 he was supplanted by his cousin, Indravarman I. Indravarman topped the architectural achievements of his predecessors by building the largest temple yet at Hariharalaya: the Bakong "temple mountain." Made primarily of stone, it used a hundred times more material than any previous temple. More valuable, in a practical sense, was Indravarman's construction of a vast reservoir, one of many that would be built over the centuries along with a widespread, sophisticated system of irrigation canals. Water collected in

the reservoirs during the monsoon season could be released in the dry months, allowing for multiple rice harvests.

Succeeding Indravarman was Yasovarman, who established the city for which the empire is famous, Angkor Thom (Great

> ## "As if out of fear of drought, he placed in the heart of all creatures the ambrosia of his charm, which the eyes of women drank insatiably."
>
> **HINDU HOLY MAN**, ABOUT INDRAVARMAN I

City), at the end of the ninth century. Built on the banks of the Siem Reap River, just north of the Tonle Sap lakeshore, the city became both a religious center, filled with temples, and the core of a thriving agricultural civilization. Hundreds of miles of canals and dikes connected to huge reservoirs spread out around Angkor's walls.

The walls themselves, almost two miles on a side, enclosed a metropolis the size of modern New York City that at its height might have had 750,000 inhabitants. More than a thousand temples rose within the city, which was laid out to reflect the Hindu world order. A moat symbolizing the world's oceans surrounded the walls. In the center, sacred Mount Meru was represented by the Bakheng temple, five stories tall with 109 towers; 33 towers are visible from each side of the temple, possibly representing the 33 gods living on Mount Meru. Tens of thousands of priests, workers, and dancers served Angkor's temples and in turn were supplied by a sizable population of rice farmers in the countryside.

Despite occasional periods of conflict, the kingdom was for the most part calm and prosperous under Yasovarman's successors. As the 11th century began, Suryavarman I reestablished control over breakaway areas and took over portions of Thailand to the west. After some dynastic struggles, Suryavarman II (unrelated to the previous Suryavarman) took the throne in the early 12th century. Also a vigorous soldier, he is better known today for beginning the magnificent temple complex of Angkor Wat, just south of Angkor Thom. Dedicated to the god Vishnu, its central temple represents Mount Meru. Miles of bas-reliefs along its walls show

This 11th-century bronze figure of Vishnu reclining, from Angkor, is one of thousands of images of Hindu deities from the Khmer capital.

Khmer Empire

- Khmer Empire, circa 800
- Khmer Empire, circa 1100
- Khmer Empire, circa 1210
- ← Khmer incursion
- ← Cham incursion
- ○ Town with inscriptions and monumental religious buildings

0   150   300 mi
0   150   300 km

scenes from Hindu sacred texts, vignettes of daily life (men playing a board game, for instance), and victorious battles against warriors from the neighboring kingdom of Champa in Vietnam.

Throughout the centuries, the Khmer rulers struggled with their neighbors, but during the 11th and 12th centuries, they were largely victorious. At their greatest extent, the leaders of the Khmer Empire expanded their rule over parts of what are now Thailand, Burma, Malaysia, Vietnam, and Laos, as well as Cambodia. Cham invaders destroyed parts of Angkor in the

12th century, but they were driven out by Jayavarman VII, who conscripted hundreds of thousands of workers to build new temples in the complex. But Jayavarman VII's rule marked a major cultural change in the Khmer Empire. He was a devout Buddhist, although religiously tolerant.

A carved aspara *(celestial dancing girl) at Angkor Wat. The Khmer absorbed religious imagery from India.*

Buddhist temples joined earlier Hindu structures in Angkor Wat.

Although surrounding kingdoms nibbled away at the Khmer Empire in the next couple of centuries, Angkor remained a prosperous city and a hub of trade. As a visiting Chinese official, Chau Ju-kua, described it in the 13th century: "The officials and the common people dwell in houses with sides of bamboo matting and thatched with reeds. Only the king resides in a palace of hewn stone. It has a granite lotus pond of extraordinary beauty with golden bridges, some three hundred odd feet long . . . There are some two hundred thousand war elephants and many horses, though of small size . . . The native products comprise elephants' tusks . . . good yellow wax, kingfisher's feathers (Note: Of which this country has great store), dammar resin, foreign oils, ginger peel, gold colored incense, sapan-wood, raw silk, and cotton fabrics. The foreign traders offer in exchange for these gold, silver, porcelainware, sugar, preserves, and vinegar."

In the 14th century, Angkor began to decline. Thai peoples, pushed south by Mongol forces, began to invade the kingdom along Angkor's fine roads. Climate change and the decay of Angkor's complicated irrigation system may also have contributed to a stressed, dwindling population. By 1432, the Thais had captured the capital city, driving out the Khmer and establishing a capital farther west. The exquisite temples of Angkor Wat were overtaken by jungle vines, remaining in obscurity until they were brought to international notice by awestruck European explorers in the 19th century.

The five terraced towers of Angkor Wat's central shrine represent the five peaks of Mount Meru.

ANGKOR WAT

Mysterious Angkor Wat, strangled in jungle vines, became a romantic symbol of lost civilizations to Westerners in the 19th century. It was never, of course, truly lost: Buddhist pilgrims and stray European explorers had been visiting the temple complex for centuries. But when the French became the colonial rulers in Cambodia in the 1860s, their archaeologists and artists brought the world's attention to the remote site and its spectacular, crumbling buildings.

Enclosed by a wall 2.2 miles long and a wide moat, the temple was the world's largest religious complex. Its sandstone blocks were held together without mortar, and its central shrine represented Mount Meru, the sacred Hindu mountain. Miles of sinuous sacred and historical bas-reliefs covered walls and passageways. Much of the complex had fallen to rubble since the Khmer Empire vanished.

French archaeologists set to work in the late 19th century to restore the site. During the wars of the later 20th century, the temple again suffered neglect, but it gained protection in 1992 after being named a UNESCO World Heritage site. Researchers from many countries now collaborate to study and preserve the temple and uncover the remains of the surrounding civilization. In 1994, the area was even scanned by radar from the space shuttle *Endeavour*. Scientists believe that many more artifacts of ancient Khmer culture remain to be found. ✂

A 13th-century Khmer relief depicts Shiva and his wife, Devi.

MONGOLS
Nomad Conquerors

In the early 13th century, north of the medieval civilizations of China and Southeast Asia, a collection of nomadic clans coalesced into one of the largest and most fearsome of all empires: the Mongols. For centuries, nomads on horseback had roamed the high plateaus of Central Asia. Their chilly, windswept lands ran from the Siberian tundra south to the Gobi Desert and from the Altai Mountains in the west to the Great Khingan Range in the east. In the center were grasslands, steppes that just barely fed the cattle, sheep, and goats that the nomads drove north and south with the seasons.

Mongol clans shared the steppes with Turkic tribes to the west and Tatars to the east. In the 12th century, these Altaic-speaking peoples consisted of feuding groups ruled by chiefs, or *khans*. Around 1162, a boy named Temujin was born to one of the clans. According to the 13th-century *Secret History of the Mongols,* Temujin's father, the tribal chief, was poisoned when Temujin was a child, and the boy, his mother, and his siblings struggled to survive by scavenging berries and rodents on the steppes. Captured by an enemy clan and imprisoned in a

A bronze paisa *(above) offered safe passage across Mongol trade routes. Genghis Khan (right) is portrayed by a 13th-century Chinese artist.*

wooden collar, Temujin supposedly escaped by using the collar to knock his enemy senseless.

Whatever the accuracy of the early tales, there is no doubt that by the time he was a young man, Temujin had acquired a wife, a household, and a leadership position among the clans. Through force and alliance, he pulled rival groups together under his sole control and built an army. Among the first to fall to his warriors was the rival Merkit tribe, which had brought Temujin's wrath upon themselves when they had stolen his young wife, Borte.

Next to succumb to Temujin's force were the Tatars; in a typical combination of ruthlessness and inclusiveness, Temujin ordered the killing of all Tatar males taller than the linchpin of a cartwheel, while adopting other Tatars as full members of his tribe.

By 1206, Temujin had conquered the Mongolian steppes. At an assembly of Mongol khans, he was named Genghis Khan, or Universal Ruler. According to the *Secret History,* the chieftains pledged: "We will make you Khan; you shall ride at our head, against our foes. We will throw ourselves like

1206–1227 Genghis Khan, first universal Mongol leader, reigns.

1211–1234 Mongols conquer northern China.

1219–1221 Persia falls to Mongols.

1237–1241 Russia added to Mongol conquests.

1258 Mongols capture Baghdad in brutal siege.

1264–1294 Khubilai Khan reigns in China.

1275 Marco Polo arrives in court of Khubilai Khan.

1279–1368 Yuan dynasty rules China.

1295 Conversion to Islam of Ilkhan ruler Ghazan.

Novgorod

Legnica
1241

Kamenets

Yaroslavl

Krakow

Tver
Moscow
Suzdal
Vladimir

Vladimir

Kolomna

RUSSIAN
PRINCIPALITIES

Ryazan

Kazan

Venice

Pest

Mohi
1241

Galich

Kiev

Chernigov

Bulgar

1229-1240

1236-1237

1241

Pereyaslav

Dnieper

Don

Volga

Ural

Ural Mts.

Irtysh

1242

Kalka
1223

New Sarai

KHANATE OF THE

1223

Mongols defeat
Byzantines, 1265

CRIMEA

Sudak

Tana

Old Sarai

GOLDEN HORDE

Black Sea

1223

Astrakhan

Constantinople

Ilkhan army defeated
by Golden Horde, 1263

Aral
Sea

Lake
Balkhash

Yanikant

Ankara

SELJUK SULTANATE
OF RUM

Sivas

Trebizond

Tiflis
1221

Derbent

Caspian
Sea

Jend
1219

Signak

KHWARAZM

Ysyk
Köl

CH

Kayseri

Erzincan

Erzurum

Ilkhan army defeats
Golden Horde, 1265

Khiva

Urgench

Otrar

Talas
1219

Balasaghun

1243
1243

Mediterranean Sea

Aleppo

1258-1260

Tabriz

Ardabil

1221

1220

Tashkent

Zarnuq

Banakat

Chodjend

Kashgar

K

Homs

Mosul

Maragheh

Bukhara

Nur

Samarkand

Tarim

Acre

Damascus

Ain Jalut
1260

Abril

Sultaniyeh

Alamut

Amol

Merv

Amu Darya

Jerusalem

Euphrates

Qazvin

Rayy 1220

Sabzevar

Nishapur

Tus

Sheberghan

Balkh

Taloqan

Hamadan

Qum

1229-1230

1258-1260

Baghdad
1258

Kashan

Kabul

Parwan

Peshawar

Srinagar

Isfahan

Yazd

Herat
Ilkhan army
defeats Chaghatai
army, 1270

Ghazni
1221

KASHMIR

Lahore

Nile

Tigris

ILKHAN
EMPIRE

Red Sea

Shiraz

Kerman

Persian Gulf

Multan
1221

Indus

Hormuz

Mecca

Growth of the Mongol Empire   ■ Mongol homeland   ■ 1227   □ 1241   □ 1259

Khambhat

Somnath

Arabian
Sea

Kozhikode

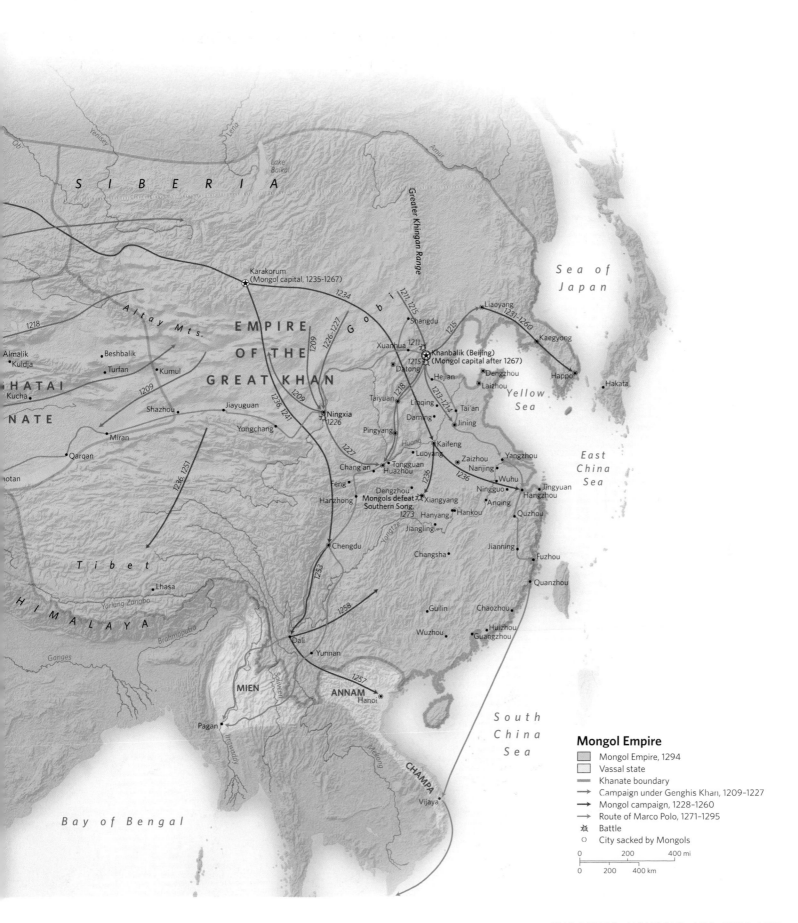

SIBERIA

Ob

Yenisey

Lena

Lake
Baikal

Amur

Greater Khingan Range

Sea of
Japan

Karakorum
(Mongol capital, 1235-1267)

1234

1211 1215

Shangdu

Altay Mts.

1218

EMPIRE

1209

1226-1227

G o b i

Liaoyang

1231-1260

Kaegyong

Almalik
Kuldja

Beshbalik

Turfan

Kumul

OF THE

Xuanhua

1211

Khanbalik (Beijing)
(Mongol capital after 1267)

Datong

Happo

HATAI

Kucha

1209

GREAT KHAN

1215

Hejian

Dengzhou

Hakata

NATE

Shazhou

Jiayuguan

Yongchang

1236 1241

1209

1227

Taiyuan

1218

Linqing

Daming

Pingyang

Ningxia
1226

1213-1274

Laizhou

Tai'an

Jining

Yellow
Sea

Miran

Qarqan

otan

1236, 1251

Huang

Luoyang

Kaifeng

Zaizhou

Nanjing

Yangzhou

East
China
Sea

Chang'an

Tongguan
Huazhou

1236

1236

Wuhu

Ningguo

Jingyuan

Feng

Hanzhong

Dengzhou
Mongols defeat
Southern Song,
1273

Xiangyang

Hanyang

Hankou

Anqing

Hangzhou

Quzhou

T i b e t

Chengdu

Jiangling

Changsha

Jianning

Fuzhou

Lhasa

Yarlung Zangbo

Yangtze

1253

1258

Quanzhou

H I M A L A Y A

Brahmaputra

Ganges

Dali

Yunnan

Gulin

Wuzhou

Chaozhou

Huizhou

Guangzhou

MIEN

Salween

1257

ANNAM
Hanoi

South
China
Sea

Pagan

Irrawaddy

Mekong

CHAMPA

Bay of Bengal

Vijaya

Mongol Empire

Mongol Empire, 1294

Vassal state

Khanate boundary

Campaign under Genghis Khan, 1209-1227

Mongol campaign, 1228-1260

Route of Marco Polo, 1271-1295

Battle

City sacked by Mongols

0   200   400 mi

0   200   400 km

THE MONGOL ARMY

The Mongol army was feared from Europe to China, and with good reason. The finest horsemen in the world, they were smart, tricky, and brutal. From infancy, Mongol children were taught to ride, to hunt, and eventually to shoot backward while standing in their stirrups. Young men participated in a great hunt in the fall, where they were organized into military units and judged on their prowess. The best hunters became elite soldiers.

On the move, the cavalry formed immense columns, signaling from front to back with flags and fires. As nomads, they knew how to travel rapidly and lightly, but they were well armed and armored: each soldier had a double-arched compound bow, a shield, a lasso, and a dagger; some also carried swords, javelins, battle-axes, or maces. Their beautifully balanced three-foot-long arrows were sometimes dipped in poison or salt to inflict extra pain. Quilted leather or mail formed their armor, and they carried hooks to snag the enemy's mail and drag the wearer to the ground. The Mongols of China, according to Marco Polo, also wore a mirror over their hearts to deflect evil.

The Mongols' scouts and spies told of weaknesses in the enemy's armament and walled cities. (The Mongols made their arrows shorter than Chinese arrows, so they couldn't be used with Chinese bows; this prevented the Chinese from reusing Mongol arrows from the battlefield.) Accompanying the fast-moving army were the support forces: wagons with food and fodder, foreign technicians to repair siege machines, and women whose duties included slitting the throats of downed enemies.

Genghis Khan holds a quiver of arrows.

Using techniques learned from Chinese captives, the Mongols besiege a Chinese fortress.

A Persian illustration depicts the tents of Genghis Khan's nomadic camp.

lightning on your enemies. We will bring you their finest women and girls, their rich tents like palaces."

Genghis Khan went on to lead one of the world's most successful armies. The warlord insisted that male children be trained in riding and archery almost from birth. By promoting soldiers on merit and forcing warriors to report to him, not to clan leaders, he broke the divisive power of the tribal groups. The army—at its peak containing no more than 125,000 Mongols—was divided into units of 10,000, 1,000, and 100 men. A new discipline was enforced. No more would raiders be allowed to invade a camp and then loot at leisure while the enemy fled; Mongol soldiers would pursue and annihilate the enemy first. Wives

and children of fallen soldiers would receive a share of the booty, ensuring their loyalty.

Genghis also molded Mongol society through his Great Yasa, a code of law governing proper behavior. The death penalty awaited adulterers, spies, sorcerers, those who defiled water, and many other transgressors. However, the code shows the leader's respect for learning and his religious tolerance as well. "Khan decided that no taxes or duties should be imposed upon fakirs, religious devotees, lawyers, physicians, scholars, people who devote themselves to prayer and asceticism, muezzins and those who wash the bodies of the

dead," noted later transcriptions of the code. "He ordered that all religions were to be respected and that no preference was to be shown to any of them. All this he commanded in order that it might be agreeable to Heaven."

Having unified their forces, the Mongols turned their attention toward their prosperous Asian neighbors with "their rich tents like palaces." Riding into northern China, the great khan was held off for a while with bribes from the Jurchen emperor, but eventually the Mongol army broke through the Great Wall. Driving refugees before them, the Mongols used captives as human shields as they besieged one city after another, starving and terrifying the inhabitants. The Mongols were not above trickery and propaganda, promising

at times to spare a city only to renege on their word, entering later and destroying it. Valuable craftsmen and specialists were captured and put to use. From Chinese engineers, the Mongols learned to build devastating siege weapons such as mangonels and trebuchets. In 1215, they razed the Jurchen capital of Zhongdu. The treacherous khan then returned to Mongolia to plan his next deadly attacks, leaving a general in charge of the Chinese territories.

For the next few years, the Mongols turned their attentions to lands to the west. Attempting to open up a trade relationship with Persia in 1218, Genghis Khan sent envoys and merchants to the Khwarazm shah. When the shah murdered his Mongol visitors, it so enraged the khan that he assembled a huge army and personally led it into Persia on a scorched-earth campaign, destroying city after city, massacring millions, even wiping out their irrigation system. Chroniclers told of mountains of skulls.

Not content with terrorizing the Persians, the Mongol armies also moved into Armenia, Ukraine, and the Crimea. There, for a time, they halted their westward expansion to look east again toward the rebellious Tanguts. Genghis handily suppressed them in 1227, but

Glazed fritware—Islamic pottery—
from the Ilkhanate era

then developed a fever and died. By the time of the great khan's death, the Mongols controlled Central Asia from Persia to northern China.

After a brief power struggle among Genghis's sons, the Mongol realm was divided among four heirs to form four khanates, in Central Asia, Persia, Russia, and China. Chief among his heirs was Ogodei, the new great khan. Building a Mongol capital city at Karakoram, on Mongolia's steppes, Ogodei encouraged traders to pass through with their textiles and jewels and welcomed practitioners of various religions, including Muslims, Christians, and Buddhists. As ambitious as his

---

ARCHAEOLOGY

SEARCHING FOR THE TOMB OF GENGHIS KHAN

In life he was a world-shaking conqueror, but in death he is a mystery. Genghis Khan died in 1227, but his tomb has never been found. Most researchers believe his body was returned to his Mongolian homeland. However, his retainers kept the location a secret, reputedly trampling traces of the burial under their horses' hooves. More recently, Russian occupiers kept the area off-limits.

In 2008, University of California San Diego researcher Albert Yu-Min Lin restarted the search using a new, noninvasive approach. Employing data-mining algorithms to scan satellite maps of northeastern Mongolia, Lin and his team are looking for unusual geometric shapes and other clues in the landscape in hopes of finding the tomb—without disturbing the sacred Mongolian land.

Researcher Albert Yu-Min Lin surveys the Mongolian wilderness with a native Mongolian.

father, Ogodei sent armies under his sons and grandsons, guided by experienced generals, in two directions: toward Europe and Russia in the west, and toward Song-dynasty China in the east. The Mongol horsemen swept ruthlessly across Russia, taking Moscow and Kiev and moving into Hungary. European observers were horrified as they watched the advance of the seemingly unstoppable "hordes," who spread "fire and slaughter wherever they went."

But Mongol politics spared Europe from what might have been a history-changing invasion: Even as the path lay open to Vienna, Ogodei died, and all Mongol chiefs were recalled to a council to choose a new great khan.

The title passed to Genghis's grandson Mongke, and after his death in 1259 to possibly the greatest of Genghis's descendants: Khubilai Khan. Khubilai represented a new kind of Mongol: cultured and settled—though just as aggressive in war. In 1271, Khubilai declared himself the new emperor of China and the progenitor of the Yuan dynasty, although it took him a few more years actually to subdue his tenacious Song opponents. Khubilai built a luxurious palace at his new capital of Khanbalik near the Yellow River—a city that eventually became Beijing. There, attended by his huge court, he received visitors from East and West and

An earthenware figure of a cheerful actor in costume, from the Yuan dynasty

Descendants of the Mongols, such as this young woman in traditional dress, form a rapidly growing, youthful society in modern-day Mongolia.

attempted to rule the resentful Chinese.

The most famous of his guests, to modern audiences, was the young Venetian merchant Marco Polo. Arriving at Khubilai's court in 1275, he became a favorite of the khan and stayed for 17 years. His admiring accounts of the Mongols, published in his *Travels,* describe the wealth of Khubilai's court, his numerous concubines, his herds of albino animals, his portable summer palace, and the curious (to Polo) use of paper currency.

Marco was impressed by the skill of Mongol warriors: "They avail themselves of bows more than of any other thing, for they are exceedingly good archers, the best in the world . . . They are good men and victorious in battle and mightily valiant and

PEOPLE

Modern Tatars pray in a temporary mosque in Ukraine.

THE TATARS

Vanquished, they ask no favor, and vanquishing, they show no compassion." In this passage from 1243, Richard Hakluyt described the Tatars, the Turkic/Mongol nomads who threatened Europe from Russia. Tatars were originally a collection of Turkic nomadic tribes conquered and partially assimilated by the Mongols in the early 13th century. As the Golden Horde, they dominated western Russia for a time but then dissolved into separate khanates in the 14th century. Unlike other Mongol peoples, they settled into stable, prosperous agricultural and trading societies. Crimean Tatars were persecuted and displaced under Joseph Stalin, but began to return to their homelands in the 1980s. Today, more than two million Tatars live in Siberia; in western Russian republics, including Tatarstan; and in Turkey. ✺

MONGOL WOMEN

The wide-ranging domestic and military skills of Mongol women impressed outsiders. According to Giovanni DiPlano Carpini, an envoy from Pope Innocent IV: "Girls and women ride and gallop as skillfully as men. We even saw them carrying quivers and bows, and the women can ride horses for as long as the men; they have shorter stirrups, handle horses very well, and mind all the property. The . . . women make everything: skin clothes, shoes, leggings, and everything made of leather. They drive carts and repair them, they load camels, and are quick and vigorous in all their tasks. They all wear trousers, and some of them shoot just like men." Marco Polo noted: "The women attend to their trading concerns, buy and sell, and provide everything necessary for their husbands and their families."

Women accompanied armies and sometimes fought in the rear guard. They could own property and were allowed to divorce their husbands. Mongol men could have many wives, if they could afford them—one reason that so many descendants of the khans are spread through the world today—but the first wife retained seniority and, in the case of royal wives, often had significant authority.

Nineteenth-century Mongolian women in their tent. Their ancestors formed the tough backbone of a warrior society.

Mongol conquerors shepherd their prisoners and loot, including livestock, during the invasion of Hungary in 1241.

they are very furious and have little care for their life, which they put to every risk without any regard." The young Polo also noted the khan's distinctly un-European welcome of various major religions—Christians, Muslims, Jews, and Buddhists—although Khubilai himself held to the shamanistic beliefs of his Mongol heritage.

Despite his accomplishments, Khubilai struggled as an administrator of his vast agricultural lands, so foreign to Mongol experience. The Mongol leaders and their Chinese subjects never blended well, holding each other in mutual disdain, and the Mongols ended the useful Confucian educational system. Khubilai's costly attempts to extend his empire east to Japan and south to Thailand, Burma, Java, and elsewhere failed repeatedly. The Japanese invasions were foiled twice by typhoons—to the Japanese, "divine winds." The Yuan dynasty faced economic problems with inflation inside China, as well as epidemics of bubonic plague, which spread to Europe. In 1368, 74 years after Khubilai's death, Chinese rebels captured the Mongol capital at Khanbalik and the Mongols returned to the steppes.

In Persia, Mongol rule started brutally with the bloody siege of Baghdad in 1258, the death of the Abbasid caliph, and the massacre of more than 200,000 inhabitants. Further advances into Egypt and Syria were foiled by the Mamluk army; reportedly, the Mamluks led the Mongol horsemen into rocky territory, where their unshod horses suffered. Meanwhile, they burned the grasslands that would feed the animals. Under Hulegu, Khubilai's brother, the Mongols settled in to rule Persia, but delegated most of the administration to

tartaroꝝ in hungariã temporibus regis Bele quarti

Persian bureaucrats. Hulegu acknowledged his allegiance to the great khan by naming his realm the Ilkhanate ("subordinate khanate"). Fairly quickly, however, the Mongol invaders were assimilated into Persian culture. By 1295, the Ilkhan ruler Ghazan converted to Islam and replaced the Mongol code with the *sharia,* Islamic law. Poor administrators there as elsewhere, the Mongols were overthrown in Persia by the nomad leader Timur and the Turks in the 14th century.

In Russia, the Mongols had a longer lasting influence. In part, this was because the societies they conquered were less sophisticated and closer to Mongol culture. Known as the Golden Horde, possibly because of Mongol leader Batu's supposedly golden

TIMUR THE LAME

With the collapse of the Mongol khanates in China and Persia, the peoples of Asia barely had time to breathe before they faced yet another conqueror. The intelligent, ruthless, limping Timur the Lame (1336–1405), or Tamerlane as Europeans came to call him, was a Turkish Muslim nomad who took inspiration from Genghis Khan. Seeing his opportunities in the power vacuum that followed the Mongol collapse, he led a growing band of nomad warriors to victory at Samarkand in 1370 and proclaimed himself the inheritor of the Chagatai khanate. Establishing his capital there, he set out for a lifetime of further conquest, rarely stopping to rest until his death. His court, including some or all of his nine wives, traveled with him.

Timur's armies moved through eastern Persia, the Near East, and the lands of the Golden Horde in Russia, where he occupied Moscow. He then turned to India, crossed the Indus in 1398, and sacked Delhi in a brutal attack—slaughtering, by some accounts, hundreds of thousands of its men, women, and children. He was preparing an invasion of China in 1405 when he died.

Like his hero Genghis, Timur had little desire to settle or administer his territories. He was interested in the treasure he could loot from wealthy conquered cities, much of which went to build his capital in Samarkand. Here, Timur's bloody victories eventually supported a renaissance of Islamic learning under his successors. ✢

The conqueror's silver coins (above), and a bronze chandelier commissioned for a mausoleum in Kazakhstan. Timur (left) enjoys a rare moment of rest in the Persian city of Balkh.

A mounted Mongol archer, shown in a lithograph from a Chinese drawing

At its height in the 13th century, the Mongol Empire controlled territory from the Arctic Ocean to the Strait of Malacca, and from the Pacific Ocean to Hungary—between 11 and 12 million square miles. Brilliant and pitiless warriors, the Mongols did not have the skills to successfully

> *"Experience certainly taught me that a good idea can do more than an army of 100,000."*
>
> TIMUR,
> FROM HIS AUTOBIOGRAPHY

rule most of the lands they conquered. ("The empire was created on horseback, but it cannot be governed on horseback," observed Ogodei.) They left little behind in terms of tangible culture: no distinctive architecture, literature, crafts, or religion. However, they appreciated skill and learning in others and went far toward integrating Eastern and Western cultures by maintaining trade routes and resettling captured peoples, particularly prized craftsmen and scholars. Religions, foods, technologies, medicine, and more spread from east to west along Mongol roads.

Perhaps the most enduring legacy of the Mongols is genetic. Researchers have traced a direct genetic link between the ruling Mongol family and approximately 8 percent of the men in the regions of the former Mongol Empire—meaning that about 0.5 percent of the world's population today may be descended from Genghis Khan.

tent, the Russian Mongols ruled from the Urals into Siberia. They prized the region's pastures but had less use for its cities, viewing them primarily as sources of tribute. They, too, became gradually Islamicized, and, like the Ilkhans, most were eventually overthrown by Timur's invading forces in 1395. In the Crimea, however, the Golden

Horde Mongols continued to occupy the land until the 20th century.

The khanate of Chagatai, smallest of the Mongol territories, encompassed the conquered cities of Bukhara and Samarkand and traditional nomadic pasturelands of Central Asia. Gradually the Chagatai Mongols, too, became assimilated and Muslim and, like their brethren in Persia and Russia, were overcome by Timur and his Turkish armies.

MING
The Brilliant Dynasty

By the middle of the 14th century, Chinese society was fracturing under the stresses of plague, famine, and the demands of an overstretched Mongol government. Rebel groups such as the Red Turbans attracted followers who sought to overthrow the Mongol Yuan dynasty, still seen as outsiders after a century and a half. Rising to the fore in these rebellions was one of China's most remarkable figures: Zhu Yuanzhang.

Zhu was a peasant and orphan whose parents had given away several of their children just to ensure their survival. Like other impoverished youths, he became a Buddhist monk and spent years begging through the countryside. In 1352, he joined the Red Turbans, where he showed a gift for command, soon collecting supporters and troops who took the city of Nanjing in 1355. Using this southern city as his base, Zhu continued to move toward the Yuan capital of Beijing. As he fought, he also studied with scholars who joined his movement. In 1367, Zhu's troops took Beijing and the former Mongol rulers fled to Inner Mongolia. He declared himself founder of a new dynasty—the Ming ("brilliant")—in

1368. Zhu is usually known as the Hongwu Emperor, a title taken from the period in which he reigned.

Unlike his Mongol predecessors, Hongwu ruled from Nanjing, where he built almost 30 miles of encircling walls. Said to be ugly and pockmarked, he was an energetic but paranoid and despotic ruler. Loyal to his peasant origins, he lowered taxes on farmers and raised them on the rich. Hongwu's control extended down to the village level, where core groups of families were assigned the task of collecting taxes and assigning labor. Through decrees read aloud in villages, the emperor attempted to bring society into order through filial piety and harmony toward neighbors.

Despite his sympathy for villagers, Hongwu resisted the idea of a meritocracy. Military leaders, including his own sons, were made into noblemen with hereditary titles, superior to civil servants. Although Hongwu eventually reinstated the Confucian exam system for the civil service, he remained intensely suspicious of scholars. "They write books to establish doctrine," he wrote, "but all this amounts to is chewing on phrases and biting on words to the ruination of their students."

Ming-era China prospered by exporting such products as glazed ceramics (above) and tea (right).

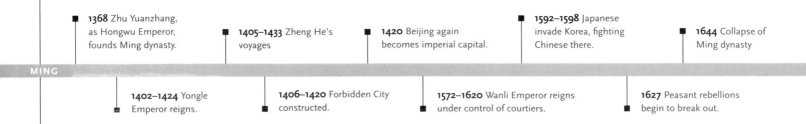

1368 Zhu Yuanzhang, as Hongwu Emperor, founds Ming dynasty.

1402–1424 Yongle Emperor reigns.

1405–1433 Zheng He's voyages

1406–1420 Forbidden City constructed.

1420 Beijing again becomes imperial capital.

1572–1620 Wanli Emperor reigns under control of courtiers.

1592–1598 Japanese invade Korea, fighting Chinese there.

1627 Peasant rebellions begin to break out.

1644 Collapse of Ming dynasty

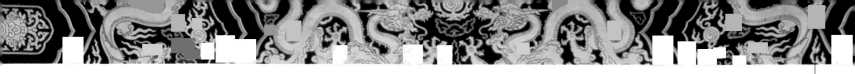

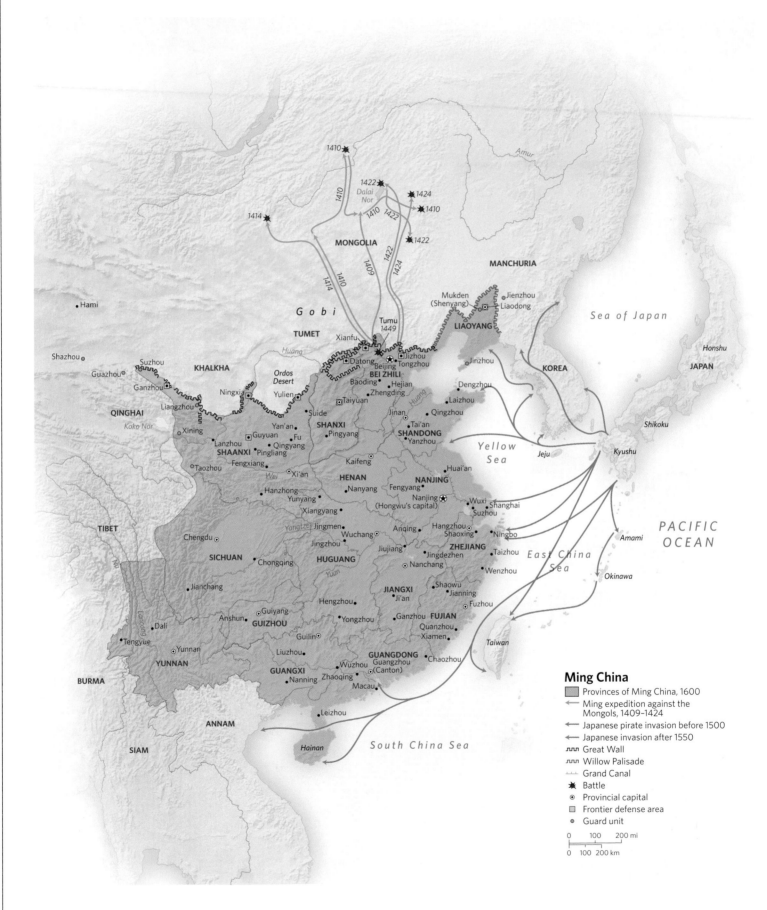

1410 ✹

1422 ✹
Dalai Nor
✹ 1424

1414 ✹
1410
1422
1410 ✹ 1410

1409
1422
1424

1422 ✹ 1422

• Hami

G o b i

TUMET

MONGOLIA

MANCHURIA

Mukden
(Shenyang) • • Jienzhou
Liaodong

Tumu
1449

• Shazhou

KHALKHA

Xianfu

LIAOYANG

• Jinzhou

KOREA

Sea of Japan

Honshu

JAPAN

Suzhou •
• Guazhou
Ganzhou

Huang

Datong •
Beijing ★ • Jizhou
• Tongzhou

• Dengzhou

QINGHAI

Liangzhou

Koko Nor

Ningxia •
*Ordos
Desert*
Yulien •

Baoding • • Hejian
Zhengding •

BEI ZHILI

• Laizhou

Taiyuan •

Huang

Jinan •

• Qingzhou

Shikoku

• Xining

Lanzhou •
• Guyuan
Qingyang •

Suide •

SHANXI
Pingyang •

• Tai'an
SHANDONG
Yanzhou •

*Yellow
Sea*

• Jeju

Kyushu

SHAANXI
Taozhou •

Yan'an •
Fu •

Pingliang •
Fengxiang •

Wei
• Xi'an

Kaifeng •

• Huai'an

*East China
Sea*

PACIFIC
OCEAN

TIBET

Hanzhong •
Yunyang •

HENAN
• Nanyang

Xiangyang •

Fengyang •
NANJING
Nanjing ★
(Hongwu's capital)

• Wuxi
Suzhou • Shanghai

Amami

Yangtze
Chengdu ☉

Jingmen •
Wuchang •

Jingzhou •

Anqing •
Hangzhou •
Shaoxing •

• Ningbo

• Okinawa

SICHUAN
Chongqing •

HUGUANG

Yuan

Jiujiang •

ZHEJIANG
Jingdezhen •

• Nanchang

Taizhou •

• Wenzhou

• Jianchang

Hengzhou •

JIANGXI
Ji'an •

Shaowu •
• Jianning

Lancang

Anshun •
• Guiyang
GUIZHOU

Yongzhou •

Ganzhou •
FUJIAN

• Fuzhou

• Dali
Tengyue •

Guilin •

Liuzhou •

Quanzhou •
Xiamen •

Taiwan

• Yunnan

GUANGDONG
Wuzhou • Guangzhou
(Canton)

• Chaozhou

YUNNAN

GUANGXI
• Nanning
Zhaoqing •

BURMA

Macau •

• Leizhou

ANNAM

Hainan

SIAM

South China Sea

Ming China

⬛ Provinces of Ming China, 1600

→ Ming expedition against the
Mongols, 1409–1424

← Japanese pirate invasion before 1500

← Japanese invasion after 1550

〰 Great Wall

〰 Willow Palisade

⊥ Grand Canal

✹ Battle

☉ Provincial capital

⬜ Frontier defense area

• Guard unit

0   100   200 mi

0   100 200 km

> *"The Yuan dynasty had risen from the desert to enter and rule over Zhongguo [China] for more than a hundred years . . . and the affairs of Zhongguo were in a state of disorder . . . But when the nation began to arouse itself, We, as a simple peasant of Huai-yu, conceived the patriotic idea to save the people."*

HONGWU EMPEROR, MANIFESTO OF ACCESSION AS FIRST MING EMPEROR

He also raised political paranoia to new heights. Not content with executing his prime minister in 1380 for suspected crimes, Hongwu also investigated and executed some 30,000 others in a 14-year purge. A general who spoke up in 1393 was killed along with his suspected associates and all of their extended families: 14,000 people in all. Others who came under suspicion during Hongwu's reign were slightly luckier, suffering only savage beatings with bamboo rods.

It was tiring and thankless work, Hongwu complained. "In the morning I punish a few; by evening others commit the same crime. I punish these in the evening and by the next morning again there are violations. Although the corpses of the first have not been removed, already others follow in their path . . . Day and night I cannot rest."

Militarily, Hongwu extended Ming control through former Mongol territories as well as into tribal realms in the southwest, eventually controlling the area of modern northern and eastern China. When his powerful and—to that point, successful—envoys ventured into Samarkand in Central Asia, however, they were imprisoned by the nomad warrior Timur; only Timur's death in 1405 spared China from an invasion by this destructive conqueror.

It's hard to imagine that anyone mourned Hongwu when he died in 1398. After a bloody three-year scrimmage among claimants to the throne, Hongwu's fourth son deposed the rightful, teenage heir and seized control under the name Yongle. The new emperor then moved the capital away from Nanjing (burned during the struggle for succession) and back to Beijing.

Yongle, who reigned from 1402 until 1424, appears to have been as strong-willed as his father, but more inclined to extravagant projects. In 1406, he commissioned

In the Ming dynasty, a woman's domain was typically limited to the household, but there she could wield considerable power.

The Palace's Hall of Supreme Harmony, reached by three tiers of steps, was by law the tallest building in the Chinese empire.

Dragon Throne. Emperor's gilded, dragon-shaped chair.

Double-eaved hipped roof signified the highest-ranking edifice.

Exposed beams, intricately painted.

Terrace. Nobility kowtowed in front of the emperor.

Imperial Way. Restricted to the emperor alone.

The emperor receives supplicants from his sandalwood throne.

THE FORBIDDEN CITY

China's Forbidden City, once off-limits to all but a few, is now the Palace Museum and one of the world's most visited sites. The rectangular palace complex sits at the very heart of Beijing, its 183 acres surrounded by 33-foot-high walls and a moat. Laid out according to the principles of feng shui, it is oriented north-south, with the most important buildings along the central axis. Each of the four sides is accessed by a gate—the Wu (Meridian) Gate being the formal entrance on the south.

Almost 10,000 rooms make up the vast, symmetrical complex. In the Ming era, the northern portion formed the inner court, the emperor's private residences. The southern, or outer, court was public, featuring a plaza large enough for parading troops or throngs of adoring subjects, and three major administration buildings, including the soaring Hall of Supreme Harmony, which housed the emperor's throne.

In the northeast, three halls hold the Treasure Gallery, containing porcelain, silver and gold, imperial silk robes, jewelry, and other rare artifacts. Beyond the Gate of Terrestrial Tranquility, the Imperial Garden's trees, flowers, sculptures, and pavilions once offered respite to the imperial family.

The Forbidden City is open to visitors year-round, for a fee. To avoid the worst of the crowds, go during spring or fall and avoid weekends and Chinese holidays.

Bronze lions guard the Gate of Supreme Harmony.

Ming-dynasty porcelain was
valued around the world.

the building of the
Forbidden City imperial
palace complex in the center of Beijing. The con-
struction of this impressive
set of buildings took up
most of his remaining life,

and he moved into the vast, graceful palace
only in 1420. Because the reinstated capital
of Beijing needed grain supplies from the
south, Yongle also ordered the restoration
of the 1,085-mile Grand Canal that linked
Hangzhou in the south, on the Yangtze
River delta, to Beijing. A transport army
of 160,000 soldiers pulled grain barges
through the canal's 15 locks.

But perhaps the most remarkable of
Yongle's ventures was the series of sea voyages he sponsored. Beginning in 1405 and
ending under a successor in 1433, vast
fleets of huge ships sailed on seven expeditions from the Chinese coast as far as the
Persian Gulf and Kenya. All were commanded by the outstanding admiral Zheng
He. A Muslim, Zheng had been captured

A vast Chinese armada fills the waters behind admiral Zheng He's flagship. As many as 317 ships took part in Zheng's seven voyages.

the fleet around Southeast Asia and into the Indian Ocean, with stops in Vietnam, Java, Sri Lanka, Sumatra, India, and elsewhere. The last three expeditions ventured even farther to Hormuz and the east coast of Africa. An inscription ordered later by Zheng reads: "We have traversed more than one hundred thousand *li* of immense water spaces and have beheld in the ocean huge waves like mountains rising sky-high, and we have set eyes on barbarian regions far away hidden in a blue transparency of light vapors, while our sails loftily unfurled like clouds day and night."

The armada was intended neither for exploration nor for warfare. Although it carried soldiers, its main purpose was to exchange gifts and collect tribute from other states, as well as to impress the world with the might of the Ming. Spices, gems, and exotic animals returned to China. Particularly valued were the giraffes, believed to resemble the legendary *qilin,* a unicorn-like creature. "From the edge of the sky to the ends of the earth there are none who have not become subjects and slaves," reads Zheng's inscription. "The barbarians from beyond the seas, even those who are truly distant . . . have come to court bearing precious objects and presents."

Zheng He's voyages were the first and last great seafaring ventures of any Chinese empire. In one of history's enduring mysteries, China

as a boy during Hongwu's early campaigns, castrated, and placed into the service of the young prince who would become Yongle, for whom he became a close adviser.

At what must have been great expense, Yongle built a flotilla of roughly 300 ships, the largest of which, the *baochuan,* were five times as big as any other vessel in the world at the time. Each two-year voyage took

THE GREAT NAVY OF ZHENG HE

Zheng He's huge fleet encompassed ships of all sizes, from water tankers and supply ships to the great *baochuan,* the treasure vessels. Built to carry riches ranging from porcelain to giraffes, these great ships would have made Columbus's fleet look like three of their dinghies. Close to 500 feet long, the largest of the bulky vessels displaced 10,000 tons and carried nine masts. No intact ships remain for study, but one rudderpost, unearthed in a Ming shipyard, measured 36 feet long. Although most Chinese ships of the time had flattened, pan-shaped hulls, Zheng's fleet was probably built by a Nanjing shipyard that specialized in the more seaworthy V-shaped hulls.

More than 27,000 soldiers and sailors crewed the fleet, accompanied by their horses. The entire armada, more than 300 ships at its greatest extent, would have filled the ocean's horizon from end to end. A contemporary account does not seem to exaggerate when it states, "The ships which sail the Southern Sea are like houses. When their sails are spread they are like great clouds in the sky."

An 18th-century Chinese map, supposedly a copy of one from 1418, showing that Zheng He sailed to North America. Most experts believe it is a fake.

canceled any further voyages after 1433, and the naval fleet was left to rot (although commercial shipping continued in Asia). Certainly the expense was a factor, as were the distractions and costs of various land wars. China became increasingly isolationist, suspicious of foreigners, and uninterested in seaborne exploration.

Yongle's military campaigns undoubtedly used up men and resources. Ill-considered attacks on Vietnam and Cambodia dragged on for 20 years until the Ming withdrew in 1427, three years after Yongle's death. In the last years of his life, he also countered the ever-present threat

---

PEOPLE

TANG SAI'ER

Secret societies were often at the heart of Chinese rebellions. The messianic Buddhist White Lotus society was one such, arising in the 13th century and lasting until the 1800s in various incarnations. Among its most remarkable leaders was a woman, Tang Sai'er, who remains wreathed in mystical legend.

A native of Shandong, Tang was a devout Buddhist and religious teacher. In 1420, she joined and eventually led an army in an uprising that spread throughout local provinces. According to contemporary accounts, she possessed magical powers. A spell book and a magic sword, found near her husband's grave, allowed her to feed and provide for her followers. She could command supernatural creatures in battle and once defeated the enemy by changing paper dolls into flying demons.

Authorities put down her uprising, but Tang managed to elude them (either through sorcery or disguised as a nun, depending on the account). Despite an extensive search ordered by the Yongle Emperor himself, she was never found—ensuring her lasting fame as a supernatural heroine.

"Even after repeated Ming punitive attacks, more than a million Mongol warriors continued to use their bows and arrows... the Mongols still covered several thousand li [kilometers]."

GU YINGTAI

of the Mongols to the north by setting up expensive defensive posts. The Mongol menace became even more apparent in the reign of Yongle's hapless great-grandson, the Zhengtong Emperor. On the advice of his chief adviser, the eunuch Wang Zhen, the 21-year-old emperor personally led a campaign against the formidable Mongol leader Esen Taiji in 1449. In a humiliating episode known as the Tumu Incident, the Mongols routed the Ming troops at a station called Tumu. The emperor got off his horse and sat on the ground, where he was promptly captured. His brother took the throne as the Jingtai Emperor, only to face further embarrassment when the Mongols returned the unharmed, unwanted, and unransomed Zhengtong. Now there were two emperors—a convenient redundancy when plotters decided to depose Jingtai in 1457 and reinstate Zhengtong. The once and future emperor acquired a new reign name—Tianshun—and ruled as his eunuchs' puppet for another seven years.

The continuing Mongol threat inspired another of the Ming dynasty's great works: the reconstruction of the Great Wall. Begun as early as the Qin dynasty, the intermittent

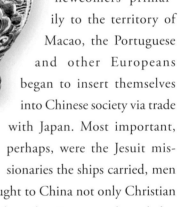

All Ming porcelain, such as this vase, had to meet high standards.

wall had fallen into disrepair. Under the later Ming emperors, thousands of miles of wall were rebuilt and extended along the northern frontier, dotted with forts and signaling stations.

Meanwhile, foreigners of another stripe were arriving via the sea. In 1514, a Portuguese fleet sailed into Guangzhou. Though the mistrustful Chinese officials confined the newcomers primarily to the territory of Macao, the Portuguese and other Europeans began to insert themselves into Chinese society via trade with Japan. Most important, perhaps, were the Jesuit missionaries the ships carried, men who brought to China not only Christian doctrine but also European knowledge and technology, such as clocks, maps, and astronomy. In turn, Jesuit scholars such as Matteo Ricci reported back to Rome on the insular wonders of Chinese society. "The extent of their kingdom is so vast, its borders so distant," he wrote, "and their utter lack of knowledge of a transmaritime world is so complete that the Chinese

---

Jesuit priest Matteo Ricci and another Christian missionary. Ricci recorded his observations of Chinese society in his reports to Rome.

Glazed Ming figurines depict the expiring Buddha and his attendants. At least six schools of Buddhism coexisted in the Ming era.

imagine the whole world as included in their kingdom."

Ricci also noted the influence of scholars on Chinese policy. "Another remarkable fact and quite worthy of note as marking a difference from the West, is that the entire kingdom is administered by the Order of the Learned, commonly known as The Philosophers. The responsibility for the orderly management of the entire realm is wholly and completely committed to their charge and care. The army, both officers and soldiers, hold them in high respect and show them the promptest obedience and deference, and not infrequently the military are disciplined by them as a schoolboy might be punished by his master."

Ricci was observing the effects of the educated civil service and its exam system. Abandoned during the Yuan dynasty, Confucian schools and rigorous examinations for official positions were revived under the Ming. Students had to master the contents of the "Four Books" of Confucian philosophy: *The Analects,*

Mencius, Doctrine of the Mean, and *Great Learning.* Hundreds of thousands of male students from every province studied the ancient texts to pass the tough exams; successful candidates then had to pass even more difficult tests, the *jinshi,* to ascend to higher and more prestigious ranks of government bureaucracy.

Despite occasional upheavals, the Ming era was productive. The population more than doubled to about 275 million, supported by a stable government. Agriculture included crops imported from the New World—corn, groundnuts, sweet potatoes,

cotton, sugarcane. Kilns such as those at Jingdezhen produced the famous Ming porcelain, which became a prime export, along with tea and silk. Wealthy families lived in elegant walled homes and became connoisseurs of the visual arts, theater, and literature. Painting and calligraphy thrived; artists such as Shen Zhou, Dong Qichang, and Wen Zhengming depicted refined and delicate landscapes.

The popular novel flourished as well. *The Water Margin,* for example, celebrates the heroism of 108 outlaws who fight corrupt officials during the Song dynasty. *Romance of the Three Kingdoms* is a complex tale of conflict during the late Han dynasty. And the racy *Plum in the Golden*

"The simplicity of Chinese printing is what accounts for the exceedingly large numbers of books in circulation here and the ridiculously low prices at which they are sold."

FATHER MATTEO RICCI, FROM HIS JOURNALS

THE GREAT WALL

Running some 4,500 miles east to west across northern China, from the Gulf of Chihli to southern Mongolia, China's Great Wall is really an overlapping line of multiple walls. Built and rebuilt over the course of 2,000 years, it began as a disconnected series of short walls in early Chinese history. Fearing the eternal threat of warriors from the north, the First Emperor, Qin Shi Huangdi, put hundreds of thousands of laborers to the brutal task of linking and extending the wall in the early third century B.C. During subsequent dynasties, the wall was alternately repaired or allowed to crumble, and when the Mongols took control during the Yuan dynasty, it was neglected: They, of all people, had little to fear from northern nomads.

That fear returned with a vengeance to Ming rulers, particularly during the reign of the Hongzhi Emperor (1487–1505), who ordered the wall strengthened and towers added. Twenty-one feet wide at its base and about 23 to 26 feet high, it was constructed from earth, bricks, stone, and wooden boards and featured crenellations at the top to shield archers. West of Juyongguan Pass, it was split into outer and inner walls, with signal towers every 600 feet and strategically located fortresses. Advances in warfare eventually rendered the wall useless as a defense, but today it is a UNESCO World Heritage site and a major source of pride and tourist revenue in China. ❧

The crenellations of the Great Wall catch the afternoon light at Juyongguan Pass, near Beijing.

Ming-dynasty children at play. The population grew during the Ming era, straining the country's resources.

Vase depicts the exploits, erotic and otherwise, of a merchant and his wives and concubines. Father Ricci commented that, despite the difficulty of carving printing blocks involving thousands of Chinese characters, "a skilled printer can make copies with incredible speed, turning out as many as fifteen hundred copies in a single day." Many of the books were illustrated with intricate woodcuts, some in color.

But the arts were largely created and enjoyed by the upper ranks of society. By the 17th century, the majority of the Chinese populace was struggling. The growing population strained agricultural capacities. The extended imperial family, all living on stipends from the government, began to eat at the budget. So, too, did military campaigns against Japanese invaders in Korea.

Meanwhile, conflicts between Japanese officials and foreign traders led to an abrupt drop in the flow of silver into

China, leading to deflation and food hoarding. Adding to the stresses were natural disasters. The "little ice age" that brought harsh winters worldwide reduced harvests, while epidemics swept through China in the early part of the century. Famine spread.

Ming authorities were unable to combat the fiscal and natural collapse. A succession of feeble emperors controlled by eunuchs had weakened the government. The situation hit a low point under the Wanli Emperor, who isolated himself within the Forbidden City and relied on a corrupt cadre of eunuchs to deal with the outside world.

> *"Your letter says: 'Recent scholars have devoted themselves to external things and have lost interest in the internal.' . . . My disciple, you thoroughly apprehend the defects of the present age."*
>
> WANG YANGMING, LETTERS

Unemployed soldiers and other disaffected men and women formed rebel groups. In the 1630s, a laid-off postal worker named Li Zicheng took control and led what had become a widespread rebellion. Like a Chinese Robin Hood, he took from the landowning rich and gave to the starving poor, building a loyal following. In 1644, Li and his troops took Beijing. Chongzen, the 16th and final Ming emperor, was betrayed by his own eunuchs and hanged himself as the rebels entered the undefended city.

But Li did not enjoy his victory for long. Even as he began a program of reforms, China's perpetual nemesis—invaders from

MAKING PORCELAIN AT JINGDEZHEN

Among the Ming dynasty's most valuable products were the exquisite pieces of porcelain produced by the kilns at the city of Jingdezhen, in Jiangxi Province. The kilns had been in use for centuries. They were ideally located next to deposits of the particular white clay (kaolin) and grayish stone needed for the porcelain, with stands of pine trees nearby for fuel and the Chang River for transport.

Jingdezhen was a clockwork operation. During the Ming era, at least 58 official kilns and additional private ones were kept in business making the delicate ware. The kilns were overseen by a government office that ensured high-quality production. Researchers have found great piles of shards nearby—pottery broken and discarded because it did not meet standards. Workers were specialists: Some shaped the pottery, others applied underglaze; some sketched outlines while others painted. Official reign-marks or inscriptions were added at the end.

A portion of the porcelain was created exclusively for the court, and some was profitably exported. A Portuguese observer noted: "The clay is so fine and transparent that the whites outshine crystal and alabaster, and the pieces which are decorated in blue dumbfound the eyes, seeming a combination of alabaster and sapphires." Even when the xenophobic Hongwu Emperor prohibited overseas trade, smugglers managed to sneak porcelain to coastal vessels and out to the wider world. Semiofficial trade continued through the Qing dynasty, with hundreds of thousands of pieces leaving China through Dutch and Portuguese traders, destined for the tables of Europe.

During the Ming era, the kilns at Jingdezhen were known for their blue-and-white porcelain, glazed using both imported and locally mined cobalt.

WEI ZHONGXIAN

With the exception of the seafarer Zheng He, eunuchs have largely figured as villains in Chinese history. The worst of them, by most accounts, was the notorious Wei Zhongxian (1568–1627). Starting his career as a servant to the mother of the Tianqi Emperor, he befriended the young monarch's nurse and gained the boy's trust.

The boy was uninterested in ruling, and after he reached the throne at the age of 15, he gave control of the government to the eunuch. Wei instituted his own corps of eunuch troops and spies, enriched himself with taxes, and had temples erected in his own honor around the country. In 1624, when Confucian scholars from the Donglin Academy submitted a protest accusing Wei of major crimes, hundreds of their leaders and supporters were arrested and tortured to death. Wei continued to wield power until the emperor's death in 1627, after which he was forced to commit suicide. ✑

A Chinese hand puppet from the era of plays criticizing Wei Zhongxian

A 17th-century ink drawing of one of the ten Daoist Kings of Hell, Dushi Huang. He runs the Grand Noisy Hell, also known as the Suffocation Hell.

the north—made their move. This time it was not the Mongols who swept in, though, but the Jurchens.

The Jurchens were agrarian tribes living in what is now Manchuria, where they were influenced by both Mongol and Han (Chinese) culture. In the 12th century, as the Jin dynasty, they had ruled northern China before being ousted by the Mongols and the Song. They began to set their sights on China again under the command of Nurhaci, an impressive Jurchen general. In the early 17th century, Nurhaci had gained control of trade between the Ming and the Jurchen and then moved on to military ventures. He collected a diverse army of Chinese and Mongol soldiers into banner units, each with its own flag but reporting to him. His son, Huang Taiji, took over from him and managed to defeat a Mongol descendant of Khubilai Khan and claim the title of great khan for himself. Commanding a Mongol/Chinese army stocked with defecting Ming soldiers, he renamed his people the Manchu and declared himself the head of a new Chinese dynasty, the Qing. After he died in 1643, his five-year-old son inherited, but Huang's brother Dorgon was the regent and real ruler.

As Li Zicheng's rebel armies moved into Beijing, Ming loyalists asked the Manchu for help and got more than they bargained for. After a Ming general opened up the Great Wall to their troops, the Manchu rode into Beijing and drove out Li, but then took the capital for themselves and left the Ming in the cold. By 1644, the almost 300-year-old Ming dynasty had ended and the Qing had begun.

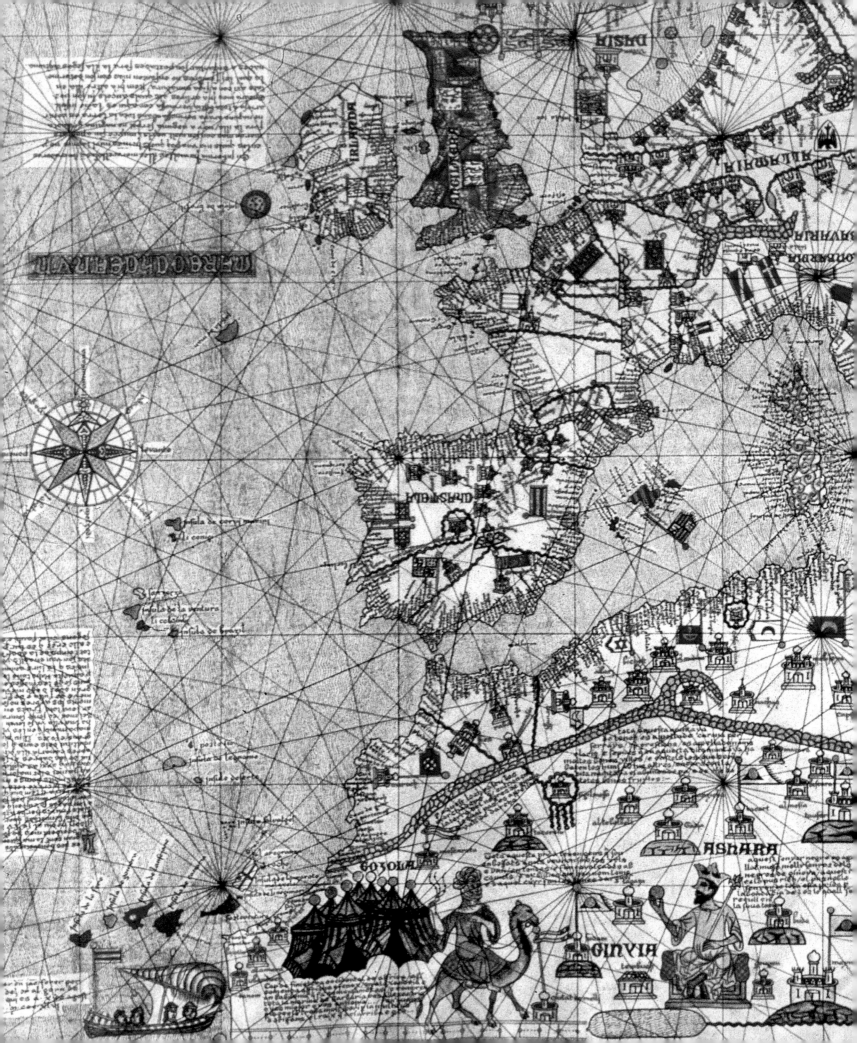

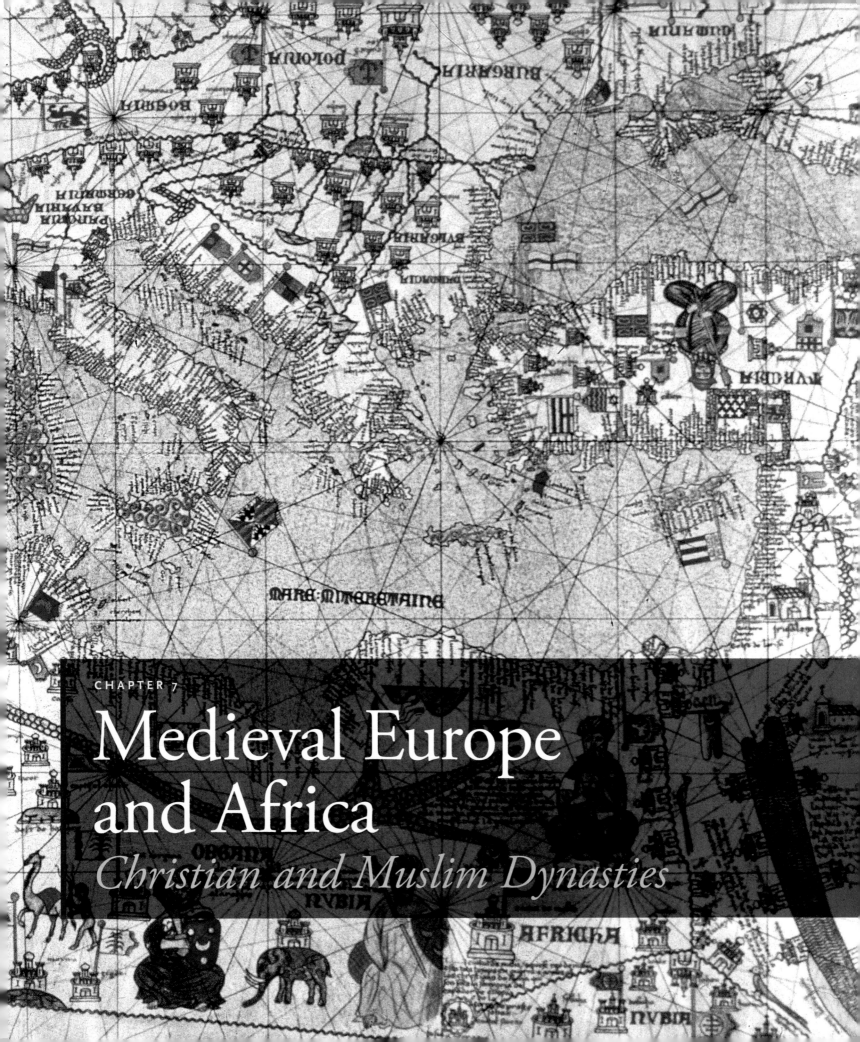

CHAPTER 7

Medieval Europe
and Africa
Christian and Muslim Dynasties

HOLY ROMAN EMPIRE
New Powers, Old Institutions

On Christmas Day 800, at St. Peter's Basilica in Rome, King Charlemagne of the Franks was crowned Imperatore Romanorum (emperor of the Romans) by Pope Leo III. The old Roman Empire had collapsed in 476 when the city fell to Germanic invaders, but the idea of Roman supremacy lived on. Many of those invaders, including the Franks, adopted Roman Catholicism and worshiped in Latin, the language in which Charles the Great, or Charlemagne, was hailed at his coronation. As emperor, he was honored as Augustus, like Roman rulers of old. But unlike his pagan predecessors, he was "crowned by God," meaning that he was elevated to his position by the pope in God's name. From this ceremony uniting worldly might with spiritual authority came the Holy Roman Empire, a great power in medieval Europe.

Charlemagne and later Holy Roman emperors were not without rivals. A similar combination of ambition and piety led Muslim commanders to cross from North Africa and conquer most of Spain. At the same time, Muslim

This bust of Charlemagne contains part of the emperor's skull and was carried during coronations in Aachen, Germany. His life is retold in 12th-century stained glass (right) at Chartres Cathedral in France.

traders were traversing the Sahara Desert and providing rulers in West Africa with new sources of wealth and inspiration, contributing to the rise of Islamic empires there. Not until the late Middle Ages did expansive new kingdoms emerge in western Europe that overshadowed the Holy Roman Empire, ended Muslim rule in Spain, and began imposing themselves on Africa.

The rise of the Franks began in earnest in 481, when a dynamic ruler named Clovis became king and greatly expanded the domain of his people. The collapse of the Roman Empire in the West allowed the Franks to advance south from their homeland along the Rhine River and occupy the former Roman province of Gaul, the country known today as France after the Franks. Many Germanic tribes made similar advances during that time, but none did more to consolidate their gains politically than the Franks under Clovis.

Clovis recognized that, while Roman power had waned, Roman institutions endured—notably the Catholic Church, which was organized hierarchically like the Roman Empire. Local priests were supervised by bishops under the

481 Clovis becomes king of the Franks.

732 Charles Martel wins Battle of Tours and founds Carolingian dynasty.

800 Pope Leo III crowns Charlemagne at St. Peter's in Rome.

962 Otto crowned emperor by Pope John XII.

1273 Rudolf I becomes emperor, first of Habsburg dynasty.

511 Clovis dies, bequeathing power to his four sons.

771 Charlemagne becomes sole ruler of Frankish kingdom.

844 Charles the Bald divides empire with Lothar and Louis the German.

1077 Barefoot and penitent, Emperor Henry IV reenters Catholic fold.

1519–1556 Charles V rules Holy Roman Empire.

A 15th-century parchment shows the capture of Frankish hero Charles Martel at the battle of Cologne. The sapphire talisman at right was found in Charlemagne's tomb.

supreme authority of the pope, who held the Roman title *pontifex maximus,* chief priest. Clovis's wife Clotilda, a devout Catholic, encouraged him to convert, and political considerations supported the idea, as well. His conversion reassured Catholics in Gaul and helped reinforce his alliance with the Byzantine Empire in Constantinople, where Christians had not yet formed an Orthodox Church distinct from the Roman Church. Clovis also adopted a legal code based partly on Roman law, which helped him and his successors maintain order.

The Franks were not able to avoid the political turmoil that afflicted other Germanic kingdoms, however. Clovis, who died in 511 and was buried at a church in Paris that he and Clotilda established, followed the Frankish custom of bequeathing power to all four of his sons, who expanded the domain of their Merovingian dynasty while at the same time vying with each other for supremacy. Eventually, the kingdom was divided between heirs who lost power to officials known as mayors of the palace, supported by nobles. In the early eighth century, a mayor of the palace called Charles Martel ("the Hammer") reunited the Franks by force of arms and challenged Muslims who had advanced from Spain into France, defeating them in 732 at the Battle of Tours. Charles founded the Carolingian dynasty, which reached its peak under his energetic grandson Charlemagne.

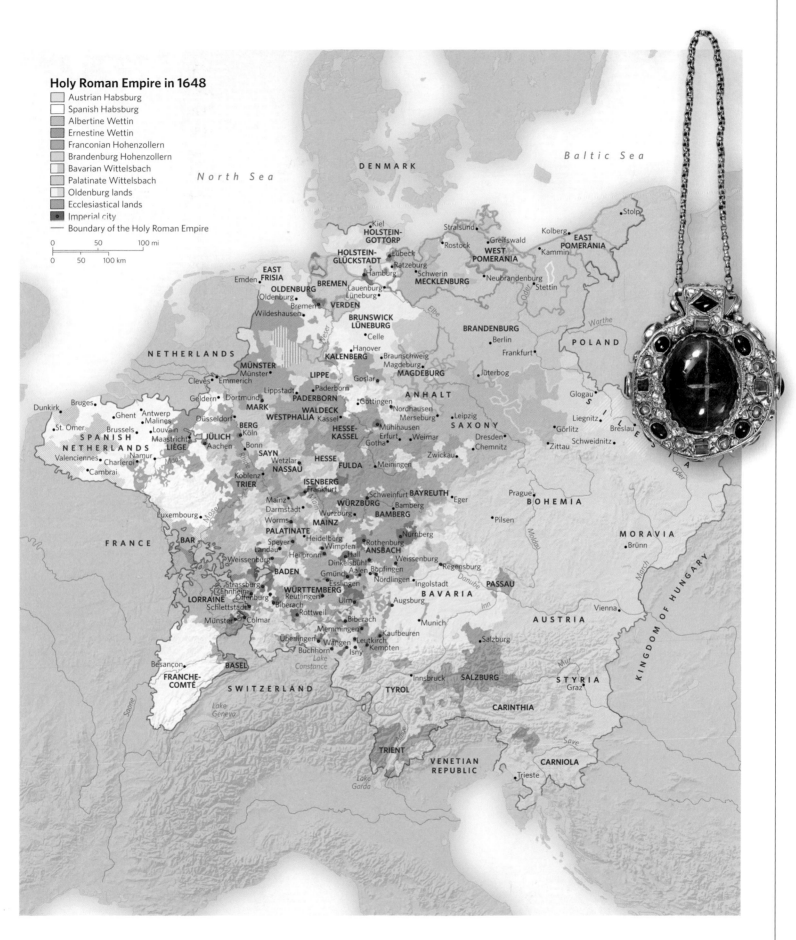

Holy Roman Empire in 1648

- Austrian Habsburg
- Spanish Habsburg
- Albertine Wettin
- Ernestine Wettin
- Franconian Hohenzollern
- Brandenburg Hohenzollern
- Bavarian Wittelsbach
- Palatinate Wittelsbach
- Oldenburg lands
- Ecclesiastical lands
- Imperial city
- Boundary of the Holy Roman Empire

0   50   100 mi
0   50   100 km

North Sea

Baltic Sea

DENMARK

Kiel
HOLSTEIN-GOTTORP
Stralsund
Rostock
Greifswald
Kolberg
Stolp
EAST POMERANIA
Kammin
HOLSTEIN-GLÜCKSTADT
Lübeck
Ratzeburg
Schwerin
WEST POMERANIA
Neubrandenburg
Stettin
Hamburg
EAST FRISIA
Emden
BREMEN
Lauenburg
Lüneburg
MECKLENBURG
Oldenburg
OLDENBURG
Bremen
VERDEN
Wildeshausen
BRUNSWICK LÜNEBURG
BRANDENBURG
Celle
Berlin
Frankfurt
POLAND
Hanover
Oder
Worthe
NETHERLANDS
MÜNSTER
Münster
KALENBERG
Braunschweig
Magdeburg
Jüterbog
LIPPE
Goslar
MAGDEBURG
Cleves
Emmerich
Lippstadt
Paderborn
ANHALT
Glogau
Geldern
Dortmund
PADERBORN
Göttingen
Nordhausen
Leipzig
Görlitz
Liegnitz
MARK
WALDECK
Merseburg
SAXONY
Breslau
Dunkirk
Bruges
Ghent
Antwerp
Malines
Düsseldorf
BERG
WESTPHALIA
Kassel
Mühlhausen
Erfurt
Weimar
Dresden
Chemnitz
Zittau
Schweidnitz
St. Omer
Brussels
Louvain
JÜLICH
Köln
HESSE-KASSEL
Gotha
Zwickau
SILESIA
SPANISH NETHERLANDS
Maastricht
Aachen
Bonn
SAYN
HESSE
FULDA
Meiningen
Valenciennes
LIÈGE
Namur
Wetzlar
NASSAU
Charleroi
Maas
Koblenz
ISENBERG
Prague
Cambrai
TRIER
Frankfurt
Schweinfurt
BAYREUTH
BOHEMIA
Luxembourg
Mainz
Darmstadt
WÜRZBURG
Bamberg
Eger
Mosel
Worms
MAINZ
Würzburg
BAMBERG
Pilsen
FRANCE
PALATINATE
Heidelberg
Rothenburg
Nürnberg
MORAVIA
BAR
Speyer
Wimpfen
ANSBACH
Brünn
Landau
Hall
Weissenburg
Heilbronn
Dinkelsbühl
Regensburg
Moldau
Weissenburg
BADEN
Gmünd
Aalen
Bopfingen
Nördlingen
Ingolstadt
March
Strassburg
Esslingen
BAVARIA
PASSAU
Lehnheim
WÜRTTEMBERG
Ulm
Augsburg
Danube
Inn
LORRAINE
Offenburg
Biberach
Vienna
Schlettstadt
Reutlingen
Munich
AUSTRIA
Münster
Colmar
Rottweil
Biberach
Überlingen
Memmingen
Kaufbeuren
Salzburg
Buchhorn
Wangen
Leutkirch
Kempten
Besançon
Isny
Lake Constance
BASEL
Innsbruck
SALZBURG
STYRIA
FRANCHE-COMTÉ
Saône
SWITZERLAND
TYROL
Graz
Lake Geneva
CARINTHIA
TRIENT
CARNIOLA
Lake Garda
VENETIAN REPUBLIC
Trieste
Adige
Mur
Save
KINGDOM OF HUNGARY

After sharing power for three years with his brother, Carloman, who died in 771, Charlemagne took sole possession of a kingdom encompassing most of France, the Low Countries to the north, and neighboring portions of Germany. Beyond that German frontier lurked tribes such as the Saxons, some of whom had migrated to Britain in recent centuries. A determined warrior-king who tolerated no rivals at his borders, Charlemagne campaigned intermittently for three decades against the defiant Saxons before finally crushing them and forcing them to convert to Christianity. In between those punishing campaigns, he conquered Bavaria, defeated the Lombards in northern Italy, and served as patron and protector of Rome and other papal states in central Italy. A Byzantine church in Ravenna was the model for the ornate Palatine Chapel he built at Aachen, his capital in the Rhineland. That shrine, which contained a majestic throne room situated above the altar, proclaimed his dual role as defender of the faith and ruler of an empire that grew to embrace most of western Europe,

Charlemagne, shown monitoring the construction of his chapel at Aachen, in an illuminated 15th-century manuscript history of French kings known as the Chroniques de St.-Denis *or* Grandes Chroniques de France

apart from the British Isles, Scandinavia, and Spain, where he challenged Muslim forces but made few gains.

Charlemagne did not proclaim himself emperor because he did not wish to antagonize Byzantine rulers, who considered themselves the rightful heirs to the Roman Empire. According to Alcuin, a scholar at his court, Charlemagne was surprised when Pope Leo III placed a crown on his head at St. Peter's in 800; the emperor declared afterward that "if he had known in advance of the pope's plan, he would not have entered church that day." It seems unlikely, however, that this calculating monarch would

The enameled golden imperial crown made for the coronation of Otto I as Holy Roman emperor in 962

have allowed Pope Leo to foist on him an honor he did not seek. Shifting responsibility for the ceremony to the pontiff may have been Charlemagne's way of deflecting the wrath of Byzantine rulers even as he acquired a title that made him their equal. He was a shrewd diplomat as well as an avid warrior and managed to appease his rivals in Constantinople. "By dint of frequent embassies and letters, in which he addressed them as brothers," Alcuin related, "he made their haughtiness yield to his magnanimity, a quality in which he was unquestionably much their superior." Charlemagne also made diplomatic overtures to the Abbasid caliph in Baghdad while continuing to battle Muslims in Spain.

Charlemagne managed his realm by holding court throughout the empire as he campaigned, placing counties under the authority of loyal aristocrats called counts—whose duties included collecting taxes and raising troops—and sending out inspectors to see that they and other local authorities carried out their tasks properly. He left his successors a solid foundation for imperial rule when he died at Aachen in 814 and was laid to rest in the Palatine Chapel.

But the Carolingian Empire, like many others, was undone by struggles among heirs.

Emperor Charlemagne was succeeded by his son, Louis the Pious, who had his first wife crowned empress and gave their first son, Lothar, priority in succession over his younger brothers. That arrangement broke down when Louis remarried and fathered another prospective heir, Charles the Bald. Following the death of Louis in 840, the Franks were once again convulsed by battles between competing princes. In 844, the empire was divided, with Charles the Bald claiming the western portion in France; Lothar receiving the middle kingdom from the Netherlands down through northern Italy; and his younger brother, Louis the German, acquiring Saxony and other eastern provinces.

In years to come, those kingdoms were assailed by raiders and invaders, including Magyars from Hungary and Vikings from Scandinavia. The impact on France was staggering, as Vikings stormed Paris and occupied the coastal region that became known as Normandy, after the Norsemen. But all parts of the former Carolingian Empire were subject to stresses that fractured kingdoms into principalities

THE PALATINE CHAPEL

Charlemagne's grandest palace was located in Aachen, the western German city where he was born. One of its glories, the Palatine Chapel, is the best surviving example of Carolingian architecture, uniting elements of classical, Byzantine, and Germanic styles (a "palatine" chapel is one for private use, usually by an emperor). Its architect, Odo of Metz, borrowed heavily from the Byzantine-influenced church of San Vitale in Ravenna, Italy. The chapel's central octagon is topped by a dome more than 100 feet high. When it was consecrated in 805, the chapel was the tallest domed building north of the Alps.

The chapel is now the core of Aachen Cathedral, a UNESCO World Heritage site. The cathedral grew around it over the centuries, and changes have been made to the interior, including a mosaic added to the dome in the 19th century. Charlemagne was buried in the chapel in 814. His remains were moved in 1215 to the elaborate golden Karlsschrein, or Shrine of Charlemagne, also in the cathedral.

Charlemagne's marble throne. For centuries after his death, emperors were crowned on it.

or duchies, whose aristocratic overlords defended their districts and became powers unto themselves.

That fragmentation was soon reversed in Germany, however, when dukes there chose one of their own as king to deal with the invading Magyars, setting the stage for a remarkable imperial revival. King Otto I of Germany came from Saxony, the region that defied Charlemagne for decades and yielded to him only after spilling much blood. When Germans were at risk of being overrun by Magyars in the tenth century, they turned to dukes of the warlike Saxons to repel the invaders. Otto's father, Henry I,

> ## *"The best man on earth and the bravest was Charles: Truth and good faith he established and kept."*
>
> JULES SYLVAIN ZELLER,
> *HISTOIRE D'ALLEMAGNE,* II, 32

had preceded him as king and won a victory over the Magyars in 933. But those relentless Hungarians remained a threat to Otto, as did German dukes who elected him king but resisted his efforts to make them his compliant vassals. They allied themselves

with resentful members of Otto's family, including his rebellious brother Henry, and tried in vain to topple him. Otto pardoned Henry but ousted the defiant dukes and replaced them with loyal relatives. He secured his hold on Germany by defeating the Magyars decisively in 955. He then followed in the path of Charlemagne by advancing into Italy to defend the Papal States at the invitation of the pope, who crowned him emperor in 962.

The realm of Otto and his successors—which encompassed much of Charlemagne's old domain except for central and western France—became known

Crusaders in the 13th century constructed this sea castle for use as a fortress off the coast of Sidon, Lebanon.

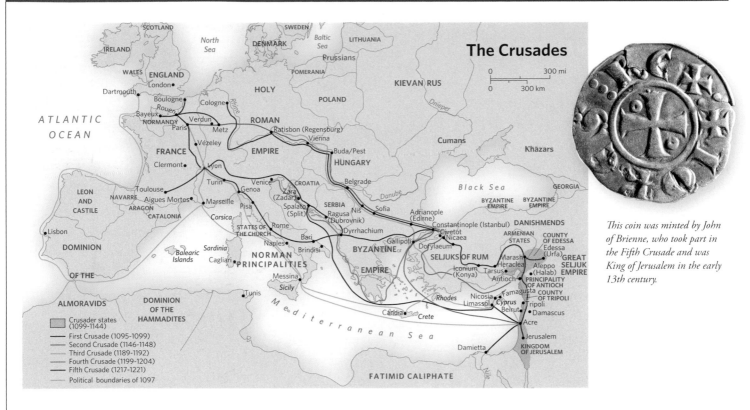

The Crusades

0 ——— 300 mi
0 ——— 300 km

- Crusader states (1099-1144)
- First Crusade (1095-1099)
- Second Crusade (1146-1148)
- Third Crusade (1189-1192)
- Fourth Crusade (1199-1204)
- Fifth Crusade (1217-1221)
- Political boundaries of 1097

This coin was minted by John of Brienne, who took part in the Fifth Crusade and was King of Jerusalem in the early 13th century.

THE CRUSADES

In the 11th century, Christian Europe went to war against Islam in the Middle East in a series of Crusades that lasted for two centuries. "Christ commands it," Pope Urban II said in 1095, when he called for knights to take the Holy Land from the Muslims, who had controlled Palestine since the seventh century. About 100,000 men marched, many searching for individual salvation under banners marked with crosses. The First Crusade captured Antioch, Edessa, and finally, in 1099, Jerusalem. The victors established outposts called the crusader states.

The Muslims fought back, and the Second Crusade was called in 1147 to wrest away land that had fallen back under Muslim control. It failed. When Muslim warlord Saladin then conquered Jerusalem in 1187, Europe responded with the Third Crusade. That campaign was led by storied kings—Frederick Barbarossa, who died before his army reached the Middle East; Richard the Lion-Hearted of England; and Philip II of France—but Jerusalem remained under Muslim control. Several lesser Crusades

followed. The holy wars ended in 1291 with the fall of the Christian city of Acre, in what is now Israel.

The Crusades produced enduring artistic images and persistent historic debates. Some argue that the crusaders were motivated primarily by religious fervor; others maintain that political

and economic forces were more important, such as political expansionism and the desire to extend trade. Disagreement also persists about how large a role the Crusades played in propelling Europe out of the Dark Ages, and how important the language and legacy of holy war remain in relations between West and East.

A barefoot army of crusaders marches around the walls of besieged Jerusalem.

as the Holy Roman Empire. But its proud Catholic rulers seldom deferred to the pope in matters of either church or state. They chose bishops and invested them, which meant presiding over ceremonies that installed them in office. They even deposed popes who defied them and replaced them with obedient figures, until one strong pope refused to tolerate such interference. In 1076, Emperor Henry IV defied Pope Gregory VII, who had ordered him to stop investing clergy. Pope Gregory then excommunicated him and released "all Christian men" from any oath of allegiance to him. This was an invitation for Catholics to rebel against Henry, and some did. In 1077, the emperor appeared barefoot before the pope in penitence and reentered the Catholic

The flag of the Imperial Habsburg dynasty, circa 1700, on painted silk, features a double-headed eagle.

fold. His successors, however, continued to feud with Rome over investiture until 1122, when the two sides agreed that each would play a part in choosing and installing bishops.

In 1095, Pope Urban II enhanced the political clout of the Church by launching

the First Crusade. But that did not stop rulers of the Holy Roman Empire from trying to reassert authority. Frederick I, known as Barbarossa ("red beard"), clashed frequently with the papacy after being crowned in 1155. He went so far as to install his own candidate as an antipope in opposition to Pope Alexander III, who responded by excommunicating Frederick and setting other European monarchs against him. Ultimately, Frederick came to terms with Alexander, acknowledging him as the one true pontiff. In 1189, the elderly emperor sought to restore his reputation as a holy Roman ruler by leading the Third Crusade, a failed attempt to reclaim Jerusalem from the sultan Saladin that cost Frederick his life.

During the 13th century, his successors faced challenges from within Germany and

---

DAILY LIFE

Schönbrunn Palace and its elaborate gardens are meant to complement each other. The gardens have been open to the public since 1799.

THE SCHÖNBRUNN PALACE

Austria's Habsburg family ruled some form of empire for more than 600 years, from 1273 when Rudolf I took the title of Holy Roman emperor until 1918, when the Austro-Hungarian Empire collapsed with the defeat of the Central Powers in World War I. With its 1,441 rooms and elaborate gardens—including the site of Europe's first zoo—the Habsburgs' Schönbrunn Palace in Vienna is Austria's most visited tourist site. The baroque edifice, meant to rival France's Versailles Palace in grandeur, was built in the late 17th and early 18th centuries as a relatively modest summer home, then expanded over time. It's now owned by the Austrian government; 40 state rooms and private apartments are open to the public, as are the acres of gardens. Many rooms are furnished in the lavish, heavily gilded style favored by Empress Maria Theresa, who reigned from 1840 to 1870.

Image labels within the painting:

FERDINANDVS. I. IMP.
ARCHIDVX AVSTRIÆ.

CAROLVS. V. IMP.
ARCHIDVX AVSTRIÆ.

LVDOVICVS REX
HVNG MASS

856

Holy Roman Emperor Maximilian I of Habsburg, who lived from 1459 to 1519, shown with his family

granted its various princes and principalities some measure of autonomy. Once the most unified country in medieval Europe, Germany fragmented while France, England, and other western European countries coalesced under strong kings.

A new ruling family, the Habsburg dynasty, emerged in Austria in the late Middle Ages and laid claim to what remained of the Holy Roman Empire before expanding their domain through marriage alliances with other royal families. Yet their hold on Germany's many small states was fragile. They lost control of northern Italy and Switzerland, where a confederation of self-governing districts known as cantons emerged. Habsburg rulers continued to pose as Holy Roman emperors for centuries to come, but as the French author Voltaire remarked in the 1700s, the great imperial power of medieval Europe had been reduced to something that was "neither holy, nor Roman, nor an empire."

MUSLIM EMPIRES IN SPAIN
Clashes Across the Iberian Peninsula

No country in medieval Europe was closer to Africa geographically or culturally than Spain. The narrow Strait of Gibraltar was easily traversed, enabling wave after wave of Muslims to cross from North Africa and colonize the Iberian Peninsula. The first such colonists were led by Arabs of the Umayyad dynasty, who presided over a vast Islamic empire from Damascus. Later, the Almoravids and Almohads—Berbers from the northern fringe of the Sahara Desert—established two successive Islamic empires embracing northwest Africa and Spain. Like the Umayyads, they faced challenges from Christians in northern Spain, who struggled to regain control of the country in campaigns known collectively as the Reconquista, or Reconquest.

Muslim forces first entered Spain in the early 700s, following earlier invasions by Vandals and then Visigoths—Germanic invaders who overran the Iberian Peninsula and converted to Christianity. When some rebellious Visigoths appealed for aid against a king they opposed, an Arab emir (commander) named

The Muslim Almohads issued elaborate coins (above). At right, an 1863 view of Gibraltar by German landscape painter Fritz Bamberger.

Tariq ibn Ziyad crossed the strait from Morocco, in the process lending his name to Jabal Tariq (Mount Tariq), or Gibraltar. After toppling the disputed Visigoth king, his army, composed largely of Berbers, was reinforced and remained in the country, conquering all but the northern part of Spain. The Muslims called their new Spanish domain al-Andalus ("land of the Vandals").

Al-Andalus was part of the Islamic empire ruled by caliphs of the Umayyad dynasty until the middle of the eighth century, when power shifted to the Abbasid dynasty in Baghdad. An Umayyad refugee, Emir Abd al-Rahman I, then took charge of al-Andalus, which became an independent emirate, beyond the control of Abbasid caliphs in Baghdad. Spain's sizable Jewish population, which had been subject to persecution by Christian Visigoths, fared better under Muslim rule and enjoyed freedom of worship, as did Christians who remained in al-Andalus. Many of those Christians adopted the language of their Arab overlords and became known as Mozarabs (people "like Arabs").

Relations between Muslims in southern Spain and the

700s Muslim forces enter Spain.

778 Basques ambush and annihilate Charlemagne's rear guard.

958 Christian leaders pay homage to Abd al-Rahman III in Cordoba.

1085 Christian troops from Castile seize the city of Toledo.

1099 El Cid (Rodrigo Díaz de Vivar) dies.

1142 Almohads seize Marrakech and al-Andalus.

1212 Christian forces win Battle of Las Navas de Tolosa.

1469 Isabella of Castile marries Ferdinand of Aragon, unifying Spain.

1492 Granada, a Muslim stronghold, falls to Christian Spain.

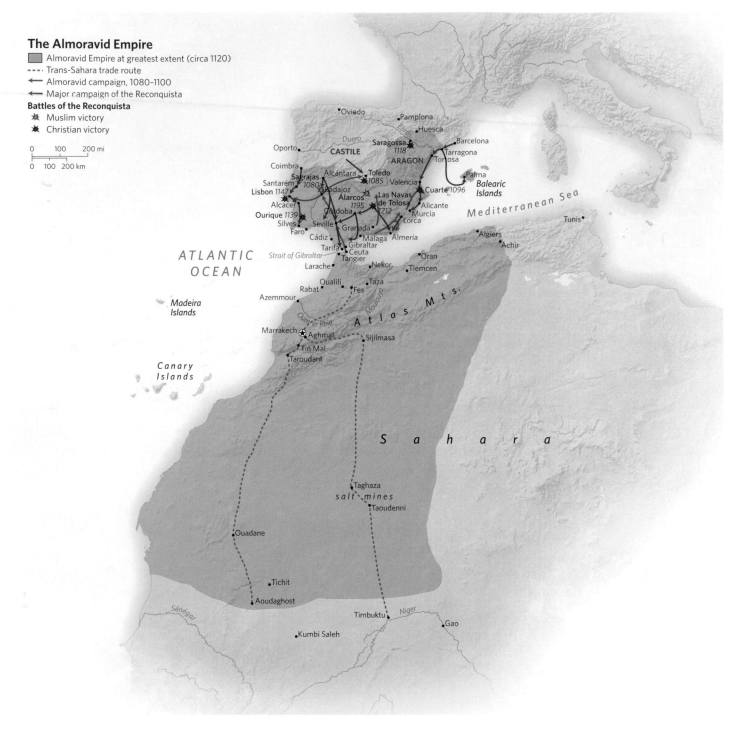

The Almoravid Empire

▢ Almoravid Empire at greatest extent (circa 1120)
- - - Trans-Sahara trade route
← Almoravid campaign, 1080–1100
← Major campaign of the Reconquista

Battles of the Reconquista
✴ Muslim victory
✴ Christian victory

0   100   200 mi
0   100   200 km

Oviedo *Pamplona*
Huesca
Barcelona
Oporto **CASTILE** Saragossa *1118* *Tarragona* *Tortosa*
Coimbra **ARAGON**
Alcántara *Toledo* *Valencia* *Palma* *Balearic Islands*
Santarém Sagrajas *1080* *1085* *Cuarte 1096*
Lisbon 1147 Badajoz Alarcos *1195* *Alicante* *Murcia*
Alcacer *Córdoba* Las Navas de Tolosa *1212* *Lorca*
Ourique *1139* *Seville* *Granada* *Almería*
Silves *Málaga*
Faro *Cádiz* *Algiers* *Achir*
Tarifa *Gibraltar* *Tunis*
Strait of Gibraltar *Ceuta* *Tangier*
Larache *Nekor* *Oran*
Taza *Tlemcen*
Oualili *Fes*
Rabat
Azemmour

Duero *Ebro*

ATLANTIC OCEAN

Mediterranean Sea

Madeira Islands

A t l a s   M t s.

Marrakech *Aghmat* *Sijilmasa*
Tin Mal
Taroudant

Canary Islands

Oum er Rbia *Moulouya*

S a h a r a

Taghaza
s a l t   m i n e s
Taoudenni

Ouadane

Tichit

Aoudaghost

Sénégal *Timbuktu* *Niger* *Gao*

Kumbi Saleh

---

unconquered Christians in the north, on the other hand, were bitter and bloody, with each side attempting to seize territory from the other. Christians built castles along their frontier with al-Andalus —a borderland that became known as Castile and evolved into a combative kingdom that would ultimately unite Spain under Christian rule. For now, however, northerners were unable to form an alliance strong enough to overpower the Muslims. The Basques living around the Pyrenees had not yet embraced Christianity and remained independent. In 778, as Charlemagne and his Franks were withdrawing through the Pyrenees after an unsuccessful campaign against Spanish Muslims, Basques ambushed and annihilated his rear guard—a debacle for the Franks that was later portrayed as a heroic feat in the French medieval epic "The Song of Roland."

After two centuries of intermittent warfare, northern leaders sought peace in 958 by paying homage to Abd al-Rahman III in Cordoba, the splendid capital of al-Andalus. He had assumed the title of caliph and sent troops abroad to vie for control of northwest Africa with forces of the Fatimid dynasty, which had gained power as the Abbasid dynasty declined. His own dynasty would not last long, but Cordoba would continue to outshine other cities in Europe for some time to come, dazzling visitors with its thousands of shops and well-lit streets and a court filled with brilliant scholars and poets whose ballads inspired troubadours in France and other Christian countries.

During the 11th century, the caliphate in Cordoba collapsed amid civil strife, and Muslim Spain splintered into competing *taifas,* or petty kingdoms. Christians in the north gained ground, but those advances were halted by the arrival of a new wave of Muslim conquerors—the Almoravids.

The Almoravid Berbers came to power in northwest Africa at a time when the region was no longer under the influence of either Cordoban caliphs or Fatimid rulers, who had shifted their attention eastward to Egypt, Arabia, and Syria. Berbers had submitted to Arab forces only after a long struggle, and even then remote Berber tribes such as the Sanhajah, who herded camels and crossed the Sahara as traders, were slow to embrace Islam. In 1035, however, a Sanhajah chieftain named Yahya ibn Ibrahim fulfilled his obligation as a Muslim by making a pilgrimage to Mecca. He returned filled with the same devotion and determination that once led the prophet Muhammad to fight for his faith,

> *"In the glittering reign of the Arabs the towers of the basilicas of the city [i.e., Cordoba] were destroyed, the vaults of the temples pulled down, and the pinnacles of the churches cast down."*
>
> **EULOGIUS,** CHRISTIAN WRITER

gathering followers at a garrison like those established earlier in Arab-occupied lands. The Almoravids ("garrison-dwellers") were strengthened in their beliefs by a militant cleric, Abd Allah ibn Yasin, and launched a holy war that within a few decades made them masters of Algeria and Morocco.

In 1085, after Christian troops from Castile seized the city of Toledo in central Spain, Muslims there appealed for help to the Almoravid ruler, Yusef ibn Tashufin, who made his capital at Marrakech. In 1086, Almoravids overcame King Alfonso VI of Castile, who had proclaimed himself "emperor" of Spain and brought some Muslims there under his authority. Alfonso might have fared better had he not lost the services of his brilliant commander, Rodrigo Díaz de Vivar, known as El Cid, who was exiled for insubordination and offered his talents to Muslim leaders. Recalled by Alfonso after the defeat, El Cid indeed may have helped the king avoid further losses, but he was also serving his own interests. That led him to seize Valencia, a prosperous kingdom in eastern Spain formerly ruled by Muslims. Not long after El Cid died in 1099, Almoravid forces took Valencia and reunited al-Andalus. As before when the Visigoths had called for help, African forces summoned to Spain in an emergency chose to stay.

The semilegendary 11th-century French knight Roland battles the Saracen giant Ferragus, in an illustration from about 1820.

Under Almoravid rulers, Andalusian culture flourished both in Spain and in northwest Africa, where towns like Marrakech and Algiers came to resemble Spanish cities such as Cordoba and Seville with their ornate palaces and mosques. Andalusian artists, as Muslims, were prohibited from portraying human or animal figures that might be viewed as idols.

convert. Once firmly established in Spain, however, the Almohads emulated earlier Muslim rulers there by patronizing artists, poets, scientists, and philosophers, thus enhancing Andalusian civilization.

The Almohad conquest presented a fresh challenge to Christian rulers in northern Spain, who responded forcefully, In the early 13th century, King Alfonso VIII

> *"The Moors were not pleased—in fact, they were downright troubled. The Cid remained there for fifteen weeks. Seeing that Minaya was delayed in getting back, the intrepid warrior and all his men withdrew from the Hill, marching away by night and leaving nothing behind."*
>
> *THE EPIC OF THE CID,*
> FIRST BOOK: EXILE (VERSES 1-1085)

Instead, they used alluring floral and geometric patterns and verses from the Koran to adorn their buildings.

The Almoravids began as Muslim purists who favored simplicity and austerity in their homes and places of worship. With power, however, came wealth and splendor, which made them targets for a more puritanical sect of Muslims known as the Almohads, who swept down from the Atlas Mountains and seized Marrakech in 1142 before conquering al-Andalus. They were stricter than the Almoravids at enforcing such traditional Muslim customs as the veiling of women in public and the prohibition of alcohol. And they were less tolerant of non-Muslims, forcing some to

Hundreds of striped columns and arches adorn the interior of the Great Mosque of Cordoba, a gem of Spanish-Islamic architecture.

of Castile and the Archbishop of Toledo prevailed on Pope Innocent III to declare a crusade against the Moors, or Spanish Muslims. French crusaders answered that call, but the bulk of the fighting was done by Alfonso's Castilians and troops from neighboring Aragon and other Iberian lands, including Portugal, which would remain distinct from the powerful Spanish kingdom fostered when Castile united with Aragon. In 1212, Christian forces won the pivotal Battle of Las Navas de Tolosa and humbled the Almohads, who soon lost their empire. Granada, at the southern tip of the Iberian peninsula, remained a Muslim bastion until 1492, when it, too, fell to Christian Spain—an emerging imperial power that would soon establish colonies around the world.

EL CID

Rodrigo Díaz de Vivar (circa 1043–1099) was a Castilian military leader who became a legend, better known as El Cid (a nickname that comes from the Spanish Arabic *al-sid*, "lord"). Over his storied military career, he switched allegiances several times, serving both Spanish kings and their Muslim enemies, as well as his own self-interest in his conquest of Valencia. While he was one of the greatest generals of his time, it's not the historical details of his life that made him a national hero of Spain. Instead, his fame was secured for the ages by the epic poem *Song of El Cid (Cantar de Mio Cid* or *Poema del Cid)*, written about 50 years after his death. It's considered a masterpiece of medieval literature. In it, an idealized soldier who personifies feudal virtues of bravery and loyalty triumphs through trials and adventures and serves as the great defender of Castile and Christianity.

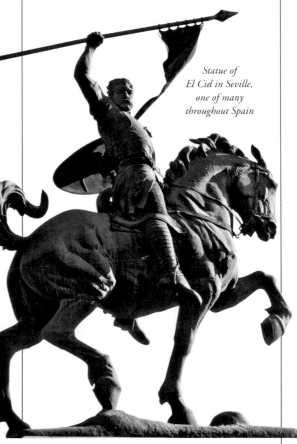

Statue of El Cid in Seville, one of many throughout Spain

WEST AFRICAN EMPIRES
Dominions of the Mali and Songhai

Like Spain, kingdoms in West Africa were greatly affected by the spread of Islam, which advanced west from Arabia and Egypt across North Africa before branching north to the Iberian Peninsula and south across the Sahara. The first Muslims to cross that desert were not troops but traders, traveling in caravans and seeking gold, ivory, and other precious goods along the Niger and Senegal Rivers—a populous region encompassing modern-day Senegal, Mauritania, Mali, and lands to their south. By the tenth century, rulers of the ancient kingdom of Ghana (situated northwest of modern-day Ghana) had profited hugely from that trade and adopted Islam. But they did not impose their new religion on their people, who worshiped ancestral spirits and nature gods. Neither did they abandon all such pagan rites themselves.

Their wealth and their tolerance for paganism made Ghana a target for the Almoravid forces, who invaded the kingdom and seized its capital, Kumbi, in 1076. That campaign was part of a wide-ranging holy war by the

Almoravids, who sought both spiritual and material gains in Africa, Spain, and other lands they occupied. The Berbers did not remain long in Ghana, but they undermined the kingdom and hastened its collapse, as tribal groups ceased paying tribute to Ghana's rulers and broke free. The trans-Saharan trade continued, though, offering wealth and power to any West African leader strong enough to control the supply of gold and other assets sought by Muslim merchants.

In the early 13th century, a prince named Sundiata, heir to a small kingdom along the upper Niger River, went into exile after his homeland was invaded by Sumanguru, a neighboring ruler intent on dominating the region. Sumanguru did himself no favor by spurning Islam and alienating Muslim traders. Sundiata, in contrast, combined two traits shared by many successful empire-builders: combativeness and diplomatic skill. After raising an army and defeating Sumanguru in 1235, he extended his authority over the former kingdom of Ghana and neighboring lands rich in gold and other assets. He then embraced Islam and welcomed Muslim traders, while remaining a cult figure

Terra-cotta horse and rider excavated in Mali (above). A 1375 map (right) shows the King of Mali at the center of his realm.

1076 Almoravid forces invade Kumbi, capital of kingdom of Ghana.

1235 Sundiata defeats Sumanguru and founds Mali Empire.

1324 Sundiata's grandnephew, Mansa Musa, makes pilgrimage to Mecca.

1468 Timbuktu seized by Sunni Ali, founder of Songhai Empire.

1473 Sunni Ali conquers trading center of Djenne.

1493 Muhammad I ousts Ali's son.

1591 Moroccan forces cross Sahara and destroy Songhai Empire.

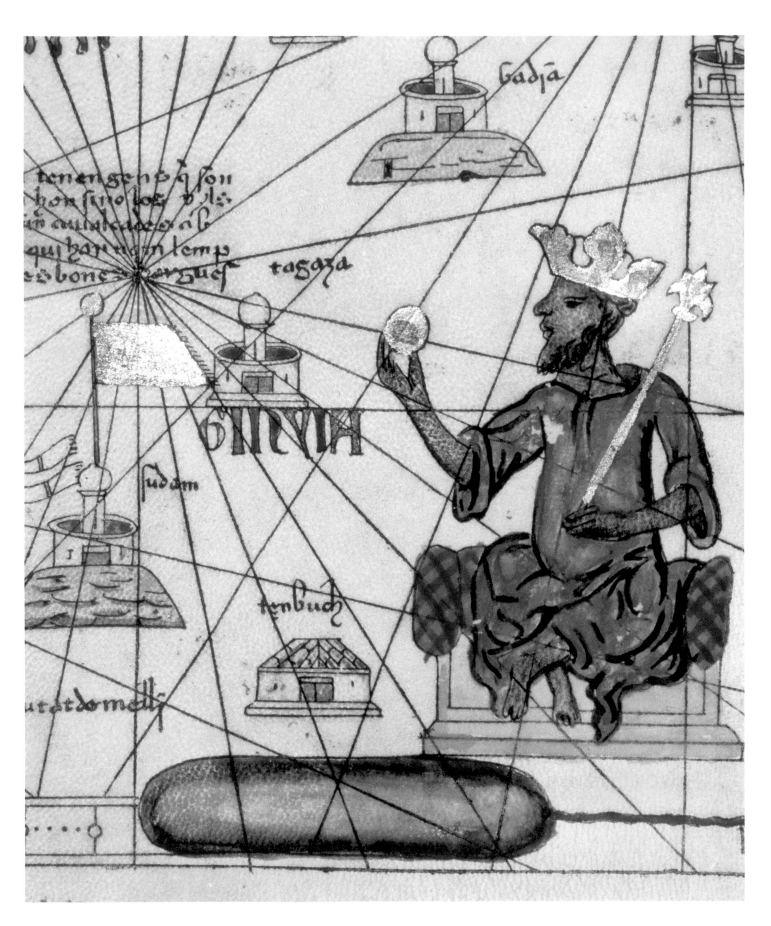

to his non-Muslim followers, who had long considered their rulers to be close to the gods, from whom they obtained power and prosperity.

The Mali Empire founded by Sundiata was largely pagan or polytheistic, but Islam took hold there among wealthy people, including merchants who acquired the language and beliefs of Muslims they dealt with. In 1324, Sundiata's grandnephew, Mansa Musa, left his capital, Timbuktu, and embarked on a celebrated pilgrimage to Mecca that focused attention on Mali and its wealthy emperor. His party numbered in the thousands and included some 500 slaves, each carrying four pounds of gold, which the emperor and his attendants spent so freely in Cairo that they devalued the metal there for years to come. Merchants of Mali exported black captives as slaves to North Africa and beyond and

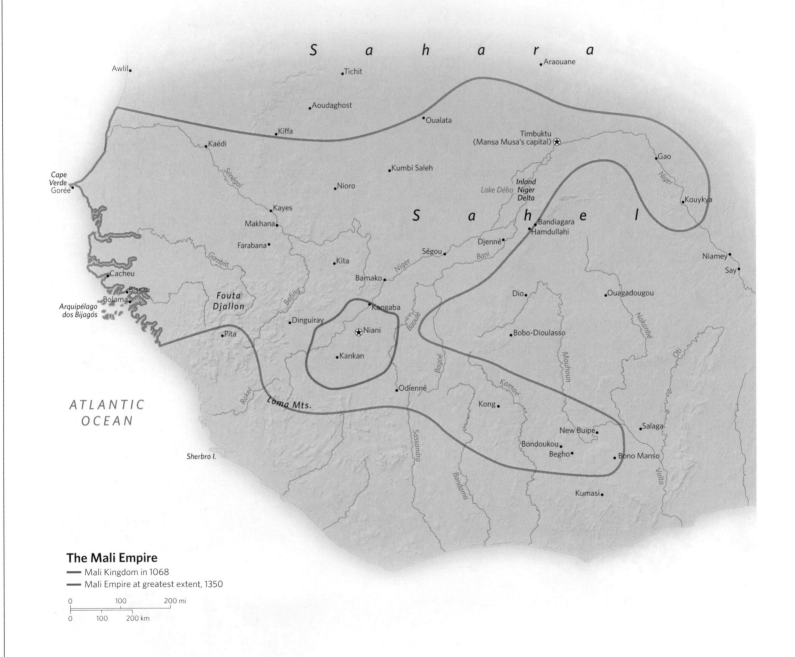

The Mali Empire

— Mali Kingdom in 1068
— Mali Empire at greatest extent, 1350

| 0 | 100 | 200 mi |
| 0 | 100 | 200 km |

obtained white slaves in return. One visitor to the emperor's court found him attended by "a score of Turkish or other pages which are bought for him in Cairo." Musa and his successors also purchased Arab horses for their army, which included some 10,000 cavalrymen, and lured scholars from the Arab world to their capital, which was adorned with mosques, a university, and an Arabic library that Musa brought back from Mecca.

Timbuktu remained a commercial and cultural hub for centuries, but it slipped from the grasp of Mali's rulers in the 1400s when their empire crumbled. Desert-dwelling Berbers known as the Tuareg swept in from the north and

Bartaga village on the Niger River in Mali (above) at the southern boundary of the Sahara. Below, manuscripts preserved in a scholar's home in Timbuktu.

occupied the city, but they did not long remain its masters. Seeking a champion to liberate their city from the Tuareg, residents of Timbuktu sent envoys to Sunni Ali, founder of the Songhai Empire, in the city of Gao on the Niger River east of Timbuktu. With the collapse of the Mali Empire, Ali and his Songhai warriors had emerged as the region's dominant military force. In 1468, he ousted the Berbers from Timbuktu and

reportedly massacred Muslims who failed to aid him as promised.

Ali was an imposing commander who supplemented his formidable cavalry by establishing a naval fleet that patrolled the Niger River, a vital artery linking Gao to Timbuktu and the trading center of

*"I have been to Timbuktu,
a place situated beyond Barbary in very
arid country. Much business is done there
in selling coarse cloth, serge,
and fabrics like those made in Lombardy."*

BENEDETTO DEI, FLORENTINE TRAVELER

Djenne, which he conquered in 1473. That secured access to nearby gold mines, the chief source of wealth and power in West Africa. Later Muslim historians portrayed Sunni Ali as a tyrant, but their accounts may have been colored by the fact that, like Sundiata, he was not strictly devoted to Islam and engaged in traditional tribal rites that devout Muslims regarded as idolatry.

The Songhai Empire was consolidated by the clever Muhammad I, who ousted Sunni Ali's son in 1493 and took the title Askia ("he will not be") because some people had mistakenly scoffed at the idea that he would ever become emperor. A shrewd administrator, he created a cabinet of officials at court to handle such matters as justice and finance. One of his

ministers oversaw white tribes, including bands of Tuaregs, who were now subject to the Songhai and served as camel-mounted cavalry, patrolling the empire's northern frontier.

Unlike Ali, Muhammad I was a devout Muslim. He went on a pilgrimage to Mecca and made efforts to propagate the faith among his people, sending out scholars to instruct villagers in the teachings of the Koran. Little instruction was required in Timbuktu and other cities of the region, which were now largely Muslim. Women of Timbuktu observed "the custom of veiling their faces, except for the slaves who sell all the foodstuffs," observed Leo Africanus, a traveler and scholar from the Spanish Muslim kingdom of Granada

ARCHAEOLOGY

The wooden beams sticking out of the distinctive pyramidal shape of this mosque allow easy regular access to restore the mud brick.

THE SANKORE MOSQUE

The Sankore Mosque in Timbuktu, Mali, was one of the Islamic world's most renowned centers of learning in the Middle Ages, with perhaps 25,000 students. The school was not organized the way modern universities are, with central bureaucracies and prescribed degrees. Rather, it was a collection of respected teachers, known as imams, who each gathered students around himself. Classes focused on the Koran but also included secular subjects such as mathematics and astronomy. The mosque itself is built of mud bricks, reinforced with wood, and known for its pyramidal shape. Although it has stood for centuries, it and other important historic spots in Timbuktu are threatened by desertification brought on by climate change, according to UNESCO's World Heritage program. Efforts are under way to preserve both the buildings and the hundreds of thousands of old manuscripts that survive in Timbuktu.

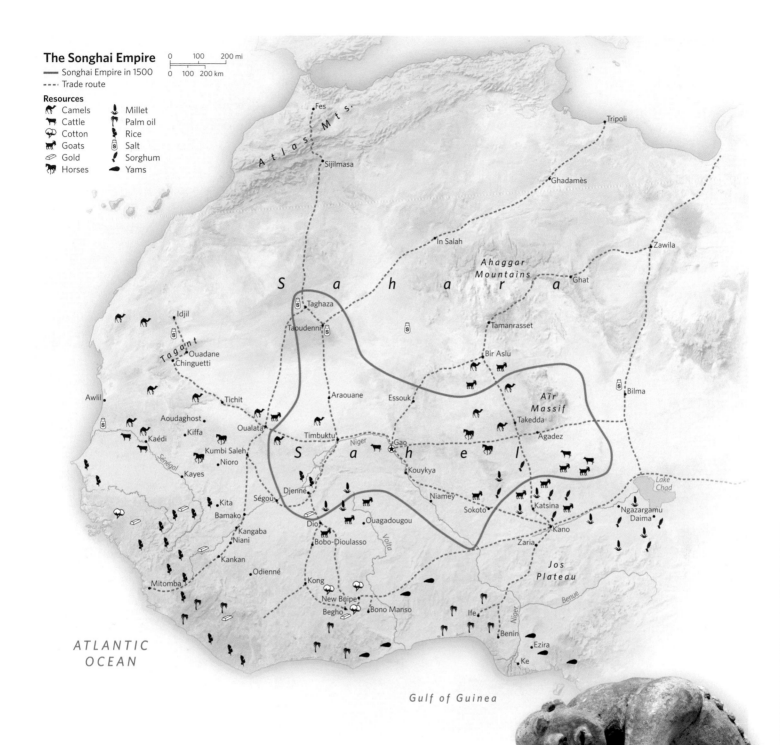

The Songhai Empire

— Songhai Empire in 1500
- - - Trade route

Resources

🐫	Camels	🌾	Millet
🐄	Cattle	🌴	Palm oil
🐑	Cotton	🌾	Rice
🐐	Goats	Ⓢ	Salt
🪙	Gold	🌾	Sorghum
🐎	Horses	🌿	Yams

Atlas Mts.

Fes

Tripoli

Sijilmasa

Ghadamès

S a h a r a

In Salah

Zawila

Ahaggar Mountains

Ghat

Taghaza

Taoudenni

Ⓢ

Tamanrasset

Idjil

Tagant

Ouadane
Chinguetti

Bir Aslu

Aïr Massif

Bilma

Awlil

Tichit

Araouane

Essouk

Takedda

Aoudaghost

Kiffa

Oualata

Timbuktu

Niger

Gao ★

Agadez

Kaédi

Kumbi Saleh

S a h e l

Nioro

Kayes

Kouykya

Sénégal

Djenné

Niamey

Sokoto

Katsina

Ngazargamu
Daima

Lake Chad

Kita

Ségou

Bamako

Dio

Ouagadougou

Volta

Kano

Kangaba
Niani

Bobo-Dioulasso

Zaria

Kankan

Odienné

Jos Plateau

Mitomba

Kong

New Buipe

Begho

Bono Manso

Ife

Benue

Benin

Ezira

Niger

Ke

ATLANTIC OCEAN

Gulf of Guinea

0   100   200 mi
0   100   200 km

---

who was freed by Pope Leo X in the early 1500s after being captured and enslaved by Christians and who composed a vivid account of Africa.

This was an age of widespread religious intolerance. Both Christians and Muslims had grown increasingly hostile toward people of other beliefs as they waged holy wars during the late Middle Ages. Among the victims were Jews, who had to convert to Christianity or flee Spain and were also persecuted in some Muslim lands, including the Songhai Empire. The

Seated 13th-century terra-cotta figure found in the Djenne/ Mopti region of Mali

GRIOTS

"I teach kings the history of their ancestors so that the lives of the ancients might serve them as an example, for the world is old, but the future springs from the past." So Mamadou Kouyate, a 20th-century griot, introduces the epic tale of 13th-century West African ruler Sundiata, as transcribed by author D. T. Niane. Griots are hereditary West African musicians and oral historians, often described as praise singers. Tradition holds that when Sundiata was a child, his father gave him Balla Fasseke as his griot, just as Fasseke's father had been griot to Sundiata's father, and his grandfather to Sundiata's grandfather.

Like Homeric poets in ancient Greece or troubadours in medieval Europe, griots pass along wisdom and stories to largely illiterate audiences. The tradition of the griot, though, remains alive. West African practitioners still pass along the words of their ancestors, and their music has been a major influence on contemporary African and African-American artists.

ruler appointed by the Songhai emperor to govern Timbuktu was "a declared enemy of the Jews," Leo Africanus observed. "He will not allow any to live in the city. If he hears it said that a Berber merchant frequents them or does business with them, he confiscates his goods." The author noted that Timbuktu remained a magnet for Muslim scholars and was filled with "numerous judges, teachers, and priests, all properly appointed by the king. Many hand-written books imported from Barbary [North Africa] are also sold. There is more profit made from this commerce than from all other merchandise."

Like Ghana and Mali, the Songhai Empire profited greatly from trade with North Africa. But trade routes could also serve as avenues of invasion, and the Songhai were not immune to that threat, which increased after the fall of Granada in 1492. Christian forces from Spain and Portugal soon crossed the Strait of

The turreted mud Great Mosque of Djenne, Mali, was rebuilt in 1907 on the site of a 13th-century house of worship and study.

Gibraltar and established outposts on the Moroccan coast. Muslims there rose up in response and overthrew their rulers in favor of a combative new regime, which ousted foreigners from coastal enclaves and

> *"In all these villages Sundiata recruited soldiers. In the same way as light precedes the sun, so the glory of Sundiata, overleaping the mountains, shed itself on all the Niger plain."*
>
> **GRIOT OF MALI,** *THE EPIC OF SUNDIATA,* 13TH CENTURY

transformed Morocco into an imposing military power, with a professional army equipped with firearms. Morocco proved strong enough to avoid the fate of other North African countries that fell subject to the Ottoman Empire, and embarked on its own conquests. In 1591, Moroccan forces crossed the Sahara and used their guns to defeat and destroy the Songhai Empire.

A new age had begun in which powers that long dominated their neighbors using age-old weapons could be shattered with staggering speed by invaders equipped with superior military technology. The consequences for West Africa and other places where kings and emperors had little or no access to that technology would be catastrophic.

Griots can be male or female; many play a traditional instrument, the kora, *a long-necked harp lute.*

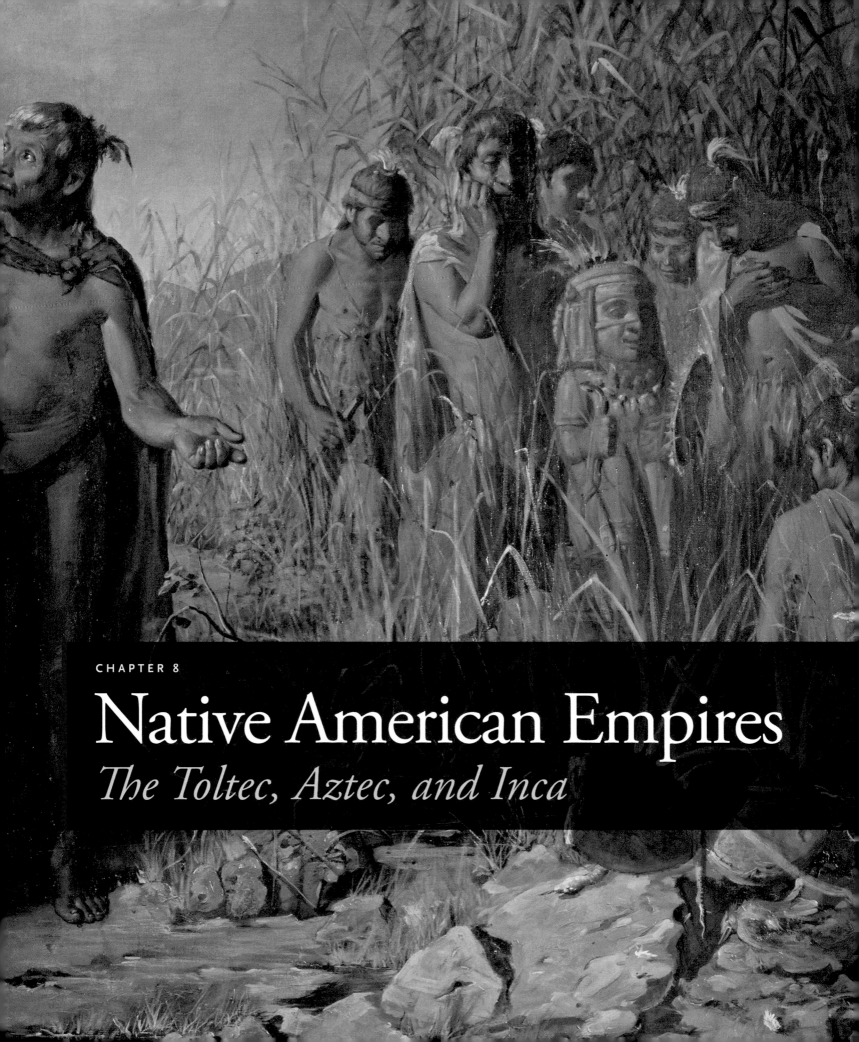

CHAPTER 8

Native American Empires
The Toltec, Aztec, and Inca

TOLTEC
People of Legend

When Spanish conquistadores under the command of Hernán Cortés approached the Aztec capital of Tenochtitlan in 1519, they could hardly believe what they saw. Before them lay one of the greatest cities in the world, home to more than 200,000 people, surpassing the population of Paris. Built on an island in Lake Texcoco in the fertile Valley of Mexico, where Mexico City now stands, Tenochtitlan was laced with canals and linked to surrounding communities by causeways. At its hub rose the Great Pyramid, crowned by twin temples devoted to the Aztec war god Huitzilopochtli and the rain god Tlaloc. Cortés and his men, who considered Native Americans primitive, were astounded by this bustling city and the civilization that built it. "Buildings rising from the water, all made of stone, seemed like an enchanted vision . . . Indeed some of our soldiers asked if it was not all a dream," wrote conquistador Bernal Díaz del Castillo.

The Aztec Empire came as a revelation to Spaniards unaware of the dynamic history of the Americas, where complex societies had

Aztec mask (above) is believed to represent either Quetzalcoatl, the feathered serpent, or Tlaloc, the rain god. Pyramid (right) at Tula, Mexico.

been developing for thousands of years. As early as 1200 B.C., an industrious people called the Olmec living along Mexico's Gulf Coast had begun building ceremonial centers with pyramids, temples, and ball courts where contestants played a game of ritual significance.

The Maya living in and around the Yucatán Peninsula later built on that cultural foundation by erecting impressive cities with lofty pyramids and palaces and recording their exploits in writing. Mayan city-states vied fiercely with each other, but no single power dominated the region. The first empires in Mesoamerica—a cultural zone extending from central Mexico to just above the isthmus of Panama—were forged in and around the Valley of Mexico between about A.D. 1000 and 1500 by the warlike Toltec and their Aztec successors. Similar advances occurred during that period along the west coast of South America, where the Inca drew on the accomplishments of earlier Peruvian societies such as the Moche and Chimu and amassed a sprawling empire even more vast than the Aztec domain, extending for some

ca 750 Great city of Teotihuacan devastated by fire.

ca 900 Toltec people gain power in Valley of Mexico.

ca 950 Tula emerges as capital of Toltec Empire.

ca 987 Legendary Toltec leader Quetzalcoatl reportedly driven into exile.

ca 1000–1170 Toltec continue to induct warriors into military societies and wield power.

ca 1170 Tula sacked and burned; Toltec Empire collapses.

Toltecs

- ▢ Toltec Empire, circa 1150
- → Influx of Toltecs, circa 900
- → Toltec migration, circa 980–1200
- ∘ Important Toltec site

0   50   100 mi
0   50   100 km

2,500 miles from present-day Ecuador south to Chile.

Much of what we know about the Toltec comes from legends passed down by the Aztec and other Mesoamerican peoples, making it difficult to distinguish fact from fiction. By one account, the Toltec destroyed the city of Teotihuacan, a great commercial and ceremonial center in the Valley of Mexico that reached a population of some 150,000 in A.D. 500 before collapsing a few centuries later. Another possibility is that the Toltec were refugees from Teotihuacan who rebuilt the society that flourished there. They probably entered the region some time after Teotihuacan was reduced to rubble, however, and settled at Tula, not far north of what is now Mexico City.

The Aztec traced many of their own traditions and beliefs back to the Toltec,

Tlaloc, the god of rain, shown here in a 16th-century manuscript, was one of the most important Aztec deities.

including the custom of inducting honored warriors into military societies devoted to the jaguar and the eagle. Society members wore distinctive costumes mimicking those creatures. According to the Aztec, Toltec rulers were god-kings with mystical titles and supernatural powers. One such king, the legendary destroyer of Teotihuacan, was called Mixcoatl ("cloud serpent"). His son and successor was known as Quetzalcoatl ("feathered serpent") and acquired great wealth and prestige before he was ousted by a sinister and calculating rival and driven from his land into exile. He supposedly had several houses in Tula where he stored gold and

silver, turquoise, precious feathers, and other treasures that the Toltec acquired through trade or as tribute from the people they conquered. Both the Aztec and the Maya told of a fabled journey that brought colonizers to the Yucatán Peninsula led by Quetzalcoatl.

How large an empire the Toltec possessed remains unclear. Toltec power or influence may have extended as far as the Yucatán Peninsula, where late Maya cities

TULA

Just as the history of the Toltec Empire is shrouded in myth, so is the precise location of its capital, known as Tollan. The most widely accepted site is believed to lie near the modern-day town of Tula de Allende, northwest of Mexico City. It has been the target of exploration since Aztec days, even though the Aztec likely dug more for treasure than for knowledge.

The city was first settled about A.D. 800, but the most remarkable archaeological finds date from around 1000. As in the larger cities of ancient Mesoamerica, the main civic area, called Tula Grande, includes a plaza, temples, pyramids, a palace complex, and ball courts, all decorated with images of snakes, birds, and jaguars. There are 15-foot-tall stone images of warriors with feather headdresses as well as sculpted scenes of human sacrifice, indicating that the Toltec, like the Aztec, were merciless toward their foes.

Shell head from Tula shows Quetzalcoatl rising from the jaws of the earth, depicted as a coyote.

The famous stone figures known as Los Atlantes, among the main archaeological attractions at Tula, stand 16 feet high.

such as Chichen Itza and Mayapan had much in common with Tula. However, their capital at its peak did not have more than about 50,000 inhabitants, far less than the population of Tenochtitlan in later times. The area under their control may have been considerably smaller than the Aztec domain. Yet the Toltec served as models for the Aztec, who remembered them as "all good, all perfect, all marvelous" and credited them with bringing order, artistry, and civilization to the lands they ruled.

Such was the ideal of empire, but the unfortunate reality for people under imperial domination was often far less inspiring, to say the least. Mesoamerican conquerors such as the Toltec and Aztec demanded heavy tribute from those they subjugated and brutally sacrificed captives as offerings to their gods. Here as in other parts of the world, people believed that sacrifices of some kind were required if they were to retain heaven's blessing and regarded warfare and bloodshed as sacred duties.

That did not make the burden any easier for victims of conquest. When pressed too hard, they often rebelled. A drought in the 12th century weakened the Toltec and convulsed the region. Around 1170, Tula was sacked and burned, either by rebellious subjects or by invaders who swept down from the north in waves. Among those who invaded the region after Tula was destroyed were the Aztec, who outdid the Toltec and built a mighty empire through conquest and coercion, only to fall victim themselves to Spanish conquerors.

"The people have been well informed,
they have been enriched.
There has been a sowing,
there has been a great
scattering of jades."

FLORENTINE CODEX, VI, 205V

AZTEC EMPIRE
Complex Culture, Bloody Sacrifices

The Aztec traced their origins to a place called Aztlan, located somewhere in what is now northwest Mexico. During the 13th century, they migrated south, led by a fabled hero called Huitzilopochtli who served as their Moses, guiding them through the wilderness to their promised land. He may well have been a historical figure, but he was later deified by the Aztec and worshiped both as a war god and as a supreme being associated with the sun. Their journey brought them to the ruins of Tula, where they marveled at monuments erected by the Toltec before the city was laid waste.

Not all Toltecs perished in that disaster. Some fled and settled at Culhuacan on the south shore of Lake Texcoco, where Aztecs encountered their descendants after arriving in the area around 1300. Lakes and marshes in the Valley of Mexico abounded with fish and fowl and could be converted into lush fields where corn and beans were cultivated, making the region a magnet for migrants and refugees.

Gold (above) tantalized the Spanish, hastening the downfall of the last Aztec emperor, Moctezuma (right), depicted in a 16th-century painting.

As impoverished newcomers, the Aztec had to reckon with well-established groups such as the Toltec and find a niche in that populous land of plenty.

Not strong enough yet to defeat rivals living around Lake Texcoco, Aztec placed themselves under the protection of the Toltec living in Culhuacan and served that city as soldiers, absorbing Toltec lore and culture until they antagonized their hosts and were forced out. According to legend, Aztecs caused that breach by inviting the daughter of one of Culhuacan's leading figures to serve ceremonially as their queen and become the "wife of Huitzilopochtli." Her father consented to send her to participate in the ceremony, not realizing that they intended to sacrifice her to that god. After her death, an Aztec priest flayed her and cloaked himself in her skin—a grim ritual that was still being performed when Spanish conquistadores arrived two centuries later. Her horrified father waged war on the Aztec and drove them into Lake Texcoco, where they took refuge on an uninhabited island.

1325 Tenochtitlan founded by the Aztec, later becoming their capital.

1426–1428 Itzcoatl conquers Valley of Mexico and establishes Aztec Empire.

1487 Ahuitzotl reportedly sacrifices 20,000 prisoners on the Great Pyramid in Tenochtitlan.

1502 Moctezuma II succeeds Ahuitzotl.

1519 Hernán Cortés reaches Tenochtitlan.

1520 Moctezuma II dies after being taken prisoner by Cortés.

1521 Cortés and allies conquer Aztec Empire.

Aztec Empire

Growth of the Aztec Empire

- Itzcoatl, 1427–1440
- Moctezuma I, 1440–1468
- Axayacatl, 1469–1481
- Ahuitzotl, 1486–1502
- Moctezuma II, 1502–1520
- • Triple Alliance city

0   50   100 mi
0   50   100 km

Valley of Mexico

Huehuetoca
Coyotepec
Lake Zumpango
Tepozotlan
Lake Xaltocan
Teotihuacan
Cuautitlan
Sierra of Guadalupe
Lake Texcoco
Texcoco
Tenayuca
Tepeyac
Atzcapotzalco (Tepanec capital)
Xochimanca
Tacuba
Tlatelolco
Tenochtitlan
Chimalhuacan
Mazatzintamaico
Chapultepec
Isolte
Tlacopan
Huitzilopochco
Iztapalapa
Coyoacan
Mexicaltzingo
Culhuacan
Iztapalapa Peninsula
Xochimilco
Lake Xochimilco
Isla Cuitlahuac
Lake Chalco
Chalco
Mixquic

Las Flores
Tamuín
San Miguel Allende
Xacalta
Ranas
Zimapan
Moctezuma
Teayo
Chiquihuitillo
Toliman
San Juan del Río
El Tajín
Cojumatlan
Lerma
Tollantzinco
Yohualichan
Xiuhquilpan
Zacapu
Tzinapecuaro
Xiuhtetelco
Ixtlahuacan
Perote
Jalapa
Chachalacas
Apatzingán
Valle de Bravo
Ixhuacán
Remojadas
Bay of Campeche
Tetela del Volcán
Tepeaca
Orizaba
Cerro de las Mesas
Atazta
Huetamo
Xocotitlan
Chalcatzinco
Mexiquito
Tres Zapotes
Matacapan Piedra
Comalcalco
Tanganhuato
Balsas
Ixcaquíztla
Acatlan
Catemaco
Zacatollan
Teotitlan
Tuxtepec
Petatlan
Tzilcayoapan
Cuicatlan
San Lorenzo
Catzacoalcos
Sierra Madre del Sur
Yanhuitlan
Ville Alta
Isthmus of Tehuantepec
Acapulco
Ayutla
Tilantongo
Yagul
San Miguel Quetzaltepec
Coyac
Sierra Madre
Tehuantepec
Tonala
Pacific Ocean
Gulf of Tehuantepec
Huiztlan

Whatever prompted them to settle on that desolate spot, it proved to be a haven for the Aztec. It offered them shelter from hostile neighbors and sustenance as they fished, hunted, and reclaimed land from the swamp—a feat they achieved by digging drainage canals and piling up earth to form raised fields called *chinampas.* Soon after arriving, they built a temple that evolved into the Great Pyramid. It was constructed at a spot where they saw an eagle perched on a cactus in fulfillment of a prophecy attributed to Huitzilopochtli. That perching eagle was later depicted on the flag of Mexico, a nation born in the early 1800s that derived its name from the Aztec, who called themselves the Mexica. According to a calendar kept by Aztec priests, the founding of that temple— the first structure in the fledgling city of Tenochtitlan—occurred in 1325.

"Is it true that on earth one lives?
Not forever on earth, only a little while.
Though jade it may be, it breaks;
though gold it may be, it is crushed;
though it be quetzal plumes, it shall not last.
Not forever on earth, only a little while."

POEM BY AZTEC PHILOSOPHER-KING **NEZAHUALCOYOTL**,
TRANSLATED FROM NAHUATL BY LEÓN-PORTILLA

Over the next century, the Aztec dealt shrewdly and tactfully with their powerful neighbors around Lake Texcoco, biding their time until they could grow strong enough to more aggressively assert themselves. They traded and intermarried with other groups and made peace with Culhuacan by inviting a part-Aztec dignitary there to become their leader. They bowed to the might of the Tepanec—who held sway over much of the Valley of Mexico from their capital, Atzcapotzalco, on the western shore of the lake—and served them as soldiers as they had Culhuacan earlier. King Tezozomac of the Tepanec, who took power in 1371, used Aztec troops to subjugate rivals in the region. By the time he died in 1426, however, the Aztec were so accomplished at warfare that his successor could no longer control them. Much like the Turks who served as soldiers under caliphs in Baghdad before surpassing them and forging their own Muslim empire, the Aztec turned on their former masters and took charge of one of the most densely populated areas in the Americas. They achieved supremacy with help of two allied city-states, Texcoco and Tlacopan, but they soon dominated that alliance as they did the region at large.

The Aztec Empire was founded by King Itzcoatl, who joined with those allies to defeat the Tepanec and reigned from 1428 to 1440. His successor, Moctezuma I, expanded the empire east to the Gulf Coast. Subsequent rulers added to the Aztec domain until it stretched from the Gulf to the Pacific, encompassing 80,000 square miles and six million people. Like the Romans, the Aztec owed their success in battle to well-motivated troops who served in effect as citizen-soldiers. Tenochtitlan was divided into 80 wards or neighborhoods, each of which had its own governing council, schools, and temples and owned land communally. Each ward also had civic obligations, including providing 400 men for military service when called upon. The pride Aztec felt in their

The deity Tlaloc, painted on parchment

TEMPLO MAYOR

Sometimes it seems that great archaeological finds are made only in remote and hard-to-find places—deep in the jungle or desert. But one of the most important Aztec sites lay hidden for centuries right in the middle of one of the world's biggest cities.

When the Spaniards conquered the Aztec, they built what's now Mexico City over the ruins of the Aztec capital, Tenochtitlan. They even erased the location of the Templo Mayor, or Great Temple, a huge pyramidal structure topped with two shrines dedicated to Huitzilopochtli, the god of war, and Tlaloc, the rain god. Over the centuries, construction

crews or archaeologists in Mexico City made occasional finds of statues or such, providing a strong indication of where the temple must have been. But in 1978, utility company workers digging near the Zócalo, the city's main plaza, found ancient stone sculptures.

Archaeologists and others undertook a painstaking multiyear excavation of the Templo Mayor, which had been constructed in phases over time, eventually rising to 196 feet. Some remains of the temple were uncovered, including walls with traces of original murals

Sculpture of the eagle Cuauhxicalli, one of the offerings excavated at the Templo Mayor

now visible to visitors. The teams found about 7,000 artifacts. Many of them are offerings that worshippers had made to the gods; there are also objects related to human sacrifice. Most of these smaller objects, as well as some larger stone pieces, have been removed from the rubble and are exhibited in a museum adjacent to the archaeological site. ✦

Lights illuminate the ruins of the Templo Mayor in downtown Mexico City for nighttime visitors. Thousands of artifacts are on display in the adjacent museum.

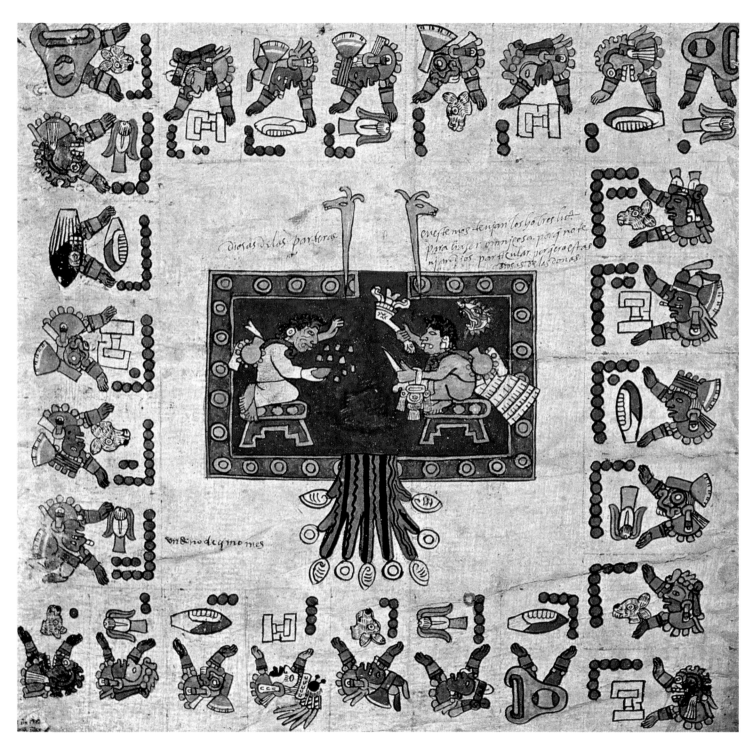

communities made them more willing to serve than if they had been lowly subjects of the king who had no stake in the empire.

The military might of the Aztec was matched by their commercial prowess. Tenochtitlan became the site of one of the world's busiest marketplaces, located

Oxomoco and Cipactonal, the first man and woman, are depicted creating agriculture and calendars in a scene from a facsimile of an Aztec codex.

in the district of Tlateloco, which was a separate island before the intervening land was reclaimed. Goods from throughout Mesoamerica were sold there, including

embroidered cotton fabric and paper made from bark, used by Aztec priests to compose accounts and keep calendars on which they recorded important mythical, historical, and astronomical events. Officials inspected the merchandise to make sure no one was cheated, and any disputes that arose were settled in a nearby courthouse. When Cortés and his men entered this vast marketplace in 1519, he estimated the crowd at 60,000. "We were astounded at the number of people and the quantity of merchandise it contained," wrote Bernal Díaz, "and at the good order and control that was maintained."

The Spaniards were also astounded and appalled to learn that the Aztec engaged in mass human sacrifice. Each new Aztec king embarked on a coronation war intended to demonstrate his prowess, exact tribute from conquered people, and seize captives, who were hauled backed to Tenochtitlan and sacrificed to the gods. King Tizoc, who took power in 1480, returned from his coronation war with only about 40 captives—a paltry number compared with that of other Aztec rulers. That poor showing may have caused people to doubt his resolve, for he soon faced rebellions from subjects who no longer wished to pay him tribute. In 1486, he was poisoned to death, perhaps by his brother Ahuitzotl, who launched his reign with a war that brought thousands of captives. Like other sacrificial victims, they were put to death atop the Great Pyramid by priests wielding razor-sharp knives, who cut open their chests and extracted their hearts. Their skulls were displayed on a giant rack.

Cortés and his men considered such ritualized slaughter barbaric, even though

conquest and carnage were intrinsic to their own culture and other powerful societies around the world. Europeans inflicted excruciating deaths on suspected traitors or heretics, and conquerors on various continents waged campaigns in which entire cities were destroyed and

A 16th-century image features a phonetic character for the town of Tula and, below it, an image of two men playing the ceremonial ball game.

thousands of men, women, and children were butchered.

The wholesale sacrifices conducted by the Aztec were indeed exceptional in the Americas, however. Warfare was common, and captives were sometimes put to death

in ritual fashion. But the Aztec practiced human sacrifice on a prodigious scale, as if the very magnitude of their success called for bloodlettings beyond compare. Their chief purpose was to honor and nourish the gods on whom they depended for victory and sustenance, but they may also have staged those murderous ceremonies to intimidate their foes and discourage subjects from rebelling. If so, they failed to achieve their goal, for many people antagonized by relentless Aztec demands for tribute and sacrificial victims turned against them and backed the Spanish conquistadores who shattered their empire.

The threat posed by Cortés and his men was not immediately apparent to King Moctezuma II, who welcomed them to Tenochtitlan and presented them with gifts, including a disk of gold "as large as a cartwheel," which only heightened the Spaniards' desire to sack the city and carry off its treasures. Moctezuma knew that these strangers with their fearsome horses, firearms, swords, and lances were potentially dangerous. Nonetheless, he tried to win them over using hospitality and diplomacy. A native woman named Malinche served Cortés as his mistress and interpreter, allowing him to communicate with the king. "Tell Moctezuma that we are his friends," he instructed her, according to an Aztec account. "Tell him that we love him well and that our hearts are contented."

Through such assurances, Cortés gained the king's confidence and caught him off guard. Seized by the treacherous Spaniards and held hostage, Moctezuma was disgraced and eventually deposed by the Aztec. He died while trying to ward off an attack carried out by troops loyal to his brother, the ruler who replaced him. Cortés managed to escape and went on to organize a far-reaching campaign against the Aztec, recruiting not only their sworn enemies and embittered subjects but also their disaffected allies, including the ruler of Texcoco, who resented being bossed by

Stone figurette of Xilonen, the Aztec corn goddess

> *"This great city of Temixtitlan [Mexico] ...*
> *is as large as Seville or Cordova;*
> *its streets, I speak of the principal ones,*
> *are very wide and straight."*

HERNANDO CORTÉS,
LETTER TO THE EMPEROR CHARLES V, 1520

Tenochtitlan and aided the Spaniards as they laid siege to that city.

By the time Tenochtitlan fell in 1521, the Aztec Empire had already collapsed. It was done in not just by a few hundred well-armed Spanish conquistadores but also by thousands of native people determined to overthrow their imperial masters. Other factors contributed to the outcome, including the technological advantages of the Spaniards and the ruinous diseases they introduced, notably smallpox, which ravaged Tenochtitlan as the siege wore on. But existing native societies had strong traditions of independence and resistance to outside authority. The Aztec Empire might soon have crumbled even without European interference, as had happened before to the Toltec.

AHUITZOTL

The eighth and greatest emperor of the Aztecs has also been remembered as the bloodiest. Ahuitzotl, who reigned from about 1486 to 1502, extended the empire west to the Pacific Ocean and south to Guatemala. Conquered people were expected to send tribute to the capital Tenochtitlan—riches and human captives, many of whom became human sacrifices.

At the dedication of the Templo Mayor in 1487, according to one account, Ahuitzotl led the sacrifice of 20,000 people, who were marched up the four sides of the pyramid in lines that stretched for miles. While that story may be exaggerated, human sacrifice was both an important part of Aztec religion and a tool for domination of subject lands.

Legend has it that Ahuitzotl's ashes were buried at the Templo Mayor after he died. In 2007, archaeologists in Mexico City began slowly excavating a spot where artifacts indicate that a great king may indeed have been interred in 1502.

Featherwork shield, supposedly the shield of Ahuitzotl, depicts a water beast holding a sacrificial knife in his jaws.

INCA EMPIRE
Conquerors From the Andes

Like the Aztec, the Inca rose over time to become a great imperial power in the 15th century, shortly before Spanish colonizers reached the New World. They began their quest for power high in the Peruvian Andes, where rainfall was sparse, crop yields were low, and conflict was frequent as neighboring groups vied for access to better land, located in river valleys or basins where fields could be irrigated. Competing in this challenging environment, Inca rulers led campaigns of conquest and plunder, waged by warriors drawn from a population made up largely of farmers who cultivated potatoes, tomatoes, and corn and herders who tended llamas and alpacas. By the 1300s, the Inca had taken control of the Cusco Valley and were eyeing the fertile fields and prosperous settlements around Lake Titicaca to the south, which was fed by rivers streaming down from snowcapped peaks.

The Inca domain expanded dramatically under a dynamic king named Pachacuti Inca Yupanqui, who took power in 1438. Before asserting his authority

Figurine (above) from an Inca sacrificial burial holds a wad of coca in her left cheek. Ancient Inca agriculture experimental station (right) near Cusco.

abroad, he first had to contend with opposition at home, waging a civil war against members of his family while repelling an invasion by powerful neighbors, the Chanca. A shrewd and ruthless infighter, he vanquished one brother who stood in his way and executed another. Thereafter, he relied largely on his sons, who fanned out with Inca armies, conquering the populous Titicaca Basin to the south and advancing northeast against the Chimu, who held sway over the Peruvian coastal plain from their capital, Chanchan. Pachacuti's son and heir apparent, Topa Inca Yupanqui, seized that city by dividing his forces and descending on his foes from several directions—a classic Inca stratagem. By defeating the Chimu, the Inca extended their empire from the Andes to the Pacific and went on to dominate much of the west coast of South America.

Pachacuti and Topa, who took power in 1471 when his father abdicated in his favor, not only conquered a huge area containing as many as 12 million inhabitants but also consolidated and organized their realm on a grand scale. Unlike Aztec kings, Inca rulers exacted little in the way of tribute from their foreign subjects, instead

■ **ca 1300** Inca take control of the Cusco Valley.

■ **1471** Topa Inca Yupanqui succeeds his father, Pachacuti, as emperor.

■ **1525** Huayna Capac perishes in an epidemic that ravages Cusco, the Inca capital.

■ **1533** Atahualpa executed by Spaniards, who join with native allies and capture Cusco.

■ **1438** Pachacuti Inca Yupanqui takes power and forges Inca Empire.

■ **1493** Topa dies and is succeeded by Huayna Capac.

■ **1532** Atahualpa defeats rival heir Huascar.

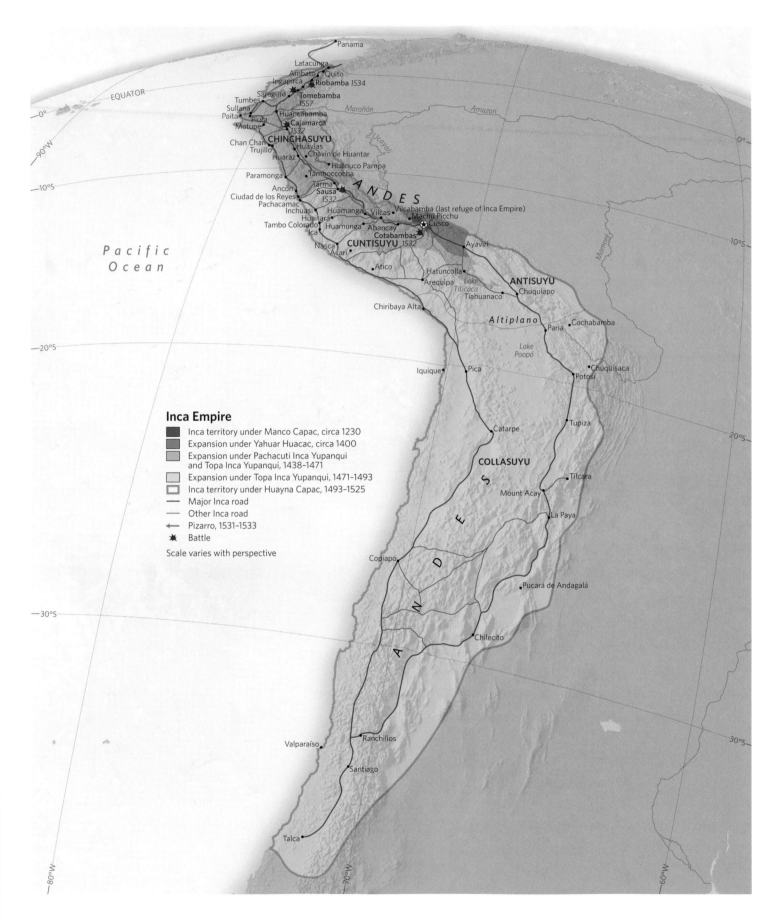

Panama

Latacunga
Ambato · Quito
Ingapirca · Riobamba *1534*
EQUATOR
Saraguro · Tomebamba *1557*
Tumbes
Sullana Huancabamba
Paita · Viura · Cajamarca *1532*
Motupe
CHINCHASUYU
Chan Chan Huaylas
Trujillo Chavín de Huantar
Huaraz
Huánuco Pampa
Paramonga Tamboccocha
Ancón Tarma
Ciudad de los Reyes Sausa *1532*
Pachacamac
Inchuasi Huamanga Vilcas Vilcabamba (last refuge of Inca Empire)
Huaitará Machu Picchu
Tambo Colorado Huamunga Abancay Cusco
Ica Cotabambas *1532*
Nasca CUNTISUYU Ayaviri
Acari
Atico
Hatuncolla
Arequipa ANTISUYU
Lake Chuquiapo
Chiribaya Alta Titicaca Tiahuanaco

Altiplano Cochabamba
Paria
Lake
Poopó
Iquique Pica Chuquisaca
Potosí

Tupiza
Catarpe

COLLASUYU
Tilcara
Mount Acay
La Paya

Copiapó

Pucará de Andagalá

Chilecito

Valparaíso Ranchillos

Santiago

Talca

Marañón
Amazon
Ucayali
ANDES
Mamoré

A
N
D
E
S

Pacific
Ocean

Inca Empire

- ▉ Inca territory under Manco Capac, circa 1230
- ▉ Expansion under Yahuar Huacac, circa 1400
- ▉ Expansion under Pachacuti Inca Yupanqui and Topa Inca Yupanqui, 1438–1471
- ▉ Expansion under Topa Inca Yupanqui, 1471–1493
- ▢ Inca territory under Huayna Capac, 1493–1525
- —— Major Inca road
- —— Other Inca road
- ← Pizarro, 1531–1533
- ✳ Battle

Scale varies with perspective

Two wooden cups found in the Peruvian Andes

demanding labor and military service. Conquered people who resisted those demands and threatened to rebel were resettled near the Inca homeland, where they were closely watched. Other subjects continued to live in their ancestral territory but were visited regularly by imperial inspectors, who made sure they were fulfilling their obligations. Those inspectors also compiled census reports, using knotted cords called *quipu* in place of writing, which the Inca and other South American cultures lacked. Officials and troops moved efficiently throughout the empire on a remarkable highway system consisting of two main arteries, one along the coast and another along the Andes, and numerous spurs. Tunnels, bridges, way stations, and storehouses facilitated traffic and furnished travelers with shelter and supplies.

Under imperial rule, the Inca capital Cusco developed into a majestic city, with a population exceeding 100,000. By one account, Pachacuti had the area vacated during his reign so that he could rebuild the capital, enhancing it with temples, plazas, and palatial residences for royalty, nobles, and priests. Overlooking the city was a great stone fortress, on which 20,000 men reportedly labored in

shifts. Spanish observers who arrived in the 16th century declared that they had never seen "a more powerful castle. Five thousand Spaniards might be able to fit inside." An extensive reclamation and irrigation project conducted by Pachacuti increased the productivity of the Cusco Valley and filled the capital's warehouses, which contained "everything that is made and grown in this realm," another Spanish witness reported.

Historians have likened the phenomenal ascent of the Inca under Pachacuti and Topa—who transformed their state from a small kingdom into a vast and coherent empire within 60 years—to the rise of the Macedonian Empire under King Philip II and his son, Alexander the Great. Like Alexander and other ancient emperors, Inca rulers were objects of cult adoration, closely identified with the Inca sun god Inti and creator god Viracocha. Reminiscent of the Roman ruler Constantine's vision of the True Cross that he believed brought him victory and led him to embrace Christianity, Pachacuti dreamed of Viracocha before defeating the invading Chanca and proclaimed that god his divine patron and protector, while also worshiping Inti as his father in heaven. He and

Manco Capac, the mythical first Inca king who supposedly founded Cusco centuries before the Spanish conquest, is depicted in a 19th-century painting.

QUIPU

The Inca didn't have a written language, but they tracked things such as taxes, births, and deaths using devices made of knotted strings, called *quipu* (also spelled *khipu* and derived from the Quechua word for knots). Quipu usually consisted of a main horizontal rope from which many pendant ropes dangled. About 600 quipu survive, most from the century or so before the Spanish encountered the Inca in 1532.

Scholars believe that numbers were recorded in a decimal system, with the position of the knot on each string indicating ones, tens, or hundreds. Other details— the color of the string, the type of fiber, the style of knot—are thought to record information that goes beyond numbers, such as names and places. Scientists are still studying quipu, using computers to untangle the ancient codes. ✺

The kneeling figure holds a quipu, a device for recording information via knots in string.

"All the people of Cuzco came out ... sat down on benches [and] passed the day in eating and drinking, and enjoying themselves; and they performed the tanqui ... [a dance] in red shirts."

CRISTÓBAL DE MOLINA, *THE FABLES AND RITES OF THE INCAS*, 16TH C.

other Inca kings were hailed as "sons of the sun."

When a ruler died, his body was mummified and buried with treasures, much like the deceased kings of ancient Egypt. Mourners declared that he had gone to heaven to join "his father, the sun." The Inca honored their gods and their present or past kings with offerings of food and drink as well as animal or human sacrifices. A Spanish chronicler told of a sacrificial ceremony that occurred when a new Inca king came to power. Boys and girls from throughout the realm were sent to Cusco, where they were dressed as young married couples and sacrificed to Viracocha by priests who asked the god to grant the ruler victory and prosperity. Inca sacrifices typically involved far fewer victims than the Aztec put to death atop their Great Pyramid and often occurred at shrines near mountaintops such as Machu Picchu, which were held sacred and served as the setting for temples as well as royal retreats.

Although the Inca sometimes sacrificed captured chiefs, most of the victims were honored members of their own society, including virgins known as Chosen Women, who were selected as young girls

Six-inch gold statue dressed as an Inca girl, found on Nevado Ampato

for their beauty and lived in seclusion at temples, where they tended sacred fires and practiced domestic arts such as cooking and weaving. Most were not sacrificed and went on to become priestesses or the wives or concubines of nobles. High-ranking Incas had many consorts and were free to cast them off, but their marriage to their principal wife was paramount and permanent. The king's principal wife was hailed by the Inca as Qoya ("queen") and Mamancik ("our mother"). Children born to her were first in line to succeed the king and belonged to her kinship group rather than his. Some Inca rulers married their sisters, a practice reportedly inaugurated by Pachacuti's son Topa. Royal wives and mothers were influential figures and were targeted along with princes and kings when rivals challenged them for supremacy.

Power seldom passed peacefully from one Inca king to another. One such succession crisis occurred following Topa's death in 1493 when supporters of young Huayna Capac, the son of Topa's sister and principal wife, clashed with those

An unwrapped Inca mummy. The Inca mummified their leaders and buried them with treasures.

The setting sun casts into relief the ruins of Machu Picchu, the magnificent abandoned Inca city high in the Peruvian Andes.

MACHU PICCHU

Some visitors to Machu Picchu speak of spirituality, others of the physical challenge of a high-altitude trek, but almost all say their first reaction upon seeing the ancient Inca city is awe. A 15th-century stone city tucked into a mountain-ringed valley high in the Andes, Machu Picchu is about 50 miles from Cusco, the Inca capital. Its great stone buildings and terraces, invisible from the valleys below, are obviously those of an advanced civilization. It is reached today by a four-hour train ride, then

a few miles of winding mountain road, or by a three- to six-day hike along the famed Inca Trail.

The Spanish conquistadores who toppled the Inca Empire never found Machu Picchu. Instead, it was rediscovered in 1911 by U.S. explorer Hiram Bingham, who was supported by Yale University and the National Geographic Society. In 2010, Yale's Peabody Museum reached an agreement with the Peruvian government to return to Cusco many of the artifacts that Bingham excavated a century ago.

Some skeletal finds were initially identified as mostly women, so Bingham postulated that Machu Picchu served as a center for priestesses. In recent years, though, more of the remains have been identified as male. Current thinking is that the city may have been the vacation retreat of late 15th-century emperor Pachacuti Inca Yupanqui, whose conquests stretched his domain from southern Peru to Quito, Ecuador. Exactly when and why the Inca abandoned Machu Picchu is unknown.

who backed another candidate, born to a secondary wife. That rival was banished and his mother was executed, as was the man who later served as Huayna Capac's regent and tried to oust him in favor of his own son. The prince overcame those early challenges and grew up to become an accomplished monarch who expanded the Inca domain north to what is now the border of Ecuador and Colombia. While campaigning there in the 1520s, he learned that a terrible epidemic had struck Cusco and hurried back to the capital. There he, too, died of the disease, which was most likely smallpox or measles introduced to the Americas by Spanish conquistadores who would soon invade the Inca Empire.

That Spanish conquest was facilitated by the ravages of disease and a tumultuous civil war that erupted following the death of Huayna Capac, whose sister and principal wife had no children. Two of his sons by secondary wives—Atahualpa and Huascar—engaged in a ruinous power struggle that weakened the empire. As in the overthrow of the Aztec, some groups subject to the Inca defied their masters and backed the Spaniards, led by Francisco Pizarro, who arrived in Peru with a few hundred soldiers shortly before Atahualpa defeated Huascar in 1532. After receiving assurances of friendship from Pizarro, Atahualpa entered his camp hoping to forge an alliance and was instead taken prisoner like the ill-fated Aztec ruler Moctezuma II. Pizarro offered to spare Atahualpa's life in exchange for a huge sum

in gold, then reneged on his promise and had him put to death, offering as justification Atahualpa's execution of Huascar.

By 1536, Spaniards and their native allies had captured Cusco and driven the last Inca emperor into exile. The treacherous feats of Pizarro, Cortés, and other conquistadores laid the foundation for the Spanish-American Empire, which drew on the resources and traditions of native kingdoms and lasted for nearly three centuries.

Illustration from the Historia y Genealogía Real de los Reyes Incas del Peru (History and Royal Genealogy of the Inca Kings of Peru), *attributed to a Spanish priest from about 1590*

PART III

1500s-1900s

It turns out that cultures armed with art and ancient wisdom are no match for invaders with guns. In the modern era, great distances were no longer a barrier to imperial expansion. In the Americas and in Africa, empires that had themselves conquered or united so many tribes were subjugated or wiped out by technologically advanced Europeans.

Imperialists grew rich around the world. Nations that increasingly honored democracy at home refused to recognize the rights, or even the humanity, of those they conquered. Westernization pushed at even the empires that could still defend their independence, such as the Ottomans in the Middle East.

But no single empire ruled the world. Instead, conflicting ideologies faced each other in bloody clashes. As the 20th century began, autocrats held tight to power in Asia, although revolution would eventually shake Russia and China. Even the British, who had built the most extensive empire yet, needed to defend their position against both enemies who wanted resources and subjects who yearned for freedom.

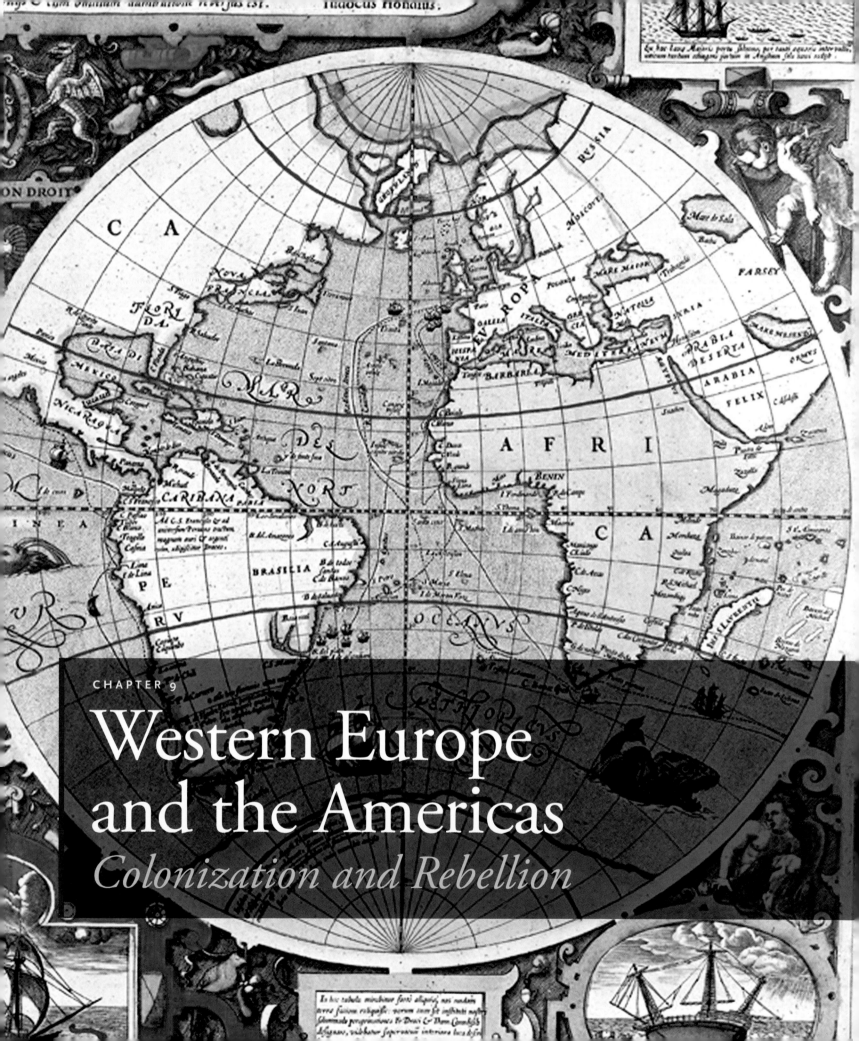

CHAPTER 9

Western Europe
and the Americas

Colonization and Rebellion

SPANISH-AMERICAN EMPIRE

Seeking Wealth in a New World

King Philip II of Spain, who came to power in 1556, had one overriding purpose as ruler of what was then the world's largest empire: to uphold Roman Catholicism, which he regarded as the only true faith. "I would prefer to lose all my dominions and a hundred lives if I had them rather than be lord over heretics," he said. Yet many of his subjects refused to conform to his beliefs, including Protestants who rebelled against Spanish rule in the Netherlands in the 1560s and Indians in his American colonies who worshiped various gods and resisted efforts by Spanish priests and soldiers to confine and convert them. Even if Philip had been granted those hundred lives, he could never have imposed his creed on everyone in his vast and diverse realm.

One factor that prevented his mighty Spanish Empire from thoroughly dominating Europe and the Americas was the growing power of England, which had officially embraced Protestantism following the death in 1558 of English Queen Mary I, Philip's wife and a fervent Catholic. Her

Coat of arms (above) granted in 1493 to Christopher Columbus, who is depicted at right being received by Ferdinand II of Aragon and Isabella of Castile

sister and successor, Queen Elizabeth I, aided Protestant rebels in the Netherlands, sent privateer Francis Drake to raid Spanish treasure fleets in the New World, authorized the founding of the North American colony known in her honor as Virginia, and withstood an attempted invasion by the powerful Spanish Armada. Other expansive kingdoms vied with Spain and established colonies in the Americas, too, among them France, Portugal, Russia, and the Netherlands. But it was England that ultimately surpassed Spain and took the lead in a global contest for imperial supremacy having less to do with religion than with wealth, power, and prestige.

The united kingdom of Spain emerged in 1469 when Queen Isabella of Castile wed King Ferdinand II of Aragon, bringing together the two largest Christian states on the Iberian Peninsula. Portugal remained distinct, but Granada—the last Muslim kingdom on the peninsula—fell to Spain in 1492, the same year in which three Spanish ships commanded by Christopher Columbus made landfall in the Caribbean. That voyage was among the most

---

1469 Queen Isabella of Castile weds King Ferdinand II of Aragon.

1494 Treaty with Portugal grants Spain most of New World.

1556 Philip II assumes Spanish throne and upholds Roman Catholicism.

1588 Spanish Armada is rebuffed by English defenders.

Early 1800s Spanish-American colonies rebel; Spain retains only Cuba and Puerto Rico.

1492 Christopher Columbus makes landfall in Caribbean.

1522 Ferdinand Magellan's crew completes circumnavigation of Earth.

1560s Protestants rebel against Spanish rule in Netherlands.

1680 Pueblo Indians drive Spanish settlers out of New Mexico.

1769 Franciscan friars found San Diego.

Arctic Ocean

ARCTIC CIRCLE

60°N

NORTH AMERICA

Manila to Acapulco with silk, spices, porcelain, ivory, lacquerware

Spanish Louisiana (1763-1800)

Havana to Cadiz and Seville with silver, silk, spices, porcelain, ivory, lacquerware

San Francisco 1776

1608 Santa Fe

Los Angeles 1781

Pensacola 1719, 1781, 1783

Pensacola 1698

New Orleans

30°N

1731 San Antonio

St. Augustine 1565

TROPIC OF CANCER

Viceroyalty of New Spain

1548 Zacatecas

Saltillo 1577

Havana 1748

Spanish West Indies

1521 **Tenochtitlan**

Tampico 1554

Havana 1515

1542 Guadalajara

Mérida 1542

Santo Domingo 1496

1521 Mexico City

Veracruz 1519

San Juan 1509

Puebla 1531

Cadiz and Seville to Cartagena, Veracruz, and Portobelo with supplies and luxury trade goods

1550 Acapulco

Trujillo 1525

Cartagena 1741

Santa Marta 1525

Acapulco to Manila with silver

1510 Nombre de Dios

Maracaibo 1529

Caracas 1567

Acapulco to Callao with silk, spices, porcelain, ivory, lacquerware

1597 Portobelo

Cartagena

Cumaná 1522

1519 Panamá

1533 **Viceroyalty of New Granada**

Callao to Panamá with silver

Bogotá (Santa Fé de Bogotá) 1538

Callao to Acapulco with silver

EQUATOR

Quito 1534

1538 Guayaquil

Riobamba 1534

Amazon

1526 Tumbes

Cuenca (Tomébamba) 1557

SOUTH AMERICA

1532 Paita

1532 Cajamarca

Cajamarca 1532

1534 Trujillo

Viceroyalty of Peru

1537 Callao

Lima 1535

1572 Huancavelica

Cusco 1533

Cusco 1533

1540 Arequipa

La Paz 1548

1541 Arica

Sucre (La Plata, Chuquisaca) 1538

Arica to Callao with silver

Potosí 1545

Corumbá 1788

TROPIC OF CAPRICORN

1537 Asunción

Ciudad Real 1630

Viceroyalty of Rio de la Plata

1550 Coquimbo

Córdoba 1573

Viceroyalty of Peru

1544 Valparaíso

Mendoza 1561

Buenos Aires 1536

1541 Santiago

Montevideo 1724

1550 Concepción

1552 Valdivia

1767 San Carlos de Ancud

Carmen de Patagones 1779

Pacific Ocean

Atlantic Ocean

AFRICA

Canary Islands

(Fernando Po) Bioko

Rio Muni

Spanish Guinea (Bioko 1778-1827, 1844-1959) (Rio Muni 1885-1959)

1588 Gravelines

Breda 1625

Rocroi 1643

(1579-1713) **Spanish Netherlands**

Nördlingen 1634

(1555-1648) **Franche-Comté**

Besançon

Bicocca 1522

Milan

Landriano 1529

Pavia 1525

Madrid

Rome

Sardinia

Naples

Kingdom of Naples (1504-1714)

(1581-1640) **Spanish Portugal**

Seville

Almansa 1707

Lepanto 1571

1702 Cadiz

Cadiz

Sicily

Cape Passaro 1718

60°S

120°W

90°W

ANTARCTICA

30°W

0°

30°E

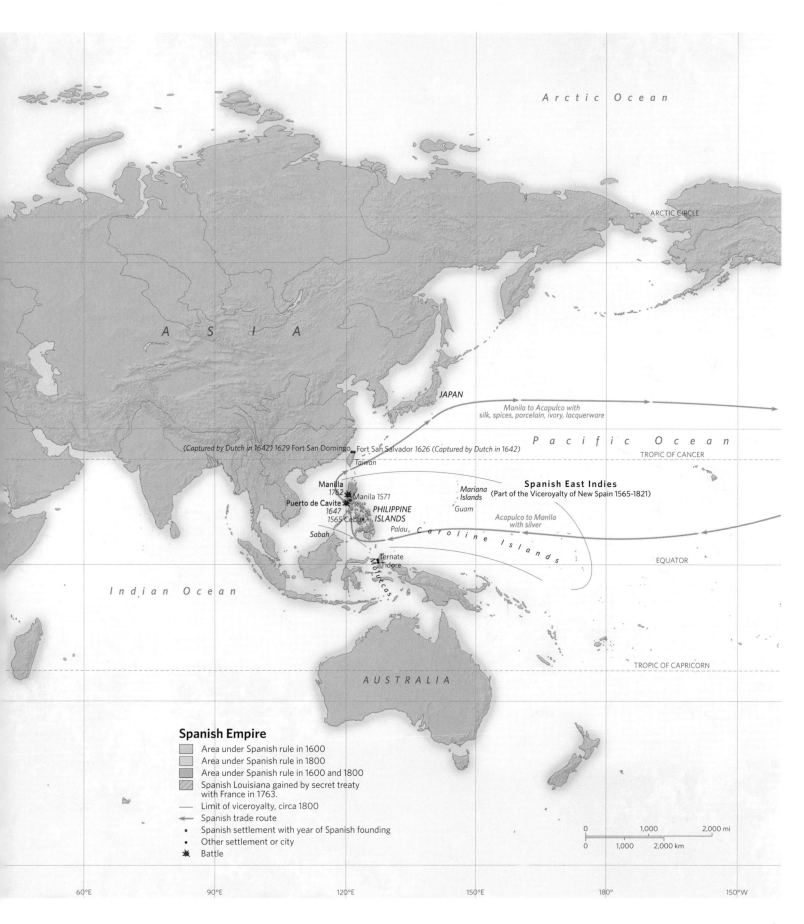

Arctic Ocean

ARCTIC CIRCLE

A S I A

JAPAN

Manila to Acapulco with
silk, spices, porcelain, ivory, lacquerware

P a c i f i c   O c e a n

TROPIC OF CANCER

(Captured by Dutch in 1642) 1629 Fort San Domingo   Fort San Salvador 1626 (Captured by Dutch in 1642)

Taiwan

Spanish East Indies
(Part of the Viceroyalty of New Spain 1565-1821)

Manila
1762   Manila 1571

Mariana
Islands

Puerto de Cavite
1647
1565 Cebu

*PHILIPPINE
ISLANDS*

Guam

Acapulco to Manila
with silver

Sabah

Palau

C a r o l i n e   I s l a n d s

Indian Ocean

Ternate
Tidore

Moluccas

EQUATOR

TROPIC OF CAPRICORN

AUSTRALIA

Spanish Empire

- Area under Spanish rule in 1600
- Area under Spanish rule in 1800
- Area under Spanish rule in 1600 and 1800
- Spanish Louisiana gained by secret treaty
  with France in 1763.
- ─── Limit of viceroyalty, circa 1800
- ◄── Spanish trade route
- • Spanish settlement with year of Spanish founding
- • Other settlement or city
- ✷ Battle

| 0 | | 1,000 | | 2,000 mi |
| 0 | 1,000 | 2,000 km | | |

60°E   90°E   120°E   150°E   180°   150°W

The Age of Exploration yielded a new source of commodities for western European countries. The world's richest silver deposits were discovered in 1545 at Mount Potosí, in what is now Bolivia.

significant feats of the so-called Age of Exploration, when venturesome Europeans drew on the know-how of earlier mariners, including Arab and Chinese navigators, whose advances included the magnetic compass and, for determining latitude, the astrolabe.

It was not technological superiority but geography and imperial rivalries that set Spain and other western European kingdoms on global paths of exploration and conquest. The recent expansion of the Ottoman Empire, whose forces conquered Constantinople in 1453 and took control of the Balkans, gave Muslim merchants a tight grip on trade between Asia and Europe in silk, spices, and other luxuries. Intent on obtaining those goods without relying on Muslims with whom they were at odds, western Europeans sought new maritime routes to the Far East. In the process, they came upon new lands and fresh sources of wealth.

Maritime exploration was spurred not just by conflict between the Christian and Muslim worlds but also by keen competition among western European kingdoms. Spain had a rival next door in Portugal, whose mariners rounded Africa and reached India in the late 1400s. Spain matched those feats with the help of foreign-born navigators such as Columbus, from the Italian city-state of Genoa, and Ferdinand Magellan of Portugal, who launched the first circumnavigation of the globe—completed in 1522 without Magellan himself, who died in the Philippines.

The Philippines became a Spanish colony engaged in profitable trade with China. Spain's largest and most lucrative colonies, however, were established in the Americas

Columbus brought corn from the Americas to Europe.

following expeditions by Columbus and later conquerors. A treaty between Spain and Portugal, worked out in 1494 by Pope Alexander VI, granted Spain nearly all of the New World except easternmost South America, where Portugal ruled Brazil. Other European kingdoms ignored that agreement and colonized lands in North America and the Caribbean. Nevertheless, Spain long remained preeminent, overseeing a huge area from Mexico south for centuries to come.

Spanish colonization of the New World began inauspiciously on Caribbean islands with the devastation of Native Americans, known as Indians because Columbus initially believed he had reached India. Some Indians perished in clashes with Spaniards or were forced to labor for them in grueling conditions that shortened their lives. Many died of smallpox and other European diseases to which they had no immunity. In the Caribbean, the indigenous population was all but annihilated. Colonists then turned to imported slaves from Africa to work their sugar plantations, and the population of Cuba and other islands became predominantly black.

The great lure for Spanish conquistadores such as Hernán Cortés and Francisco Pizarro was mineral wealth, which they acquired by probing the interior of Mexico and South America in the early 1500s and conquering the Aztec and Inca Empires (see chapter 8). Vast amounts of silver poured into Spanish coffers from mines such as those at Potosí in present-day Bolivia, a boomtown that swelled to a population of

- Main entrance
- Basilica
- Museo de Arquitectura
- Pantheon Real (below church)
- Museo de Pintura
- Patio de los Evangelistas
- Salas Capitulares
- Monastery with four arcaded courtyards
- Grand entrance
- Patio de los Reyes
- College with four courtyards

ROYAL MONASTERY OF SAN LORENZO DE EL ESCORIAL

When the highly religious monarch Philip II set out to construct a grand monument to his reign, he built not a palace, but a monastery. But the Royal Monastery of San Lorenzo de El Escorial is no humble retreat. It has 15 cloisters, 13 oratories, 86 staircases, 88 fountains, more than 1,600 paintings, nine towers, and 73 sculptures (and yes, a palace was eventually included in the complex, as well as a church, a library, and a museum).

Philip built the monastery to provide a burial place for his father, Charles V, as well as to atone for attacking a French church—dedicated to St. Lawrence, an early Christian martyr—during a battle. The layout of the complex is based on the shape of a griddle, the cruel device upon which Lawrence was killed. The monastery took 21 years to build. Construction began in 1563 under the direction of architect Juan Bautista de Toledo and continued after his death under Juan de Herrera, who expanded upon the original plan. The vast, austere gray granite building is considered the first example of the Herreran style of architecture, which influenced numerous Spanish churches. Most of Spain's kings, including Philip, are buried at El Escorial in the Pantheon of the Kings.

The monastery sits on a hill over the town of El Escorial, about an hour outside Madrid. It is open most days to visitors, who can wander the rooms on their own or join guided tours. Highlights include not only the church, crypts, and Renaissance art but also the library, which has more than 40,000 documents, including thousands of manuscripts from the 15th and 16th centuries.

The ornate Pompeian Room, a section of El Escorial renovated in the 18th century as a palace for Bourbon kings

Tupac Amaru II

At the same time the British faced revolt in their North American colonies, rebellion challenged the Spaniards in South America. An estimated 100,000 Indians in what is now Peru, Bolivia, and Argentina joined in the south Andean revolt, which lasted from 1780 to 1783. It was begun and led by Tupac Amaru II (1741–1781), born José Gabriel Condorcanqui, a wealthy Jesuit-educated chief who lived in southern Peru, near Cusco. He was a descendant of Tupac Amaru, the rebellious last Inca king, and he adopted his ancestor's name to proclaim his Inca heritage.

Tupac Amaru II and his followers wanted, among other things, to end the brutal colonial system of forced labor. At first, the rebels were successful, drawing tens of thousands of natives to the cause. But Tupac Amaru II was captured in 1781 as his army battled to take Cusco. He was killed in a ghastly bloody public execution, and although the rebellion simmered another two years after his death, it was eventually unsuccessful. His last words, in response to a question from a Spaniard about the identity of his accomplices, reportedly were: "There are no accomplices here but you and I. You, the oppressor and I, the liberator. Both of us deserve death!"

TUPAC AMARU II

150,000. To work those mines, Spanish officials conscripted Indian laborers. Viceroys serving as representatives of the king ruled Spanish colonies from Lima, within the former Inca domain, and Mexico City, built on the ruins of the Aztec capital, Tenochtitlan.

Mineral wealth from the Americas enriched the Spanish Crown, which claimed one-fifth of the silver shipped from the colonies. King Philip II used that treasure to finance wars against France, England, and rebels in the Netherlands—a country endowed to Spain by his grandfather, King Philip I of the Habsburg dynasty, who wed the daughter of Ferdinand and Isabella in 1496. Unwilling to surrender Holland to Protestant insurgents, Philip II sent troops to pound them into submission. That heightened resistance to Spanish rule among the Dutch, who eventually won independence. Philip's efforts to topple the defiant Queen Elizabeth went awry as well when the Spanish Armada was rebuffed by English defenders in 1588 and shattered by storms.

Treasure from the Americas did not bring Philip victory nor his people prosperity. The influx of silver caused inflation and did little to stimulate the Spanish economy because much of it went to buy goods made abroad. Spain remained a poor country when the devout Philip II died in 1598. He had expanded his empire by incorporating Portugal when its king died without an heir. But his own heir, Philip III, proved inept, bearing out his father's bleak assessment: "God, who has given me so many Kingdoms to govern, has not given me a son fit to govern them."

Spain's great imperial legacy was not economic or military but cultural. Like

> *"All these islands and territories, abounding in gold, spices and treasure, situated west and south of a line that runs from the North to the South Pole, a hundred leagues west of the Isles of the Azores and Cape Verde, are allocated to the Catholic Kings."*
>
> **ALEXANDER VI,** *INTER CAETERA*

Roman conquerors, Spanish colonizers bequeathed their language, laws, and beliefs to millions of people in distant lands. Spanish traditions blended with Indian customs to produce a new Hispanic-American society, where European imports such as wheeled vehicles, horses, and cattle enhanced a way of life based on native staples such as corn and tomatoes and native crafts such as pottery and adobe architecture. Colonists of pure Spanish ancestry formed the elite, but a large class of mestizos, people of mixed race, emerged through intermarriage.

Missionary priests gradually converted much of the native population to Catholicism, aided by Spanish officials and troops, who guarded missions and pursued Indians who fled them. Tribal resistance

Native cultures were often forced to follow the religious beliefs of Spanish missionaries, in monasteries such as Igaraszo in Brazil.

to colonization and conversion remained high, however, particularly along the rugged northern frontier of Spanish America. In 1680, Pueblo Indians rose up in New Mexico and drove out Spanish settlers and missionaries. Colonists returned there a decade later and reached an accommodation with the Pueblo, who then served with them as troops in campaigns against hostile tribes such as the powerful Comanche living in and around Texas.

In the 1700s, control of Spain and its colonies passed from Habsburg monarchs to Bourbon kings of French ancestry. Spain and France, which had long been rivals, found common cause against the British, who expanded rapidly in North America and took Canada from France in 1763. Intent on bolstering the Spanish-American Empire against the British and the Russians, who had recently colonized Alaska, Spain's King Charles III (Carlos III) expelled the Jesuits, whom he considered disloyal, and entrusted to Franciscan friars in Baja California the task of colonizing Alta California. Aided by Spanish troops, they founded San Diego in 1769 and went on to settle San Francisco, one of the finest ports in North America.

Colonial expansion in the New World only made this and other European empires harder to govern, however, and many colonists grew dissatisfied with their distant imperial masters. Spanish America soon faced a threat that proved greater than any foreign foe—a flood of rebellion that swept British colonies along the Atlantic in the 1770s and engulfed Mexico and South America in the early 1800s, producing new independent nations and leaving only Cuba and Puerto Rico in Spain's possession.

BRITISH EMPIRE
A Truly Global Realm

Like Spain, England embarked on imperial expansion at a time of bitter religious controversy. During the reign of Queen Elizabeth I, English troops crushed rebellions by Catholics in Ireland—a country that long resisted English rule—and confiscated their land, which went to Protestant colonists. Unlike Spain, however, England did not try to impose religious uniformity on its American colonies, which were organized by companies or founders with varying beliefs and objectives. Among the English colonists who settled in North America in the 1600s were Catholics in Maryland, Quakers in Pennsylvania, Anglicans (members of the Church of England) in Virginia, and Puritans (at odds with the Church of England) in Massachusetts.

Politically as well as spiritually, English colonists had more latitude than Spanish colonists. For a time, Massachusetts was practically self-governing. Eventually, English monarchs asserted greater authority over their American subjects—including Dutch settlers in New York, seized from

The Armada Jewel (above) depicting Queen Elizabeth I (right, during the Spanish Armada) in gold, diamonds, rubies, and rock crystal

the Netherlands in 1664—by appointing royal governors and imposing trade restrictions. But English colonists retained their own representatives, who met in assemblies, fostering a spirit of independence that led to the American Revolution.

By 1700, there were some 250,000 English settlers in North America. They seldom intermarried with Indians or relied on their labor. Instead, they occupied tribal lands and fought wars with natives who resisted their incursions. Some English colonists of means hired indentured servants from Europe, who gained their freedom after fulfilling their contracts. But many preferred to purchase African slaves, who remained the property of their masters for life, along with any children born to them. Slave labor proliferated in Virginia and other southern colonies, where tobacco, rice, and cotton were cultivated on large plantations. African slaves were also shipped to Jamaica and other islands in the Caribbean that England wrested from Spain in the 1600s.

Beginning in the early 18th century, England—known as Great Britain following its union with Scotland in 1707—engaged in an

1600s Catholics, Quakers, Anglicans, and Puritans colonize North America.

1664 England seizes New York from the Netherlands.

1707 Great Britain formed by England's union with Scotland.

1759 Gen. James Wolfe seizes Quebec.

1776 American colonies declare independence from Great Britain.

1781 George Washington achieves decisive victory at Yorktown.

1788 Australia founded as a penal colony.

1857 British forces impose direct imperial rule on India.

1910 Britain grants South Africa dominion status.

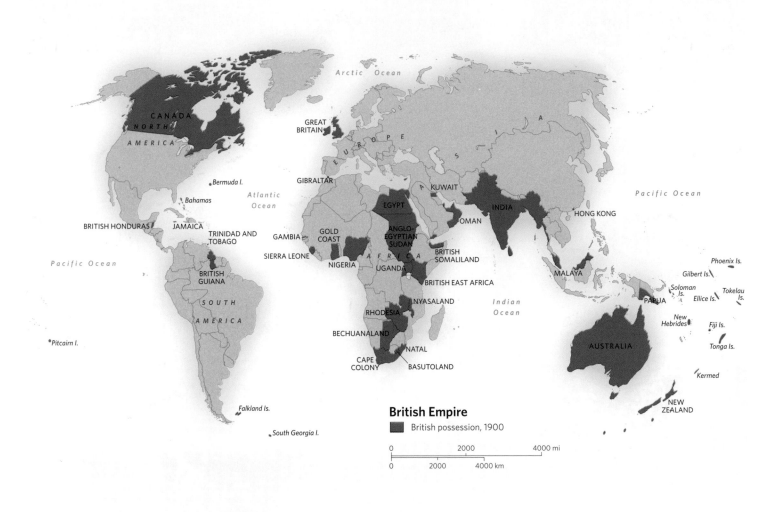

British Empire

■ British possession, 1900

```
0          2000         4000 mi
0     2000      4000 km
```

epic struggle with France in Europe, North America, and Asia. The two nations were old foes; during the late Middle Ages they had waged one of the longest-running conflicts in history, known as the Hundred Years' War. Their rivalry was suppressed in the 16th and 17th centuries by their mutual animosity toward Spain but resurfaced as that once-great power declined and came under French influence. Britain and France were now competing for imperial supremacy and clashed repeatedly, beginning with the War of the Spanish Succession (1701–1713), during which the British and their allies prevented King Philip V of Spain, a Bourbon monarch born in France, from also inheriting the French throne.

France lost that conflict and fared even worse in the Seven Years' War (1756–1763), waged on several continents and known to the British in America as the French and Indian War. By that time, French settlers in Canada and Louisiana were vastly outnumbered by British colonists along the Atlantic, but had forged alliances with Indians of many tribes, who backed them in the war, hoping to halt British advances into tribal territory. The French suffered an irreparable loss when troops led by Gen. James Wolfe seized Quebec in 1759. At the conclusion of the Seven Years' War, France temporarily ceded Louisiana to its ally Spain and surrendered Canada and all its claims east of the Mississippi River to Britain, retaining

only Haiti and a few other colonies around the Caribbean.

This proved to be a costly victory for Great Britain, which imposed new taxes on its American colonists to cover its war debts. Those taxes and other British measures, including an effort to avoid further Indian wars by curbing the westward expansion of settlers, drove colonists to rebel. The American Revolution began in Massachusetts in 1775 and became official when representatives from 13 colonies met in Philadelphia in 1776 and broke with Great Britain. Their Declaration of Independence denounced King George III as a tyrant. Thomas Jefferson of Virginia and other founders of the American Republic drew inspiration from the English political philosopher John Locke, who helped draft the Bill of Rights requiring British monarchs to honor the will of Parliament and respect its laws. The success of the

During the Seven Years' War, the French and Indian allies attacked British and American troops as they attempted to reach Fort Duquesne (above). The Treaty of Utrecht (left) of April 11, 1713, ended the War of the Spanish Succession.

An American Revolutionary War reenactor tightly grips his musket.

MUSKETS

The musket was the firearm on the shoulders of the earliest American settlers, the rebels of the American Revolution, and British redcoats who fought against them. The first muskets were developed by the Spanish in the 16th century. They were the dominant guns until the rifle became widespread in the 19th century.

Muskets were a major advance over their predecessors, the hard-to-aim, hard-to-fire hand cannons. They were muzzle loaded, meaning the gunpowder and projectile, usually a lead ball, were put into the muzzle, the front-facing open end of the gun's barrel. With the earliest muskets, called matchlocks, the powder was ignited when a lever or trigger lowered a smoldering match cord into the flash pan, at the end of the barrel away from the muzzle. Later flintlock models struck sparks to ignite the powder.

Muskets were sometimes clumsy, and in the time it took to reload, a skilled Indian archer could launch several arrows. But the musket had a greater range and, when a gunman found his target, the result was deadly.

Gen. George Washington crosses the Delaware River, leading troops to the Battle of Trenton, during the American Revolutionary War.

American Revolution and the nation that emerged from it owed much to British constitutional principles—and military aid from France, which struck back at Britain by supporting the American rebels. French intervention helped Gen. George Washington achieve a decisive victory at Yorktown in 1781, leading the British to acknowledge American independence two years later.

Far from dealing a fatal blow to the British Empire, the American Revolution demonstrated the empire's resilience and led British authorities to seek ways to retain the allegiance of distant colonists without using military force. Tens of thousands of Anglo-Americans remained loyal to Britain and emigrated to Canada, which eventually became a self-governing British dominion. Other countries that achieved self-rule as dominions without rebelling

Louis XVI, was exhausting the royal treasury. He and the old aristocratic regime he upheld collapsed during the tumultuous French Revolution, which began in 1789. Napoleon Bonaparte seized power a decade later, restored law and order to France, and led his formidable army of citizen-soldiers on brilliant campaigns that brought much of Europe under his imperial rule. To finance those conquests, he reclaimed Louisiana from Spain and sold it to the United States in 1803. A year later, he withdrew French forces from Haiti and allowed that rebellious colony to go free, staking all he had on his bid for European supremacy.

Despite Napoleon's smashing victories on the Continent, he remained hemmed in by the British navy, which shattered his fleet at Trafalgar in 1805. When Russia joined the British in opposing him, he launched a disastrous invasion of that country in 1812 and was forced into exile. Attempting to return to power, he was crushed at Waterloo in 1815 by Britain's Duke of Wellington. "Had I succeeded," Napoleon declared afterward, "I would have died with the reputation of the greatest man that ever existed." In truth, he was one of the many meteoric conquerors with supersize egos throughout history who dazzled the world briefly before they came crashing down, achieving little of lasting significance compared with those who built enduring empires.

Following the downfall of Napoleon, Great Britain solidified its position as the world's leading imperial power—the first ever to gain preeminence

included Australia, founded as a penal colony in 1788, and New Zealand, where British settlers arrived in the early 1800s.

While Great Britain rebounded quickly from its American defeat, the French gained little from intervening there and could ill afford to finance a revolution abroad while their absolute monarch, King

VISITING THE PAST

THE JAMESTOWN COLONY

Jamestown, Virginia, the first permanent English settlement in America, is now an active archaeological site. Since excavation began in 1994, the project has uncovered most of the foundations of the original James Fort, begun in 1607, plus more than a million artifacts from early settlers.

Those settlers came in search of wealth on a voyage financed by the private Virginia Company. Their first years were difficult, including a winter of near starvation. The settlement eventually grew into the hub of a wealthy tobacco-growing region. Jamestown was the capital of colonial Virginia until 1699, when nearby Williamsburg took over that role and Jamestown itself was nearly abandoned.

The original Jamestown site, on what's now an island in the James River, is overseen by the National Park Service. It's part of Colonial National Historical Park, a collection of historic locations that also includes the Yorktown Battlefield, where the last major battle of the Revolution occurred. Visitors can tour the archaeological site, Jamestown Settlement—a living history museum that includes a recreation of a native Powhatan village—and nearby Colonial Williamsburg.

At Jamestown Settlement, visitors can see life-size re-creations of the homes where early colonists lived.

THE ENGLISH LANGUAGE

At the time English settlers came to Virginia in 1607, their language was spoken almost exclusively in England, with a population of less than five million. Shakespeare was still alive and the first English dictionary was three years old. As England's empire spread, it spread its language to the Indian subcontinent, Australia, and elsewhere. The language the American colonists imported has been exported as the language of entertainment, business, and most Internet sites. Even in famously anti-Anglophone Paris, subway ads urge riders to learn English to get better jobs.

According to Robert McCrum, author of several books on the language: "English is now used, in some form, by approximately 4 billion people on earth—perhaps two thirds of the planet—including 400 million native English speakers. As a mother tongue, only Chinese is more prevalent, with 1.8 billion native speakers—350 million of whom also speak some kind of English." ✍

A scrap from the epic poem Beowulf, *written about* A.D. *1000 in Old English, the Germanic ancestor of today's language*

on a truly global scale and rule countries in Europe, Asia, Africa, the Americas, and the Pacific. This was an empire unprecedented both in its extent and in the means by which its colonies were acquired and governed. Most earlier empires were built largely if not entirely through conquest and consisted of contiguous states or provinces subject to a supreme ruler whose military and political authority was absolute. The British Empire was forged not just by soldiers or sailors but also by settlers, traders, missionaries, officials, and engineers who colonized distant lands and imposed British traditions and technology on their native inhabitants. It was ruled not just by kings or queens but also by parliamentary leaders, who unlike hereditary rulers had to compete publicly for power. They were often more skilled and energetic in promoting British imperial interests than were the monarchs they served. Queen Victoria, who reigned over Britain and its far-flung colonies from 1837 to 1901, was an enthusiastic imperialist who proudly bore the title Empress of India. But it was elected leaders such as Prime Minister Benjamin Disraeli who truly ruled the empire and worked to expand it.

No colony proved more important to Britain economically and strategically than India, acquired not by the British navy or army but rather by the British East India Company, which hired its own soldiers and gradually took control of the subcontinent in the 18th century as the Mughal Empire fractured (see chapter 11). Not until Indian troops called sepoys

rebelled against that company in 1857 did British forces intervene and impose direct imperial rule on India, a major source of cotton and other raw materials for British industries. Britain's economic and strategic interests as a great industrial power led to the colonization of other countries in Asia and Africa, including Egypt, where British troops intervened in 1882 to secure the Suez Canal, a vital conduit linking Britain to India, Burma, and more distant colonies.

Boosters like author Rudyard Kipling hailed the British Empire as a civilizing force that would bring peace, prosperity, and the blessings of modern technology such as railroads

A cameo of Queen Victoria and Prince Albert

> *"We have done with Hope and Honour, we are lost to Love and Truth, We are dropping down the ladder rung by rung, And the measure of our torment is the measure of our youth. God help us, for we knew the worst too young!"*
>
> RUDYARD KIPLING, "GENTLEMEN-RANKERS," 1892

and electric power to lands cloaked in medieval gloom and convulsed by ethnic and religious strife. But imperialism often heightened tensions within colonial societies and proved more disruptive than constructive. The British abolished slavery in their empire in 1833, but the grim legacy endured in colonies such as South Africa. There British troops clashed with defiant tribes such as the Zulu, who resisted encroachment by white settlers, and with colonists of Dutch origin called Boers or Afrikaners, who sought independence. When Britain granted South Africa dominion status in 1910—a privilege denied to India and other colonies without large numbers of white settlers—it left Afrikaners in control there, free to impose on the country's black majority a rigid policy of segregation and discrimination known as apartheid.

Reforms such as self-rule or constitutional government did not bring to an end the age-old desire of strong states or societies to dominate other groups. Even the United States, which began by throwing off British colonial rule and espoused freedom and equality, subjugated many Indian nations as it expanded west to the Pacific. It later colonized Hawaii and the Philippines, occupied by American troops in 1898 along with Cuba and Puerto Rico in a war that all but obliterated the once-mighty Spanish Empire.

Poster (right) produced for the Colonial and Empire Exhibition of 1886 showing Britannia surrounded by various images representing the broad reach of the British Empire.

PEOPLE

THOMAS STAMFORD RAFFLES

Thomas Stamford Raffles (1781–1826) spent most of his life in the service of one of the most influential nongovernmental colonizers ever, the British East India Company. His career embodied the British belief that conquerors could profit while "improving" the lives of the inhabitants of faraway civilizations.

Raffles, later Sir Stamford, began working for the East India Company at age 14 as a clerk in London. After a decade, he was posted to Penang in the Malay Peninsula, where he learned the language and culture. After the British ousted the French and Dutch from Java, he set up the system of colonial administration there. He was also a naturalist and ethnographer, but is best known for founding the city of Singapore, which began as a Company trading post. His name lives on there at the famous colonial-era Raffles Hotel, opened some 60 years after his death.

IMPERIAL TRIBES OF NORTH AMERICA
Ruling Without Capitals or Kings

History affords many examples of tribal groups that rose to imperial glory, including the Franks under Charlemagne and the Mongols under Genghis Khan. In Mexico and South America, the Aztec and Inca grew from tribal societies to imperial powers. No such indigenous empire, with a great urban capital and a centralized political system that brought millions of people under the authority of one ruler, rose north of Mexico. But several Native American societies within what is now the United States, notably the Comanche of the southern Plains, exercised imperial power in other ways.

English colonists who settled at Jamestown, Virginia, in the early 1600s confronted a formidable chief called Powhatan who asserted authority over about 30 tribes in the region, using armed force or diplomatic means such as marriage alliances (he reportedly had 100 wives). In the words of one English emissary, Powhatan exuded "such a majesty as I cannot express." Capt. James Smith of the Jamestown Colony told of being captured by Powhatan

Comanche (above) with shield, lance, bow, and arrows. Comanche warriors showed feats of horsemanship by dropping from the saddle during battle (right).

and rescued from execution by his daughter Pocahontas. She was later kidnapped by the English, under whose supervision she converted to Christianity and wed John Rolfe, a pioneering tobacco planter who helped make the colony profitable and populous. Powhatan refused to bow to the English and bequeathed his tribal empire to his brother, Opechancanough, who waged a determined war on the colonists before his defeat in the 1640s.

Paramount chiefs such as Powhatan who ruled over many tribes were not the only Native American imperialists. Other tribal leaders enhanced their own power and that of their people by forming confederacies that dominated distant groups and controlled areas far larger than Powhatan's domain. The formidable Iroquois Confederacy took shape in upstate New York not long before Dutch and English colonists arrived there in the 17th century. It consisted originally of five tribes—the Seneca, Cayuga, Onondaga, Oneida, and Mohawk—living between Lake Ontario and the Hudson River. They offered beaver pelts to Dutch and English traders in exchange

---

- **Early 1600s** Chief Powhatan asserts authority over about 30 tribes in Virginia.

- **Late 1600s** Iroquois Confederacy gains power through warfare, trade, and diplomacy.

- **1786** New Mexico governor reaches accord with Comanche chief.

- **1845** Texas annexed by United States, which seeks to confine Comanche.

- **1870s** Sherman forces Comanche and other Plains tribes onto reservations.

- **1640s** Opechancanough, Powhatan's successor, defeated by English colonists.

- **Mid-1700s** Comanches defeat their rivals, the Apache, and dominate southern Plains.

- **1821** Texas passes from Spain to newly independent nation of Mexico.

- **1867** William Tecumseh Sherman helps negotiate Medicine Lodge Treaty.

Comancheria

- Comancheria, 1750–1845
- Kiowa, Comanche, and Apache Reservation in Indian Territory, 1890
- Republic of Texas
- Mexico (Spain)
- United States
- Disputed between Texas and Mexico
- □ Fort, with date of establishment
- ○ Comanchero trade site
- ✸ Battle
- → Comanche campaign
- → Campaign against the Comanche
- --- Santa Fe Trail
- — Boundary, 1846

0   50   100 mi
0   50   100 km

for firearms and gained supremacy over neighboring tribes such as the Mohican, from whom they demanded tribute. When beaver grew scarce in their territory, they raided tribes hundreds of miles away for pelts and other booty. One vulnerable southern tribe, the Tuscarora, sought protection from the Iroquois, who adopted them and brought them north to join their confederacy.

Trading ties led to a formal covenant, or alliance, between the British and the Iroquois, enhancing their status as Indian nations, capable of dealing with European powers on equal terms. That covenant brought them into sharp conflict with the French and their Indian allies, however, and the fighting took its toll. By the late 1700s, the Iroquois were losing strength, and the ties binding them were beginning to fray. Their chiefs met annually in

"It was a spectacle never to be forgotten ...
Both horses and riders
were decorated most profusely ...
Red ribbons streamed out from their horses' tails
As they swept around us, riding fast ...
Exhibiting feats of horsemanship and daring
None but a Comanche ... could perform."

JOHN HOLLAND JENKINS, PLUM CREEK

council, but it became increasingly difficult for them to reach a consensus. During the American Revolution, two of the Six Nations backed the rebels while the other four remained loyal to Great Britain and suffered devastating reprisals by the victorious Americans. Their confederacy was shattered, but for nearly two centuries they had matched European empires at their own game.

No tribal group within the present United States controlled a larger territory or dealt more forcefully with European or Anglo-American colonists than the Comanche, who ruled the southern Plains for more than a century. They arrived there from the vicinity of the Rocky Mountains in the early 1700s, not long after Pueblo Indians rebelled against Spanish settlers in New Mexico. Following that revolt, many Spanish horses found their way into the hands of Plains Indians, including the Comanche, who were among the first to master the arts of mounted warfare and hunting buffalo on horseback. By the mid-1700s, they had defeated their formidable rivals the Apache and laid claim to one of the richest buffalo-hunting grounds in North America, extending south from the

Arkansas River for more than 500 miles. Although their population was only about 15,000, their domain was as large as the Aztec Empire, and they cast a long shadow over Spanish settlements in Texas and New Mexico.

Comanches alternately raided and traded with Spanish colonists, who gained a grudging respect for them. One Spaniard noted in 1778 that they were acquiring iron weapons as well as horses and showed "so much skill in handling both that they surpass all nations in agility and courage. They have made themselves the lords of all the buffalo country." Spanish authorities barred the sale of firearms to Comanches, but they obtained guns from French merchants. Among the items they offered in trade were slaves they seized from rival tribes. Spanish officials found it hard to stop that illegal slave trade, for if the Comanche were denied access to Spanish markets, they would attack settlements and seize goods and captives.

Spanish commanders conducted punitive raids on the Comanche, but could not defeat them. In 1786, New Mexico governor Juan Bautista de Anza reached a peace accord with a Comanche chief named Ecueracapa, who did not represent

Pocahontas throws herself over Capt. John Smith, preventing Opechancanough from striking a death blow, while Powhatan raises his hand to stay the execution.

COMANCHE RULE

The Comanche tribe traditionally was a loose organization of nomadic bands—groupings based on extended families. Band chiefs would meet to work out issues. A series of treaties among the Plains tribes and the U.S. government culminated in 1867 with the Treaty of Medicine Lodge, which was soon broken. Despite resistance, the Indians were placed on reservations, the horsemen who once roamed the Plains allotted relatively small tracts of Oklahoma land.

For much of the century, the government treated the neighboring Kiowa, Comanche, and Apache as one entity. But in 1966, the Comanche split into a separate tribe, the Comanche Nation, with its own constitution and elected council. There are about 14,600 enrolled members, of whom about 7,800 live in the Lawton–Fort Sill area of southwestern Oklahoma. The council oversees public services and economic development, including managing revenue from the tribe's four casinos.

the tribe as a whole but had enough influence with other chiefs to make the agreement stick. The Comanche were made up of various bands, each with its own leaders. Like the Iroquois, their chiefs often met in council, allowing them to function loosely as a nation or confederacy. Had they recognized a single ruler, they might have been better equipped to defeat the Spaniards. But they had no desire to occupy settlements and live as the colonists did. Their seminomadic life of hunting, trading, and raiding was a better strategy for them than settling in towns, whose inhabitants were vulnerable to attack and prone to communicable diseases. They were content with what they had—an empire with no emperor to obey, no capital to defend, and no cumbersome code of laws to enforce.

During the 19th century, as the United States expanded west and subdued many other tribes, the Comanche

Steve Street (right), a Comanche, garbed in ceremonial clothing, participates in the modern Red Earth Festival in Oklahoma City, Oklahoma.

resisted incursions by Anglo-Americans. Officially, control of Texas passed from Spain to the newly independent nation of Mexico in 1821, and then from Mexico to the Republic of Texas, which broke free in 1836 before being annexed by the United States in 1845. In reality, much of Texas and what is now Oklahoma remained Comanche country, open to traders who dealt fairly with the tribe but closed to white settlers, who came under attack if they intruded.

Anglo-Americans called this obstacle to their territorial ambitions the "Comanche barrier" and were determined to break it. But not until after the Civil War—which ended slavery in the United States while enhancing the power of the federal government to impose on Indians and confine them to reservations—were the Comanche subdued. Gen. William Tecumseh Sherman, who had crushed Confederate resistance to the Union by waging total war on the South and its economy, applied the same scorched-earth policy to the Comanche and other defiant Plains tribes, attacking bands in their winter villages and inviting professional hunters with high-powered rifles to annihilate the buffalo herds that were vital to the Indians' way of life.

Forced onto reservations, the tribes were subsumed within the American nation that Thomas Jefferson called an "empire for liberty." It would be many years, however, before the Indians were recognized as U.S. citizens and granted the liberties Jefferson and other Founders promised Americans.

Comanche delegation (which may also have included Kiowa members), photographed in Washington, D.C., in the late 1800s

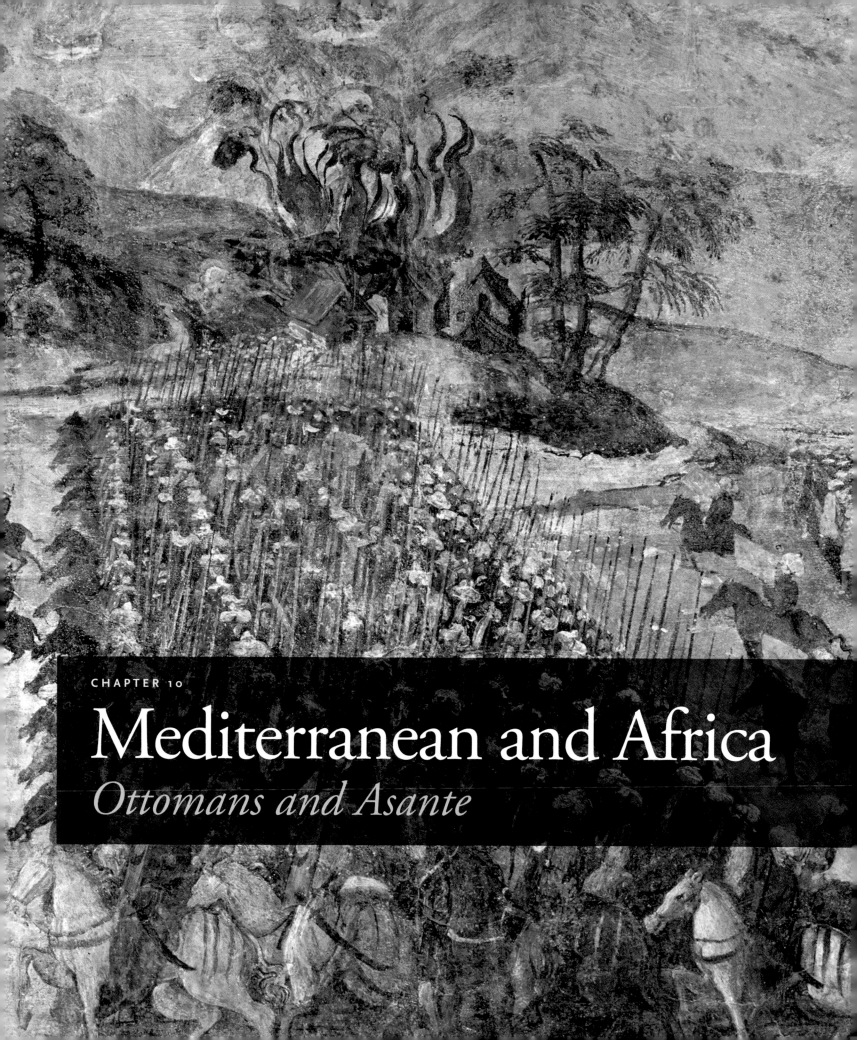

Mediterranean and Africa
Ottomans and Asante

OTTOMAN EMPIRE
Bridging Asia, Africa, and Europe

The fall of Constantinople in 1453 to the Muslim forces of the Ottoman Empire shocked Europeans, who saw it as a catastrophe for their civilization. "What a misery for Christendom!" wrote the future Pope Pius II, who thought the conquerors would persecute Greek Orthodox Christians and destroy what remained of classical Greek culture. "Homer and Plato have died a second death," he declared.

Yet his worst fears were not realized. Sultan Mehmed II, the dynamic Ottoman emperor who seized Constantinople, converted the Hagia Sophia and other Orthodox churches there into mosques but did not force Christians to convert. Far from disdaining Europeans and their culture, Mehmed spoke Greek, read Homer, and studied history under Italian tutors. "He aspires to no less fame than that of Alexander the Great," wrote one Italian observer. "Eager for information about the Western world, he possesses a map showing the realms and provinces of Europe," which he hoped would soon be part of the Ottoman Empire.

Mehmet III's Koran case (above), made of wood, ivory, and nacre. Selimiye Mosque (right) in Turkey, was built by the Ottoman sultan Selim II.

Mehmed and his successors had a profound impact on the modern world through their own imperial accomplishments and those of competing kingdoms in western Europe such as Spain and Portugal, which advanced in new directions in response to the Ottoman challenge. Ottoman rulers of Turkish origin reunited much of the Muslim world—which had fractured when the Abbasid dynasty in Baghdad declined in the 11th century—and forged bonds between far-flung countries in Europe, Asia, and North Africa. At the same time, their dominance of the eastern Mediterranean impelled western Europeans to seek new trade routes to the Far East and to sail around Africa, where they established coastal trading posts. That commerce proved devastating for some African societies but strengthened others, notably the wealthy and opportunistic Asante of the Gold Coast, who, like the Ottomans and their western European rivals, acquired firearms, embarked on imperial expansion, and sold captives into slavery.

The Ottoman dynasty was founded around A.D. 1300 by Osman, a Turkish chieftain in northwestern Anatolia, now Turkey. His

ca 1300 Osman, a Turkish chieftain, founds Ottoman dynasty.

1453 Ottoman emperor Mehmed II conquers Byzantine Empire by seizing Constantinople.

1501 Ismail becomes shah of Iran and leads Shiites against Sunni Muslim Ottomans.

1514 Ottoman troops defeat the army of Shah Ismail at Chaldiran.

1520 Sultan Suleyman I begins reign that brings Ottoman Empire to its peak.

1683 Ottomans repulsed at Vienna.

1807 Conservatives in the Janissary corps overthrow Sultan Selim III.

1908 Young Turks impose constitutional rule and leave Ottoman sultan powerless.

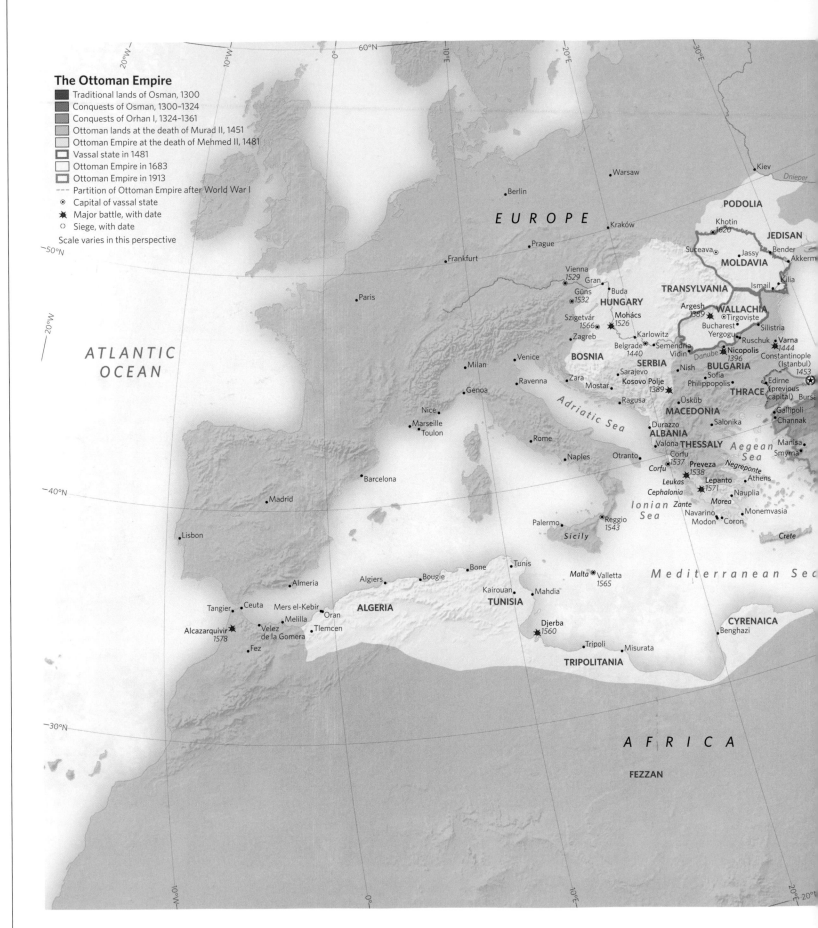

The Ottoman Empire

- Traditional lands of Osman, 1300
- Conquests of Osman, 1300–1324
- Conquests of Orhan I, 1324–1361
- Ottoman lands at the death of Murad II, 1451
- Ottoman Empire at the death of Mehmed II, 1481
- Vassal state in 1481
- Ottoman Empire in 1683
- Ottoman Empire in 1913
- - - Partition of Ottoman Empire after World War I
- ⊙ Capital of vassal state
- ✹ Major battle, with date
- ○ Siege, with date

Scale varies in this perspective

EUROPE

ATLANTIC OCEAN

Mediterranean Sea

AFRICA

Warsaw
Berlin
Kraków
Prague
Frankfurt
Paris
Vienna *1529* Gran
Güns *1532* Buda
HUNGARY
Szigetvár *1566* Mohács *1526*
Zagreb Karlowitz
Belgrade *1440* Semendria
BOSNIA Vidin
Venice SERBIA Nish
Milan Sarajevo
Ravenna Zara Kosovo Polje *1389*
Genoa Mostar
Ragusa
Nice Üsküb
Marseille Durazzo MACEDONIA
Toulon ALBANIA Salonika
Rome Valona THESSALY
Naples Corfu *1537*
Otranto Corfu Preveza *1538*
Barcelona Leukas *1571* Lepanto
Madrid Cephalonia Morea
Navarino Modon Coron
Lisbon Palermo Reggio *1543*
Sicily
Bone Tunis
Almeria Algiers Bougie Malta ⊙ Valletta *1565*
Tangier Ceuta Mers el-Kebir Kairouan Mahdia
Melilla Oran ALGERIA TUNISIA
Alcazarquivir *1578* Velez Tlemcen Djerba *1560*
de la Gomera Tripoli Misurata
Fez TRIPOLITANIA

Kiev
Dnieper
PODOLIA
Khotin *1620* JEDISAN
Suceava Jassy Bender Akkerm
MOLDAVIA Ismail Kilia
TRANSYLVANIA
Argesh *1389* WALLACHIA
Tirgoviste
Bucharest Silistria
Yergogu Ruschuk Varna *1444*
Nicopolis *1396*
Danube Constantinople (Istanbul) *1453*
BULGARIA
Sofia Edirne (previous capital) Bursa
Philippopolis THRACE
Gallipoli
Channak
Aegean Sea Manisa
Smyrna
Negreponte Athens
Zante Nauplia
Ionian Sea Monemvasia
Crete

Adriatic Sea

FEZZAN

CYRENAICA
Benghazi

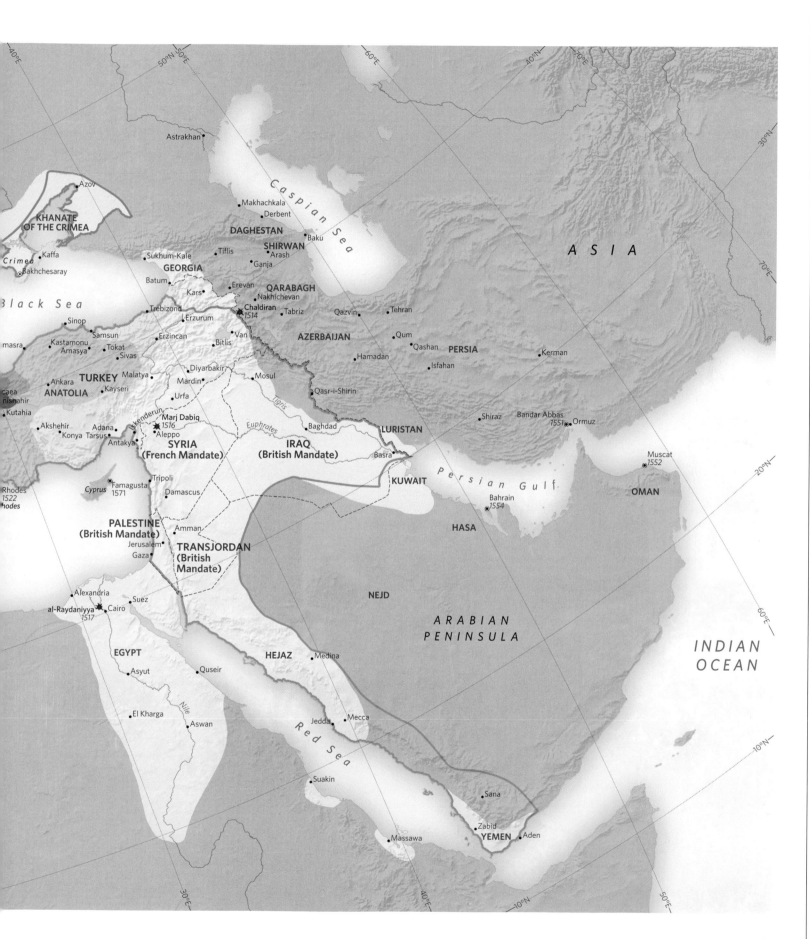

KHANATE
OF THE CRIMEA

Azov

Crimea

Kaffa

Bakhchesaray

Black Sea

Sinop

Kastamonu
Amasya

Samsun

masra

Tokat

Sivas

Ankara

TURKEY

Kayseri

ANATOLIA

caea
nishahir

Kutahia

Akshehir

Konya

Adana

Tarsus

Antakya

Cyprus

Famagusta
1571

Rhodes
1522
hodes

Tripoli

Damascus

PALESTINE
(British Mandate)

Jerusalem

Gaza

Alexandria

al-Raydaniyya
1517

Suez

Cairo

EGYPT

Asyut

Quseir

El Kharga

Aswan

Nile

Astrakhan

Makhachkala

Derbent

DAGHESTAN

SHIRWAN

Arash

Baku

Tiflis

Sukhum-Kale

Ganja

GEORGIA

Batum

Kars

Erevan

QARABAGH

Nakhichevan

Trebizond

Chaldiran
1514

Tabriz

Erzurum

Erzincan

Van

Bitlis

AZERBAIJAN

Diyarbakir

Mardin

Mosul

Malatya

Urfa

Iskenderun

Marj Dabiq
1516

Aleppo

Euphrates

Tigris

Qasr-i-Shirin

Baghdad

SYRIA
(French Mandate)

IRAQ
(British Mandate)

Basra

Caspian Sea

ASIA

Qazvin

Tehran

Qum

Qashan

PERSIA

Hamadan

Isfahan

Kerman

Shiraz

Bandar Abbas
1551

Ormuz

Muscat
1552

LURISTAN

KUWAIT

Persian Gulf

Bahrain
1554

HASA

OMAN

Amman

TRANSJORDAN
(British
Mandate)

NEJD

ARABIAN
PENINSULA

INDIAN
OCEAN

HEJAZ

Medina

Jedda

Mecca

Red Sea

Suakin

Sana

Massawa

Zabid

YEMEN

Aden

homeland lay between two declining imperial powers—the Mongol Empire to the east and the Byzantine Empire to the west. Osman and his immediate successors did not yet have sufficient strength to expand east, where other Turkish forces were challenging Mongol rulers. Instead, Ottoman warriors advanced west across the Bosporus Strait into Europe and carved up the vulnerable Byzantine domain.

Byzantine rulers had long faced challenges from inside and outside their empire, including incursions by Catholic crusaders from western Europe, who did not confine themselves to fighting Muslims and sacked Constantinople in 1204. Emperors there now had little control over their provinces in the Balkans, which fell one after another to the advancing Ottomans.

Devout Muslim soldiers known as *ghazi* contributed to those conquests, believing that if they died in battle against foes considered infidels they would gain eternal life. Ottomans also conscripted Christian boys in conquered lands, converted them to Islam, and trained them as warriors known as Janissaries. Officially, they served sultans as mamluks (slaves), but their masters grew increasingly dependent on them and could ill afford to lose the support of this elite military force.

By the mid-15th century, Ottoman armies had advanced north through

Enamel and engraved copper pitcher, Turkey, 18th century

the Balkans to the Danube River, bypassing Constantinople, which was bounded on three sides by water and heavily fortified against assault by land. Intent on overcoming those defenses, Sultan Mehmed II, who came to power in 1451 at the age of 18, assembled a large fleet that besieged Constantinople and massive artillery that shattered its walls. Like many conquerors, Mehmed allowed his victorious troops to pillage the fallen city and punish its populace, but he spared Constantinople from wholesale destruction and transformed it into the Ottoman capital, renamed Istanbul.

Many of the hundreds of rooms in the harem section of Topkapi Palace are decorated with elaborate tiles and mosaics.

VISITING THE PAST

TOPKAPI PALACE

Beginning in 1459, soon after he conquered Constantinople, Sultan Mehmed II began construction of a majestic palace on a hill overlooking the Bosporus. It grew to become the primary residence of the Ottoman sultans until 1853 and an administrative center of their empire. The walled complex of courtyards, gardens, and buildings is among the world's grandest examples of Islamic architecture. It became a museum in 1924 and is one of the most visited sites in Istanbul.

Although the museum houses a collection of artistic treasures dating back centuries, as well as holy relics of the prophet Muhammad, one of its biggest draws is the harem. Far more than a lounge for the sultan's concubines, it was an elaborate private quarters for the rulers and their families, where women were secluded from the business around them. The harem contains more than 300 rooms, nine Turkish baths, two mosques, a laundry, and a hospital.

Courtiers assemble in strict fashion in front of the gate of Topkapi Palace, Istanbul, at a reception at the court of Sultan Selim III.

The policy of Mehmed and his successors toward non-Muslims was similar to that of earlier Arab rulers of the Umayyad and Abbasid dynasties. Conversion to Islam was sometimes encouraged, but seldom required. Christians and Jews who adhered to their own faiths were subject to a special tax—a price that many Jews who faced persecution in Christian countries were willing to pay in exchange for official tolerance. Tensions between people in the Balkans who embraced Islam and those who remained Christian contributed to ethnic conflict in later times when the Ottoman Empire declined.

The tolerance Ottoman rulers showed Christians and Jews was not, however, extended to dissident Shiite Muslims, who denied the legitimacy of Sunni sultans in Istanbul. The split between Sunnis and Shiites had originated as a dispute over whether the prophet Muhammad's son-in-law, Ali, was his only rightful successor, from whom all future caliphs who ruled the Islamic world should be descended, as Shiites believed. The quarrel between these two branches of Islam had expanded to include other religious differences and resulted in fierce power struggles between imperial dynasties.

In 1501, Shiites seized the city of Tabriz, a former Mongol stronghold in northwestern Iran, and proclaimed their leader Ismail shah, or king. Unlike Ottoman sultans, who were political rather than spiritual leaders, Shah Ismail was hailed as a Shiite imam—a divinely inspired ruler in the mold of Muhammad and Ali. Through conquest and conversion, he gained a large following in Iran and neighboring Anatolia and posed a growing threat to Sultan Selim I, who launched a brutal campaign against

Ismail's Shiite devotees. In 1514, Ottoman troops wielding firearms overpowered the shah's army at Chaldiran, near what is now the Turkish-Iranian border. That pivotal battle left Ismail and later rulers of his Safavid dynasty on the defensive and cleared the way for Selim's forces to advance south through Syria and Palestine to Egypt, which fell to the Ottomans in 1517. They also gained control of Mecca and other Muslim holy places in Arabia, enhancing the stature of Selim and his successors as guardians of Islam.

The Ottoman Empire reached its peak under Selim's son, Sultan Suleyman I, who took power in 1520. Known as Suleyman the Magnificent, he campaigned energetically to expand his

Copper basin decorated with enamel and engravings

> *"I will make no change in the government now. Obey me while I live. The one who disobeys will be guilty of treason. After that, all will be between you as God wills."*
>
> SULEYMAN THE MAGNIFICENT

domain but recognized the danger of overreaching. He used diplomacy when necessary to appease his foes and consolidate his gains. His dedicated army advanced through Hungary into Austria and laid siege to Vienna, defended by Holy Roman Emperor Charles V, a Catholic monarch who made concessions to dissident Protestant princes in Germany in return for their support against the Turks. Unable to break through,

Suleyman withdrew from Vienna but later negotiated a treaty upholding his claim to the fertile Danube River valley in Hungary. He showed similar flexibility in the Middle East, where his troops advanced to the Tigris River before encountering stiff resistance from Iranian forces of the Safavid dynasty: Suleyman reached a pact with the Safavids that left Ottomans in possession of Mesopotamia but allowed Shiite pilgrims to visit Mecca.

Suleyman made further gains in North Africa and the Mediterranean, where an accomplished Turkish pirate named Khayr al-Din—known to his European foes as Barbarossa ("red beard")—served as his naval commander. After ousting Spanish forces and seizing Algiers in 1529, Barbarossa secured Tunisia for the Ottomans and defeated a fleet organized by Emperor Charles V off the coast of Albania, leaving the Turks in firm command of the eastern Mediterranean.

Like Augustus Caesar, Suleyman worked to unify and enhance his empire politically and culturally as well as militarily. Known to Ottomans as the Lawgiver, he issued many edicts concerning legal matters not covered by sharia, Islamic religious law.

Suleyman I, also known as Suleyman the Magnificent, was the tenth and longest-reigning sultan of the Ottoman Empire and is known for his military and cultural talents.

PEOPLE

ROXELANA

The woman known as Roxelana in the West and Hürrem Sultan ("the cheerful one") in Turkey was born about 1550 and taken into slavery during an Ottoman raid on her Crimean village. She is variously said to be of Ukrainian, Russian, or Polish ethnic heritage. Despite that grim beginning, she became one of the most powerful and important women in the Ottoman Empire. As a slave in the royal harem, she caught the attention of Suleyman the Magnificent and soon became his favorite concubine. She bore several of his children, and eventually he took her as his legal wife—a rarity for an Ottoman sultan, and a clear sign that he valued her counsel. She is usually portrayed as strategizing successfully against grand viziers and other concubines to ensure that her son Selim II followed his father on the throne.

JANISSARIES

The military elite of the Ottoman Empire, the Janissary corps, was formed in the late 14th century based on a system called *devşirme*, the "child levy." Ottoman troops occupying the Balkans took sons from Christian families—preferably 12 to 14 years old—marched them to Istanbul, converted them to Islam, and then raised them as state-educated slaves. Some sources estimate that boys were taken at the rate of one per 40 families.

Some boys went to school and others worked on farms or in public works projects before they received military training. All were raised to be devout Muslims and dedicated supporters of the state. They were known for their well-armed and aggressive, if not always disciplined, performance in battle.

Although they were classified as slaves, they were paid and had many privileges. At first, Janissaries were celibate, which prevented the formation of a hereditary class. In time, that requirement was dropped, as was the child levy and the prohibition against Turks' and other Muslims'

becoming Janissaries. What developed was a corrupt, violent, and often rebellious armed class. Through the 17th and 18th centuries, they staged numerous bloody palace coups. In June 1826, they rebelled against attempts by Sultan Mahmud II to modernize the military. But the sultan wisely maintained his own loyal military elite, which crushed and killed thousands of remaining Janissaries in what is known as the Auspicious Incident.

Depictions of Janissaries from the 16th century show richly dressed, well-armed, and prosperous-looking men.

A great builder, he commissioned mosques, palaces, madrassas (religious schools), hospitals, aqueducts, and public baths throughout the empire. Many of those structures were designed by his chief architect, Sinan, a Greek Orthodox Christian by birth who converted to Islam as a Janissary before distinguishing himself as a military engineer and winning the sultan's favor. Suleyman was likened by Muslims to the biblical King Solomon for the splendid monuments he raised and the justice he dispensed. Before he died in 1566, he left an inscription that was closer to the truth than many boastful proclamations by emperors: "Slave of God, master of the world, I am Suleyman and my name is read in all the prayers in all the cities of Islam. I am the Shah of Baghdad and Iraq, Caesar of all the lands of Rome, and the Sultan of Egypt."

Like the Caesars who ruled Rome after Augustus with varying degrees of competence, Ottoman sultans were sometimes decadent or inept. But their empire proved remarkably durable, lasting for more than 350 years after reaching its zenith under Suleyman. His successors suffered occasional setbacks, including a stinging defeat for the Ottoman fleet at the Greek port of Lepanto, where the allied naval forces of Spain and Venice emerged triumphant in 1571. That battle deprived the Turks of their aura of invincibility, but did little to loosen their grip on the eastern Mediterranean or the lands surrounding it.

Not until the late 1600s did the Ottoman Empire begin to decline perceptibly. One factor behind that decline was the increasing isolation of sultans from their soldiers in the field and their subjects

At the 1789 Battle of Focsani during the Russo-Turkish War, the Russians, supported by Austrians, defeated the Ottomans.

in the provinces. Earlier rulers had been outgoing figures who sometimes served as officers or governors before taking power and often campaigned with their armies as sultans. By the 17th century, however, princes were confined to the palace to prevent them from battling each other openly for the right to succeed the reigning ruler. The prince who prevailed owed his success less to his own merits than to the machinations of his supporters at court, including high officials such as the grand vizier—the

> **"Those who saw Suleiman's face in this hour of triumph failed to detect . . . the slightest trace of undue elation."**
>
> OGIER GHISELIN DE BUSBECQ

sultan's chief adviser and administrator—commanders of the Janissaries, and women of the sultan's harem. New rulers often continued to live sheltered lives and were not always well served or well informed by their advisers.

Such was the situation of Sultan Mehmed IV, whose deranged father, known as Ibrahim the Crazy, was murdered by palace officials in 1648 when Mehmed was just six years old. He remained under the guardianship of his mother and grandmother until he matured, and even then his authority was limited. He proved more energetic than some sultans and took an active interest in warfare, occasionally joining his forces in the field. But he did not control the army and failed to prevent his overzealous grand vizier from launching a risky campaign in the 1680s to crush the Habsburg dynasty in Austria and seize Vienna. That goal, which had eluded the determined troops of Suleyman the Magnificent, was beyond the capacity of

*Sixteenth-century Ottoman art demonstrates
an appreciation of leisure and music.*

the less imposing army of Mehmed IV, and it was driven back and lost ground to Austria in the northern Balkans. Mutinous soldiers ousted the ill-fated sultan in favor of his more popular brother, Suleyman II, who repaired some of the damage done to the empire with the help of a grand vizier wiser than Mehmed's.

Economic problems also contributed to the decline of the Ottomans, who lost tax revenue when western Europeans opened maritime trade routes to West and East Africa as well as the Far East, reaping profits at the expense of Middle Eastern merchants. That increased the tax burden on poor people in the Ottoman Empire, who grew increasingly resentful of sultans and their impositions. Measures such as "tax farming"—entrusting revenue collection to private agents who kept part of what they extracted from the populace as a fee for their services—led to abuses that caused some people to rebel or throw their support to local landlords or warlords over whom the government had little control. Meanwhile, the Ottoman Empire, which once boasted some of the world's best-equipped armed forces, was falling behind European countries in military and industrial technology. Sultan Selim III, who came to power in 1789, made efforts to modernize the army, but met with opposition from the conservatives in the Janissary corps and was overthrown in 1807.

By the late 1800s, nationalist uprisings in Greece and other Balkan countries as well as advances by Great Britain, France, and Russia had whittled down the Ottoman Empire, stripping it of possessions in North Africa, Europe, and the Crimea. Reformers known as Young Turks tried to halt the decay by imposing a constitutional government in 1908 and reducing the authority of the sultan to that of a mere figurehead. But they kept a tight rein on Arabs, Armenians, and other ethnic groups within their empire who hoped for greater freedom.

Six centuries of Ottoman rule came to a bitter end during World War I, when Armenians, considered disloyal by Turkish authorities, were evicted from their homeland in death marches that claimed half a million lives. Such persecution did nothing to strengthen the faltering Ottomans or stop Arabs from joining with Allied forces in defeating them. Their once great empire had lost its way. But from its wreckage emerged a new nation, Turkey, a democratic society that reached out to its old foes in Europe and forged close bonds with the West.

MEN'S CLOTHING

Modern Westerners might regard clothing as a mode of self-expression, but in the Ottoman Empire, dress was dictated by law and served to mark each person's place in the social structure. In the 16th century, Suleyman the Magnificent put forth laws that dictated the size, color, and design of robes and headgear, especially turban styles. One style of headgear was reserved for the sultan himself, others for various ranks at court and in the military, and commoners wore simple turbans. Clothing colors were designated for Muslims, Christians, and Jews. "One glance at the robes informed all—rivals and allies alike—of the precise rank and place of an official," explains Donald Quataert, a modern scholar of the Ottomans.

Men wore baggy trousers, a waist sash, and a shirt, with a kaftan over them when weather required, sometimes in multiple colorful layers. Those who could afford it wore luxurious silks, golden cloth, and elaborate decoration. By the 18th century, a new round of laws regulated ostentation—for instance, only the most elite could wear ermine. Sultan Mahmud II's modernization in the 1820s also changed clothing. After he crushed the Janissary corps in 1826, he decreed that the fez—a felt hat that looks like an overturned flower pot—was part of the new military uniform, and then required it for all civil and religious officials. With that hat seen as a symbol of his authority, the remnants of the Janissary class refused to wear it.

1808 painting of Amurath (Murad) IV (1612–1640), sultan of Turkey from 1623 to 1640

Velvet skullcap embroidered with metallic thread, from the Ottoman Empire, 19th century

Hasseki Baltaci Valet del Sultani, Ottoman period, third quarter of 18th century

ASANTE EMPIRE
Uniting the Chiefdoms

In Africa, as in other parts of the world, trade provided rulers with wealth, weaponry, and the means to overpower their rivals. During the late Middle Ages, trade with Muslim merchants from North Africa who crossed the Sahara in caravans contributed to the rise of the Mali and Songhai Empires in West Africa, a region rich in gold. Beginning in the late 15th century (see chapter 7), merchants from Portugal, Holland, England, and other European countries established trading posts along the Gold Coast of modern-day Ghana and offered firearms in trade. As a result, power in West Africa shifted south from lands near the Sahara, where the Mali and Songhai had prevailed, to the Gold Coast and vicinity. Here, the Asante forged an empire that remained formidable well into the 19th century.

It was not just guns that strengthened the Asante and others who traded with Europeans. Among the crops merchants introduced from the Americas to West Africa were tomatoes, cassava, and corn, which flourished in land cleared from the tropical rain forest along the Gold Coast by African

Asante swords (above) from Ghana. A head made of gold (right) symbolizes the Asante emperor.

inhabitants and their slaves. The brutal transatlantic slave trade carried millions of Africans to the Americas in bondage. But before black slaves were shipped across the ocean in large numbers, some were sold to West Africans by the Portuguese, who obtained them elsewhere along the coast. Slaves in Africa had a better chance of gaining freedom than did slaves in American colonies, but toiled at similar tasks: clearing land, hauling loads, digging in mines, and performing other chores that allowed free Africans to devote time to trade, crafts, and warfare, all of which enhanced the prospects of societies wealthy in gold and other assets sought by European merchants.

The Asante were divided into chiefdoms and did not acquire great wealth and power until King Osei Tutu Opemsoo united them under his authority around 1690. He was aided by Okomfo Anokye, a shrewd priest who helped him impress his majesty on other Asante leaders and their followers. According to legend, the priest received a gift from heaven that he endowed to Osei Tutu: the Golden Stool, which served as the king's throne. This miraculous gift signaled that the

Late 1400s European merchants establish trading posts on Gold Coast.

ca 1700 Osei Tutu's warriors defeat the Denkyira and take control of Gold Coast.

1824 Asante forces defeat and behead British commander Sir Charles MacCarthy.

1896 Asante king deposed and arrested by British governor.

1690 Osei Tutu Opemsoo unites Asante under his authority.

1720 Opoku Ware succeeds Osei Tutu.

1831 British and Asante agree to a pact.

1957 Kwame Nkrumah leads Ghana to independence.

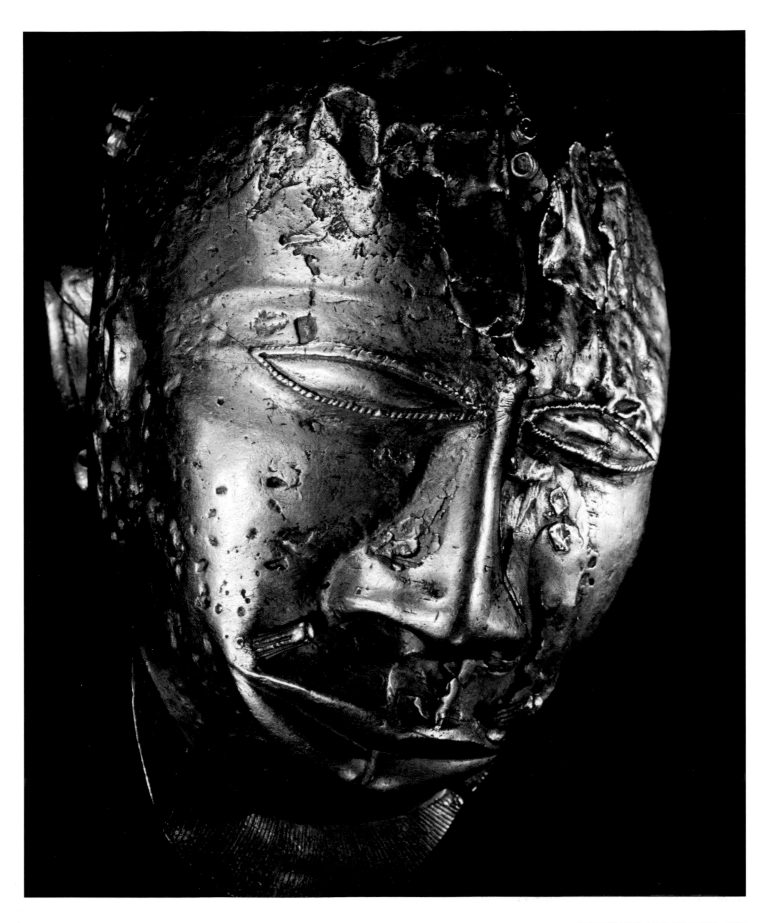

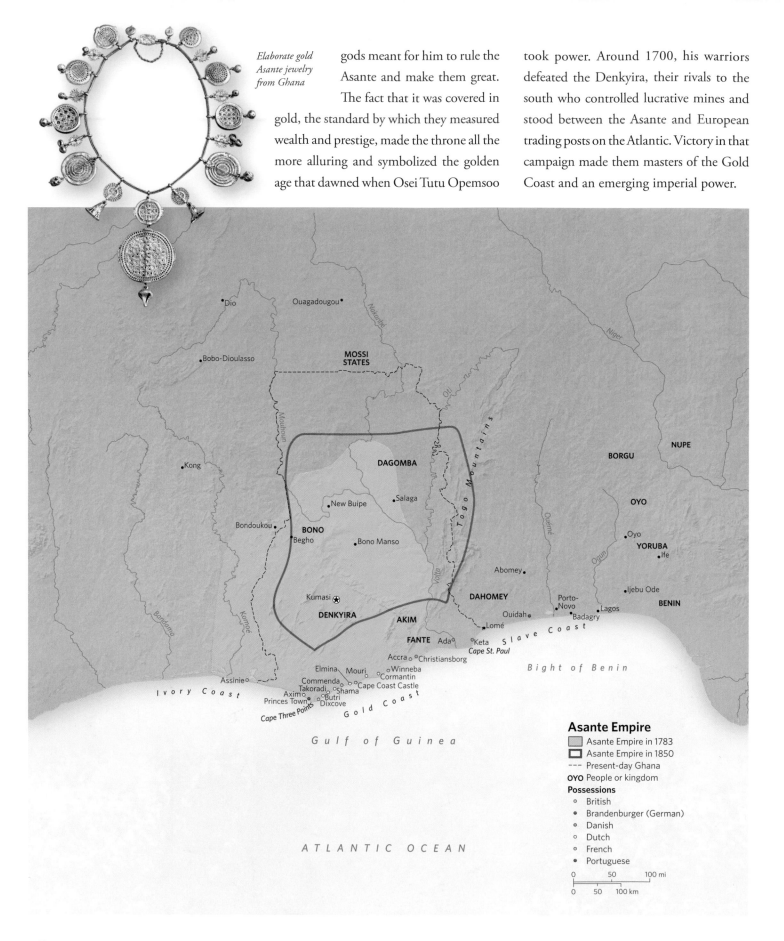

Elaborate gold Asante jewelry from Ghana

gods meant for him to rule the Asante and make them great. The fact that it was covered in gold, the standard by which they measured wealth and prestige, made the throne all the more alluring and symbolized the golden age that dawned when Osei Tutu Opemsoo took power. Around 1700, his warriors defeated the Denkyira, their rivals to the south who controlled lucrative mines and stood between the Asante and European trading posts on the Atlantic. Victory in that campaign made them masters of the Gold Coast and an emerging imperial power.

Dio
Ouagadougou
Bobo-Dioulasso
MOSSI STATES
Kong
DAGOMBA
New Buipe
Salaga
Bondoukou
BONO
Begho
Bono Manso
Togo Mountains
BORGU
NUPE
OYO
Oyo
YORUBA
Ife
Abomey
Ijebu Ode
Kumasi
DENKYIRA
AKIM
DAHOMEY
Porto-Novo
Ouidah
Badagry
Lagos
BENIN
Lomé
FANTE
Ada
Keta
Cape St. Paul
Slave Coast
Bight of Benin
Accra
Christiansborg
Elmina
Mouri
Winneba
Cormantin
Commenda
Cape Coast Castle
Assinie
Takoradi
Shama
Aximo
Butri
Princes Town
Dixcove
Cape Three Points
Gold Coast
Ivory Coast
Gulf of Guinea

ATLANTIC OCEAN

Asante Empire
- Asante Empire in 1783
- Asante Empire in 1850
- Present-day Ghana
- **OYO** People or kingdom
- **Possessions**
  - British
  - Brandenburger (German)
  - Danish
  - Dutch
  - French
  - Portuguese

0   50   100 mi
0   50   100 km

> *"The King mediated great improvements and embellishments in his capital, on his return from the war, when it was intended that every captain should be presented with an extraordinary sum of the treasury for adorning or enlarging his house."*

T. E. BOWDICH, 1817 ON KING OSEI BONSU'S *ABAN* (STONE PALACE)

During the 18th century, the Asante conquered an area extending inland from the Gold Coast for several hundred miles and containing more than two million inhabitants. Slaves they seized in battle or claimed in tribute from subordinate chieftains toiled for the Asante or were traded to Europeans in exchange for firearms, which made the Asante all the more formidable. King Opoku Ware, who succeeded Osei Tutu Opemsoo around 1720 and reigned for three decades, waged wars that extended his domain north to lands where Islam had been introduced by Muslim traders. Following his death, one Muslim remarked bitterly: "May Allah curse him and place his soul in hell . . . He ruled violently, as a tyrant, delighting in his authority. People of all the horizons feared him greatly."

Conquerors often inspired such dread, but empires based strictly on fear and intimidation seldom lasted long. Asante rulers preserved and prolonged their empire by employing diplomacy as well as force. They governed with the help of responsible officials, including literate Muslims, whose beliefs were not shared by the monarchs they served. Asante kings continued to worship their ancestral gods and engage in rituals that Muslims and

British art depicting the torture of an Asante man prior to his sacrifice during an Asante religious ceremony, a practice in Ghana that both Muslims and Christians found abhorrent.

MATRILINEAL SOCIETY

Traditional Asante clans were matrilineal, meaning family heritage traced through the mother, not the father. Extended matrilineal clans often lived together in the same part of a village. In that system, a man's property passed down not to his son, but to the sons of his sisters. Leadership positions passed down the same way. Mothers or sisters played an important behind-the-throne role, often nominating chiefs.

One of the most famous of Asante women was Yaa Asantewaa, queen mother of the Edweso tribe, who was born about 1850. She helped lead resistance against British brutality, at one point concealing the location of the Golden Stool, the traditional Asante throne. She was an inspiration and leader in the last Asante uprising in 1900–1901, sometimes called the Yaa Asantewaa war.

These dolls, known as akua'ba, *carried by young women to promote their fertility, have broad flat heads, achieved by massaging a baby's forehead.*

Christians found abhorrent, such as sacrificing humans to honor men of high rank when they died (the deceased also received offerings of gold and kente cloth, colorful fabric woven of cotton or silk obtained through trade). Despite such pagan practices, King Osei Tutu Kwame, who ruled in the early 1800s, was admired by Muslims living in Kumasi, the Asante capital, and considered "a good man, and wholly undeserving of the name of tyrant." He and other Asante monarchs were guided by an assembly of some 200 district chiefs and a royal council that included such dignitaries as the queen mother, an influential figure in this matrilineal society. Police kept order in the capital and patrolled the well-built roads that brought trade goods and tribute to Kumasi.

In 1817, envoys dispatched by a British company operating on the Gold Coast negotiated a treaty of "perpetual peace and harmony" with the Asante. That agreement was negated a few years later, however, when British authorities abolished the company and sent Sir Charles MacCarthy to govern the Gold Coast as a crown colony. MacCarthy recruited warriors among the Fante, a tribe at odds with their Asante overlords, to bolster his own troops. He then embarked on a reckless campaign that ended disastrously on January 21, 1824, when Asante forces routed his men and beheaded MacCarthy.

Peace was restored when the British and the Asante agreed to a new pact in 1831. In years to come, however, Great Britain and other industrialized European nations were no longer content with securing treaties or trading rights. Instead, they took control of many countries in Africa and

Relief sculpture on the shrine of a spirit medium, once common in Asante palaces, near Kumasi, Ghana

Asia. A British assault on Kumasi in 1874 encouraged rebellions by tribes subject to the Asante, who suffered the ultimate humiliation in 1896 when their king was arrested and removed by the British governor. In 1902, their domain was officially subsumed within the British Empire, which was beginning to feel the strain of maintaining its grip on large parts of the world. In 1957, Ghana—once home to an African empire that held its own against European powers for nearly two centuries—became the first black African country under colonial rule to win independence, led by Kwame Nkrumah, who was born to a goldsmith in the Gold Coast and transformed that British possession into a sovereign nation.

An Asante soldier (right) from Ghana holds a gun in one hand and a horn with holes—possibly a musical instrument—in the other.

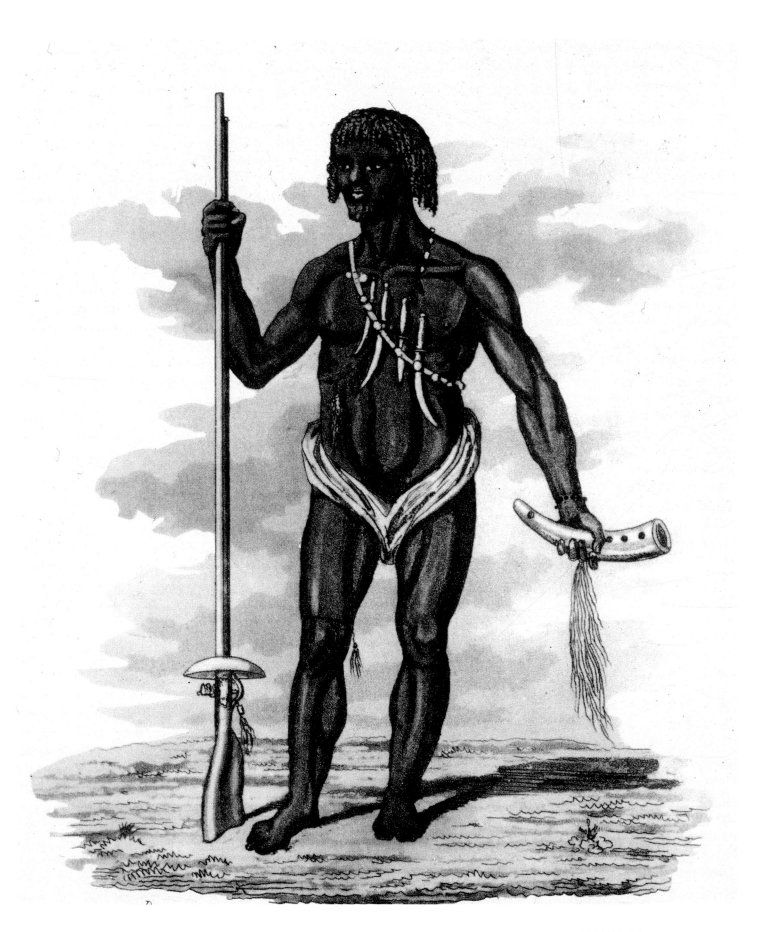

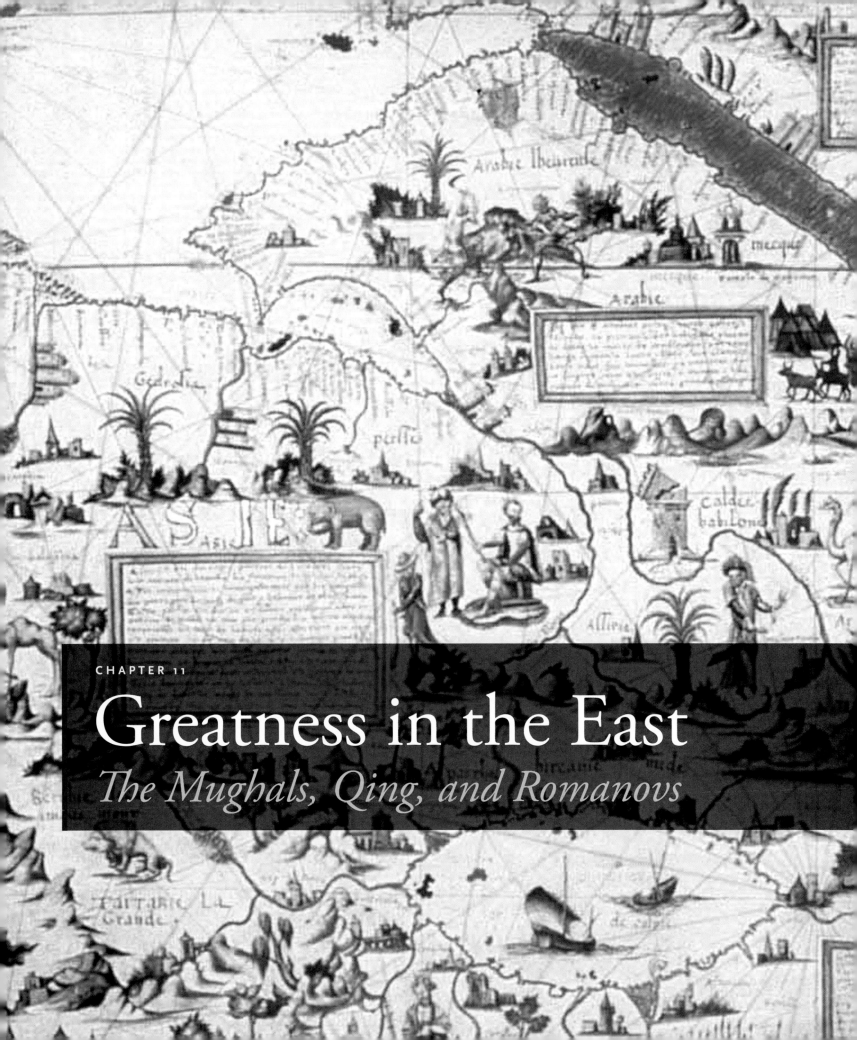

CHAPTER 11

Greatness in the East

The Mughals, Qing, and Romanovs

MUGHALS
Conquerors of India

When Babur invaded India in 1526 and founded the Mughal dynasty, he was simply carrying on an illustrious family tradition. Born in 1483 in what is now Uzbekistan, he claimed descent on his mother's side from Genghis Khan and on his father's from Timur, the fabled Turkish conqueror whose empire reached from the Indus River to the Black Sea before crumbling after his death in 1405. Babur ("tiger" in Arabic) began life as Zahir al-Din Muhammad. He was raised as a Muslim and steeped in rich Turkish culture. But he was also immersed in the proud military tradition of the Mughals (a variant on Mongols) through his membership in the clan of Chagatai, a son of Genghis Khan. In a remarkable memoir he composed in later years, Babur recalled an event that served as a kind of initiation into the warlike Mughal fraternity: "My uncle Kichik Khan bestowed on me arms of his own, a saddled horse from his private stable, a full suit of Mughal attire, a Mughal cap, a long embroidered coat of Chinese satin, and Chinese armor."

A Mughal glass hookah base (above). Prince Khurram (right) was the young successor to the Mughal throne after the death of Emperor Jahangir.

The imperial dynasty that Babur established was not the only one in the East shaped or influenced by the far-ranging Mongols. The Manchu, who swept down from Manchuria in the 1600s and founded the Qing dynasty in China, were following the forceful example of earlier Mongol invaders. They were even aided by Mongol warriors, who enlisted in Manchu armies and helped overthrow the Ming dynasty. Mongols also had a profound impact on Russia, which became a power in its own right in 1480 when Grand Prince Ivan III of Moscow refused to pay tribute to his Mongol overlord, the khan of the Golden Horde, and forged an alliance with another khan in Crimea. Schooled in ruthless Mongol tactics, Ivan's successors emerged as Russia's first tsars, a title derived from "Caesar."

Babur did not set out at first to conquer India. Instead, his goal was to capture the ancient Uzbek city of Samarkand, which had been ravaged by Mongols when it defied Genghis Khan. Later, it was restored to glory as Timur's capital, and the lord of Samarkand could claim to be Timur's successor. Babur's forces challenged Uzbeks who held

---

1526 Babur invades India and founds Mughal dynasty.

1530 Babur dies and is succeeded by his son Humayun.

1555 Humayun recaptures Delhi and regains power.

1562 Akbar, Humayun's heir, courts non-Muslims by wedding a Hindu princess.

ca 1632 Taj Mahal commissioned by Emperor Shah Jahan in memory of his late wife.

1658 Aurangzeb imprisons his father, Shah Jahan, executes relatives, and seizes throne.

1739 Invaders from Iran sack Delhi.

1757 British oust defiant nawab of Bengal and take control there.

1857–1858 British troops crush Indian Mutiny and exile last Mughal emperor.

1877 Queen Victoria proclaimed Empress of India.

1947 Independence granted to India.

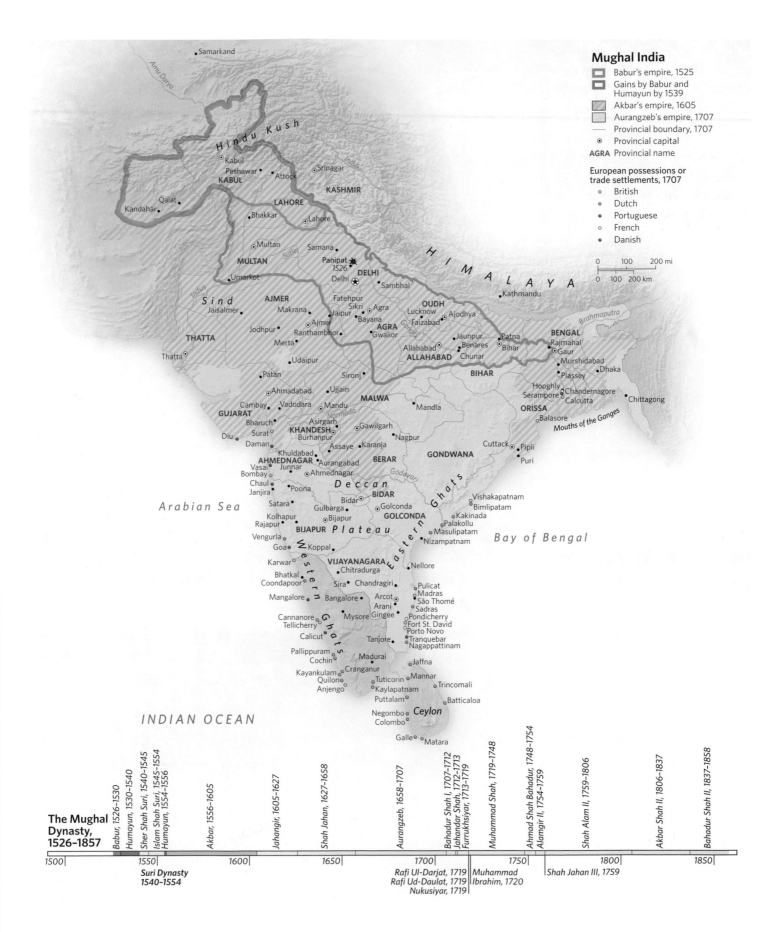

Mughal India

- ☐ Babur's empire, 1525
- ☐ Gains by Babur and Humayun by 1539
- ▨ Akbar's empire, 1605
- ☐ Aurangzeb's empire, 1707
- — Provincial boundary, 1707
- ⊙ Provincial capital
- **AGRA** Provincial name

European possessions or trade settlements, 1707
- ○ British
- ◐ Dutch
- ● Portuguese
- ○ French
- ● Danish

Samarkand

Amu Darya

Hindu Kush

Kabul
Peshawar • Attock
KABUL
Qalat
Kandahar
Srinagar
KASHMIR
Indus

Bhakkar
LAHORE
Lahore
Sutlej

Multan
MULTAN
Umarkot
Samana
Panipat
1526
Delhi **DELHI**
Sambhal
Kathmandu
H I M A L A Y A

Sind
Jaisalmer
AJMER
Makrana
Fatehpur
Sikri
Jaipur
Bayana
Agra
OUDH
Lucknow
Ajodhya
Faizabad

0   100   200 mi
0   100   200 km

Jodhpur
Ajmer
Ranthambhor
AGRA
Gwalior
Jaunpur
Patna
BENGAL
Rajmahal
Gaur
Murshidabad
Dhaka

THATTA
Merta
Udaipur
Allahabad
Benares
Bihar
Plassey
Thatta
Sironj
ALLAHABAD
Chunar
BIHAR
Hooghly
Serampore
Chandernagore
Calcutta
Chittagong

Patan
Ujjain
Ahmadabad
MALWA
Mandla
ORISSA
Balasore
Mouths of the Ganges

Cambay
Vadodara
Mandu
Narmada
GUJARAT
Bharuch
Asirgarh
Gawilgarh
Nagpur
Cuttack
Pipli
Diu
Surat
KHANDESH
Burhanpur
Puri
Daman
Khuldabad
Assaye
Karanja
GONDWANA

Vasai
AHMEDNAGAR
Junnar
Aurangabad
BERAR
Godavari
Vishakapatnam
Bombay
Ahmednagar
Bimlipatam
Chaul
Poona
Deccan
BIDAR
Kakinada
Janjira
Bidar
Palakollu
Satara
Golconda
Masulipatam
Arabian Sea
Kolhapur
Gulbarga
GOLCONDA
Nizampatnam
Rajapur
Bijapur
Plateau
Vengurla
BIJAPUR
Eastern Ghats
Bay of Bengal
Goa
Koppal
Karwar
VIJAYANAGARA
Chitradurga
Nellore
Bhatkal
Coondapoor
Sira
Chandragiri
Pulicat
Mangalore
Bangalore
Arcot
Madras
São Thomé
Arani
Sadras
Western Ghats
Mysore
Gingee
Pondicherry
Cannanore
Fort St. David
Tellicherry
Porto Novo
Calicut
Tanjore
Tranquebar
Nagappattinam
Pallippuram
Madurai
Cochin
Jaffna
Kayankulam
Cranganur
Mannar
Quilon
Tuticorin
Trincomali
Anjengo
Kaylapatnam
Puttalam
Batticaloa

INDIAN OCEAN
Negombo
Ceylon
Colombo
Galle
Matara

The Mughal Dynasty, 1526–1857

Babur, 1526–1530
Humayun, 1530–1540
Sher Shah Suri, 1540–1545
Islam Shah Suri, 1545–1554
Humayun, 1554–1556
Akbar, 1556–1605
Jahangir, 1605–1627
Shah Jahan, 1627–1658
Aurangzeb, 1658–1707
Bahadur Shah I, 1707–1712
Jahandar Shah, 1712–1713
Furrukhsiyar, 1713–1719
Muhammad Shah, 1719–1748
Ahmad Shah Bahadur, 1748–1754
Alamgir II, 1754–1759
Shah Alam II, 1759–1806
Akbar Shah II, 1806–1837
Bahadur Shah II, 1837–1858

1500   1550   1600   1650   1700   1750   1800   1850

Suri Dynasty 1540–1554

Rafi Ul-Darjat, 1719
Rafi Ud-Daulat, 1719
Nukusiyar, 1719
Muhammad Ibrahim, 1720
Shah Jahan III, 1759

the city and briefly gained possession. "For nearly 140 years Samarkand had been the capital of our dynasty," he recalled, speaking as a descendent of Timur. "It had slipped from our hands; but God gave it back!" He could not hold the city, however, and was soon ousted by the Uzbek khan, who then seized territory Babur inherited from his father. Rebounding from that abject setback, he took a new direction, advancing south with his followers into Afghanistan,

sultan, who commanded an estimated 100,000 men and 1,000 war elephants. But Babur's force included infantry armed with muskets and artillery, giving him firepower his opponent lacked. Ibrahim was "ruled by avarice," Babur remarked, and reluctant to share his wealth with his troops. Babur's avid warriors, in contrast, were amply rewarded with plunder and tribute from cities they seized as they advanced. On April 20, 1526, they crushed

> "By God, I'll not see that day when our empire
> will become the toy of a rake prince!
> Mann Singh, remove the veil of his mother's love
> on his head and put an iron cover on his head.
> Take him, raise and teach him in
> the hot deserts of war. Today, I hand over to you
> the future of the Mughals."
>
> EMPEROR AKBAR (AKA AKBAR THE GREAT),
> AFTER SEEING HIS SON MISBEHAVING

where they took Kabul in 1504. After solidifying his hold there and strengthening his forces, he set his sights on the Punjab, a fertile land along the modern border of Pakistan and India.

Since the 13th century, the Punjab and neighboring lands in northern India had been ruled by the sultans of Delhi, Muslims of Turkish heritage like Babur. Their hold on the region had been weakened by Timur, who sacked Delhi around 1400. Sultan Ibrahim Lodi of Delhi was now at odds with many of the nobles who served under him, including the rebellious governor of the Punjab, who appealed to Babur for help. The army Babur led into India was much smaller than that of the

the sultan's army at Panipat, north of Delhi. Ibrahim's body was found in a pile of dead by one of Babur's men, who "brought in his head."

Babur took Delhi a short time later and went on to vanquish other foes before defeating Ibrahim's brother. That triumph in 1529 made him the master of northern India, but he had little time left to savor his accomplishment. A gifted poet, he reflected in verse on the fate awaiting all conquerors: "We took the world by courage and might, / But we could not take it with us to the grave." When his son and heir, Humayun, contracted a fever and lay near death, Babur reportedly prayed to Allah, asking him to spare the boy and take the father instead.

BABUR'S ARMY

The odds appeared to be against Babur and his army as they confronted the forces of Sultan Ibrahim Lodi at Panipat, about 50 miles north of Delhi, on April 20, 1526. Babur had fewer than 12,000 soldiers, he recalled in his autobiography, the *Baburnama*. His enemy had 100,000, plus 1,000 elephants.

But Babur's men were trained in cavalry maneuvers. Moreover, some were armed with cannon and muskets. As the sultan attacked Babur's line, Babur's mounted forces wheeled to the right and left, attacking their foes from the rear. The guns and cannon panicked the elephants. Babur's army killed 15,000 or more of the enemy, including Ibrahim.

The clash had begun at dawn, when "the sun was spear-high," Babur wrote. "Till mid-day fighting had been in full force; noon passed, the foe was crushed in defeat . . . By God's mercy and kindness, this difficult affair was made easy for us!"

Parchment painting of Akbar receiving drums and standards captured from Abdullah Uzbeg, governor of Malwa, in 1564

Humayun recovered, and Babur soon fell ill, dying in 1530.

Humayun faced fierce opposition from Afghans who had infiltrated northern India before the Mughals arrived and had no intention of yielding without a struggle. They forced Humayun into exile and installed their leader as shah of northern India. But Humayun recaptured Delhi in 1555. Like his father, he died soon after vanquishing his foes and was succeeded by his son, Akbar.

Lasting imperial dynasties require not only dynamic founders like Cyrus the Great of Persia but also brilliant successors like Darius I, possessing both the military and organizational skills needed to build on the foundation and bequeath to his heirs a durable political structure. Akbar was the Mughal equivalent of Darius—a ruler who solidified the empire. Just 13 years

A gold mohur (coin) minted by Jahangir has Capricorn on one side, an inscription on the other.

old when he succeeded Humayun, Akbar was well served by his regent, who guided him until he was 18. Taking command of a domain consisting originally of little more than the capital district around Delhi and the Punjab to the north, Akbar expanded his realm through conquest as well as diplomacy. He reached out to Hindu lords called *rajputs,* who were adept at warfare and often at odds with earlier Muslim rulers. In 1562, he married the daughter of one prominent rajput, who pledged loyalty to

Akbar, as did other Hindu nobles. Those who defied him received no mercy from his troops, who brought much of central India under his authority.

An ingenious administrator, Akbar divided his empire into 15 provinces, each of which had officials with distinct responsibilities and separate powers, including a governor, a military commander, and a judge. The separation of powers discouraged those officials from interfering in each other's business or taking personal command of the province and posing a threat to the emperor. With Hindus making up the majority of his subjects, Akbar not only tolerated these non-Muslims but even gave prominence in his administration to Hindus. He also limited the power of Muslim clerics by declaring himself the ultimate authority in matters of Islamic doctrine—a stance resembling that of assertive European monarchs like King Henry VIII, who broke with the pope and declared himself head of the Church of England. In his later years, Akbar introduced a cult of his own called the Divine Faith, which combined elements of Islam, Hinduism, and other faiths. It cast him in the role of a uniquely inspired and prophetic ruler, and later emperors had no use for it.

Akbar and his successors were great builders and patrons of the arts. They did not confine themselves to Delhi, but constructed palaces, offices, and mosques at various sites that served as alternative capitals, administrative centers, or royal retreats. Mughal architecture was influenced by Hindu as well as Persian Islamic

Akbar (right), also referred to as Shahanshah ("king of kings"), Akbar-e-Azam, and Akbar the Great, was the third Mughal emperor of India.

PEOPLE

NUR JAHAN

As a strong woman married to a weak king, Nur Jahan (1577–1646) became one of the most powerful women in Indian history. Born as Mihrunnisa, the child of a noble Persian family living in India, she was a widow with a daughter when she joined the imperial Mughal harem. In 1611, when she was 34, Emperor Jahangir fell in love with her and took her as his 20th and last wife. He gave her the name Nur Jahan, "light of the world." But Jahangir was a drunk and an opium addict, and his new wife was not only beautiful but also brave, intelligent, and ambitious. She ruled from the harem in Agra, shrewdly manipulating both court politics and foreign affairs.

After Jahangir's death in 1627, she ended up on the wrong side of a succession fight among the emperor's sons and eventually died in exile. ⁒

traditions and featured majestic domes that rose like crowns to a peak, as well as enticing pools, fountains, and gardens evoking thoughts of paradise. Akbar's grandson, Shah Jahan, raised two of the greatest Mughal monuments near his capital, Agra: the Red Fort and the Taj Mahal, the latter built as a memorial and mausoleum for his beloved wife, Mumtaz Mahal, who died in childbirth. Mughal rulers maintained extensive harems, which included concubines as well as various female relatives of the emperor who looked after the emperor's young children. But a ruler's principal wife had high standing in the palace, exceeded only by the queen mother while she was alive.

The problem of succession haunted imperial dynasties throughout history. That problem was complicated for rulers of Turkish origin such as the Mughals and the Ottomans because their culture did not favor the custom of primogeniture, or bequeathing wealth and power to the eldest son. Instead, princes often vied among themselves for supremacy. This had the virtue of producing a proven leader who might be better at waging war than an heir chosen simply because he was born first, but the system could be counterproductive for established dynasties that were no longer devoted exclusively to warfare and needed stability from one generation to the next. Some Mughal rulers tried to avoid a succession struggle by

designating an heir, but their sons did not always abide by those wishes.

Such was the case with Aurangzeb, the third son of Mumtaz Mahal and Shah Jahan. When Shah Jahan fell ill in 1657 and his death appeared imminent, Aurangzeb waged war on his eldest brother, who had been appointed as heir by their father, and defeated him. Shah Jahan recovered, however, negating Aurangzeb's claim to power. Aurangzeb then imprisoned his father, had other relatives executed, and seized the throne in 1658. Such ruthlessness could be an asset for an emperor intent on enlarging his domain. Aurangzeb had the added advantage of being a devout Muslim, which kept him from leading a dissolute life, as

The Taj Mahal, the famous domed mausoleum, was built by Mughal emperor Shah Jahan in memory of his third wife, Mumtaz Mahal.

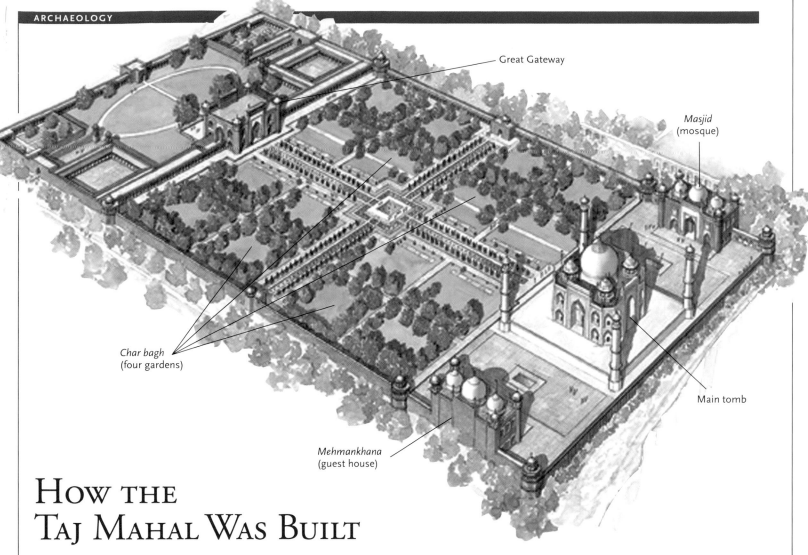

Great Gateway

Masjid
(mosque)

Char bagh
(four gardens)

Main tomb

Mehmankhana
(guest house)

HOW THE TAJ MAHAL WAS BUILT

The Taj Mahal in Agra is the grandest monument to the Mughal Empire and, by some reckonings, the loveliest building in the world. It was built by Shah Jahan as a tomb for his beloved wife Mumtaz Mahal, who died in 1631 giving birth to her 14th child. (Taj Mahal is a variant on her name, which meant "chosen one of the palace.")

Construction of this massive complex on the bank of the Yamuna River began soon after her death and, according to legend, required as many as 20,000 laborers and craftsmen from Europe, Persia, and the Ottoman Empire as well as India. The main mausoleum was completed in 1648, the gardens and support buildings in 1653—a total of 22 years in construction. Not surprisingly given the region, the architecture combines elements of Hindu and Islamic design.

The grand domed white marble mausoleum is set off by four minarets. It is flanked by two identical red sandstone buildings: an east-facing mosque and a west-facing structure known as the *jawab* ("answer"), built for aesthetic symmetry and used as a meeting hall. The image of the dome reflects in a long north-south pool that runs down the center of the gardens. The white dome glows in the sunlight; the jeweled inlays that adorn the walls of the central building epitomize the use of line and color in Mughal art. Those inlays show intricate and beautiful geometric shapes, flowers, and verses from the Koran. The tomb chamber itself is at the core of the main building, and the emperor and his wife are buried in a lower chamber.

Millions of people from around the world visit each year, and many complain of the crowds and the persistent hawkers. But sometimes, perhaps just at sunrise, it's possible to get an unspoiled view and realize what beauty humans can build. ❧

Marble walls at the Taj Mahal are decorated with intricate inlays.

died. The British sent a relief expedition led by Robert Clive, an army officer and company official, who secured Calcutta and gained control of Bengal, replacing its defiant nawab with a compliant one. The term nawab, or nabob, was soon applied to British officials such as Clive who took charge of one province after another with the help of local recruits, called sepoys, established order, and emerged as India's real governors.

The East India Company remained the instrument of British rule in India until the sepoys rebelled in 1857, igniting a widespread revolt. Marching on Delhi, insurgents proclaimed as their emperor the 82-year-old Mughal heir Bahadur Shah II, a mere figurehead before the uprising.

British troops eventually crushed the Indian Mutiny, imposed direct colonial rule on India, and exiled the last Mughal emperor.

In 1877, Britain's Queen Victoria was proclaimed Empress of India. Among her crown jewels was the fabled Koh-i-Noor diamond, which once adorned the Peacock Throne. Victoria prized the diamond, but India was the true jewel in her crown.

ARCHAEOLOGY

THE RED FORT AT DELHI

Shah Jahan, who built the Taj Mahal, began construction on the Red Fort in Delhi in 1638 when he moved his capital to that city from Agra, where he had rebuilt an earlier Red Fort captured by his Mughal forebears. The Delhi fort, known as Lal-Qila, has red sandstone walls that surround what were gardens, public halls, military fortifications, and marble palaces. Portions are elaborately decorated in the Mughal style, with ornate stone carvings. The walls run for nearly a mile and a half around a roughly octagonal shape. Portions of the interior structures have deteriorated over the years, although some have been partially restored. During the British occupation, significant areas of the complex were destroyed to provide military barracks for colonial troops.

The fort has become a symbol of India—the new nation's independence was proclaimed there in 1947, and Independence Day is celebrated each year. The complex, a UNESCO World Heritage site and a tourist highlight, is in the Old Delhi portion of India's capital, near some of the city's other most visited spots: Jama Masjid, the nation's largest mosque, also built by Shah Jahan; and Qutb Minar, an ornate Islamic tower that dates in part to 1193.

Ornate red sandstone arches and decorative carvings are among the artistic highlights of the Red Fort in Delhi.

It served her nation as a major source of cotton and other raw materials and as a market for British manufactured goods such as cotton cloth, which flooded India and swamped that country's own textile trade. During World War I, as pressure

An 18th-century watercolor painting of a Mughal couple and attendants on a terrace at sunset

mounted for an end to colonial rule in return for India's hefty contributions to the Allied cause, Britain promised Indians

"self-governing institutions." But this jewel was seemingly too precious part with. Independence would not be granted until 1947, and it would come at a steep price— the partition of predominantly Hindu India from largely Muslim Pakistan.

QING
China's Last Emperors

The people of China conceived of the world as a compass, at the center of which lay their own country, known as the Middle Kingdom. The four cardinal points of the compass, at the outer limits of the world, were occupied by mythical creatures representing the four seasons—the Green Dragon of spring in the east, the Red Bird of summer in the south, the White Tiger of autumn in the west, and the Black Tortoise of winter in the north. The Black Tortoise, encased in a protective armor-like shell, was sometimes called the Black Warrior—a fitting emblem for China's far northern frontier, from which wave after wave of invaders came like fierce winter winds, toppling old dynasties to make room for new ones. Among those invaders were the Jurchens, who descended from Manchuria in the 12th century and seized northern China from the Song dynasty; the Mongols, who conquered the Middle Kingdom in the 13th century and held power

Traditional Chinese porcelain dog, 17th century (above). Massive red doors of the Forbidden City, Beijing (right).

until their Yuan dynasty fell to the Ming dynasty in the 14th century; and the Manchu (Manchurians akin to the Jurchens), who did away with the Ming in the 17th century and founded the Qing dynasty, China's last imperial regime.

Like the Germanic tribes that descended on the Roman Empire, invaders of imperial China were considered barbarians, but that term was misleading. Conquerors with no knowledge of the language, customs, beliefs, or technology of the people they subdued had little chance of ruling their country effectively, as the Manchu did China for more than a century before gradually losing their grip in the 1800s amid rebellions by their subjects and incursions by foreigners. Long before they occupied China, they had been exposed to Chinese culture by the Chinese occupation of southern Manchuria, instigated in the 15th century by Ming rulers who hoped by expanding northward to secure their frontier against further invasions. Instead, the Chinese presence in Manchuria made its inhabitants more

- **Early 1600s** Manchu ruler Nurhaci unites Manchuria under his authority.
- **1644** Manchus seize Beijing and replace Ming dynasty with their own Qing dynasty.
- **1689** Kangxi settles China's boundary dispute with Russia.
- **1839** Opium War launched by British against China.
- **1864** Taiping Rebellion against Qing dynasty crushed after 14 years of turmoil.

- **1626–1643** Huang Taiji, Nurhaci's successor, conquers Mongolia and invades China.
- **1661** Kangxi succeeds Emperor Shunzhi and reigns for 61 years.
- **1735** Emperor Qianlong begins 60-year reign.
- **1842** Treaty of Nanjing requires China to cede Hong Kong to Britain.
- **1912** Sun Yat-sen and his revolutionaries oust last Chinese emperor.

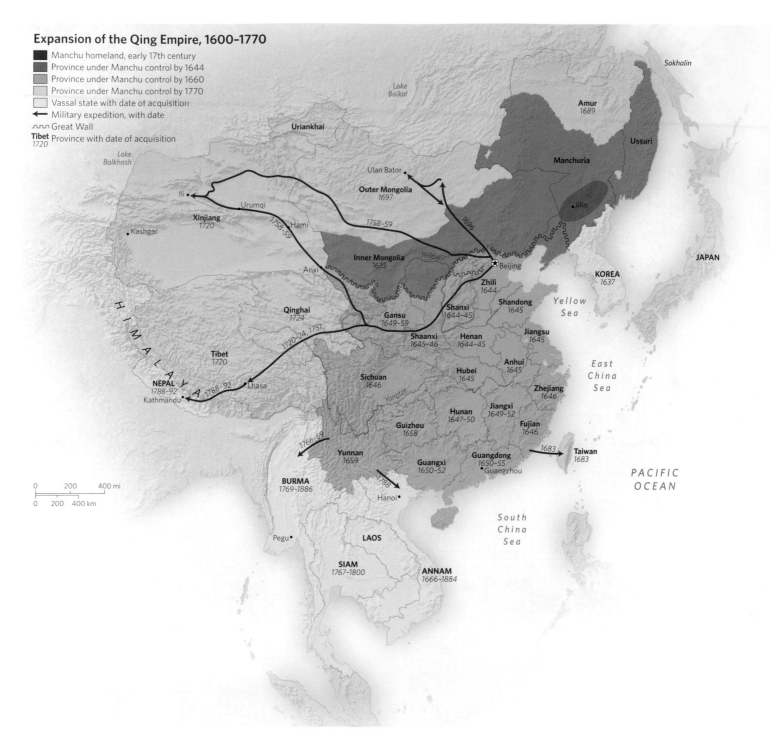

Expansion of the Qing Empire, 1600–1770

- ■ Manchu homeland, early 17th century
- Province under Manchu control by 1644
- Province under Manchu control by 1660
- Province under Manchu control by 1770
- Vassal state with date of acquisition
- ← Military expedition, with date
- Great Wall
- **Tibet** Province with date of acquisition
  1720

formidable challengers in the long run. Some Chinese soldiers and officers went native and became part of Manchurian society, enhancing its military prowess. Many Manchurians learned to speak Chinese, and some became literate in the language. Contacts with Chinese traders increased

their understanding of the great kingdom to their south.

The Manchu emerged as a force in the early 1600s, when their tribes were united by a chieftain named Nurhaci, using an ingenious banner system that brought warriors of various origins together in tightly

knit companies. Each company was identified by a distinctive banner and constituted a community. Members lived together with their families in peacetime, paid taxes as a unit, and provided a certain number of soldiers to fight for Nurhaci in wartime. At his death in 1626, he bequeathed to his heir,

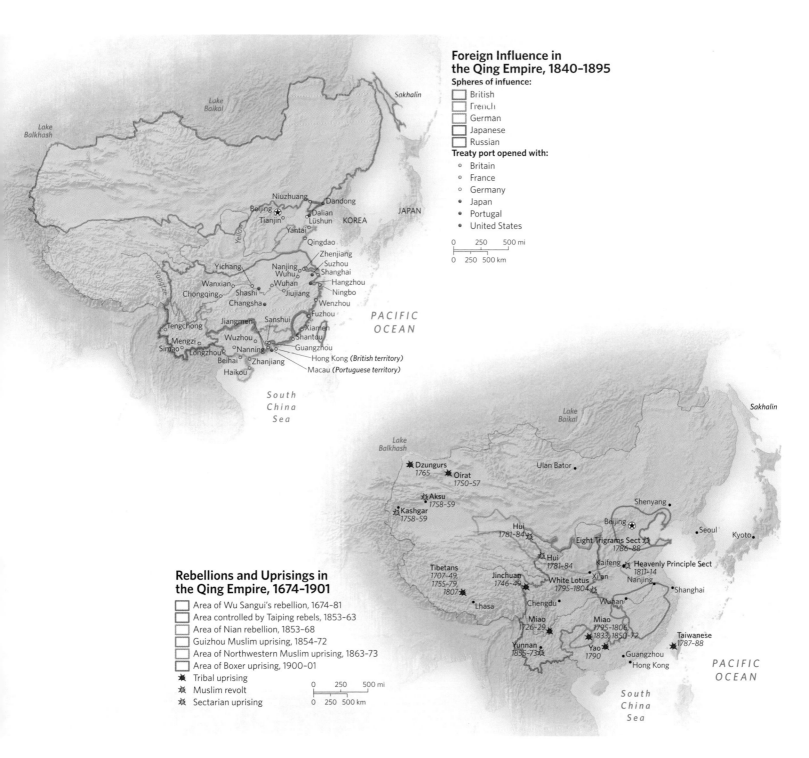

Foreign Influence in the Qing Empire, 1840–1895

Spheres of influence:
- British
- French
- German
- Japanese
- Russian

Treaty port opened with:
- Britain
- France
- Germany
- Japan
- Portugal
- United States

Rebellions and Uprisings in the Qing Empire, 1674–1901

- Area of Wu Sangui's rebellion, 1674–81
- Area controlled by Taiping rebels, 1853–63
- Area of Nian rebellion, 1853–68
- Guizhou Muslim uprising, 1854–72
- Area of Northwestern Muslim uprising, 1863–73
- Area of Boxer uprising, 1900–01
- Tribal uprising
- Muslim revolt
- Sectarian uprising

Huang Taiji, a well-organized state, with its own Manchu script, a code of laws, and a powerful army that eventually invaded Mongolia and northern China. By 1643, when Huang Taiji died—leaving his five-year-old heir, Shunzhi, under the care of a regent named Dorgon—the eight original Manchu banners had been joined by eight Mongol and eight Chinese banners.

China's decrepit Ming dynasty was now threatened both by the Manchu and by the forces of Chinese rebel leader Li Zicheng, who won support by redistributing food and property seized from landlords to peasants devastated by famine and neglect. Li's troops entered Beijing practically unopposed in early 1644 and overthrew the last Ming emperor, who had been abandoned by his generals. One Ming commander, Wu Sangui, refused to yield to the rebels after they seized Beijing, and he sought aid from Dorgon. Backed by his formidable bannermen, Dorgon took precedence over Wu and ousted Li in June 1644 to become the first Manchu ruler of China. Not until after Dorgon's death in 1650 did his ward, Emperor Shunzhi, assume authority.

In the early years of this Qing dynasty, many people in China regarded their new masters in Beijing as illegitimate and remained loyal to Ming holdovers such as Wu Sangui, who pledged loyalty to the new regime but later rebelled. The arduous task of reuniting China under Manchu authority fell to Shunzhi's dynamic heir, Emperor Kangxi, who was six years old when his father died in 1661. Like Shunzhi, he was dominated as a youngster by his regent, a ruthless overseer named Oboi who remained in command after Kangxi turned 13, the age at which he was supposed to begin ruling the realm. At 15, aided by his paternal grandmother—who served as empress dowager and wielded great influence—he had Oboi arrested, showing the resolve that would make him one of the most accomplished Chinese rulers of all time.

Over the next two decades, Kangxi and his forces defeated Wu and two other rebellious generals in southern China, invaded Taiwan and seized that island from Ming loyalists, and rebuffed Russian forces along the northern frontier, leaving Kangxi in a strong position to settle China's boundary dispute with Russia by treaty in 1689. Before he died in 1722 after ruling China for more than a half century, Kangxi extended authority over Korea and Tibet and rebuilt one of the world's greatest empires, extending for more than 2,000 miles from the Yellow Sea to the Himalaya.

As demonstrated by their success in winning Mongol support, the Manchu

Ceramic dish, Kangxi period, Qing dynasty

Chinese peasants in front of the towering walls of the Western Gate of Beijing. Though the walls were demolished in the 1950s, the bridge remains.

> *"[The Jesuits] gave him an insight into optics by making him a present of a semi-cylinder of a light kind of wood ... The emperor was greatly pleased with so unusual a sight."*
>
> PÈRE DU HALDE,
> *TEACHING SCIENCE TO THE MANCHU EMPEROR, CA 1680*

were adept at dealing with foreigners and inducing them to cooperate. Chinese resistance to Manchu rule diminished during the reign of Kangxi not just because he cracked down on those who rebelled but also because he allowed those who submitted to his authority to serve under him as soldiers, officers, and bureaucrats. He appealed to Chinese scholars and officials by embracing their guiding philosophy, Confucianism, which held that a ruler should look after his people like a conscientious father. To that end, he avoided the lavish court life and expenditures of earlier emperors, reduced taxes, and used public funds and labor for vital public projects such as dredging the Yellow River to prevent ruinous floods.

Although Kangxi and his successors admired Chinese culture, they wanted Manchus to remain distinct from the rest of the populace and granted them elite status. Intermarriage between Manchu and Chinese was forbidden. As a token of submission, Chinese men were required to adopt the customary Manchu style of shaved forehead and hair worn in a queue, or pigtail. Their Chinese subjects thereafter harbored lingering resentment toward the Qing dynasty.

The Manchu dealt cautiously with Europeans, allowing them limited access to China. Jesuit missionaries had arrived in the 16th century and gained access to the Ming court, where they shared their knowledge of geography, astronomy, and other subjects with emperors and in exchange were allowed to proselytize in China. Some Manchus were suspicious of those foreign priests, but Kangxi put great trust in Ferdinand Verbiest, a Jesuit from Belgium. Verbiest performed so well when his skills as an astronomer were put to the test by Kangxi that he was named head of the imperial bureau of mathematics, whose

Cloisonné enamel moon flask from the Qing dynasty.

EMPEROR KANGXI

In the Confucian tradition, a ruler was expected to be a scholar, or at least to aid scholarship. Emperor Kangxi embraced this role. This gained him support among the intelligentsia who had resisted the ascendance of the Qing dynasty. With his backing, those scholars compiled a history of the Ming dynasty, the predecessors to the Qing; an anthology of poems from the earlier Tang dynasty; and a dictionary of Chinese characters. They also embarked on an encyclopedia, the *Gujin Tushu Jicheng (Complete Collection of Illustrations and Writings of Ancient and Modern Times)*, a name that gives a taste of its ambitious scope. It filled more than 5,000 volumes. In addition, Kangxi encouraged foreign scholarship, notably a geological survey under the direction of French Jesuits. It produced a Chinese atlas and a version in French, the *Nouvel Atlas de la Chine, de la Tartarie Chinoise et du Thibet (New Atlas of China, Chinese Tartary, and Tibet)*. ❧

chief task was to draw up an elaborate calendar for each year, including the precise times of eclipses and other astronomical events. The priest also served as a translator for the emperor in negotiations with Russia and advised him on the construction of artillery for his army.

Jesuit missionaries drew parallels between the moral teachings of Confucianism and Christianity and allowed their converts in China to continue the ancient custom of venerating their ancestors by making offerings of food and wine to the dead and seeking their blessings. "They do not recognize in the dead any divinity," wrote Matteo Ricci, the founder of the Jesuit mission in China, who concluded that this so-called ancestor worship did not amount to idolatry. Missionaries of other Roman Catholic orders seeking converts in China disagreed, however, and appealed to the pope, who ruled in the early 1700s that Christians must not engage in such rites. This angered Kangxi, who ordered missionaries in China to tolerate this ancestor veneration or leave the country. Some Jesuits heeded his wishes rather than the pope's and stayed, but their relations with the Qing dynasty deteriorated nevertheless. Christian mission efforts in China dwindled and did not revive until the 1800s.

Qing dynasty's Emperor Qianlong (top) and his first imperial concubine (bottom)

Rulers of earlier dynasties had had little need of foreign know-how because China was one of the most advanced countries in the world technologically through the Middle Ages. But when the Jesuits left China, Qing emperors no longer had access to advisers with knowledge of the quickening advances in Western science and technology. Furthermore, under Emperor Qianlong—who, like Kangxi, enjoyed remarkable longevity, reigning from 1735 to 1795—foreign trade was restricted to a single port, Guangzhou (Canton), where Chinese goods such as silk, tea, and porcelain were sold to foreign merchants for silver. This trade profited China economically but stifled the introduction of new devices and techniques to the country along with any stimulus for Chinese manufacturers to improve their methods or products in response to foreign competition.

Qianlong summed up his view of foreign trade in a letter to King George III of England, denying a British request to trade at other Chinese ports. "Our Celestial Empire possesses all things in prolific abundance and lacks no product within its own border," he declared. "There was therefore no need to import the manufactures of outside barbarians in exchange for our own produce." There was some truth to this at the time. China under Qianlong remained vibrant and industrious, with factories that turned out fine porcelain, or "china," for the world market and printing presses that produced scholarly books as well as popular novels. It did not lag far behind Europe technologically until the Industrial Revolution began in Britain in the late 18th century. Isolation from the West thereafter prevented China from closing the gap and keeping pace with the British and other European powers militarily and economically.

Rulers of the Qing dynasty grew painfully aware of their limitations when British merchants began shipping opium from India to China in large quantities in the early 1800s. Chinese efforts to halt this

Decorated fan from the Qing dynasty

IMPERIAL PALACE AT SHENYANG

Before the Qing dynasty took control of China, the Manchu established their capital in the city of Shenyang, in the nation's northeast, and there they built a palace modeled on the Forbidden City of their Ming rivals in Beijing.

Construction of the Shenyang palace began in 1625 under Nurhaci, the chieftain who united the Manchu. It was finished in 1636 by his son, Huang Taiji; later Qing emperors added onto it. At roughly 600,000 square feet, it is only a tenth of the size of the Forbidden City, but even at that size still contains 114 buildings. Three large courtyards align on the central north–south axis, just as the most important buildings align on the north–south axis of the Forbidden City. The buildings, with their glazed tile roofs and elaborate carved and painted decorations, combine elements of the Manchu, Mongol, and Han styles, showing how architecture evolved over the 17th and 18th centuries. Once the Qing toppled the Ming and moved to Beijing, this palace became auxiliary to the Forbidden City. In 2004, UNESCO extended its World Heritage recognition of that grander Beijing complex to encompass the Shenyang palace, too.

Modern Shenyang—also known over the centuries as Shenzhou, Mukden, and Fengtian—is an industrial city and the capital of Liaoning Province. The Imperial Palace is the major tourist attraction, displaying art and historic artifacts, including the swords of both Nurhaci and Huang Taiji. Visitors to Shenyang can also see Qing imperial tombs and several museums.

An exterior view of the throne room at the Imperial Palace in Shenyang. In front of the stairs is a jade chime with a golden frame, made in 1761.

SOUTHERN INSPECTION TOURS

In shows of pageantry that harked back to ancient Chinese traditions and displayed the power of the Qing rulers, both Emperor Kangxi and his grandson Emperor Qianlong embarked on several extensive inspection tours of their vast domains during their long reigns. And each of those emperors commissioned painters to commemorate one of his tours—a route south from Beijing, along the Grand Canal, to the cities of Yangzhou, Nanjing, Suzhou, and Hangzhou.

The resulting intricately painted silk scrolls are magnificent visual travelogues, linear depictions of the imperial pageantry of the trip. There are a dozen scrolls per trip, each more than two feet high and as much as 85 feet long. They roll out to show the emperor, his traveling court, and subjects, as well as the mountains, waterways, and cities under his sway. Most of the scrolls have survived. (Less elaborate ones mark other tours.) They are in museums in China, Europe, and North America; three are at the Metropolitan Museum of Art in New York City. ❧

The sixth scroll painting of Emperor Qianlong's
Southern Inspection Tour: Entering Suzhou
Along the Grand Canal

illegal trade faltered. Corrupt officials became involved and helped merchants evade inspection at Guangzhou and thus reach drug traffickers, who paid for opium in silver, which merchants used to purchase tea that could be sold in Britain at considerable profit. The opium trade had a devastating impact on China. By one estimate, four million of its 400 million people were addicted by the late 1830s, when Emperor Daoguang appointed a scrupulous official, Lin Zexu, to wipe out the trade. "Any foreigner who brings opium to China will be sentenced to death," Lin warned. "Our purpose is to eliminate this poison once and for all." He searched warehouses where foreign merchants stored their goods and seized and destroyed 20,000 chests of opium—roughly half the amount that was being shipped to China annually.

The British responded in 1839 by launching the Opium War, during which their modern navy, equipped with steam-powered gunboats, shattered China's antiquated fleet and penetrated its interior waterways. China yielded in 1842 and signed the humiliating Treaty of Nanjing, which ceded Hong Kong to Britain; nullified China's claims to Korea, Indochina, and Burma; and opened five additional ports to British merchants, free from China's legal jurisdiction. The opium trade continued, and a second conflict in the 1850s, during which France joined Britain against China, resulted in legalization of the drug.

Defeat in the Opium War exposed the weakness of the Qing dynasty and the moral decay within its bureaucracy.

Corruption in China was not limited to officials involved in the drug trade. Revenue that should have been used to strengthen the army and navy or repair dikes and canals was embezzled by bureaucrats whose flagrant disregard for the public welfare violated the Confucian principles they were supposed to uphold. "Approach your duties with reverence and be trustworthy,"

Confucius advised. Instead, some wealthy candidates for office passed the grueling civil service test by bribing examiners, then used their positions to enrich themselves or give preferential treatment to powerful landlords and nobles at the expense of downtrodden peasants and laborers.

In 1850, a massive upheaval known as the Taiping Rebellion erupted in China under the leadership of Hong Xiuquan, a messianic figure inspired in part by visions he experienced after repeatedly failing the civil service exam. (Unlike some candidates, he was too poor to bribe his way to success, even if he had been so inclined.) Hong had some exposure to Christianity and attracted followers with a revolutionary gospel that combined Christian and

Emperor Kangxi's tour of Kiang-Han in 1699, drawn with ink and color on silk-backed paper

Chinese concepts of justice, benevolence, and a better world to come. He preached that those who did evil, such as dealing in opium or prostitution, would be punished, while those who lived justly would enter a heavenly kingdom on earth, where all

would share equally in God's blessings. The promise of equal rights and rewards appealed to China's peasants. They enlisted in large numbers along with miners and other laborers when Hong launched his rebellion against the Qing dynasty and proclaimed himself ruler of a new celestial empire known as the Heavenly Kingdom of Great Peace (Taiping Tianguo). Women

> ## *"Our dynasty's majestic virtue has penetrated unto every country under Heaven."*
>
> EMPEROR QIAN LONG,
> LETTER TO GEORGE III, 1793

were promised equality with men and formed their own regiments in the rebel army, which captured the city of Nanjing in 1853.

The Taiping Rebellion was fueled by growing resentment of China's Manchu rulers, who maintained their distinct Manchurian identity and were reviled by their foes as oppressive foreigners. In fact, the Qing dynasty relied on Chinese as well as Manchu officials, and members of both groups engaged in corrupt practices. But Manchu emperors oversaw the bureaucracy and failed to end the favoritism, embezzlement, and incompetence that hampered their government and armed forces, which took more than a decade to crush the stunning uprising by Hong's untrained army.

Empress Cixi (left), a powerful and charismatic de facto ruler of the Qing dynasty in China and mother of the Tongzhi Emperor.

To achieve that victory, they still needed help from Hong and other rebel leaders—who feuded among themselves—and aid from foreigners like Charles George "Chinese" Gordon, a British officer who helped repulse a rebel attack on Shanghai in 1860. Hong committed suicide in 1864, shortly before government forces reclaimed Nanjing. Losses suffered by both sides in battle, combined with the ravages of disease and famine in chaotic war zones, left more than 20 million people dead, making this one of the greatest catastrophes in China's history.

The dominant figure of the Qing dynasty in the late 19th century was the woman behind the throne, Empress Dowager Cixi, whose son, Emperor Tongzhi, reigned from 1861 to 1875, followed by her nephew and adoptive son, Emperor Guangxu. Both rulers were boys when they took the throne, and Cixi acted as their regent. Following the wrenching Taiping Rebellion, she and her brother-in-law, Prince Gong Qinwang, tried to accommodate Western powers and use their technology. This program, known as the Self-Strengthening Movement, included industrializing the production of weapons and warships and establishing a foreign office to deal diplomatically with other countries. Cixi resisted political reform, though, and spent lavishly on her gorgeous and decadent Summer Palace near Beijing with funds intended for naval development.

Efforts to modernize China proved far less successful than those undertaken in Japan, where Emperor Meiji became head of a constitutional government and the nation rapidly industrialized, emerging as an imposing military power. Imperial

HONG XIUQUAN

China's difficult civil service examinations were the door to an elite career. So, it's understandable that when Hong Xiuquan (1814–1864) failed it for the third time, he suffered an emotional collapse, during which he had visions of an old man with a golden beard. Years later, after reading some Christian tracts, Hong decided the man was God, and that he himself was the brother of Jesus Christ. He founded a sect that combined elements of folk religion, Christianity, and politics, and it appealed to oppressed peasants.

Hong's vision evolved into a disciplined military movement named Taiping Tianguo, or Heavenly Kingdom of Great Peace; Hong was Heavenly King. Multitudes joined the Taiping Rebellion that began in 1850. They fought government troops around the country for more than a decade. But the leadership feuded, and Hong had opposing generals killed, then retreated into his religion. The rebellion, which cost the lives of millions, ultimately collapsed in 1864 after Hong's suicide.

A 19th-century watercolor showing Taiping rebels capturing a British soldier

> ## "...your reverence for Our Celestial dynasty fills you with a desire to acquire our civilisation."
>
> **EMPEROR QIAN LONG,** LETTER TO GEORGE III, 1793

China was too conservative, corrupt, and inefficient to achieve such an overhaul and suffered the consequences in 1895 when it was defeated by Japan, which seized Taiwan and the Liaodong Peninsula in Manchuria and claimed supremacy over Korea.

That shocking loss brought renewed calls in China for wholesale changes. Emperor Guangxu, now in his 20s, asserted himself in 1898 by backing reforms that would have made him a constitutional monarch and revamped the educational and bureaucratic systems that allowed China's privileged elite to dominate society and use high offices for their own benefit. But conservatives at court, led by Cixi, opposed those plans and staged a coup. They imprisoned Guangxu in the palace and executed leading reformers. Ruling in place of her powerless nephew, Cixi encouraged the xenophobic Boxer Rebellion in 1899, aimed at ridding the country of Christian missionaries and other "foreign devils." International forces entered Beijing in 1900 and put down the uprising, imposing another humiliating defeat on the discredited Qing dynasty. Cixi died in 1908, shortly after Guangxu was poisoned to death, a deed for which she may have been responsible.

In 1912, the last Chinese emperor, Guangxu's six-year-old nephew Puyi, yielded to revolutionaries led by Sun Yat-sen and abdicated. So deep were the divisions within Chinese society that the revolutionary upheaval that began under the Qing dynasty—and persisted when it failed to reform—continued for much of the 20th century before China coalesced as a nation and regained its place among the world's great powers.

Three-year-old Puyi (right), widely known as the "Last Emperor" of China, sits to the right of his father, Prince Chun, and his infant brother.

SO WHAT?

Images of Mao Zedong were ubiquitous throughout China during his decades as head of the Chinese Communist Party.

REVOLUTIONS

Although the Qing dynasty ruled China for almost 300 years, the populace saw the Manchu as an occupying force. Throughout the second half of the 19th century, many revolts erupted. The Sino-Japanese War of 1894–95 exposed how Qing conservatism had let China fall behind other nations. In 1895, a former doctor named Sun Yat-sen led the failed nationalist Canton Uprising. In 1898–1900, the Boxer Rebellion, a peasant revolt, tried to drive out foreigners; international armies quashed the rebellion and imposed a humiliating settlement on the Qing royalty. Half-hearted reforms fueled more unrest. In 1911, a revolution succeeded, the boy-emperor Puyi abdicated, and Sun Yat-sen became president. He was soon unseated, though, and years of turmoil ensued. The fight between the Nationalists, led by Chiang Kai-shek, and the Communists, led by Mao Zedong, culminated in 1949 with Mao's victory and the founding of the People's Republic of China.

RUSSIA
Realm of the Tsars

Ivan III laid the foundation for the Russian Empire in the late 1400s by defying his Mongol overlord and asserting authority over a large area around Moscow, which became known as the "third Rome." The first Rome had fallen to Germanic invaders a thousand years earlier. The second Rome—Constantinople—was conquered by the Ottoman Empire shortly before Ivan became grand prince of Moscow in 1462. By wedding Sofia, niece of the last Byzantine emperor, he laid claim to the imperial legacy of Rome and Constantinople, from which Orthodox Christianity had spread to Russia during the Middle Ages. Ivan and his successors would uphold that faith, but their empire would be less like the Orthodox Byzantine Empire and more like the polytheistic Roman Empire that preceded it. Like ancient Rome, which ruled provinces in Europe, Asia, and Africa, imperial Russia at its peak would span three continents (Europe, Asia, and North America) and embrace people of various creeds, races, and tribes.

Ivan III was known to posterity as Ivan the Great, but his historical accomplishments were overshadowed

Jeweled Fabergé egg (above) created to celebrate 300 years of Romanov rule in Russia, which began with Tsar Michael Romanov (right)

by the grim reputation of his grandson, Ivan IV, dubbed Ivan the Terrible. That title was well deserved, but Ivan IV could not have overcome the daunting challenges he faced in 1547 when he became the first Russian ruler to be proclaimed tsar without possessing ruthlessness and cunning. Proud nobles called boyars had been vying murderously with each other to gain control over him at court ever since his widowed mother—who served as his regent—died of suspected poisoning when he was eight. Now the 16-year-old tsar had to avoid being dominated by those aristocrats, a goal he achieved by forming a council of advisers who achieved prominence not through inheritance but through loyal service to him. Ivan also had to contend with Mongols along the Volga River who blocked Russian expansion to the south and east. After defeating them at Kazan in 1552, he advanced down the Volga to Astrakhan, which fell to his forces in 1556, giving Russia access to the Caspian Sea.

That triumph tempted Ivan to expand west to the Baltic Sea, which unlike the land-locked Caspian

- **1462–1505** Ivan III, grand prince of Moscow, lays foundation for Russian Empire.
- **1570** Novgorod city destroyed by Ivan IV and his henchmen, the oprichniki.
- **1762** Catherine the Great takes power in a coup.
- **1812** Tsar Alexander I withstands invasion by Napoleon Bonaparte.
- **1917** Communist Bolsheviks, led by Vladimir Lenin, seize power.

- **1547** Ivan IV becomes first Russian ruler proclaimed tsar.
- **1696** Peter the Great takes sole command of Russia.
- **1774–1775** Emelian Pugachev, the rebellious Cossack, is captured, butchered in Moscow.
- **1861** Alexander II frees Russia's serfs.

offered Russia an outlet to the Atlantic and western Europe. The war he waged on Livonia (Latvia and Estonia) blighted his promising reign by drawing his forces into ruinous conflict with Lithuania, Poland, and Sweden. Ivan blamed losses he suffered in battle—and the death of his wife, Anastasia Romanovna—on treacherous boyars and lashed out at them and others he considered disloyal. The attacks were carried out by henchmen called *oprichniki,* who received land from the tsar in return for their bloody services and made little distinction between his confirmed enemies and innocent bystanders. In 1570, Ivan led oprichniki against Novgorod—a city that once rivaled Moscow and now chafed under its rule—and laid waste to it, massacring thousands. While Ivan was busy assaulting his own people, Crimean Tatars of Mongol and Turkish ancestry advanced up the Volga. In 1571, they sacked Moscow, leaving much of it in ruins.

Ivan the Terrible died in 1584 with no competent heir, having murdered his

Russian military campaign successfully captures the Azov in 1696 (left). The double-headed eagle (right) continues to be used by Russia as a national symbol.

EXPANSION OF RUSSIA

Bit by bit, from 1462 to 1914 Russia expanded to cover most of northern Eurasia. By the end of his reign in 1505, Ivan the Great had overcome the previously dominant Golden Horde and had tripled the size of the Russian Empire (map 2). Expansion continued down the Volga and into Siberia (maps 3 and 4). With Peter the Great's 1721 victory against Sweden in the Great Nothern War, Russia gained access to the warm-water ports on the Baltic Sea (map 5). With its vast territory now stretching from the Baltic to the Pacific Ocean, Russia needed a way to connect and consolidate its empire: the Trans-Siberian Railway. And while the 1991 breakup of the Soviet Union resulted in a reduction of the overall size of Russian-controlled lands (see graph on page 335), Russia today remains the largest country in the world.

1462 **1**

Moscow

0   400   800 mi
0 400 800 km

☐ Russia in 1462
Map shows modern boundaries.

> *"You see, lad, even though I am the Tsar I have calluses on my hands, all in order to show you an example so that I may see fitting helpers and servants of the fatherland, even if I have to wait until I am old."*

PETER THE GREAT

eldest son in a fit of rage three years earlier. Russia soon descended into a chaotic period of contested leadership known as the Time of Troubles, continuing until 1613 when Michael Romanov, the grandnephew of Ivan's wife Anastasia, was crowned tsar. Under the Romanov dynasty, which endured for three centuries, Russia resumed its territorial expansion, aided by Cossacks. Many of these mounted warriors were Slavs of peasant stock who avoided being reduced to serfdom by migrating onto the steppes of southern Ukraine and Russia. There they clashed with Tatars and refined their equestrian skills. Some venturesome bands of Cossacks advanced east into Siberia, where they served as agents of Russian expansionism by subduing tribal groups. Others remained in and around Ukraine and fought to free that land from Polish rule. In 1654, those Cossacks made a pact

with Russia, which claimed eastern Ukraine in 1667 and later annexed the entire country. Cossacks were long dreaded by Jews, Muslims, and others who felt their fury, and they sometimes turned on their Romanov masters in violent uprisings.

Russia emerged as a major power under Peter the Great. Born in 1672 to Tsar Alexis and his second wife, Peter was overshadowed in his youth by his half-sister, Sophia, who governed as regent for her sickly young brother, Ivan IV. Peter was named co-ruler with Ivan but was kept away from court by Sophia, who was at odds with his side of the family. Exclusion from the palace did wonders for Peter, who lived with his mother on the outskirts of Moscow and spent much of his time among European merchants nearby at a colony called Germantown. He developed a lifelong fascination with Western technology and inventions and studied navigation and military engineering. In 1689, after plotting unsuccessfully against Peter, Sophia was confined to a convent. Peter took sole command of Russia when Ivan died in 1696.

After touring Europe and inspecting workshops and shipyards, Peter began building a navy and strengthening his army,

which expanded to become the largest force in Europe, furnished with arms and equipment from Russian factories he established. He signaled his determination to modernize and westernize his government by moving it from Moscow to St. Petersburg. The new capital sat at the mouth of the Neva River, which was open to the Gulf of Finland for much of the year, offering access to the Baltic Sea and the Atlantic. Peter tightened his grip on the Baltic coast by succeeding where Ivan the Terrible had failed and annexing Latvia and Estonia. In honor of that triumph he was proclaimed emperor by the newly established Russian Senate, which he dominated as thoroughly as Emperor Augustus Caesar did the old Roman Senate. Proud boyars, who had caused earlier tsars much trouble, were required to serve in Peter's government and reside in St. Petersburg, where they paid court to him at his handsome Winter Palace. They and other men of note had to cut off their long beards and appear clean-shaven like European gentlemen or pay a steep beard tax.

Modernization and expansion continued under Catherine the Great, the wife of

> *"Who among you, my brothers, would have dreamed 30 years ago that we would be here together, on the Baltic Sea . . . in a land won from them by our labors and courage, erecting this city in which we live."*
>
> **PETER THE GREAT,**
> *ILYA PROROK* SHIP LAUNCHING

Peter the Great's grandson, Peter III, who was ousted by Catherine and her supporters soon after he was crowned in 1762. She and her husband were both of German birth. But whereas he remained a foreigner at heart and backed Frederick the Great of Prussia—the most powerful German state and Russia's former enemy—she was devoted to Russia and won the army's support against Peter. The coup that toppled

him was organized by Catherine's lover Grigory Orlov. Catherine's involvement in that plot and her affairs with various men at court made her notorious. But her behavior was much like that of her male counterparts in other European kingdoms, who did not keep harems like Turkish or Chinese rulers but often consorted with women other than their wives and sometimes plotted against members of their own family to gain or retain power.

One man intimate with Catherine was Grigory Potemkin, who served as her field marshal and waged war on the Ottoman Turks, seizing the Crimea and the warm-water port of Sevastopol, home to Russia's Black Sea Fleet. With his conquests, Catherine's empire reached from Belarus, or eastern Poland—obtained when Russia, Prussia, and Austria carved up that country—all the way to Alaska, colonized by Russian fur traders. Most of her realm lay in Asia, but like Peter the Great she looked for inspiration to the West and hoped to make Russia as powerful and prosperous as Britain and France. She sympathized with the Enlightenment, an intellectual movement that favored reforming and

1598-1689   **4**

Moscow

SIBERIA

Russia in 1598
Land added 1598-1689
Map shows modern boundaries.

1689-1799   **5**

St. Petersburg

Moscow

Sevastopol

Russia in 1689
Land added 1689-1796
Map shows modern boundaries.

rationalizing Europe's old aristocratic regimes. But her interest in improving the lot of Russia's serfs—who were tied to the land and at the mercy of their masters—evaporated when she faced a peasant rebellion led by the Cossack Emelian Pugachev, who was captured in 1774 and publicly butchered in Moscow. In her last years, Catherine reacted against the French Revolution and abandoned any pretense of reform, cracking down on Poles who sought independence and Ukrainians who resisted serfdom.

Imperial crown (above) made for Catherine the Great

Imperial Russia in the early 19th century was a study in contrasts. Militarily, it flourished under Catherine's grandson, Tsar Alexander I, who withstood invasion by Napoleon Bonaparte in 1812 and emerged triumphant. Yet economically, Russia remained backward, with a huge

Empress Catherine the Great of Russia (right) in her coronation robe and Great Imperial Crown

6

1799–1914

St. Petersburg

Moscow

Trans-Siberian Railway (constructed 1891–1916)

Russia in 1796
Land added 1796–1914
Map shows modern boundaries.

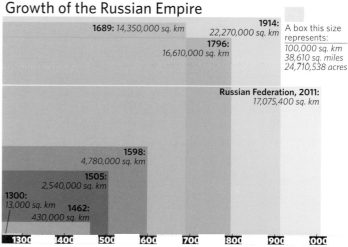

Growth of the Russian Empire

1689: *14,350,000 sq. km*

1914: *22,270,000 sq. km*

1796: *16,610,000 sq. km*

A box this size represents:
*100,000 sq. km
38,610 sq. miles
24,710,538 acres*

Russian Federation, 2011: *17,075,400 sq. km*

1598: *4,780,000 sq. km*

1505: *2,540,000 sq. km*

1300: *13,000 sq. km*

1462: *430,000 sq. km*

1300   1400   1500   1600   1700   1800   1900   2000

DEAD SOULS

Serfs were peasants who worked a hereditary plot of land for the benefit of the landowner. They weren't slaves—they couldn't be bought and sold—but they weren't free, either. They couldn't move from the land, and if the master sold the land, the serf transferred along with it. Serfs owed their master much of what they produced, and often they were treated brutally.

Serfdom disappeared from western Europe in the 14th and 15th centuries, but persisted in eastern Europe. In Russia, the westernization led by Peter I and his descendants did not change the system, despite debates over its efficiency and morality. In 1767, Catherine the Great decreed that serfs "owe their landlords proper submission and absolute obedience in all matters." It wasn't until 1861 that Alexander II emancipated the serfs.

Nikolai Gogol satirized the system in his 1842 novel *Dead Souls*. The protagonist, Chichikov, attempts to better his social position by trading in "dead souls"—dead serfs who are still carried on the census rolls, meaning the landowners still owe taxes on them. Chichikov figures he can use these serfs as collateral on a loan—a scheme that collapses, and in so doing skewers a system that treated humans so callously.

"Dinner at the Zemstvo," painting, 1872. A zemstvo was a rural government unit established following the emancipation of the serfs in 1861.

The 1896 coronation of Tsar Nicholas II and Empress Alexandra Feodorovna at the Church of the Assumption

gap between its aristocratic elite and abject serfs, whose inability to leave their masters and seek employment elsewhere hampered the development of Russian cities and industries.

Alexander's archconservative successor, Tsar Nicholas I, crushed an uprising called the Decembrist Revolt and used secret police to spy on dissidents and arrest them. Not until 1861 did his reform-minded son, Alexander II, free Russia's serfs. That was one of several steps he took to catch up with industrialized European rivals such as Britain and France, which had sided with the Ottoman Empire during the Crimean War (1853–1856) and inflicted a humiliating defeat on Russia. Despite Alexander's reforms, his realm made only fitful progress. From its educated elite emerged artists of worldwide renown such as composer Pyotr Ilich Tchaikovsky and novelist Leo Tolstoy, author of *War and Peace,* a monumental novel set in the Napoleonic era. But Russian culture could not save Russian society, torn by discord between reactionaries, reformers, and revolutionaries. Among the radicals seeking to topple the old imperial regime were communists, anarchists, and terrorists like those who assassinated Alexander II in 1881.

Tsarist Russia collapsed under Alexander's reactionary grandson, Nicholas II, who took power in 1894 and led his country into a calamitous war with Japan a decade later. That

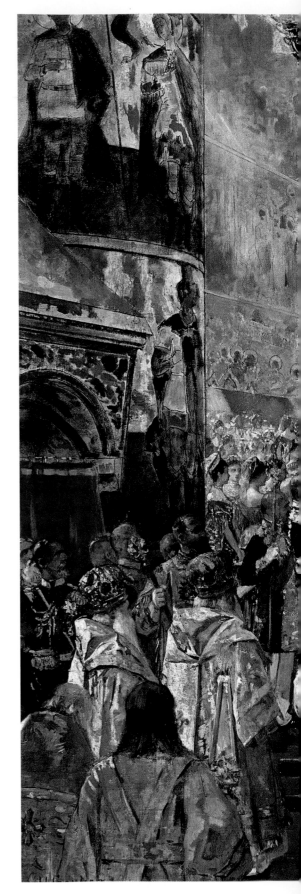

debacle triggered a revolution against him in 1905. Belatedly, Nicholas allowed constitutional reforms, but revolutionary workers' councils called soviets remained defiant. His troops managed to restore order, but they were ill prepared for the global conflict that loomed when Russia allied with Britain and France in 1907. That compact set Russia against imperial Germany and its ally Austria-Hungary, which like Russia was a declining empire that courted disaster by continuing to act provocatively like a great power. After the Ottoman Empire lost control of the Balkans, Austria-Hungary annexed Bosnia in 1908, and Russia became patron and protector of neighboring Serbia.

In 1914, following the assassination in Bosnia of Archduke Franz Ferdinand and the Archduchess Sofia by a Serbian terrorist, Austria-Hungary challenged Serbia and clashed with Russia, igniting World War I, known then as the Great War. Ottoman

> *"What is the true End of Monarchy? Not to deprive People of their natural Liberty; but to correct their Actions, in order to attain the supreme Good."*
>
> CATHERINE II (CATHERINE THE GREAT), PROPOSALS FOR A NEW LAW CODE

Turks sided with the Central Powers of Germany and Austria-Hungary, increasing the pressure on Russia, whose troops were poorly led, inadequately supplied, and dangerously cut off from their Allied partners to the west. Dreadful losses to the seemingly unstoppable advancing German forces doomed Nicholas II, who faced another uprising and abdicated in March 1917. Communists called Bolsheviks, led by Vladimir Lenin, seized power later that

year, withdrew from the war, and extinguished the Romanov dynasty by executing Nicholas, his wife Alexandra, and members of their family. Bolsheviks posed as anti-imperialists but capitalized on the collapse of the Central Powers at war's end and rebuilt the Russian Empire in the early 1920s. That revolutionary imperial regime, known as the Union of Soviet Socialist Republics (U.S.S.R.), was ruled from the Kremlin in Moscow, home to Russia's first tsars.

PEOPLE

RASPUTIN'S POWER

Grigory Yefimovich Rasputin (circa 1872–1916, originally Grigory Yefimovich Novykh) was a self-declared holy man whose influence over Russia's last imperial family is near legendary. An illiterate peasant, he acquired the name Rasputin, usually translated as "debauched one," because of his drinking and womanizing. In photographs and descriptions from the time, his eyes fascinate—bright, intense, hypnotic. It is thought that hypnosis allowed him to ease the pains of Alexei, the hemophiliac son of Tsar Nicolas II and Empress Alexandra. The empress, deaf to talk of his scandals and misdeeds, became his patroness. For years, he wielded great power over political decisions. In December 1916, a group of his noble enemies conspired to kill him, first with poison, then gunshots, and finally drowning.

Rasputin, who could not read or write, poses with pen in hand.

The last Russian imperial family. Tsarina Alexandra Feodorovna and Tsar Nicholas II are surrounded by their children (clockwise, from bottom) Alexei, Maria, Olga, Tatiana, and Anastasia.

THE COLLAPSE OF MODERN EMPIRES

In January 1919, representatives of 27 nations met in Paris to bring a formal end to World War I. Imperial rivalries had ignited that terrible conflict, and it left several empires in ruins, including the defeated Central Powers—Germany, Austria-Hungary, and the Ottoman Empire—as well as their opponent Russia, which withdrew from the war after the Bolsheviks overthrew Tsar Nicholas II.

One question hanging over the Paris Peace Conference was whether peace could be preserved in a world still dominated by imperial powers. Great Britain and France, having defeated the Central Powers at great cost, felt entitled to retain their own colonies and acquire mandates over the colonies of their opponents. The British Empire remained the world's largest, and France had reasserted its imperial ambitions following the defeat of Napoleon by colonizing much of North and West Africa as well as Indochina. The United States, which joined the war in 1917 and helped secure the Allied victory, had the makings of an imperial power, too, with overseas possessions or protectorates such as the Philippines, as well as predominance over Latin America. President Woodrow Wilson had sent American troops into Mexico during the tumultuous revolution that erupted there in 1910. But he believed that great nations should use their authority over other countries to foster self-determination rather than dependence or subservience. He envisioned a new world order, imposed not by imperial powers but by a cooperative League of Nations.

When Wilson arrived in Paris for the conference, he was greeted as a hero by crowds who shared his hope for lasting peace. Behind closed doors, however, he met with skepticism from European leaders such as French prime minister Georges Clemenceau, who believed that conflict between great powers was inevitable and that security lay in military strength. "I have come to the conclusion that force is *right,*" he remarked. Clemenceau praised Wilson for his "lofty aspirations" and went along with his proposed League of Nations, but doubted that it would stop strong nations from imposing on weak ones. "I like the League," he declared, "but I do not believe in it."

Wilson's hopes were dashed when the U.S. Senate rejected the Treaty of Versailles that had been drawn up at Paris, thus keeping America out of the League of Nations. The League was further hampered because it lacked enforcement powers to curb aggression against vulnerable new nations such as Czechoslovakia and Yugoslavia, created out of the remains of the old empires and made up of diverse ethnic groups with conflicting aspirations. Those countries would eventually succumb to a new empire: the German Reich forged by Adolf Hitler, an embittered veteran of World War I. Hitler's relentless campaign to restore Germany to imperial might and punish those he blamed for its defeat led his nation and the world to an even greater disaster in World War II. The Versailles Treaty gave him some ammunition against leaders of Germany's democratic postwar government, the Weimar Republic, by requiring them to accept blame for the war and pay reparations.

The terms imposed on Germany were not that punishing by historical standards, though, and do not fully explain why it became one of several nations ruled by aggressive imperial regimes following World War I—among them Italy, Japan, and the Soviet Union, a resurgent Russian Empire forged by Bolshevik leader Vladimir Lenin. What those regimes had in common was a desire to create their own new orders using old imperial tactics, as Lenin's successor, Joseph Stalin, did by wielding tsarist powers with the help of secret police. Economic turmoil in postwar Europe and the global distress caused by the Great Depression in the 1930s spurred those regimes, which promised their followers a bright future while exploiting their longing to recapture lost imperial glory and their fear of the changes their societies were undergoing.

A New Caesar

In Italy, Benito Mussolini seized power in 1922 as leader of the Fascists, who derived their name from an emblem symbolizing the authority of ancient Roman rulers. Unified in 1870, Italy was a young nation with few colonies, but Fascists drew inspiration from the Roman Empire of old and made Mussolini their Caesar, hailing him with stiff-armed salutes. Like other neo-imperial dictators of the 20th century, Mussolini reveled in dominating opponents and had little interest in enhancing the material welfare of those he conquered—a redeeming feature of great empires in the past. His brutal invasion of Ethiopia in 1935 exemplified his exploitive imperial agenda.

Unlike Italy, Japan entered the 20th century as an imperial state, having restored authority in 1868 to the young Emperor Meiji, whose predecessors were mere figureheads. He and his successors served as commander in chief and head of state. Initially, imperial rule and a new constitution that established a parliament called the Diet had a bracing impact on Japan, which pulled together as a nation and rapidly industrialized. With modernization came rearmament and expansion at the expense of the declining Chinese and Russian empires. By World War I, Japanese forces had occupied Korea and Taiwan and infiltrated Manchuria. Japan was on the winning side in that war and was awarded control over some of Germany's colonies in the South Pacific. The Great Depression convinced Japanese militarists that only though further conquests could they meet the needs of their fast-expanding population. Politicians who opposed that risky course were attacked and discredited. Emperor Hirohito, who failed to restrain his generals, remained a revered figure and lent prestige to a reckless military regime that invaded China in 1937 and would soon lead imperial Japan into a disastrous conflict with the United States and its allies.

The Third Reich

Like Japan, Germany had an imperial heritage that served as a pretense for aggression and expansion in the 1930s. Hitler's Third Reich harked back to the Holy Roman Empire forged by Otto I of Saxony in the tenth century and the modern German Empire that arose in 1871 under Kaiser Wilhelm I and collapsed in 1918 when Wilhelm II faced defeat and was toppled by revolutionaries. Promising to avenge that humiliation, Hitler rose to power through the electoral process, then used emergency powers to crush political opposition to his Nazi Party. He became Germany's unchallenged *Führer* ("leader"), to whom generals swore loyalty as they did earlier to the *kaiser* ("Caesar"). Britain and France, weary of war and fearful of losing blood, treasure, and colonies in another global conflict, remained passive as Hitler defied the Versailles Treaty, annexed Austria, and seized Czechoslovakia. Not until he invaded Poland in September 1939 did they rise to his imperial challenge and declare war.

One reason the Axis Powers of Germany, Italy, and Japan faltered as empires and lost World War II was that they were locked into aggression. Unlike successful empire-builders in ancient times, such as Cyrus the Great and Augustus Caesar, they were unable to shift from conquest to conciliation. Japan's vicious occupation of China drew rival Nationalist and Communist forces there into an alliance against the invaders that kept large numbers of Japanese forces tied down in China throughout World War II and undermined their wider war effort. Hitler's racial and ideological obsessions—which included eliminating communists, annihilating Jews, and dispossessing and brutalizing other "non-Aryans" such as Slavs (who made up much of the population of eastern Europe)—embroiled German forces in costly guerrilla warfare after they invaded the Balkans and the Soviet Union, which Hitler mistakenly thought would collapse under assault within months.

Despite the damage Stalin did to his Red Army by eliminating many of its top officers in murderous purges during the 1930s, the Soviets withstood the German invasion in 1941 and turned the tide, motivated more by hatred of the invaders than by devotion to Stalin and his commissars. Meanwhile, Americans had entered the war in response to Japanese attacks on their own bases at Pearl Harbor and the Philippines as well as on British, French, and Dutch colonies in Southeast Asia. The Axis could contend with the old imperial powers of western Europe. But its fate was sealed when it took on both the U.S. and the U.S.S.R., the world's two emerging superpowers. Significantly, neither of those nations had extensive overseas colonies, which were hard to defend in wartime and could prove to be liabilities. Their strength lay within their borders, with their vast populations and immense resources.

Among the casualties of World War II was the notion that empires had any constructive purpose or justification. Britain and other imperial powers that were not defeated in the conflict gave up their colonies afterward or were forced to relinquish them. Wars of independence like that waged by communist insurgents against the French in Vietnam—where the U.S. later intervened and lost—demonstrated that the world was entering a postimperial era. During the Cold War, some former colonies that won independence, such as India, avoided alignment with either the U.S. and its Western allies or the Soviet Bloc to keep from falling once again under the authority of an imposing foreign power. The breakup of the Soviet Union in 1991 dismantled the world's last major empire by stripping Russia of Eastern European satellites such as Poland and Hungary, occupied by Soviet troops during World War II, and of countries such as Ukraine and the Baltic States, annexed by Russian tsars in earlier times.

IMPERIAL AFTERMATH

The political, ethnic, and religious strife that followed the disintegration of empires in Africa, Asia, and eastern Europe could not be blamed entirely on the bitter legacy of imperialism. Many empires throughout history left turbulence behind when they failed, but that does not mean they all were inherently unstable or bent on destruction. Before the exploitive modern Age of Imperialism ended with the wrenching global conflicts of the 20th century, great empires often played a constructive role by imposing peace, repressing religious and ethnic hostilities, and furthering commerce and communications. The question facing the world in the 21st century, following the collapse of empires, is whether multinational organizations such as the European Union and the United Nations are strong and cohesive enough to take up that constructive role and preserve global order and prosperity. If not, the world might yet witness a resurgence of imperial aggression or destructive great-power rivalries, making the prospect of lasting peace that glimmered at the conclusion of the Cold War look as fleeting as the hopes raised and dashed at Paris in 1919.

	3500-2751 B.C.	2750-2501 B.C.	2500-2251 B.C.	
AKKADIAN EMPIRE	**ca 3500 B.C.** Cities develop in Sumer, forming the basis for Mesopotamian civilization.		**ca 2500 B.C.** Royal burials at the Sumerian city-state of Ur include human sacrifices. **ca 2330 B.C.** Sargon of Akkad conquers Sumer and goes on to expand his domain. **ca 2280 B.C.** Sargon dies, bequeathing control of his empire to his heirs.	
BABYLONIAN EMPIRES				
OLD & MIDDLE KINGDOMS	**ca 3100 B.C.** Egypt unified by Narmer.	**ca 2600 B.C.** Djoser of Egypt's 3rd dynasty buried in Step Pyramid at Saqqara. **ca 2550 B.C.** Khufu of 4th dynasty erects Great Pyramid at Giza.		
NEW KINGDOM				

2250-2001 B.C.	2000-1751 B.C.	1750-1401 B.C.	1400-1001 B.C.
ca 2250 B.C. Naram-Sin, Sargon's grandson, takes power. **ca 2220 B.C.** Akkadian Empire collapses following the death of Naram-Sin. **ca 2100 B.C.** Ur-Nammu of Ur takes command of Sumer and Akkad.	**ca 2000 B.C.** Ur destroyed by invading Elamites. **ca 1800 B.C.** Babylon, a city-state in Akkad, emerges as an imperial power.		
	1792 B.C. Hammurabi becomes king of Babylon and begins forging an empire. **ca 1750 B.C.** Hammurabi dies, leaving his code of laws as his chief legacy.	**1595 B.C.** Hittites descend from the north and conquer Babylon.	**ca 1120 B.C.** Nebuchadnezzar I takes power and launches a brief Babylonian revival.
ca 2150 B.C. Old Kingdom collapses and Egypt fractures. **ca 2050 B.C.** Mentuhotep II of Thebes reunites Egypt, inaugurating Middle Kingdom.		**ca 1650 B.C.** Hyksos invasion brings Middle Kingdom to an end. **ca 1550 B.C.** Ahmose I of Thebes expels Hyksos and reunites Egypt.	
		ca 1550 B.C Ahmose I of Thebes expels Hyksos, reunites Egypt, and ushers in New Kingdom. **1479 B.C.** Queen Hatshepsut becomes regent for King Thutmose III and later clings to power. **ca 1457 B.C.** Thutmose III, now ruler in his own right, secures Palestine and Syria for Egypt.	**ca 1350 B.C.** Amenhotep IV, renamed Akhenaten, devotes himself exclusively to god Aten. **ca 1275 B.C.** Ramses II leads Egyptian forces against Hittites in great chariot battle at Kadesh. **1156 B.C.** Ramses III dies, marking beginning of the end for New Kingdom. **1070 B.C.** New Kingdom breaks apart.

	1000-926 B.C.	925-851 B.C.	850-776 B.C.	
THE BABYLONIAN EMPIRE		**ca 900 B.C.** Assyrians emerge as the dominant force in Mesopotamia and surrounding lands.		
PERSIAN EMPIRE				
CARTHAGE			**ca 800 B.C.** Phoenician colonists establish Carthage.	
NEW KINGDOM				
QIN/HAN				

775-701 B.C.	700-626 B.C.	625-551 B.C.	550-510 B.C.
	689 B.C. King Sennacherib of Assyria destroys Babylon, which is later rebuilt.	**612 B.C.** Babylonians defeat Assyrians and inherit their empire. **586 B.C.** Jerusalem falls to the Babylonian army of Nebuchadnezzar II.	**539 B.C.** Babylon falls to Cyrus the Great of Persia.
		559 B.C. Cyrus the Great becomes king of the Persians and leads them against their overlords, the Medes.	**546 B.C.** Cyrus defeats King Croesus of Lydia. **539 B.C.** Cyrus takes Babylon and becomes master of Mesopotamia. **529 B.C.** Cyrus dies in battle and is succeeded by his son Cambyses. **525 B.C.** Persian troops led by Cambyses conquer Egypt. **522 B.C.** Darius I seizes power following the death of Cambyses.
ca 750 B.C. Nubians from kingdom of Kush take control of Egypt.	**667 B.C.** Assyrians invade Egypt, ending Nubian rule.		
		551–479 B.C. Life span of Confucius (Kong Fuzi).	

	509-426 B.C.	425-340 B.C.	339-276 B.C.	
PERSIAN EMPIRE	**490 B.C.** Greek troops repulse Persian invaders at Marathon. **480 B.C.** Persian fleet led by Darius's successor, Xerxes, defeated by Greeks at Salamis.		**330 B.C.** Alexander the Great shatters Persian Empire.	
PERSIAN DYNASTIES			**323 B.C.** Alexander the Great dies, triggering a power struggle between Seleucus and other Macedonian generals. **301 B.C.** Seleucus defeats Antigonus and extends his domain from Iran to the Mediterranean. **281 B.C.** Seleucus I dies, bequeathing power to his son, Antiochus I, of the Seleucid dynasty.	
ALEXANDER'S EMPIRE		**356 B.C.** Alexander is born to King Philip II of Macedonia. **ca 342 B.C.** Greek philosopher Aristotle serves as Alexander's tutor. **ca 340 B.C.** Philip II conquers Greece.	**336 B.C.** Alexander becomes king. **334 B.C.** Alexander begins campaign against Persian Empire. **331 B.C.** Alexander's army defeats Persians. **327 B.C.** Alexander invades India. **325 B.C.** Alexander leaves India. **323 B.C.** Alexander dies of fever.	
CARTHAGE	**ca 500 B.C.** Carthaginians occupy Cadiz and colonize other places in Spain.			
ROMAN EMPIRE	**509 B.C.** Rome achieves independence from Etruscans and becomes a republic.			
MAURYA AND GUPTA EMPIRES			**325 B.C.** Alexander the Great's troops leave India. **ca 321 B.C.** Mauryan dynasty begins as Chandragupta Maurya takes the throne. **300 B.C.–A.D. 100** Buddhism spreads throughout India.	
QIN AND HAN				

275-201 B.C.	200-126 B.C.	125-51 B.C.	50 B.C.-0
	165 B.C. Jewish rebels led by Judas Maccabeus defy Antiochus IV and take Jerusalem. **139 B.C.** Mithradates I leads Parthians to defeat Demetrius II and supplant the Seleucids.	**64 B.C.** Romans conquer Syria and threaten Parthians in Mesopotamia. **53 B.C.** Parthians crush invading Roman army at Carrhae in Mesopotamia.	
264 B.C. Rome challenges Carthage for control of Sicily, begins First Punic War. **241 B.C.** First Punic War ends with Rome in control of Sicily. **218 B.C.** Second Punic War begins. **216 B.C.** Hannibal defeats Roman army. **202 B.C.** Romans defeat Carthaginians at Zama, ending Second Punic War.	**149 B.C.** Romans set out to annihilate Carthage, launching Third Punic War. **146 B.C.** Third Punic War ends with destruction of Carthage.		
ca 275 B.C. Southern Italy comes under Roman rule.	**146 B.C.** Romans destroy Carthage and complete conquest of Greece and Macedonia.		**49 B.C.** Julius Caesar crosses the Rubicon with his army and becomes Rome's dictator. **44 B.C.** Assassination of Caesar leads to civil war. **31 B.C.** Octavian (Augustus Caesar) defeats Mark Antony and Queen Cleopatra of Egypt and becomes emperor.
268–232 B.C. Ashoka rules Mauryan Empire.	**200 B.C.–A.D. 650** Ajanta caves decorated by Buddhist artisans. **185 B.C.** Mauryan dynasty comes to an end.		
221–210 B.C. Qin empire consolidated by Qin Shi Huangdi. **206 B.C.–A.D. 9** Western Han dynasty rules from Chang'an.		**124 B.C.** Emperor Wudi founds the first imperial university. **ca 85 B.C.** Sima Qian writes *The Records of the Grand Historian*.	

		1-149	150-299	300-449	
	PERSIAN DYNASTIES		**224** Persian rebels led by Ardashir I, founder of the Sasanid dynasty, oust last Parthian king.		
	ROMAN EMPIRE	**117** Emperor Trajan dies, with Roman Empire at its greatest extent.	**212** Roman citizenship extended to all within the empire who are not slaves.		
	MAURYA AND GUPTA EMPIRES			**320** Gupta dynasty founded by Chandra Gupta I. **ca 380** Chandra Gupta II comes to the throne.	
	QIN AND HAN	**9–23** Wang Mang, a reformer, rules during an interregnum. **25–220** Eastern Han dynasty rules from Luoyang.	**189** Palace eunuchs slaughtered. **184–208** Yellow Turban rebels attack the Han government.		
	BYZANTINE EMPIRE			**330** Emperor Constantine founds city of Constantinople.	
	HOUSE OF ISLAM				
	KHMER	**First–sixth centuries** Indian culture comes to Cambodia via traders.			
	HOLY ROMAN EMPIRE				
	MUSLIM EMPIRES IN SPAIN				
	TOLTEC				

450-599	600-749	750-899	900-999
	651 Arab conquerors bring Sasanid rule to an end.		
476 Rome falls to Germanic invaders.			
ca 550 Gupta dynasty ends.			
527–565 Emperor Justinian rules, with Theodora as empress. **537** Hagia Sophia, the great church, built by Justinian. **550s** Silk production begins after empire gains secret from China.	**717–741** Leo III reigns as emperor. **726–843** Icon controversy splits Byzantium.		**976–1025** Basil II, the Bulgar Slayer, reigns.
ca 570 Prophet Muhammad born in Mecca; he dies in Medina in 632.	**661–750** Islam expands under the Umayyad dynasty.	**750–1258** Abbasid dynasty rules from Baghdad. **756** Abd al-Rahman makes Cordoba, Spain, his capital. **786–809** Caliph Harun al-Rashid rules in Baghdad.	**969** Fatimids, a Shiite dynasty, conquer Egypt.
		802–835 First Khmer king, Jayavarman II, reigns. **877–ca 890** Indravarman I fills the throne. **881** "Temple mountain" of Bakong dedicated in Angkor. **ca 890–ca 910** Yasovarman I rules and builds Angkor Thom.	
481 Clovis becomes king of the Franks. **511** Clovis dies, bequeathing power to his four sons.	**732** Charles Martel wins Battle of Tours and founds Carolingian dynasty.	**771** Charlemagne becomes sole ruler of Frankish kingdom. **800** Pope Leo III crowns Charlemagne at St. Peter's in Rome. **844** Charles the Bald divides empire with Lothar and Louis the German.	**962** Otto crowned emperor by Pope John XII.
	700s Muslim forces enter Spain.	**778** Basques ambush and annihilate Charlemagne's rear guard.	**958** Christian leaders pay homage to Abd al-Rahman III in Cordoba.
		ca 750 Great city of Teotihuacan devastated by fire.	**ca 900** Toltec people gain power in Valley of Mexico. **ca 950** Tula emerges as capital of Toltec Empire. **ca 987** Legendary Toltec leader Quetzalcoatl reportedly driven into exile.

		1000-1099	1100-1249	1250-1289	
	BYZANTINE EMPIRE	**1054** Schism splits Roman Catholic and Orthodox Churches.			
	HOUSE OF ISLAM	**1055** Seljuk Turks under Tughril Beg oust Shiites from Baghdad.	**1187** Saladin retakes Jerusalem from Christian crusaders.	**1258** Mongols invade, ending the Abbasid dynasty.	
	KHMER	**ca 1004–1050** Suryavarman I rules, extending empire into Thailand.	**1113–ca 1150** Angkor Wat built in reign of Suryavarman II. **1177** Jayavarman VII retakes Cambodia and promotes Buddhism.		
	MONGOLS		**1206–1227** Genghis Khan reigns. **1211–1234** Mongols conquer north China. **1219–1221** Persia falls to Mongols. **1237–1241** Russia falls to Mongols.	**1258** Mongols capture Baghdad in siege. **1264–1294** Khubilai Khan rules China. **1275** Marco Polo meets Khubilai Khan. **1279–1368** Yuan dynasty rules China.	
	MING				
	HOLY ROMAN EMPIRE	**1077** Barefoot and penitent, Emperor Henry IV reenters Catholic fold.		**1273** Rudolf I becomes emperor, first of Habsburg dynasty.	
	MUSLIM EMPIRES IN SPAIN	**1085** Christian troops from Castile seize the city of Toledo. **1099** El Cid (Rodrigo Díaz de Vivar) dies.	**1142** Almohads seize Marrakech and al-Andalus. **1212** Christian forces win Battle of Las Navas de Tolosa.		
	SPANISH-AMERICAN EMPIRE				
	WEST AFRICAN EMPIRES	**1076** Almoravid forces invade Kumbi, capital of kingdom of Ghana.	**1235** Sundiata defeats Sumanguru and founds Mali Empire.		
	TOLTEC	**ca 1000–1170** Toltec continue to induct warriors into military societies and wield power.	**ca 1170** Tula sacked and burned; Toltec Empire collapses.		
	AZTEC EMPIRE				
	INCA EMPIRE				
	OTTOMAN EMPIRE				
	ASANTE EMPIRE				
	MUGHALS				
	RUSSIA				

1290-1399	1400-1499	1500-1599
	1453 Constantinople falls to Ottomans.	
	1432 Khmer routed by Thais.	
1295 Conversion to Islam of Ilkhan ruler Ghazan.		
1368 Zhu Yuanzhang, as Hongwu Emperor, founds Ming dynasty.	**1402–1424** Yongle Emperor reigns. **1406–1420** Forbidden City constructed. **1420** Beijing again becomes imperial capital. **1405–1433** Zheng He's voyages.	**1572–1620** Wanli Emperor reigns under control of courtiers. **1592–1598** Japanese invade Korea, fighting Chinese there.
		1519–1556 Charles V rules Holy Roman Empire.
	1469 Isabella of Castile marries Ferdinand of Aragon, unifying Spain. **1492** Granada, a Muslim stronghold, falls to Christian Spain.	
	1469 Queen Isabella of Castile weds King Ferdinand II of Aragon. **1492** Christopher Columbus makes landfall in Caribbean. **1494** Treaty with Portugal grants Spain most of New World.	**1522** Ferdinand Magellan's crew circles Earth. **1556** Philip II assumes Spanish throne. **1560s** Protestants resist Spanish in Netherlands. **1588** Spanish Armada rebuffed by English navy.
1324 Sundiata's grandnephew, Mansa Musa, makes pilgrimage to Mecca.	**1468** Timbuktu seized by Sunni Ali, founder of Songhai Empire. **1473** Sunni Ali conquers trading center of Djenne. **1493** Muhammad I ousts Ali's son.	**1591** Moroccan forces cross Sahara and destroy Songhai Empire.
1325 Tenochtitlan founded by Aztec, later becoming their capital.	**1426–1428** Itzcoatl conquers Valley of Mexico and establishes Aztec Empire. **1487** Ahuitzotl reportedly sacrifices 20,000 prisoners on the Great Pyramid in Tenochtitlan.	**1502** Moctezuma II succeeds Ahuitzotl. **1519** Hernán Cortés reaches Tenochtitlan. **1520** Moctezuma II dies after capture by Cortés. **1521** Cortés and allies conquer Aztec Empire.
ca 1300 Inca take control of the Cusco Valley.	**1438** Pachacuti Inca Yupanqui forges Inca Empire. **1471** Topa Inca Yupanqui succeeds Pachacuti as emperor. **1493** Topa dies and is succeeded by Huayna Capac.	**1525** Huayna Capac perishes in an epidemic in Cusco. **1532** Atahualpa defeats rival heir Huascar. **1533** Atahualpa executed by Spaniards.
ca 1300 Osman, a Turkish chieftain, founds Ottoman dynasty.	**1453** Ottoman emperor Mehmed II conquers Byzantine Empire by seizing Constantinople.	**1501** Ismail becomes shah and leads Shiites against Sunni. **1514** Ottoman troops defeat the army of Shah Ismail. **1520** Sultan Suleyman I begins reign that brings Ottoman Empire to its peak.
	Late 1400s European merchants establish trading posts on Gold Coast.	
		1526 Babur invades India and founds Mughal dynasty. **1530** Babur dies and is succeeded by his son Humayun. **1555** Humayun recaptures Delhi and regains power. **1562** Akbar weds Hindu princess.
	1462–1505 Ivan III, grand prince of Moscow, lays foundation for Russian Empire.	**1547** Ivan IV becomes first Russian ruler proclaimed tsar. **1570** Novgorod city destroyed by Ivan IV and his henchmen, the oprichniki.

	1600-1649	1650-1699	1700-1749	
MING	**1627** Peasant rebellions begin to break out. **1644** Collapse of Ming dynasty.			
BRITISH EMPIRE	**1600s** Catholics, Quakers, Anglicans, and Puritans colonize North America.	**1664** England seizes New York from the Netherlands.	**1707** Great Britain formed by England's union with Scotland.	
IMPERIAL TRIBES OF NORTH AMERICA	**Early 1600s** Chief Powhatan asserts authority over about 30 tribes in Virginia. **1640s** Opechancanough, Powhatan's successor, defeated by English colonists.	**Late 1600s** Iroquois Confederacy gains power through warfare, trade, and diplomacy.		
SPANISH-AMERICAN EMPIRE		**1680** Pueblo Indians drive Spanish settlers out of New Mexico.		
OTTOMAN EMPIRE		**1683** Ottomans repulsed at Vienna.		
ASANTE EMPIRE		**1690** Osei Tutu Opemsoo unites Asante under his authority.	**ca 1700** Osei Tutu's warriors defeat the Denkyere and take control of Gold Coast. **1720** Opoku Ware succeeds Osei Tutu.	
MUGHALS	**ca 1632** Taj Mahal commissioned by Emperor Shah Jahan in memory of his late wife.	**1658** Aurangzeb imprisons his father, Shah Jahan, executes relatives, and seizes throne.	**1739** Invaders from Iran sack Delhi.	
QING	**Early 1600s** Manchu ruler Nurhaci unites Manchuria under his authority. **1626–1643** Huang Taiji, Nurhaci's successor, conquers Mongolia and invades China. **1644** Manchus seize Beijing and replace Ming dynasty with their own Qing dynasty.	**1661** Kangxi succeeds Emperor Shunzhi and reigns for 61 years. **1689** Kangxi settles China's boundary dispute with Russia.	**1735** Emperor Qianlong begins 60-year reign.	
RUSSIA		**1696** Peter the Great takes sole command of Russia.		

1750-1799	1800-1849	1850-1899	1900-2000
1759 Gen. James Wolfe seizes Quebec. **1776** American colonies declare independence from Great Britain. **1781** George Washington achieves decisive victory at Yorktown. **1788** Australia founded as a penal colony.		**1857** British forces impose direct imperial rule on India.	**1910** Britain grants South Africa dominion status.
Mid-1700s Comanches defeat their rivals, the Apache, and dominate southern Plains. **1786** New Mexico governor reaches accord with Comanche chief.	**1821** Texas passes from Spain to newly independent nation of Mexico. **1845** Texas annexed by United States, which seeks to confine Comanche.	**1867** William Tecumseh Sherman helps negotiate Medicine Lodge Treaty. **1870s** Sherman forces Comanche and other Plains tribes onto reservations.	
1769 Franciscan friars found San Diego.	**Early 1800s** Spanish-American colonies rebel; Spain retains only Cuba and Puerto Rico.		
	1807 Conservatives in the Janissary corps overthrow Sultan Selim III.		**1908** Young Turks impose constitutional rule and leave Ottoman sultan powerless.
	1824 Asante forces defeat and behead British commander Sir Charles MacCarthy. **1831** British and Asante agree to a pact.	**1896** Asante king deposed and arrested by British governor.	**1957** Kwame Nkrumah leads Ghana to independence.
1757 British oust defiant nawab of Bengal and take control there.		**1857–1858** British troops crush Indian Mutiny and exile last Mughal emperor. **1877** Queen Victoria proclaimed Empress of India.	**1947** Independence granted to India.
	1839 Opium War launched by British against China. **1842** Treaty of Nanjing requires China to cede Hong Kong to Britain.	**1864** Taiping Rebellion against Qing dynasty crushed after 12 years of turmoil.	**1912** Sun Yat-sen and his revolutionaries oust last Chinese emperor.
1762 Catherine the Great takes power in a coup. **1774–1775** Emelian Pugachev, the rebellious Cossack, is captured, butchered in Moscow.	**1812** Tsar Alexander I withstands invasion by Napoleon Bonaparte.	**1861** Alexander II frees Russia's serfs.	**1917** Communist Bolsheviks, led by Vladimir Lenin, seize power.

BOOKS

Aldred, Cyril. *The Egyptians,* rev. ed. New York: Thames and Hudson, 1984.

Bentley, Jerry H., and Herbert F. Ziegler. *Traditions and Encounters: A Global Perspective on the Past.* Boston: McGraw-Hill, 2000.

Burbank, Jane, and Frederick Cooper. *Empires in World History: Power and the Politics of Difference.* Princeton, N.J.: Princeton University Press, 2010.

Castillo, Bernal Díaz del. *The Discovery and Conquest of Mexico, 1517-1521.,* trans. A. P. Maudsley. New York: Da Capo Press, 1996.

D'Altroy, Terence N. *The Incas.* Malden, Mass.: Blackwell Publishing, 2002.

Daniels, Patricia S. and Stephen G. Hyslop. *Almanac of World History.* Washington, D.C.: National Geographic Society, 2003.

Dunstan, William E. *The Ancient Near East.* Fort Worth, Tex.: Harcourt Brace, 1998.

Farrington, Karen. *Historical Atlas of Empires.* New York: Checkmark Books, 2002.

Freeman, Charles. *Egypt, Greece, and Rome: Civilizations of the Ancient Mediterranean.* New York: Oxford University Press, 1999.

Hämäläinen, Pekka. *The Comanche Empire.* New Haven, Conn.: Yale University Press, 2000.

Haywood, John. *Historical Atlas of the Ancient World.* Abingdon, U.K.: MetroBooks, 1998.

Heer, Friedrich. *Charlemagne and His World.* New York: Macmillan, 1975.

Herodotus. *Herodotus: The Histories,* trans. Walter Blanco. New York: Norton, 1992.

Homberger, Eric. *The Penguin Historical Atlas of North America.* London: Penguin Books, 1995.

Hourani, Albert. *A History of the Arab Peoples.* Cambridge, Mass.: Harvard University Press, 1991.

Hyslop, Stephen G., Bob Somerville and John Thompson. *Eyewitness to History: From Ancient Times to the Modern Era.* Washington, D.C.: National Geographic Society, 2010.

James, Lawrence. *The Rise and Fall of the British Empire.* New York: St. Martin's Press, 1994.

Kamen, Henry. *Empire: How Spain Became a World Power, 1492-1763.* New York: HarperCollins, 2003.

Kershaw, Ian. *Fateful Choices: Ten Decisions That Changed the World, 1940-41.* New York: Penguin Press, 2007.

Kia, Mehrdad. *The Ottoman Empire.* Westport, Conn.: Greenwood Press, 2008.

Lichtheim, Miriam. *Ancient Egyptian Literature,* vol. 2. Berkeley: University of California Press, 1976.

Livy. *Hannibal's War,* trans. J. C. Yardley. Oxford: Oxford University Press, 2006.

MacMillan, Margaret. *Paris 1919: Six Months That Changed the World.* New York: Random House, 2002.

McLeod, M. D. *The Asante.* London: British Museum Publications, 1981.

Ochoa, George. *Atlas of Hispanic-American History.* New York: Checkmark Books, 2001.

Plutarch. *Plutarch's Lives,* trans. Bernadotte Perrin. Cambridge, Mass: Harvard University Press, 1919.

Robins, Gay. *Women in Ancient Egypt.* Cambridge, Mass.: Harvard University Press, 1993.

Rowe, William T. *China's Last Empire: The Great Qing.* Cambridge, Mass: Harvard University Press, 2009.

Scarre, Christopher, and Brian M. Fagan. *Ancient Civilizations.* New York: Longman, 1997.

Time-Life Books, ed. *What Life Was Like on the Banks of the Nile.* Alexandria, Va.: Time-Life, 1997.

Time-Life Books, ed. *What Life Was Like When Rome Ruled the World.* Alexandria, Va.: Time-Life, 1997.

Townsend, Richard F. *The Aztecs.* New York: Thames and Hudson, 1992.

Weber, David J. *The Spanish Frontier in North America.* New Haven, Conn.: Yale University Press, 1992.

Wells, Colin. *The Roman Empire,* 2nd ed. Cambridge, Mass.: Harvard University Press, 1992.

Wilks, Ivor. *Forests of Gold: Essays on the Akan and the Kingdom of Asante.* Athens: Ohio University Press, 1993.

WEBSITES

Ancient Egypt: http://www.bbc.co.uk/history/ancient/egyptians/

British Empire: http://www.nationalarchives.gov.uk/education/empire/

Byzantine Empire: http://public.wsu.edu/~dee/MA/BYZ.HTM

"Inca Mummies: Secrets of a Lost World": http://www.nationalgeographic.com/inca/

Islamic History: http://www.uga.edu/islam/history.html

Metropolitan Museum of Art: Heilbrunn Timeline of Art History: http://www.metmuseum.org/toah/

Ottoman Empire: http://www.theottomans.org/english/history/empire.asp

Qing Dynasty: http://www.learn.columbia.edu/nanxuntu/start.html

Russian History: http://www.bucknell.edu/x17601.xml

Spain: al Andalus: http://countrystudies.us/spain/5.htm

The Spanish Empire: http://www.pbs.org/kcet/when-worlds-collide/essays/the-spanish-empire.html

"Unburying the Aztec": http://ngm.nationalgeographic.com/2010/11/greatest-aztec/draper-text

Chapter openers (borders): 18-19 Frieze of archers, from the Palace of Darius the Great (548-486 B.C.) at Susa, Iran, Achaemenid Period, c. 500 B.C. (glazed bricks), Persian School, (6th century B.C.) / Louvre, Paris, France/Giraudon/The Bridgeman Art Library International; 50-51, Fedor Selivanov/Shutterstock; 78-79, Cameraphoto Arte, Venice/Art Resource, NY; 112-113, Lucy Baldwin/Shutterstock; 136-137, luigi nifosi/Shutterstock; 168-169, Bill Perry/Shutterstock; 206-207, Scala/Art Resource, NY; 232-233, Lukiyanova Natalia/frenta/Shutterstock; 258-259, bpk, Berlin/Art Resource, NY; 284-285, The Newark Museum/Art Resource, NY; 304-305, Losevsky Pavel/Shutterstock.

2-3, Erich Lessing/Art Resource, NY; 4, Erich Lessing/Art Resource, NY; 7, Erich Lessing/Art Resource, NY; 8, V&A Images, London/Art Resource, NY; 14-15, Gordon Gahan; 16-17, Ms Lat 463 f.111v-112r Map of Phoenicia, Mesopotamia and Babylon (vellum), Ptolemy (Claudius Ptolemaeus of Alexandria)(ca 90-168)(after)/Biblioteca Estense, Modena, Italy/Alinari/The Bridgeman Art Library International; 18, Steve McCurry; 19, Life in Mesopotamia (wall painting)/Museum of the Jewish Diaspora, Tel Aviv, Israel/The Bridgeman Art Library International; 21 (LO LE), War chariot pulled by two horses, 2800-2300 B.C. (ivory, mother-of-pearl & mosaic), Mesopotamian/National Museum, Damascus, Syria/The Bridgeman Art Library International; 21 (UP RT), Réunion des Musées Nationaux/Art Resource, NY; 22 (LO), © The Trustees of the British Museum/Art Resource, NY; 22 (UP), Augusta McMahon, Tell Brak Project; 23 (UP), © The Trustees of The British Museum/Art Resource, NY; 23 (LO), Victory stele of Naram-Sin, King of Akkad, over the mountain-dwelling Lullubi, Akkadian Period, ca 2230 B.C. (pink sandstone), Mesopotamian/Louvre, Paris, France/The Bridgeman Art Library International; 24, Erich Lessing/Art Resource, NY; 25, bpk, Berlin/Vorderasiatisches Museum, Staatliche Museen, Berlin, Germany/Olaf M.Teßmer/Art Resource, NY; 27 (UP LE), Erich Lessing/Art Resource, NY; 27 (LO RT), Réunion des Musées Nationaux/Art Resource, NY; 28, Tablet with cuneiform script, ca 1830-1530 B.C. (clay), Babylonian/Iraq Museum, Baghdad/The Bridgeman Art Library International; 28-29, The Hanging Gardens of Babylon, from a series of the "Seven Wonders of the World" published in *Munchener Bilderbogen,* 1886 (color litho), Knab, Ferdinand (1834-1902)/Private Collection/Archives Charmet/The Bridgeman Art Library International; 30, Erich Lessing/Art Resource, NY; 31, Erich Lessing/Art Resource, NY; 33 (UP), Earring, Persian (ca 525-330 B.C.) (gold with inlays of turquoise, carnelian, and lapis lazuli), Achaemenid, (550-330 B.C.)/Museum of Fine Arts, Boston, Massachusetts, USA/Edward J. & Mary S. Holmes Fund/The Bridgeman Art Library International; 33 (LO), © The Trustees of the British Museum/Art Resource, NY; 34 (LO LE), Réunion des Musées Nationaux/Art Resource, NY; 34-35, Amir Niknam Pirzadeh/iStockphoto.com; 34 (UP RT), Daric depicting Darius as a Royal Archer (gold) (obverse), Achaemenid, (550-330 B.C.)/Tamashagah-e Pool (Money Museum), Tehran, Iran/The Bridgeman Art Library International; 36, Simon Norfolk; 37, Faravahar, Zoroastrian parsi symbol (metal), Indian School/Private Collection/Dinodia/The Bridgeman Art Library International; 38-39, Neue Galerie, Museumslandschaft Hessen Kassel, Kassel, Germany/Art Resource, NY; 39, Oldproof/Shutterstock; 40 (UP), Erich Lessing/Art Resource, NY; 40 (LO), I.T./Shutterstock; 41, Erich Lessing/Art Resource, NY; 42, Tetradrachma of Seleucus I (ca 358-280) King of Syria, minted at Persepolis, ca 300 B.C. (silver), Persian School, (4th century B.C.)/British Museum, London, UK/The Bridgeman Art Library International; 43, Réunion des Musées Nationaux/Art Resource, NY; 45 (UP), Scala/Art Resource, NY; 45 (LO), Giraudon/Art Resource, NY; 46, Dish depicting King Ardashir II (r. 379-86), from Sari, Mazandaran, ca A.D. 380 (chased and incised silver), Sasanian School, (4th century)/National Museum of Iran, Tehran, Iran/The Bridgeman Art Library International; 47, Relief depicting the investiture of King Ardashir I (ca 210-241) founder of the Sassanian empire in ancient Persia (photo)/Naqsh-e Rostam, Iran/Giraudon/The Bridgeman Art Library International; 48-49, View of Pharos at the mouth of the Nile, famous for its lighthouse built between 300 and 280 B.C., from "Le Theatre du Monde" or "Nouvel Atlas," 1645 (engraving), Blaeu, Willem (1571-1638) and Joan (1596-1673)/Private Collection/Index/The Bridgeman Art Library International; 50, Kenneth Garrett; 51, Kenneth Garrett/ NationalGeographicStock.com; 52, Statuette of the god Imhotep, the eyes inlaid with copper and gold (bronze), Egyptian, Late Period (715-332 B.C.)/Ashmolean Museum, University of Oxford, UK/The Bridgeman Art Library International; 54, Richard Nowitz/ NationalGeographicStock.com; 55, Aegyptisches Museum, Staatliche Museen, Berlin, Germany/Art Resource, NY; 56 (LE), Model of a servant grinding grain, Old Kingdom, from Saqqara (stone), Egyptian 5th Dynasty

(ca 2494-2345 B.C.)/Egyptian National Museum, Cairo, Egypt/Giraudon/The Bridgeman Art Library International; 56-57, The River Nile in Cairo (oil on panel), Frere, Charles Theodore (Bey) (1814-88)/© Dahesh Museum of Art, New York, USA/The Bridgeman Art Library International; 58, Roger Wood/CORBIS; 59 (UP), The Expulsion of the Hyksos, illustration from "Hutchinsons History of the Nations," ca 1910 (litho), Dudley, Ambrose (fl. 1920s)/Private Collection/The Stapleton Collection/The Bridgeman Art Library International; 59 (LO), Chariot and horses, from the Tomb of Princess Neferriabet, Old Kingdom (clay), Egyptian 4th Dynasty (ca 2613-2498 B.C.)/Louvre, Paris, France/Peter Willi/The Bridgeman Art Library International; 60, Kenneth Garrett; 61, Kenneth Garrett/NationalGeographicStock.com; 63 (LO), Kenneth Garrett; 63 (UP), The Rosetta Stone, from Fort St. Julien, El-Rashid (Rosetta) 196 B.C. (see also 138897), Egyptian Ptolemaic Period (332-30 B.C.)/British Museum, London, UK/The Bridgeman Art Library International; 64 (UP), Kenneth Garrett; 64 (LO), Kenneth Garrett; 65, Lori Epstein/ NationalGeographicStock.com; 66-67, "Washerwomen on the banks of the Nile" (oil on canvas), Girardet, Eugene Alexis (1853-1907)/Private Collection/The Bridgeman Art Library International; 67 (UP LE), Kenneth Garrett; 67 (LO RT), Richard Barnes; 68, Kenneth Garrett; 69 (UP), Kenneth Garrett; 69 (LO), Kenneth Garrett; 70, Kenneth Garrett; 71 (UP), Kenneth Garrett; 71 (LO), Kenneth Garrett; 72 (LO LE), Kenneth Garrett; 72 (UP), Kenneth Garrett; 72 (CTR), Kenneth Garrett; 73, Kenneth Garrett; 74 (LO RT), O. Louis Mazzatenta/ NationalGeographicStock.com; 74 (LO LE), Victor R. Boswell, Jr.; 75, Georg Gerster; 76-77, A New Map of the Roman Empire, from "A Prospect of the Most Famous Parts of the World," pub. by Bassett & Chiswell, 1676 (hand colored plate engraving), Speed, John (1552-1629)/O'Shea Gallery, London, UK/The Bridgeman Art Library International; 78, Muenzkabinett, Staatliche Museen, Berlin, Germany/Art Resource, NY; 79, James L. Stanfield; 82, Tom Lovell; 83, Richard Schlecht; 84 (LO LE), Erich Lessing/Art Resource, NY; 84 (UP CTR), © The Metropolitan Museum of Art/Art Resource, NY; 85, Cameraphoto Arte, Venice/Art Resource, NY; 86, Robert Clark; 87, Robert Clark; 89, Scala/Art Resource, NY; 90, Réunion des Musées Nationaux/Art Resource, NY; 91, Peter V. Bianchi; 92, James L. Stanfield; 93, kated/Shutterstock; 96 (UP), Scala/Ministero per i Beni e le Attività culturali/Art Resource, NY; 96 (LO), Ariy/Shutterstock; 97, Albert Moldvay; 98, Banqueting couple with a slave, from Herculaneum, ca 50-79 A.D. (fresco), Roman, (1st century A.D.)/Museo Archeologico Nazionale, Naples, Italy/The Bridgeman Art Library International; 98-99, abadesign/Shutterstock; 100, Ian McDonald/Shutterstock; 101, Scala/Art Resource, NY; 102, The Great Eruption of Mt. Vesuvius (w/c), Desprez, Louis Jean (1743-1804)/Private Collection/The Bridgeman Art Library International; 103 (UP), Maltings Partnership; 103 (LO RT), silky/Shutterstock; 103 (LO LE), O. Louis Mazzatenta; 104 (LO), Elena Elisseeva/Shutterstock; 104 (UP), "Magic" Vase, from the House of Sestilius Pyrricus, Pompeii, 1st century A.D. (pottery)/Private Collection/Accademia Italiana, London/The Bridgeman Art Library International; 105, Erich Lessing/Art Resource, NY; 106, Vanni/Art Resource, NY; 107 (LO), Slave Combing a Girl's Hair, Herculaneum, Third Style (fresco), Roman, (1st century A.D.)/Museo Archeologico Nazionale, Naples, Italy/The Bridgeman Art Library International; 107 (UP RT), Vanni/Art Resource, NY; 108, Réunion des Musées Nationaux/Art Resource, NY; 109, "Baptism of Constantine I" (270-337) (oil on canvas), Puget, Pierre (1620-94)/Musee des Beaux-Arts, Marseille, France/The Bridgeman Art Library International; 110-111, "Inside the Main Entrance of the Purana Qila, Delhi, 1823" (oil on canvas), Smith, Robert (1787-1873)/Yale Center for British Art, Paul Mellon Collection, USA/The Bridgeman Art Library International; 112, Museo Nazionale di Capodimonte, Naples, Italy/Art Resource, NY; 113, Borromeo/Art Resource, NY/Art Resource, NY; 115, Chanakaya and King Chandragupta (w/c & gouache), Indian School/Private Collection/Dinodia/The Bridgeman Art Library International; 116 (LO LE), James P. Blair; 116 (LO RT), Borromeo/Art Resource, NY; 117, Emperor Ashoka (r. 264-23 B.C.) Emperor in the Mauryan dynasty in India, Indian School/Private Collection/Dinodia/The Bridgeman Art Library International; 118-119, Monique Pietri/akg-images; 118 (LO LE), © DeA Picture Library/Art Resource, NY; 119, Wikipedia; 120, Werner Forman/Art Resource, NY; 121, Emperor Wu Ti (156-87, r. 141-87 B.C.), leaving his palace, from a history of Chinese emperors (color on silk), Chinese School, (17th century)/Bibliotheque Nationale, Paris, France/Archives Charmet/The Bridgeman Art Library International; 123, Musee du Quai Branly/Scala/Art Resource, NY; 124, Snark/Art Resource, NY; 125 (UP), O. Louis Mazzatenta/NationalGeographicStock.com; 125 (LO), O. Louis Mazzatenta/ NationalGeographicStock.com; 126 (UP LE), Confucius (photo)/Museum of Saigon, Ho Chi Minh City, Vietnam/Photo © Luca Tettoni/The Bridgeman Art

Catalunya, Barcelona, Spain/Photo © AISA/The Bridgeman Art Library International; 217, Schack-Galerie, Bayerische Staatsgemaeldesammlungen, Munich, Germany/Art Resource, NY; 219, HIP/Art Resource, NY; 220, Brandus Dan Lucian/Shutterstock; 221, Monument to El Cid (ca 1040 99) (bronze), Spanish School/Seville, Spain/Ken Welsh/The Bridgeman Art Library International; 222, Werner Forman/Art Resource, NY; 223, HIP/Art Resource, NY; 225 (LO), Brent Stirton; 225 (UP), George Steinmetz; 226, David Kerkhoff/iStockphoto.com; 227, © The Metropolitan Museum of Art/Art Resource, NY; 228, David Alan Harvey; 229, James L. Stanfield, 230-231, Scala/Art Resource, NY; 232, © The Trustees of the British Museum/Art Resource, NY; 233, David Hiser/NationalGeographicStock.com; 235, Snark/Art Resource, NY; 236, Werner Forman/Art Resource, NY; 236-237, Martin Gray/ NationalGeographicStock.com; 238, Kenneth Garrett; 239, Alfredo Dagli Orti/Art Resource, NY; 241, © DeA Picture Library/Art Resource, NY; 242 (LO), Kenneth Garrett; 242 (UP), Scala/Art Resource, NY; 243, Facsimile copy of codex Borbonicus, detail depicting the elaboration of the Oxomoco and Cipactonal calendar (vellum), Aztec/Private Collection/Jean-Pierre Courau/The Bridgeman Art Library International; 244, Snark/Art Resource, NY; 245 (LO), Werner Forman/Art Resource, NY; 245 (UP), Michel Zabé/Art Resource, NY; 246, Robert Clark; 247, Lynn Johnson/ NationalGeographicStock.com; 249 (UP), Stephen L. Alvarez; 249 (LO), Manco Capac, First Inca King, mid-18th century (oil on canvas), Peruvian School (18th century)/Brooklyn Museum of Art, New York, USA/ The Bridgeman Art Library International; 250 (LO LE), Illustration of a Quipu, from *Historia y Genealogia Real de los Reyes Incas del Peru, de sus hechos, costumbres, trajes y manera de Gobierno,* known as the *Codice Murua* (vellum), Spanish School, (16th century)/Private Collection/The Bridgeman Art Library International; 250 (UP RT), Stephen L. Alvarez; 251, Ira Block/ NationalGeographicStock.com; 252, Mike Theiss/ NationalGeographicStock.com; 253, Illustration of Manco Capac, from *Historia y Genealogia Real de los Reyes Incas del Peru, de sus hechos, costumbres, trajes y manera de Gobierno,* known as the *Codice Murua* (vellum), Spanish School, (16th century)/Private Collection/The Bridgeman Art Library International; 254-255, Victor R. Boswell, Jr.; 256-257, Geography and Map Division, Library of Congress; 258, Scala/Art Resource, NY; 259, "The Reception of Christopher Columbus (1450-1506) by Ferdinand II (1452-1516) of Aragon and Isabella (1451-1504) of Castille" (oil on canvas), Deveria, Eugene (1808-65)/Musee Bargoin, Clermont-Ferrand, France/Giraudon/The Bridgeman Art Library International; 262 (UP), HIP/Art Resource, NY; 262 (LO), tatniz/Shutterstock; 263 (LO), Erich Lessing/Art Resource, NY; 264, Georgios Kollidas/Shutterstock; 265, Erich Lessing/Art Resource, NY; 266, V&A Images, London/Art Resource, NY; 267, Elizabeth I, Armada Portrait, ca 1588 (oil on panel), Gower, George (1540-96) (attr. to)/Woburn Abbey, Bedfordshire, UK/The Bridgeman Art Library International; 268 (LO), The Treaty of Utrecht, 11th April 1713 (pen & ink on paper), French School, (18th century)/Archives du Ministere des Affaires Etrangeres, Paris, France/Archives Charmet/The Bridgeman Art Library International; 269 (LO), "The Shooting of General Braddock at Fort Duquesne," Pittsburgh, 1755 (oil on canvas), Deming, Edwin Willard (1860-1942)/State Historical Society of Wisconsin, Madison, USA/The Bridgeman Art Library International; 269 (UP), Mark Grenier/Shutterstock; 270-271, Art Resource, NY; 271, L. Kragt Bakker/Shutterstock; 272 (LO), HIP/Art Resource, NY; 272-273, Ami Vitale; 274 (LO), Sir Thomas Stamford Raffles (1781-1826), Lonsdale, James (1777-1839)/Private Collection/The Bridgeman Art Library International; 274 (UP), Victoria & Albert Museum, London/Art Resource, NY; 275, HIP/Art Resource, NY; 276, Comanche warrior with a shield, lance, and bow and arrows, ca 1835 (color litho), Catlin, George (1794-1872)/Private Collection/Peter Newark American Pictures/The Bridgeman Art Library International; 277, "Comanche Feats of Martial Horsemanship," 1834 (oil on canvas), Catlin, George (1794-1872)/Private Collection/Peter Newark American Pictures/The Bridgeman Art Library International; 279, Library of Congress; 280, Library of Congress; 281, Peter Turnley/CORBIS; 282-283, Alinari/SEAT/Art Resource, NY; 284, Réunion des Musées Nationaux/Art Resource, NY; 285, Vanni/Art Resource, NY; 288 (UP), © DeA Picture Library/Art Resource, NY; 288 (LO), Vanni/Art Resource, NY; 289, Bridgeman-Giraudon/Art Resource, NY; 290 (LO), James L. Stanfield; 290 (UP), © DeA Picture Library/Art Resource, NY; 291, The Gallery Collection/CORBIS; 292 (LO LE), Snark/Art Resource, NY; 292 (LO RT), Nicolo Orsi Battaglini/Art Resource, NY; 292 (UP), Erich Lessing/Art Resource, NY; 293, Erich Lessing/Art Resource, NY; 294, Scala/White Images/Art Resource, NY; 295 (UP), Amurath (Murad) IV (1612-40) Sultan 1623-40, from *A Series of Portraits of the Emperors of Turkey*, 1808 (w/c), Young, John (1755-1825)/Private Collection/The Stapleton Collection/The Bridgeman Art Library

International; 295 (LO LE), The Jewish Museum, New York/Art Resource, NY; 295 (LO RT), Hasseki Baltaci Valet del Sultani, probably by Cousinery, Ottoman period, third quarter of 18th century (w/c on paper), French School, (18th century)/School of Oriental & African Studies Library, University of London/The Bridgeman Art Library International; 296, Asante swords from Ghana, African/Private Collection/Photo © Boltin Picture Library/The Bridgeman Art Library International; 297, Werner Forman/Art Resource, NY; 298 (UP), Asante pectoral, from Ghana (gold), African/Private Collection/Photo © Boltin Picture Library/The Bridgeman Art Library International; 299, SCHOMBURG CENTER/Art Resource, NY; 300 (LO LE), Werner Forman/Art Resource, NY; 300 (UP RT), Werner Forman/Art Resource, NY; 301, HIP/Art Resource, NY; 302-303, Add 24065 Map of the World, Desceliers, Pierre (fl.1550)/British Library, London, UK/© British Library Board. All Rights Reserved/The Bridgeman Art Library International; 304, Base for a Hookah Pipe, Mughal Court Workshop, gilt glass, Indian, ca 18th century/Victoria & Albert Museum, London, UK/The Bridgeman Art Library International; 305, Emperor Khurram (Shah Jahan) (1592-1666), Jahangir Period, Mughal (copy of a 17th century painting)/Victoria & Albert Museum, London, UK/The Bridgeman Art Library International; 307, Akbar receiving the drums and standards captured from Abdullah Uzbeg, Governor of Malwa, in 1564, 1590-98 (gouache on parchment), Mughal School, (16th century)/Victoria & Albert Museum, London, UK/The Stapleton Collection/The Bridgeman Art Library International; 308 (LO), © 2009 Museum Associates/LACMA/Art Resource, NY; 308 (UP), © The Trustees of the British Museum/Art Resource, NY; 309, Akbar (1542-1605) (gouache on paper), Indian School, (17th century)/Prince of Wales Museum, Mumbai, India/Giraudon/The Bridgeman Art Library International; 310, Pius Lee/Shutterstock; 311 (LO), Aleksandar Todorovic/Shutterstock; 311 (UP), Maltings Partnership; 312-313, Mudassar Ahmed Dar/Shutterstock; 313 (UP), © The Metropolitan Museum of Art/Art Resource, NY; 313 (LO), Steve McCurry; 314 (LO LE), Carlos Neto/Shutterstock; 314 (LO RT), Carlos Neto/Shutterstock; 315, Ladies feasting, from the Small Clive Album, Mughal School/Victoria & Albert Museum, London, UK/The Stapleton Collection/The Bridgeman Art Library International; 316, Fo porcelain dog, 17th century/Private Collection/The Bridgeman Art Library International; 317, Justin Guariglia/NationalGeographicStock.com; 320 (LO), © The Trustees of the British Museum/Art Resource, NY; 320 (UP), Dish with famille verte decoration, Kangxi Period, 1662-1722 (ceramic), Chinese School, Qing Dynasty (1644-1912)/Musee Guimet, Paris, France/Giraudon/The Bridgeman Art Library International; 321 (LO), Moon Flask (cloisonné enamel), Chinese School, Qing Dynasty (1644-1912)/Private Collection/Photo © Heini Schneebeli/The Bridgeman Art Library International; 321 (UP), K'ang-hsi, Chinese School/Private Collection/Peter Newark Military Pictures/The Bridgeman Art Library International; 322 (LO), Fan decorated with small birds and morning glories (ink & color on paper), Chinese School, Qing Dynasty (1644-1912)/Freer Gallery of Art, Smithsonian Institution, USA/Transfer from the United States Customs Service, Department of the Treasury/The Bridgeman Art Library International; 322 (CTR), Réunion des Musées Nationaux/Art Resource, NY; 322 (UP), Réunion des Musées Nationaux/Art Resource, NY; 323, Todd Gipstein/NationalGeographicStock.com; 324 (LO LE), © Metropolitan Museum of Art/Art Resource, NY; 324-325, Réunion des Musées Nationaux/Art Resource, NY; 326, © DeA Picture Library/Art Resource, NY; 327, Rebels capture a British soldier during the Taiping Rebellion in China (w/c on paper), Scott, W. R. S. (19th century)/Private Collection/Peter Newark Military Pictures/The Bridgeman Art Library International; 328, Hung Chung Chih/Shutterstock; 329, Library of Congress; 330, Cary Sol Wolinsky; 331, Portrait of Tsar Michael Fyodorovich Romanov (1596-1645) of Russia, Russian School, (17th century)/Private Collection/Archives Charmet/The Bridgeman Art Library International; 332, "Capture of Azov, 18th May 1696" (oil on canvas), Porter, Sir Robert Kerr (1777-1842)/Central Naval Museum, St. Petersburg, Russia/The Bridgeman Art Library International; 333, Iakov Filimonov/Shutterstock; 335 (LE), RIA Novosti/The Image Works; 335 (RT), Scala/White Images/Art Resource, NY; 336 (LO LE), "Dinner at the Zemstvo," 1872 (oil on canvas), Mjasoedov, Grigori Grigorievich (1835-1911)/Tretyakov Gallery, Moscow, Russia/The Bridgeman Art Library International; 336-337, "Study for the Coronation of Tsar Nicholas II (1868-1918) and Tsarina Alexandra (1872-1918) at the Church of the Assumption, Moscow, 14th may 1896" (oil on canvas), Gervex, Henri (1852-1929)/Musee d'Orsay, Paris, France/Giraudon/The Bridgeman Art Library International; 338, Portrait of Rasputin writing (b/w photo), Russian Photographer/Private Collection/The Bridgeman Art Library International; 339, Library of Congress.

GREAT EMPIRES: AN ILLUSTRATED ATLAS
Stephen G. Hyslop, Patricia S. Daniels

PUBLISHED BY THE NATIONAL GEOGRAPHIC SOCIETY
John M. Fahey, Jr., Chairman of the Board and
 Chief Executive Officer
Timothy T. Kelly, President
Declan Moore, Executive Vice President; President, Publishing
Melina Gerosa Bellows, Executive Vice President;
 Chief Creative Officer, Books, Kids, and Family

PREPARED BY THE BOOK DIVISION
Barbara Brownell Grogan, Vice President and Editor in Chief
Jonathan Halling, Design Director, Books and Children's
 Publishing
Marianne R. Koszorus, Design Director, Books
Lisa Thomas, Senior Editor
Carl Mehler, Director of Maps
R. Gary Colbert, Production Director
Jennifer A. Thornton, Managing Editor
Meredith C. Wilcox, Administrative Director, Illustrations

STAFF FOR THIS BOOK
Susan Straight, Editor
Maryann Haggerty, Text Editor, Contributing Writer
Carol Norton, Art Director
Susan Blair, Adrian Coakley, Illustrations Editors
Linda Makarov, Designer
Miriam Stein, Illustrations Researcher, Picture Legends Writer
Matthew W. Chwastyk, Michael McNey, Gregory Ugiansky,
 and XNR Productions, Map Research and Production
Judith Klein, Production Editor
Lisa A. Walker, Production Manager
Marshall Kiker, Illustrations Specialist
Elizabeth Weiss, Intern
Jodie Morris, Design Assistant

MANUFACTURING AND QUALITY MANAGEMENT
Christopher A. Liedel, Chief Financial Officer
Phillip L. Schlosser, Senior Vice President
Chris Brown, Technical Director
Nicole Elliott, Manager
Rachel Faulise, Manager
Robert L. Barr, Manager

The National Geographic Society is one of the world's largest nonprofit scientific and educational organizations. Founded in 1888 to "increase and diffuse geographic knowledge," the Society's mission is to inspire people to care about the planet. It reaches more than 400 million people worldwide each month through its official journal, *National Geographic,* and other magazines; National Geographic Channel; television documentaries; music; radio; films; books; DVDs; maps; exhibitions; live events; school publishing programs; interactive media; and merchandise. National Geographic has funded more than 9,600 scientific research, conservation and exploration projects and supports an education program promoting geographic literacy. For more information, visit www.nationalgeographic.com.

For more information, please call 1-800-NGS LINE (647-5463) or write to the following address:

National Geographic Society
1145 17th Street N.W.
Washington, D.C. 20036-4688 U.S.A.

For information about special discounts for bulk purchases, please contact National Geographic Books Special Sales: ngspecsales@ngs.org

For rights or permissions inquiries, please contact National Geographic Books Subsidiary Rights: ngbookrights@ngs.org

ISBN: 978-1-4262-0829-4
ISBN:978-1-4262-0830-0 (Deluxe)

Printed in the United States of America

11/QGV-CML /1